HISTORICAL ENCYCLOPEDIA
OF AMERICAN WOMEN
ENTREPRENEURS

HISTORICAL ENCYCLOPEDIA OF AMERICAN WOMEN ENTREPRENEURS

1776 to the Present

JEANNETTE M. OPPEDISANO

Greenwood Press
Westport, Connecticut • London

Library of Congress Cataloging-in-Publication Data

Oppedisano, Jeannette M.
    Historical encyclopedia of American women entrepreneurs : 1776 to the present /
Jeannette M. Oppedisano.
        p.   cm.
    Includes bibliographical references and index.
    ISBN 0–313–30647–8 (alk. paper)
    1. Businesswomen—United States—Biography.   2. Businesswomen—United
States—History—Encyclopedias.   3. Businesspeople—United States—Biography.   4.
Businesspeople—United States—History—Encyclopedias.   I. Title.
HF3023.A2O64   2000
338.04'082092273—dc21   99—088204
    [B]

British Library Cataloguing in Publication Data is available.

Library of Congress Catalog Card Number: 99–088204
ISBN: 0–313–30647–8

First published in 2000

Greenwood Press, 88 Post Road West, Westport, CT 06881
An imprint of Greenwood Publishing Group, Inc.
www.greenwood.com

Printed in the United States of America

The paper used in this book complies with the
Permanent Paper Standard issued by the National
Information Standards Organization (Z39.48–1984).

10   9   8   7   6   5   4   3   2   1

Throughout the writing of this book, there has been an "angel" by my side, my sister Antoinette "Toni" Bosco. Even before I understood the enormity of the task I had opted to initiate, Antoinette knew, because of her more than thirty years of experience as a published author and editor. She encouraged, tweaked, listened, read, suggested, phoned, and, most important, unconditionally supported and loved me. She is truly one of the greatest blessings in my life.

CONTENTS

A photo essay follows page 104

PREFACE

The women in this volume and I have something important in common—we started out in one direction, and life's circumstances landed us on a whole different path. My original goal was to develop a course for my students on the entrepreneurial ventures of American women from a historical perspective. The intent was to demonstrate that these women had managed to be important economic contributors even when the odds were significantly against them. An objective was to highlight these role models so that students would be encouraged to follow their own dreams. However, I could find little resource material on the subject. The primary content of the literature was on how to start a business. The works that did speak of innovators themselves were primarily written by men, had a male focus, and, if they mentioned women, implied that female entrepreneurs were a "recent" phenomena. Both the invisibility of women and the inaccuracy of what was written redirected my effort to write a book. It was the insight of Nita Romer, an acquisitions editor at Greenwood Publishing Group, who saw, in my original proposal submission, the embryo of a more extensive work on entrepreneurial American women. For this, I am truly grateful.

The women profiled in this encyclopedia are different in many ways. They are economically, ethnically, racially, physically, spiritually, and generationally diverse; they cross cultural and social classes; and they represent different organizational entities in all regions of this country and some that reach out into other lands. These female innovators also are similar in many ways. They faced obstacles that entrepreneurial men, by virtue of their gender, did not have to face; they were women of courage, stamina, and tenacity; they were talented jugglers of the demands from multiple social roles; and they achieved against the odds. This work is a celebration of these women.

INTRODUCTION

Entrepreneurs are agents of change who take substantial risks—human, physical, and/or financial—to initiate and develop an organizational entity and to participate in these endeavors even though there is no certainty of generating personal income. These innovators are catalysts for the American economic system by impacting multiple economies—local, regional, national, and international. The classic characteristics of these women are intelligence, decisiveness, persuasiveness, a need for independence, and a need for achievement. American women have been such innovators since the beginning of this nation. The difference now is that their contributions have finally achieved greater visibility. As a case in point, according to a study conducted by Dun & Bradstreet Information Services, "women now hire more workers in the United States than Fortune 500 companies do globally" (McClain, 1995: C16). Yet, our recorded history does not demonstrate either this fact or the breadth and depth of their contributions.

Not only have women been a consistent and successful economic factor in our actual history, but they have been so in spite of constraints and circumstances additional to those normally experienced by male entrepreneurs. These extra burdens or barriers have included restrictions on the right to own property, a lack of political power because they could not vote, the absence of the civil rights that were given as a birthright to white men, the multiple responsibilities of the societally imposed role of "caregiver," and, as if that weren't enough, the suffocation of girdling garments.

Thus, the purpose of this encyclopedia is to chronicle some of the extensive entrepreneurial contributions of American women to the economy of this democracy; to demonstrate how these activities were achieved throughout the widely accepted categories of agriculture and mining, communications, construction, manufacturing, service (both for-profit and not-for-profit), transportation, and wholesale and retail trade; to correct our recorded history of American women; and to establish an extensive base of role models for girls and boys, women and men.

JANE ADDAMS (1860–1935)

"I have never been sure I was right. I have often been doubtful about the next step. We can only feel our way as we go on from day to day."
(Jane Addams, Co-founder, Hull House)

She was considered the most useful citizen in America according to President Theodore Roosevelt, labeled the most dangerous woman in America by the press, and was the first American woman to receive the Nobel Peace Prize. This was Laura Jane Addams—a woman who took on the perilous and much-criticized practical mission of bringing hope and help to the poorest of the poor in Chicago, Illinois, from 1889 until the end of her life. Her work of unrelenting social reform was an unlikely path for a nineteenth-century white woman who came from a wealthy family headed by a father she adored, State Senator John Huy Addams. Oddly enough, it was a series of painful experiences that led her in this direction, ultimately shaping her life and that of millions of others.

Jane Addams had just graduated from Rockford Seminary as the valedictorian of her class when her father died. This loss triggered a deep depression and may have also stimulated the reoccurrence of the back pain created by her childhood illness of tuberculosis of the spine. The doctors recommended that she have surgery; she consented but, as a result, was in a cast for a year. Addams subsequently traveled to Europe; it was in England that she faced the reality of urbanized poverty for the first time. She was taken to see one of the "tourist attractions" of London—a sight which revolted her—"hordes" of the East End poor bidding to purchase nearly spoiled food (Addams, 1910). She also got to see how the workers at the settlement house of Toynebee Hall were trying to help these poor. Jane Addams returned to the United States on a mission. She was determined to "aid in the solution of social problems engendered by the modern conditions of life in a great city . . . to help our neighbors build responsible, self-sufficient lives for themselves and their families" (Jane Addams Hull House Association, 1999).

With the money she inherited from her father and the assistance of her close friend Helen Gates Starr, Addams rented an old mansion in the West End of Chicago at Halsted and Polk Streets. The building was situated between a saloon and a funeral parlor in a rat-infested ghetto of immigrants from Italy, Greece, Russia, Ireland, Germany, and China. The residents had no choice but to live in squalor on garbage-strewn streets and with no plumbing in their living quarters. Addams renovated and furnished the home she now called Hull House, the place she would choose to live the rest of her life because of her dedication to the inner-city poor.

It took less than a month before the specific needs of those living around her became apparent, and she began providing programs in her settlement house. Children were the first to visit because they were often alone during the day because their parents had to work. Addams learned that sometimes they were locked in their apartments or tied to furniture when their mothers couldn't be home with them. "The first three crippled children we encountered . . . had all been injured when their mothers were at work; one had fallen out of a third-story window, another had been burned, and the third had a curved spine [because] for three years he had been tied all day long to a kitchen table, only released at noon by an older brother who hastily ran in from a neighboring factory to share his lunch with him" (Share, 1989: 3D). Her response was to start a day-care program at Hull House; this was followed by an employment bureau; vocational training program; social clubs for women, men, children; music and art classes; libraries; and America's first little theater. In the first twelve months Hull House was in operation, these women had served about fifty thousand people. "Addams herself . . . was available at any hour of the day or night to do whatever needed to be done. She delivered babies, taught classes, helped with housework, kept the books, babysat, counseled those looking for a job or those in trouble with the law, nursed the sick, and tended to the affairs of the dead" (Straub, 1992: 15).

Just four years after Hull House opened, the United States was hit with the 1893 depression. The settlement houses were even more needed as sixty percent of workers were out of a job. By 1900 there were one hundred settlement houses in the country and, within just a decade, four hundred had been started (Stivers, 1995). By this time, Jane Addams and the benefits of her Hull House programs were known here and abroad. She had a dozen buildings that housed the facilities and programs of the organization. "Eventually 70 people experienced collective living and more than 2,000 people crossed its doorway daily. It became a community center for all of Chicago" (Lundblad, 1995: 663).

A long list of firsts can be attributed to the efforts of Jane Addams and those who joined her causes. These included establishing the first settlement house in Chicago; the first successful cooperative residence for women; the first public baths, which offered the only way some of the residents could have access to such a luxury; the first public gymnasium; the first swimming pool, kitchen, and playground in Chicago; the first free art exhibits; the first women's basketball team; and the first community-based foster care program. In addition, Addams joined with others to initiate the first juvenile court, the first women's labor unions, and the first factory laws. In 1915, Jane Addams also co-founded the Women's Peace Party, which advocated pacifism. This was what caused public opinion about her to become strongly negative.

Although there can be no doubt that Addams took significant human, physical, and financial risks as she initiated and went about the business of Hull House and social advocacy, she faced a much more public risk when she refused to support U.S. World War I efforts. The consequences of her decision included widespread derision, with some people even denouncing her as a traitor. Others harassed her and even trashed the premises of the U.S. Women's Peace Party. "If a bit of mail protruded from the door, it was frequently spat upon, and, although we rented our quarters in a first class office building on Michigan Boulevard facing the lake, the door was often befouled in hideous ways" (Addams, 1983: 127). She was blacklisted by practices such as having her name on the *Spider Web Chart* and the *Who's Who of Pacifists and Radicals*. In addition, "The Lusk Commission of New York State . . . accused Addams of using both the national and international women's peace movement to foster her socialistic views . . . [however] by 1928, when the U.S. Congress ratified the Kellogg-Briand Pact, peace had become popular, and Addams something of a hero" (Alonso, 1995: 14, 15). In 1931 Jane Addams received the Nobel Peace Prize for her long-standing commitment and efforts for peace through the Women's International League for Peace and Freedom. She was the first American woman to be so honored. Addams died four years later from intestinal cancer at the age of seventy-five.

The much needed and multidimensional endeavors initiated by Jane Addams continued. By the end of the twentieth century Hull House was still vibrantly operating with six hundred employees in thirty-five locations with six community centers across Chicago, more than one hundred different programs being offered, and over 250,000 people being served annually.

SOURCES: Addams, J. (1910), *Twenty Years at Hull House* (New York: Macmillan); Addams, J. (1983), *Peace and Bread in Time of War* (Silver Spring, MD: National Association of Social Workers); Alonso, H. (1995), "Nobel Peace Laureates, Jane Addams and Emily Greene Balsh: Two Women of the Women's International League for Peace and Freedom," *Journal of Women's History* 7, no. 2: 6–26; Davis, A. (1973), *American Heroine: The Life and Legend of Jane Addams* (New York: Oxford University Press); Hart, M. (1990), "Hull House: A Landmark for the Needy," *Chicago Tribune*, November 11: 3+ [Lexis/Nexis]; Jane Addams Hull House Association (1999), *http://www.terasys.com/hullhouse/history* (accessed January 17; Lundblad, K. (1995), "Jane Addams and Social Reform: A Role Model for the 1990s," *Social Work*, Vol. 40, 5:661–669; Share, A. (1989), "The Legacy of Hull House," *The Courier Journal*, September 17: 3D [Lexis/Nexis]; Stivers, C. (1995), "Settlement Women and Bureau Men: Constructing a Usable Past for Public Administration," *Public Administration Review*, November/December: 522–533; Straub, D., ed. (1992), *Contemporary Heroes and Heroines* (Detroit, MI: Gale Research, Inc.); Swanson, S., ed. (1997), *Chicago Days: 150 Defining Moments in the Life of a Great City* (Wheaton, IL: Contemporary Books).

LINDA ALVARADO (1952–   )

"What I still hope for and long for is the day when people will truly be judged not based on where they came from, and their gender, but really on their ability. That is a dream that we can't let go. America is a country of immigrants and our success is built not on everybody being alike but on our diversity." (Linda Alvarado, Founder, Alvarado Construction Company)

An entrepreneurial "woman of the West" in the construction business is Linda Alvarado. She was born in Albuquerque, New Mexico, but moved with her family to Los Angeles, California, when she was a teenager. It was there that she was first introduced to commercial development. At the age of twenty-two, Alvarado again moved, this time to Denver, Colorado. It was here that she wanted to start a commercial general contracting firm; however, getting the necessary capital from banks presented a formidable hurdle. The year was 1975; Alvarado was refused by five banks. "It was probably more my age and lack of long-term experience than the fact that I was female," she notes (Oppedisano, 1998; all direct quotes are from this source unless otherwise cited).

Her parents, however, believed in their daughter's dream and in her ability to do what she set out to do. They took out a mortgage on their home and loaned her the remaining $2,500 that she needed. "It doesn't sound like much in today's dollar terms, but back then it was a lot of money to me," explained Alvarado. She had taken courses in surveying, estimating, and construction management, but the computing course on critical path scheduling gave her the competitive niche edge. At the time Alvarado Construction was incorporated, Linda Alvarado was only twenty-four years old. By 1998, this multimillion-dollar-a-year business specializing in commercial, industrial, environmental, and heavy engineering projects was well known and highly regarded throughout the western part of the United States and employed over four hundred people.

The owner, however, is more widely recognized. Among Alvarado's many honors is her being named by *Hispanic Business Magazine* as one of the "100 Most Influential Hispanics in America," her receipt of an honorary doctorate in commercial science from Dowling College and of the Sara Lee Corporation Frontrunner Award for exemplary achievement and leadership, and her appointment to the President's Advisory Commission on Educational Excellence for Hispanic Americans.

In addition to these opportunities Alvarado was invited in 1991 to become one of the limited partners of the Colorado Rockies baseball team. She noted, "I've been interested in sports all my life. I had lettered in softball back in high school. What for me that has been particularly a lot of fun is to take young kids who have done well in school down to the ballpark, have them sit with business leaders, and let them meet the ballplayers. It lets these kids know that they're just as important, and that all things are possible if they just work hard."

SOURCES: Alvardo, L. (1998), "Constructing a Better America," *American Dreams* *(http://www.usdreams.com/preview/alvardo.htm)*, July 20 (accessed November 23, 1998), Fowler, S. (1991), "A Major Leaguer in Denver Now Wants to Play Ball," *Chicago Tribune*, June 9; Meadow, J. (1994), "How They Got Their Starts," *Rocky Mountain News*, April 11: 3D; Oppedisano, J. (1998), interview with Linda Alvarado, March 11, Saratoga Springs, NY; Rabin, A. (1985), "The Last 'Women in Business' Story," *Denver Business*, Vol. 7, 10: Sec. 1: 16+; Richter, M. (1994), "Business Owner Laughs at Her Detractors, *Tampa Tribune*, December 14: 2+.

HELENE AN (1938–   )
HANNAH AN (1966–   )
ELIZABETH AN (1967–   )
MONIQUE AN (1971–   )

"The reason I created the Secret Kitchen is that [these special dishes are] my treasure to give to my daughters. For me, after all the many experiences in my life, I don't think that the money can exist forever— only something you create, and so I created something to pass on to

my daughters." (Helene An, Executive Chef and Owner of the Thanh
Long and Crustacean Restaurants)

Riches to rags and back to riches is the life path of Helene Thuong An and
her family—a journey that has permeated their personal philosophy with
issues of safety and security. Her life began with prosperity and promise,
as the youngest child of seventeen born into the aristocratic North Vietnamese family of the provincial governor, Tran Luu Mau, and his wife,
Duong Nguyet Thuong. But a political calamity beset the Thuongs with
the Ho Chi Minh revolution, begun in 1955, which forced them to relocate
to South Vietnam, leaving behind all the trappings of wealth, status, and
privilege.

In 1965 Helene Thuong entered into an arranged marriage with Air
Force pilot Danny An. This was a fortunate match, since he did not hold
the traditional belief in a woman's role. "Maybe I was lucky, but we got
along," she said. "He didn't think I had to listen to him like a slave. We
discussed problems together" (Karlin & Wihlborg, 1998: 90). Over the
next ten years their lives were filled with having children and establishing
roots—all to be changed in the space of one very short hour in 1975.
Helene An's husband was serving in the Philippines at the time. A friend
told her to leave South Vietnam immediately if she and her children were
to be safe. Saigon was falling to the Communist army. With little else than
the clothes on their backs, this Vietnamese family had to flee once again.
The war destroyed all that Helene An and her family had known. Fortunately, she and her daughters were able to rejoin her husband, and together
they emigrated to the United States. What they carried with them was a
fierce loyalty and commitment to family that remains as true today as then.

A stroke of luck was that they had a place to go. Danny An's mother,
Diana An, had already come to the United States and, in 1971, had opened
a small Vietnamese restaurant in San Francisco called Thanh Long. This
means "green dragon," the symbol of good luck, prosperity, and happiness.
That first year they all lived together in a one-room apartment above the
restaurant. Helene An helped with the menu and added some of the dishes
she remembered her father's chefs creating. She was also earning her second
accounting degree and having more children, daughters Jacqueline and
Katherine. The restaurant quickly became famous for a specialty dish, roast
crab, and success followed. By 1991, Helene An was able to open a second
restaurant, Crustacean—named after a main ingredient in some of their
family recipes. By 1996, their continuing success led to the launching of
their third establishment, again named Crustacean, but this time located in
Beverly Hills, California. In determining how this latest million-dollar restaurant was to be designed, Elizabeth An drew upon the family history: "I
was truly inspired by the stories of my grandmother and my mother so I

tried to recreate my grandfather's estate. He felt that all his children must live together around the courtyard [that they had in the prewar province of Tuyen Quang] so I created the essence of a courtyard in the restaurant and the atmosphere of a home in 1930 Vietnam" (*Dining in Style*, 1999).

The family used the ancient art of Feng Shui, which balances the negative and positive energies, as their theme throughout Crustacean. The combination of curves and water to bring good luck is present in the 6,000-gallon stream aquarium built into the floor that is home to an exotic and expensive collection of koi (carp). Depending on size and color, each fish can range in price from $500 to $5,000. They are named after celebrities who have dined at the restaurant, such as Sylvester Stallone and Warren Beatty. Elizabeth explained the symbolism and importance of the koi: "Grandfather believed that koi brought good fortune, honesty, and abundance—[with] plenty of food on the table" (*Dining in Style*, 1999).

For daughter Hannah An the restaurant contains two particularly precious family heirlooms—a chest of her great-grandmother's that has been passed down through the family for hundreds of years and a tapestry that depicts a legend to which this unique matriarchal family can easily relate. She explained: "As the legend goes, there were these three sisters married to three generals who were captured by the Chinese. The sisters rode elephants into the camp where their husbands were being held, fighting as they went along, and rescued them. We three An sisters identify with the determination of these three sisters" (*Dining in Style*, 1999).

The "food treasures" of the An family are kept under lock and key by Helene An to protect them from culinary espionage. She cooks from the special family recipes she learned from her grandfather's "three chefs—one French (from whom Helene learned that cooking was an art), one Chinese (who taught the aesthetics of the table) and one Vietnamese (who instructed as to native culinary culture)" (Mariani, 1998: 102). These master chefs would sometimes prepare food for lavish banquets of three hundred political dignitaries. Today, Helene An provides for even more people, cooking in her "secret kitchen"—a specially built space that only she and her daughters can enter. In fact, it has two stainless steel sliding doors, through which she slips the finished meals to the servers on the other side.

While Danny An provides consulting services for Vietnamese-U.S. businesses, Helene An plans on opening two more restaurants in California so that there will be a restaurant for each of their five daughters. The An women are thankful for what they have been able to achieve. "We feel very privileged and lucky," Elizabeth noted. "Not just for the success we've had, but because, as women, we have been able to achieve something that would have been impossible in Vietnam, where a woman's happiness depends upon her ability to be a fine host and to serve people with beauty and grace. Then again, maybe we're not so different" (Mariani, 1998: 104).

SOURCES: Bauer, M. (1999), "Thanh Long Is King When It Comes to Crab/Efficient Staff, Updated Decor," *San Francisco Chronicle* [Online], February 12: C15 (available: Proquest, accessed June 10, 1999); *Dining in Style* (1999), E-Entertainment Television: The Style Network, Spring; Karlin, B., & Wihlborg, U. (1998), "Royal Palates: Helene An Re-creates the Elegant Cuisine of her Vietnamese Youth at Beverly Hills' Crustacean," *People*, April 13: 89–90; Mariani, J. (1998), "Upper Crust," *Wine Spectator*, July 11: 102–104; Sheridan, M. (1997), "Prewar Saigon Comes to Beverly Hills via San Francisco; Restaurants: The Family-owned Crustacean, a Big Success in the Bay Area, Is Opening a Branch in the Southland," *Los Angeles Times* [Online], January 17: 20 (available: Lexis-Nexis, accessed June 10, 1999); Shindler, M. (1998), "Asian Matchmakers," *Food Arts*, July/August: 51–52; Virbila, S. (1997), "East Looking West," *Los Angeles Times* [Online], April 6: 30 (available: Lexis-Nexis, accessed June 10, 1999).

CATHERINE "KYE" ANDERSON (1946–)

"Entrepreneurs seldom know what they're getting into when they start. They are people so fired up with a vision that they are blind to everyday realities—which is a good thing since, otherwise, they would never attempt to do the impossible things they so often succeed in doing." (Catherine "Kye" Anderson, Founder of Medical Graphics Corporation and e-med.OnCall)

When she was only thirteen years old, Catherine "Kye" Anderson watched her beloved father gasping for breath, hooked up to an electrocardiogram in the hospital, then dying a few days later at the age of forty-seven. This was a life-altering event for the teenager. From then on, Kye was determined to find ways to help those with similar life-threatening diseases. All through her high school years in Crosby, Minnesota, Kye spent summers working at the hospital laboratory. Under the guidance of a strong female mentor, Sister Mary Grace, she learned how to work with patients, draw blood, and be precise. Though at the time Kye thought it was cruel—only understanding later how crucial the value was—Sister Mary Grace told her, "Whenever you do a test, I want you to pretend you're doing it on your father" (Anderson, 1994: 145).

During her years at the College of St. Scholastica in Duluth, Minnesota, Kye remained determined in her goal of one day finding noninvasive technology that would save lives. "On top of all the math and chemistry and anatomy," she recalled, "I worked my way through school in hospital labs. . . . I *knew* where I was going. I was going to prevent heart and lung disease" (Anderson, 1994: 146). After earning her degree in medical technology, Anderson worked for eight years in the cardiopulmonary laboratory of the University of Minnesota Hospital. "Kye was supervising the . . . lab during the 1970s when pulmonary function testing took hours to perform and days to manually calculate the results" ("MedGraphics Corporate Profile," 1997). She taught herself computer programming and then began to develop software programs that would much simplify complicated data so that the doctors would be better able to accurately diagnose and assist their patients. Convincing the Tektronix company that her software could benefit their sales, Anderson was able to borrow $180,000 worth of equipment from them so that she could attend medical conventions and demonstrate her innovative software. "I kept it for another month and then another, on the grounds that eventually I would start selling enough Tektronix computers along with my software that it would pay off for this company as well as for me. Eventually it did" (Anderson, 1994: 146).

Though she got only one order worth $600 at her first medical convention in 1977, within this first year of what was now her new company, Medical Graphics, sales reached $200,000, with Anderson the sole employee. "I had a mission to help save lives. I was driven to do everything I could do to realize my mission—and to do it all myself. I was a crusader, an inventor, a salesperson, an organizer, a hustler. I had been a kind of monomaniac, unconsciously, ever since my father died. Now I was becoming an entrepreneur" (Anderson, 1994: 147). One of her inventions enabled doctors to balance the level of carbon dioxide in an infant's blood, which saved his life.

With her growing success, Anderson found herself traveling extensively. Because of her emphasis on research and development, the company's profits ebbed and flowed, though sales were growing, soon soaring to seven million dollars in sales. "We introduced new systems or new software about every six months," Anderson explained (Anderson, 1994: 149). By 1981 the company had gone public and was traded on the over-the-counter Nasdaq stock market. However, by 1988, profits were not reaching ten percent. This led board members to persuade Anderson to step aside. The corporate press release contained the following explanation for her departure: "Medical Graphics has developed a complete line of advanced cardiopulmonary diagnostic systems and has gained the technological leadership position in our industry, but has had difficulty in developing its sales and marketing" ("Medical Graphics," 1988).

Anderson then sought the assistance of Earl Bakken, an entrepreneur who had founded Medtronic, Inc. He taught her that "a leader's greatest obligation is to preach. . . . With Earl's help [she] put together a statement of higher purpose. . . . 'To prevent heart and lung disease, the leading causes of death and rising healthcare costs' " (Anderson, 1994: 153). This was the rallying point for her retaking the reins of her company a year-

and-a-half later as Chair, President, and Chief Executive Officer. Anderson remained at the head of her company until 1995. At the time, annual sales had reached over $21 million; from the time she initiated the company, more than $200 million worth of medical diagnostic equipment had been sold. Medical Graphics gross revenues for the first six months of 1999 were $10.4 million, and thousands of MedGraphics systems continue to operate around the world.

Then it was time for a new venture. In 1996 Kye Anderson founded e-med.OnCall, Inc., an Internet/Intranet-based company that offers health-improvement programs to individuals and corporations. Utilizing the data garnered over the years at Medical Graphics, new software was designed that would help participants become "aware of just how much disease is preventable, if people would exercise more, eat properly, and not smoke. . . . [It also provides] tailored health improvement programs . . . to help catch people 'upstream'—before they develop medical problems" ("We're e-med.OnCall," 1999). Catherine Kye Anderson is still following her childhood mission of trying to save lives.

SOURCES: Anderson, C. (1994), "The Purpose at the Heart of Management," in Nancy Nichols, ed., *Reach for the Top: Women and the Changing Facts of Work Life* (Boston, MA: Harvard Business Review Book); "Medical Graphics Names Armour President and Chief Operating Officer" (1988), *PR Newswire* [Online] (available: Lexis-Nexis, accessed August 23, 1999); "MedGraphics Corporate Profile" (1997), Company at a Glance (*http://www.medgraph.com*); "We're e-med.OnCall" (1999), *HealthBuzz* [Online] (*http://www.healthbuzz.com/who_mid.html*, accessed August 23, 1999).

SUSAN ANDERSON (1870–1960)

"Don't trust two-faced people with any affair that involves the happiness of your life and the life that should be dearest and most protected by you." (Susan "Doc Susie" Anderson, M.D., Doctor of Grand County, Colorado, 1909–1956)

By the time she was thirty-seven, Dr. Susan Anderson was weary and seriously ill with tuberculosis. She traveled to Fraser, Colorado, in search of either a cure or an unobtrusive death. What she found was a large, widely dispersed, mostly immigrant community in serious need of her skilled, fastidious medical background—a need that brought life back into her downtrodden spirit and put her on an often physically perilous road for fifty more years of medical service to the residents of Grand County, Colorado.

Susan was the first of two children born to Joseph Anderson and Marya Pile Anderson in Nevada Mills, Indiana. Unusual for the time, her parents were divorced when she was only five years old. With legal rights and a former wife who did not have the strength to try to prevent it, her father took both children, his parents, and several other relatives to Wichita, Kansas, where he continued to be a successful farmer, as he had been in Indiana. The children learned how to be "barnyard veterinarians," while Joseph often told them how he had wanted to be a doctor. He also taught them how to shoot a gun with pinpoint accuracy. He was a domineering father, particularly critical of his son, John, who was more interested in exploring than studying. Because Susan was more focused and eager to learn, she became his favored and spoiled child. Mother love was given to the children by their grandmother, but there was always a longing in their hearts for the woman whose sad eyes were etched in their minds and hearts when they were pulled away from her and brought to a strange new home.

As a teenager, Susan learned Morse code. When she "announced she'd like to be a telegrapher, her Pa brought home a book entitled: *What Women Can Do* and urged her to set her sights considerably higher" (Cornell, 1991: 23), and so she did. While in high school, she excelled in "English, algebra and geometry, physiology, geography, U.S. history, and physics" (25). When she was twenty-one years old, as if following her father's dream, Susan went to medical school at the University of Michigan in Ann Arbor. In 1893, "it wasn't difficult to gain admission to medical school. A college degree was not required. Susan's high school performance had been first rate. . . . The four-year medical curriculum at Michigan was designed to prepare students to become country doctors—in the eyes of most people a sure ticket to an impoverished future" (28). Tuition was thirty-five dollars a semester since she wasn't a state resident, and room and board in the area ran from three to five dollars a week—not cheap in this period of history. Continuing the studious pattern she had developed in grammar school, Susan completed certification in "materia medica" and also earned a degree in literature. However, it was during these college years that two crises almost ended her career. The first was the early signs of her tubercular illness. She had been working at the Catherine Street Hospital for months on end, sometimes not having any sleep for days except for an occasional nap. The second was being told by her father, halfway through her program, that he was no longer going to support her. Joseph Anderson had taken a second and younger wife; they now had a new family to support.

Fate stepped in. A fellow student and close friend of Susan's, Mary Lapham, loaned her what amounted to $500 for the remaining years of schooling. It pained Susan that Mary had to drop out of school and move to a warmer climate because of having contracted tuberculosis. Ironically, by her senior year, Susan had the same disease and was unable to accept an internship from the Women's Hospital in Philadelphia. Instead, in 1897, she headed back to Cripple Creek to rejoin her family and set up practice. She proudly repaid Mary's loan within two years.

In 1900 two more devastating events took place in Dr. Susan Anderson's life. First, she was left at the altar by the man she loved, sure that her father was behind this grief. Then, her beloved brother John came down with pneumonia. By the time her father called for her, it was too late to help medically; she could only watch him die. She wrote in her diary, "Life seems so useless and in vain. No one now cares much whether I live or die. John was my best friend on earth and now my best friend is in heaven" (Cornell, 1991: 35).

To distract herself from her grieving, Susan took a position as private physician to a wealthy individual, traveling with him for a year throughout the eastern United States and Canada. Then she returned to Colorado, taking a job as a nurse for the next four years since such practitioners were hard to find, while doctors were not. During 1907, however, a diphtheria epidemic struck and the long hours of working with those afflicted took its toll on Susan, worsening her tuberculosis. This is when she returned to the crisp, clear air of Fraser, Colorado, an area she fondly remembered.

Susan took a little shack close to her friends the Warners. When she had regained enough health, she started to work in their general store, more for companionship than money. Then she was asked to help a seriously injured "friend" of a local young man. The friend turned out to be a horse, but her success with saving this animal brought recognition of her medical talent. Over the next few years, human patients slowly started to come to her shack for medical treatment or to request her to travel to mining and logging communities to save the lives of children and adults. To serve these many and mostly immigrant families, Dr. Susan Anderson was willing to risk her life traveling by any means, including horse and buggy or train, and risking attack by wild animals like mountain lions. The weather could range from the thick mud of spring to the violent blizzards and avalanches of Colorado winters, but she came when asked. Often, as her patients could not afford to pay, she would have meals with them or accept firewood, produce, or baked goods as payment. "Doc Susie," as they referred to her, even had to become a dentist of sorts since there were few to be found in this part of the country. She became so respected by the logging communities that when the Denver and Salt Lake Railroad management reclaimed the land on which her shack was built, the Stevens-Barr sawmill company gave her a piece of land. Next, the Swedish lumberjacks got together and built her a house and barn with a carefully laid-out floor plan to provide cubicles for patients, a luxury she had not had since she began her work in Grand County.

In 1918, a large influenza epidemic hit the county. "Doc Susie had rarely slept as people rushed her from one deathbed to the next. Her reputation for saving pneumonia patients put her in much demand, but more often than not, the Grim Reaper beat her to the patient" (Cornell, 1991: 193). A few years later, Dr. Anderson began to realize that she needed to have a steady income; after all, she was now fifty-four, so she accepted the position of county coroner in 1926. She also maintained her medical practice until 1958, since she was the only doctor in Fraser or in many of the surrounding communities. She was now eighty-eight years old. At the Colorado General Hospital in Denver, her medical colleagues and friends amputated a blackened toe, the relic of an old frostbite occurrence. She went into a rest home and died in 1960, when she was ninety years old. Doc Susie was the medical angel of Grand County, Colorado, for half a century.

SOURCE: Cornell, V. (1991), *Doc Susie: The True Story of a Country Physician in the Colorado Rockies* (New York: Ivy Books).

ELIZABETH ARDEN (1878–1966)

"Opening a fashion building in a World's Fair may not seem very important when outside the world is going to pieces [1940 World War II], but it has its significance. . . . It means that individuals are not going to pieces . . . no matter what comes or what goes, I shall go on as best I can, making women look courageous and steady." (Florence Graham, Founder, Elizabeth Arden)

As a little girl growing up in Toronto, Canada, Florence "Flo" Graham knew hardship and tragedy. She was one of five children born to William Graham and Susan Tadd Graham. Although Florence Graham's mother had come from a wealthy British family, her father hadn't. Susan Tadd's parents wouldn't approve of any such marriage, so the young couple eloped and left for a new start in a new land. The Grahams had a strong love for each other but William's unwise horse purchases, the meager living he eked out of the land as a tenant farmer, the subsequent poverty, and regular childbirths were too much for Susan; she died of tuberculosis when Florence Nightingale Graham was only six years old.

This loss led to two life-long habits for the young girl; the first was putting newspapers in her shoes to keep warm so that she could avoid getting sick, and the second was pursuing wealth with a vengeance. Graham proclaimed to her siblings: "I want to be the richest little woman in the world" (Lewis & Woodworth, 1972: 44). She learned how to sell by helping her father in the open marketplace of York. "She very quickly developed into a precociously shrewd salesgirl. She learned that if she used a babyish voice and acted cute, people would fawn and fuss and buy anything she tried to sell them" (34). Her focus on the customer never wavered once she learned how this tactic led to success.

Graham believed that providing beauty products for women was the avenue she wanted to pursue, but her potential client base was significantly different from her father's. She wanted to sell to wealthy, white women. Her kitchen experimentation began when she was a teenager but often led to such terrible smelling disasters that she and the rest of the family had to get out of the house to breathe fresh air. The neighbors began to believe that the family was so financially desperate that they were cooking rotten eggs to eat. This embarrassed her father and he put a stop to those early attempts of creating beauty products.

The dramatic change in Graham's life didn't occur until she was almost thirty, still determined to pursue her dream of amassing wealth. She decided to pursue this goal in New York City where her brother, William, then lived. Her father was vehemently opposed but she declared: "It's no use, Father. You can't stop me. But don't worry. Nothing's going to happen to me. If I haven't been wicked until now, I'm not likely to start at my age. Who'd be interested?" (Lewis & Woodworth, 1972: 41). Once she got to the city, Graham took various jobs to survive and to learn as much as she could about the industry in which she would eventually achieve her dream. First she became a bookkeeper for E. R. Squibb and Sons to be near the laboratory; then she became a cashier at Eleanor Adair's beauty parlor to learn about treatments and products, and she was a manicurist on the side to add income. In short order, Graham convinced Adair to let her become one of the "beauty culturists" and she quickly gained a reputation for having "healing hands."

The opportunity to start her first business occurred when Elizabeth Hubbard offered to join her in the venture; Hubbard had the products, Graham had the skill. They opened their establishment on Fifth Avenue, which was the first of many of Graham's wise marketing strategies—the tried and true adage of location, location, location. The rich white women she wanted to reach were "in the neighborhood." However, the Hubbard/Graham partnership was volatile from day one; in less than a few months, Graham took over the business and renamed it Mrs. Elizabeth Arden's. Since she had no funds left after paying the rent, her brother loaned her $6,000. Because of her drive, intuition, hard work, and skill at picking the right people, she was able to pay this loan back in less than six months.

Graham's marketing strategies were instinctive and right on target. Instead of naming her business a "parlor," she called it a "salon" to create the image of a European drawing room; she had the front door painted red, which became one of her symbols; her salons were plushly decorated; her products had Grecian-sounding names to evoke images of Venus, the goddess of beauty. Her advertisements were published whether she had the money to make the payroll or not—it wasn't long before meeting payroll was not a problem. She joined the Suffragettes in 1912 because of the contacts she could make. Like Lydia Pinkham, Graham invited women to write to her. She would give them "personal" guidance about beauty products. She developed a regular newspaper that was sent to her customers and created market demand for her products. For example, one article reported when Graham, who by now was referred to as Miss Arden, wanted to introduce a lipstick kit that was made up of seven shades, "she personally toured the country with a troupe of seven ballet girls . . . individually dressed in costumes matching the different shades of lipstick . . . making headlines everywhere they went" (Lewis & Woodworth, 1972: 151).

Arden had a gift for knowing which people could help her business. One of her wisest human resource decisions was to hire chemist Fabian Swanson; she would describe what she envisioned, and he created it in the laboratory. Together they were an amazing team. For example, Arden wanted a face cream that was as light as whipped cream; that doesn't sound strange to us now, but in the early part of the twentieth century face cream was greasy and hard. Swanson knew better than to argue with her; it took a while, but the challenge was met. Arden's vision led to other firsts including being an indomitable force in what could be termed a cosmetic cultural revolution in the United States: "There was a tremendous amount of resistance to cosmetics in small-town America. Every week brought fresh newspaper items about students being expelled, teachers and office workers fired, for wearing makeup" (Lewis & Woodworth, 1972:97). This was no deterrent to Arden. After a trip to Europe where she saw eye makeup used by theater women or "cheap" women, she experimented with various mixtures until she created an eye makeup that enhanced the face and could be used by the general female population. She was the first to put her name on her products. She created the makeup concept of matching colors to clothing. (Until 1932 lipstick colors came in only light, medium, or dark.) One of her products, the Eight Hour Cream, "actually did contain medical properties and worked so well on skin eruptions, abrasions, and burns that children's hospitals used it for treating these afflictions in the young" (180). It would surprise some people even today but, from the start, Arden encouraged men to use her skin products, and she was the first to open a men's boutique in a beauty salon.

Her rise to fame and fortune was swift. "By the 1920s, Elizabeth Arden boasted more than a hundred salon locations" (Vare & Ptacek, 1988: 65), and she had opened her first Elizabeth Arden factory. Then she began her international ventures: a European salon in Paris was opened in 1920; others followed—on the Riviera and in Berlin, Cannes, Rome, Rio de Janeiro, Buenos Aires, and Toronto. Her philosophy that "people valued a product more if they had to pay dearly for it" (Shukar, 1989: 39) was apparently based on the purchase of beauty products and on women beautifying themselves by means of salons and hairdressers. From its domestic wholesale division alone, the Arden Company was grossing over $2,000,000 annually (Lewis & Woodworth, 1972: 121).

Arden was offered $15 million for her business in 1929; she refused. She weathered the Great Depression with little difficulty. By the mid-thirties, she was manufacturing over a hundred different products and in almost 600 separate shapes and sizes. A few years later, she was offered $25 million for her business; the offer came from United States Steel; once again she refused. In 1943 Arden started her own clothing line and contributed to the career success of such internationally renowned designers as Oscar de la Renta, Ferdinando Sarmi, and Antonio Castillo. "Isn't it remarkable what a woman can do with a little ambition?" she commented (Lewis & Woodworth, 1972: 205).

It was socialite Elisabeth Marbury who introduced Arden to the beautiful countryside of Mount Vernon, Maine. There she bought her "retreat" property next to Marbury's summer estate and named it "Maine Chance." But when Marbury died unexpectedly, Arden's feelings about the place changed; instead of a restful getaway for herself, she turned it into a spa for other wealthy women. "At most there were twenty guests per week who were served by forty servants, including six gardeners, and who paid between $250 and $500, at the nadir of the Depression, for an average weight loss of six pounds a week. Elizabeth had spent months going over the details of how each moment of their day was to be spent" (Lewis & Woodworth, 1972: 159). Arden was not one to give up any control if she had a choice in the matter, which she almost always did.

With her retreat now turned into a business, Arden was advised to find a hobby. She decided to follow the dream of her father to own racehorses and purchased her first horse in 1931. In seven years this "hobby" was out of the red; earnings went from less than $7,000 in 1943 to almost $600,000 in less than two years under the expert guidance of trainer Tom Smith and Arden's tender loving care. "She insisted that her horses' legs be massaged for twenty minutes before and one hour after races. The Eight Hour Cream proved as good for horses as it was for women and children and began to appear in stables all over the world" (Lewis & Woodworth, 1972: 184). Her favorite color may have been pink but her touch was golden.

Up until her eighties, Arden was in complete control of her empire and worked vigorously, but as her health began deteriorating with advanced age, she made the tough decision to let the horse breeding/racing side of her life slide so that she could put what energy she had into the business. She refused to develop a succession plan, however. The Elizabeth Arden company was to be hers until the day she died, which occurred when she was eighty-eight. According to authors Lewis and Woodworth, "The will was explicit about everything except the most important item of all—the empire. . . . Large sums were to be divided among those [employees] with ten years or more of service . . . [and] the government had a claim to $37,000,000 in estate and corporate taxes" (314–15). Four years after Arden's death, the business was sold to Eli Lilly and Company for $38.5 million.

SOURCES: Leckie, J. (1970), *A Talent for Living: The Story of Henry Sell, an American Original* (New York: Hawthorn Books, Inc.); Lewis, A., & Woodworth, C. (1972), *Miss Elizabeth Arden* (New York: Coward, McCann, & Geoghegan, Inc.); Shuker, N. (1989), *Elizabeth Arden: Cosmetics Entrepreneur* (Englewood Cliffs, NJ: Silver Burdette Press); Vare, E., & Ptacek, G. (1988), *Mothers of Invention: From the Bra to the Bomb: Forgotten Women and Their Unforgettable Ideas* (New York: William Morrow and Company).

LISA ARNBRISTER (1964–   )

"Business ventures are always risky. . . . Day-to-day changes are unpredictable. . . . We need to remain unique with our products and focused on the client. That's the challenge, and that's why I enjoy what I do." (Lisa Arnbrister, Founder, Tuff Scent-Ence)

As her five-year-old daughter was playing with Mr. Sketch markers, especially the apple-scented green one, single parent Lisa Arnbrister had an inspiration: Why not put scents into nail polish? It was not unusual for her to be coming up with new ideas. She had been raised to think innovatively and entrepreneurially by her family. When her mother, Juanita Washburn, was alive, she had been a cosmetologist, an herbologist, and a retail merchant, the latter with her husband, Ken Arnbrister. An uncle had developed and patented a golf shoe, and Lisa's brother, Allen, was a pioneer of snowboarding. "Do your own thing" was a subtle, powerful message she received and welcomed (Ritorto, 1999).

The two Arnbrister children were born in San Mateo, California, but the family set its sights on Lake Tahoe, moving there in 1976 to open a health food store. Within two years, they added a high-end specialty fashion boutique, Fine 'n' Funky, to their enterprises, enabling Lisa Arnbrister to learn about merchandising while still a teenager. She later chose marketing as her focus in the business program at the University of Colorado–Boulder, where she earned her bachelor's degree.

Arnbrister immediately put this education to work in her family's fashion business as store manager, buyer, and merchandiser. "I even designed and produced lines of clothing for the store," she added. By 1987, the Arnbrister family had expanded to Reno, Nevada, opening a second location of Fine 'n' Funky there. Marriage, a child, and divorce filled in the next five years, but then came her innovative idea, and by 1995 Lisa Arnbrister had started her own company, Tuff Scent-Ence. She was thirty-two, free to do what she wanted and eager to be successful on her own. Arnbrister based her company in Reno and financed it solely with credit cards. Orders came quickly, but so did some problems.

Since she was new to how chemicals, the ingredients in her nail polish products, worked and interacted and also inexperienced about quality-assurance issues in the cosmetic industry, Arnbrister did not pay attention to these factors. After she had 70,000 bottles manufactured and was shipping large orders, the temperature rose so high that the heat from the chemical reaction in the small bottles broke many of them. Though this was a financial setback, it was temporary, because Arnbrister turned to a different manufacturer, one who could guarantee quality control and timely shipment of customer orders. A second financial loss was the not-so-wise $400,000 purchase of counter display units made of injection molding. In spite of these setbacks, Arnbrister focused on marketing and publicity. As a result, Tuff Scent-Ence was noticed and used by famous celebrities like Julia Roberts, Drew Barrymore, Fran Drescher, and Cindy Crawford. Arnbrister herself appeared on the Oprah Winfrey Show.

By 1998 gross annual sales had surpassed the $1.5 million mark. Tuff Scent-Ence had a customer base of more than 350 retail stores and had put up a Web site for individual purchases as well. Arnbrister's product is the first aromatic nail lacquer, and she estimated that the age range of her customers is as broad as from five to sixty years old. Her original line of over fifty fragranced nail polishes has been expanded to include lipsticks, lip gloss, lip liner, nail polish remover, hand and body creams, and body scrubs. Her products are available in stores like Bloomingdale's and Sephora. Arnbrister has also added other concepts to the original nail polish, including a floral-scented line with silk flowers in the bottles and a zodiac line that has bottles decorated with charms of the twelve astrological signs.

Arnbrister attributes her success to persistence, focus, and analysis of the big picture. She adds that "you need to be willing to sacrifice what you are for what you can become. However, what is most important is enjoyment of the process" (Ritorto, 1999).

SOURCES: Ritorto, M. (1999), Telephone interview with Lisa Arnbrister on March 4; Tuff Scent-Ence (1999), *http://www.tuffscentence.com.*

MARY KAY ASH (c. 1916–   )

"The question was asked, 'How did you do this? How did you get so far so fast?' Well, I was a middle-aged woman, had varicose veins, and I didn't have time to fool around! And so we started with a measly $5,000. Had I tried to go to the bank to borrow money they would have laughed me right out of there. It was years later when I found out that a bank would lend me money as soon as I proved I didn't need it." (Mary Kay Ash, Founder, Mary Kay, Inc.)

Having a sense of humor is one of the personal characteristics that helped Mary Kay Wagner Rogers Ash, better known around the world simply as Mary Kay, to survive through a difficult life and prosper in a demanding industry. She was one of four children born in Hot Wells, Texas, of entrepreneurial parents who owned a small restaurant. As a child of seven, Mary Kay became the caretaker of her siblings when her father contracted tuberculosis, since her mother had to put in fourteen-hour days in the business to keep food on the table and a roof over their heads. Mary Kay recalled, "My only contact with her was by phone. . . . She always told me in great detail how to do the things I needed to do and would end every conversation with the words, 'You can do it, honey.' That has become the guiding theme of my life" (Taylor, 1988: 67).

Mary Kay also excelled in the classroom and in extracurricular activities. She was a straight-A student and a member of the debating and drill teams. Her dream was to become a doctor, but as no money was available, she got married right after high school like other young women of her time. She and her husband, Ben Rogers, a local radio musician, soon had a daughter, two sons, and a disruption in their marriage. World War II had begun, and Rogers was drafted. When he returned from military duty, he asked for a divorce, leaving Mary Kay a single parent with three children to support. "That was the lowest point in my life. . . . I felt like a complete failure as a woman," Mary Kay noted (Shook, 1981: 107).

She went to work right away carrying two jobs, one as secretary at the

Tabernacle Baptist Church in Houston, the other as a dealer for Stanley Home Products. Though there for only a few years, this opportunity helped her hone her exceptional sales ability. At one point, Mary Kay determined that she needed to go to the company's sales convention in Dallas, but she didn't have the twelve dollars needed for the trip. She borrowed the money from a woman friend, who critically "suggested that she ought to be spending it on shoes for her children rather than going to conventions like men" (Shook, 1981: 107). She experienced many such admonitions in the years to come but always heard her mother's voice reminding her, "You can do it, honey!"

In 1953, Mary Kay was offered a position with the World Gift Company of Dallas that paid more money than she had been earning. She joined the home accessories firm and remained with them for ten years. But here she experienced the "glass-ceiling effect"—that is, women were allowed to rise only so far in the organization. "I would take a man out on the road for training, and after I'd been teaching him the business for six months, he'd come back to Dallas and end up being my superior at twice my salary. It always irked me when I was told that the men 'had families to support' so they deserved more pay because I had a family to support, too!" she pointed out. "It seemed that a woman's brains were worth only fifty cents on the dollar in a male-run corporation" (Shook, 1981: 108).

Since she had remarried by this time and had a relatively comfortable life, Mary Kay retired, but that didn't last long. Soon her restless spirit took over and she was drafting up her concept of the ideal company for women. As she wrote, the notion that this ideal could be her own company began to form. What she needed was a product. For more than ten years, she had been using a skin cream developed by a tanner and sold in homes by his daughter; both were deceased by 1963. Mary Kay bought the rights to the product from the family and, with her total life savings of $5,000, began to formulate her business with her second husband, who was taking over the responsibility for the financial management. Then tragedy hit. Her husband died one month before they were to open their new business. Advice from both her attorney and accountant not to go forward fell on deaf ears. She was determined. Then her youngest son, Richard Rogers, offered to help. He was an ex-Marine selling life insurance. As Mary Kay presented the situation: "Now I ask you, how would you like to turn your life savings over to your twenty year old? If my son Richard had a brain, I didn't know about it! . . . But it turns out that God knew more about that son of mine than I did . . . he's [now] recognized as one of those young financial geniuses across the nation" (*Outstanding*, 1993: 70).

With herself, her son, and nine cosmetic consultants, on Friday the thirteenth in September 1963, the Mary Kay Cosmetics organization was born, with one major goal being to offer "women unprecedented opportunities for financial independence, career advancement, and personal fulfillment" (Mary Kay, 1999). The mode of operation was the party plan, whereby consultants would go into homes and give lessons on skin care. "Each recruit [paid] $65 for a Beauty Kit. All orders to the company [were] paid in money orders or cashier's checks [because] Mary Kay [had] witnessed many direct sales companies go broke due to loose credit policies" (Shook, 1981: 113). In the first year, sales quickly rose to $198,000; the following year, sales soared to $800,000. Six years later, Mary Kay went international; by 1972, sales had reached $18 million. Mary Kay wrote the first of her three books in 1981, the same year that her company went public. Two years later, wholesale sales surpassed the $300 million mark. By 1986, she decided to buy back the company from stockholders for $250 million (Silver, 1994). Wholesale sales totaled more than a billion dollars by 1997, and Mary Kay had operations in twenty-nine markets.

Mary Kay Ash has received many honors and recognitions, including the Horatio Alger Distinguished American Citizen Award, Outstanding Women in Business in Dallas Award, Churchwoman of the Year Award, and the Individual Komen Award for Philanthropy, and she was the first woman to receive the Kupfer Distinguished Executive Award. In addition, Mary Kay has been a very generous philanthropist. Examples include her Mary Kay Ash Charitable Foundation, which helps fund research on cancers affecting women; her sponsorship of the Center for Retailing Studies at Texas A&M University; the Mary Kay Museum; the Mary Kay Ash Center for Cancer Immunotherapy Research; and the Mary Kay Ash–St. Paul Medical Center Mobile Cancer Screening Unit in Dallas, Texas. The company's environmental efforts have been so significant that Mary Kay, Inc., has been acknowledged by the Environmental Protection Agency, and Mary Kay has received a number of environmental excellence awards. In explanation of this phenomenal success, Mary Kay would likely note the Bible parable of the talents, Matthew 25: 14–30, as she did in her book *On People Management*: "We are meant to use and increase whatever God has given us. And when we do, we shall be given more" (Ash, 1984: ix).

SOURCES: Ash, M. (1984), *Mary Kay on People Management* (New York: Warner Books); Fucini, J., & Fucini, S. (1985), *Entrepreneurs: The Men and Women Behind Famous Brand Names and How They Made It* (Boston, MA: G. K. Hall & Co.); Mary Kay (1999), *http://www.marykay.com/marykay/about/company* (accessed August 25, 1999); *Outstanding Business Leaders* (1993) (Midland, MI: Northwood University Press); Shook, R. (1981), *The Entrepreneurs: Twelve Who Took Risks and Succeeded* (New York: Harper & Row); Silver, A. (1994), *Enterprising Women: Lessons from 100 of the Greatest Entrepreneurs of Our Day* (New York: AMACOM); Sobel, R., & Sicilia, D. (1986), *The Entrepreneurs: An American Adventure* (Boston, MA: Houghton Mifflin Company); Taylor, R. (1988), *Exceptional Entrepreneurs: Strategies for Success* (New York: Praeger).

HATTIE MOSELEY AUSTIN (1900–1998)

"Whenever anybody comes to the door, give 'em something to eat. That may be Jesus." (Hattie Moseley Austin, Founder of Hattie's Chicken Shack)

Though it is hard to imagine that an African American girl, the youngest child born to Harry and Lydia Gray of St. Francisville, Louisiana, in 1900, could have dreamed of becoming a well-known restaurateur in a famous racing city in upstate New York, this is what happened to Hattie Gray, a woman whose life began with the tragedy of her mother dying as she gave birth to this daughter. Little is known of her early years except that Hattie, who had some siblings, was raised by a local rabbi, not by her family. As a teenager, Hattie moved to New Orleans, where she learned how to sew, becoming a dressmaker for several families. When she was later able to visit a sister in Chicago, she met the A. E. Staley family, who had acquired their wealth in the starch industry. They hired Hattie, and she traveled with them, as was the custom with domestic workers at the time.

The Staleys wintered in Miami and summered in Saratoga Springs, New York. It was in the world-famous racing city of Saratoga that Hattie met the man who would become her first husband—Willy Moseley, a cigar-shop owner and alleged bookmaker. After they were married, Hattie began working in a local restaurant, but not until the 1930s, after her husband died, did she consider starting her own business. She began by making chicken and biscuits for her friends, deciding soon after to open a stand to sell these same items. She was able to use her own savings since the start-up costs were low. Her business was so successful that within a year she had earned enough income to buy property on the very populated Federal Street. In 1938 she started Hattie's Chicken Shack, which was open twenty-four hours a day in the early years because, at the time, Saratoga was a hot spot for "gambling, speakeasies, and smoky jazz clubs" (MacLean, 1993). According to Hattie, "Saratoga was fast . . . real fast. It was up all night long" (MacLean, 1993). This is when she met Bill Austin, the man who not only would become her second husband but also work the "front of the house" while Hattie ran the kitchen. He became known for his large bow tie and smooth charm.

After thirty years in the same location, Saratoga went through an ur-ban renewal project that forced Hattie to relocate, raising a general suspicion in the community about the true motivations behind this project. However, having to relocate did not negatively affect her business because she had long ago earned the loyalty of her customers. Her new location on Phila Street is where Hattie's restaurant still stands, some thirty years later.

The menu at Hattie's Chicken Shack has stayed constant for more than sixty years—ribs, cobbler, collards, corn bread, and, of course, chicken. "In the hearts and stomachs of many it's still the only place for fried chicken in August," according to restaurant critic William Dowd (Dowd, 1996: 1). Yet all who came to know her realized that Hattie didn't just serve up food; she provided work for young people regardless of color, helped some of them through school, and, on occasion, took one or two into her home as family. Current owner Christel MacLean recalled that "Hattie was also known for her sense of humor and that special quality of treating royalty and the downtrodden exactly alike, making everyone feel welcome" (MacLean, 1993).

In 1992, when she was already ninety-two but still cooking in the kitchen, Hattie met a new customer—Christel Albritton MacLean, an investment banker for Solomon Brothers. MacLean had come to Greenwich, New York, to recover from a horseback-riding accident. A friend asked her to lunch to ward off her "cabin fever." MacLean had an old travel guide to the region she had picked up in a used book store, and in this she discovered an entry for Hattie's Chicken Shack. She called to see if the restaurant was still open; since it was, she and her friend headed to Saratoga. Bill Austin was almost deaf by this time but was still taking food orders. What he brought back was not what they ordered, but they enjoyed it just the same.

Then a strange encounter with Hattie changed MacLean's life; she had asked to meet this customer, having mistaken her for a local television reporter. Hattie was not disappointed when she discovered her mistake. Instead, she predicted that MacLean would buy the restaurant. Even though MacLean tried to explain that she was in banking and had no desire to be a restaurateur, Hattie's premonition held true. MacLean kept in touch with this elderly legend for the next few years. At the age of ninety-three Hattie announced to MacLean that she was going to close the restaurant because she was too tired. At the same time, Wall Street had lost its luster for MacLean because of the "one hundred twenty hour weeks and no life outside of work." In 1995, she bought Hattie's Chicken Shack, believing that "Hattie sold it to me because she knew I would run the restaurant with the same ideals she had and would never do anything to disrupt the integrity of what Hattie had created" (Tucker, 1999). In 1998 Hattie Moseley Austin died at ninety-eight years of age, having served up food for over sixty years.

SOURCES: Dowd, W. (1996), "Faithful Ol' Hattie's Evolving," *The Times Union* [Online], August 16 (available: Lexis-Nexis); MacLean, C. A. (1993), The Story of Hattie, *http://www.hattiesrestaurant.com* (July 16; accessed January 30, 1999); Tucker, L. (1999), personal interview with Christel Albritton MacLean, March 8.

HARRIET AYER (1849–1903)

"That those weeping, groaning and shrieking, unheard voices, muffled behind thick walls, should find in mine outside an echo that would resound end to end throughout this liberty-loving land, has been a purpose to me infinitely dearer than the life so blighted by the hideous experiences to which I was subjected, owing to the iniquitous laxity of the lunacy laws." (Harriet Ayer, Founder, Harriet Hubbard Ayer Cosmetics Company)

The obstacle courses that Harriet Hubbard Ayer encountered and overcame in her fifty-four years on this earth read more like the pages of a novel than real life. She was the sixth child born into the respected Chicago household of Henry and Juliet Hubbard, a couple who had already lost three children from diseases like cholera, consumption, or "brain fever," which were rampant in this historical period. When she was only four years old, Harriet's father died from pneumonia, and her mother did what other fashionable women of the day did—she took to her bed for most of the next thirty years.

Harriet's formal schooling did not begin until she was twelve, though she had learned to read by the age of five. Her painful shyness led the nuns of the Sacred Heart School to think that she wasn't capable of learning; her mother even thought she might be "dull in brains as well as in looks" (Ayer & Taves, 1957: 23). Harriet got used to being considered an "ugly duckling" for the first twenty years of her life. No one knew what incredible spirit and talent she had. When she was fifteen, she met Herbert Ayer, the alcoholic son of the very wealthy Chicago iron tycoon John V. Ayer. Though it wasn't love at first sight, young Harriet felt privileged to have such a "good catch" court her. Shortly after their marriage, she became pregnant and ill, seriously enough to be hospitalized. During this time, she discovered two facts about herself: She loved to read the novels of Charles Dickens, and she abhorred the poverty others endured. When her doctor commented that she couldn't help everybody, Harriet responded that she could help a few people. While still recovering in the hospital, she provided anonymous gifts—such as a layette for a mother who couldn't afford one.

She even paid the hospital bill for and sent food to the family of a woman who had broken her hip and whose husband was unemployed. This latter good deed would help save her own children's lives a few years later.

The Ayer's first child was a girl; while Herbert had hoped for a boy, he accepted little Hattie lovingly. It is strangely noted that Harriet, the ugly duckling, became a beautiful woman after giving birth to this baby, much to the chagrin of her alcoholic, playboy husband. He was now fixated on having a son. When the second child born the following year was also a girl, and sickly at that, he began to act as if he blamed his wife and reverted to his past behavior, again visiting saloons. Soon after little Gertrude came, Harriet was pregnant again. Her husband was increasingly perturbed because, when pregnant, his wife was becoming an avid student, which he deplored. He had mistakenly believed that "enough babies would keep her nose out of the books" (Ayer & Taves, 1957: 50). Then there were two simultaneous and catastrophic blows to the Ayers family. The Great Chicago Fire devastated much of the city, including their home. They were not there when the fire broke out and at first thought that their children and housekeeper would perish. But suddenly a stranger with a horse and buggy appeared, ready to take them back to rescue their family. The man said he was waiting for Mrs. Ayer, that his wife told him to do so. Then he explained, "Ma'am, you helped my wife and me when she broke her hip. There was nothing we could do for you before, but you saved our lives. God willing, we'll all escape" (57). Although they got the children and housekeeper out safely, the smoke inhalation had been too much for baby Gertrude, who died the following day.

In time, Harriet, traumatized by the loss of her baby, went to Europe to try to regain her emotional and physical health. It was on this trip in Paris that she first learned of the facial product that would later make her rich and famous. She was told it was the actual formula used by the well-known beauty Julie Récamier. When she returned home, her husband had become even more jealous, and "her failure to produce a son had become an issue between them. She had gone through a series of miscarriages, which had made her weak and morose, subject to bouts of insomnia" (Ayer & Taves, 1957: 85). However, after her father-in-law, a man she loved and respected, pleaded with her to try to reconcile with Herbert and have another child, Harriet conceded. A year later, their third and last child was born, again a daughter, Margaret Mitchell, who was ignored by her father yet loved and pampered by her grandfather until his death.

The reconciliation of the Ayers was short-lived. Harriet asked for a divorce, discovering soon after that her husband had driven his father's iron business into the ground. She was left almost penniless. Then she remembered the skin cream in France, bought the formula, and began to make samples to test. At this time, she made a critical error in judgment—one that would later nearly destroy her—when she began a business relationship with Jim Seymour, a wealthy man she had known for several years. Ayer had no reason to distrust him when he offered to loan her $50,000 to start the business, taking stock as collateral for the loan. She accepted his offer. "Within six months, the cream was selling well not only in America, but in Europe. . . . Harriet then conceived the idea of persuading famous women of the time to let her use their endorsements in advertising—women like Adelina Patti, Sarah Bernhardt, Lily Langtry, Lillian Russell . . . it was not long before she was . . . planning new additions to the Recamier line: balm, freckle and mouth lotion, soap, powder, depilatory, tonic for the blood" (Ayer & Taves, 1957: 152).

Then Harriet learned that her daughter and the son of Jim Seymour were falling in love. Fearful that a marriage between them could cause problems, considering her business connections with Seymour, she went to see him to express her concern. Insulting and shocking her, he didn't respond, asking her instead to be his mistress. When she refused, he threatened to make life hell for her. He was a man wealthy enough to carry out this threat, and he did. Although the following incidents seem too bizarre and the stuff of which novels are made, they are verifiable in the respected press of the day. Harriet Hubbard Ayer was drugged while on a visit to Europe, at the bidding of Jim Seymour.

Harriet, now knowing the treachery of Seymour, took him to court. He tried to turn the tables on her by saying that she had never repaid the $50,000, but there were enough witnesses and evidence for the court to accept that Seymour had illegally entered her house and destroyed the documents. He was brazen enough not to deny that he had gone into her home and place of business. Medical testimony also verified that "being given fifteen grains of sulfonal every half hour, would weaken her mind and body and ultimately kill her" (Ayer & Taves, 1957: 190). Harriet won the case, and Seymour was ordered by the court to return her stocks. However, his revenge didn't stop here.

Harriet's alcoholic ex-husband who "was being supported by the Seymours and was installed in a luxurious suite at New York's fashionable new Holland House" (Ayer & Taves, 1957: 233) had Harriet declared mentally unfit and put in an insane asylum—illegally, but there was no one to stop him. After fourteen months, a man who was self-admitted to the institution befriended her. Speaking in French so that the attendants would not understand them, he arranged for Harriet to get word out to her attorney and other friends. She was quickly released; her business and her health had been destroyed, but not her underlying spirit. Harriet was now forty-five years old.

For a while, and understandably, Harriet was depressed, yet she began writing and talking about the abusive treatment of the mentally ill. Then one day, she happened to go into the Trinity Church, bowing her head in prayer. When she left she had no plans, but she noticed the sun reflecting off the dome of the Pulitzer building, which housed Joseph Pulitzer's *New World* newspaper. She found herself walking in and asking for a job. Since her name was so recognizable, the Sunday editor, Arthur Brisbane, agreed to see her. When she explained that she would like to write for the paper, he had her write a column on the spot. This started her on the road to widespread acclaim as a feature writer for the *New World* newspaper, "specializing in interviews of women involved in notorious crimes. . . . [She also became] editor of the woman's page" (Ayer & Taves, 1957: 15). She worked there for seven years, getting as many as 20,000 letters a year from readers. During this time, she also wrote and published *Harriet Hubbard Ayer's Book of Health and Beauty*. In 1903, after she had dutifully finished her last column, Harriet Hubbard Ayer died. The business manager at the paper, Don Seitz, had the flag on the World building flown at half mast. When two male reporters asked, "You did that for a woman?" Seitz answered, "She was the best man on the staff" (284).

SOURCE: Ayer, M., & Taves, I. (1957), *The Three Lives of Harriet Hubbard Ayer* (Philadelphia, PA: J. B. Lippincott Company).

NINNIE BAIRD (1869–1961)

"My goal is to bake a better loaf of bread today than I did the day before. We will use only the finest ingredients, and we will take no short cuts." (Ninnie Baird, Founder, Mrs. Baird's Bakeries)

In 1908, at the age of thirty-nine, Ninnie Baird found herself in the position of having to find a way to support her sickly husband, William, and their eight children. She focused on what she knew how to do well, which was bake. Baird had been taught fine baking techniques by the aunt who raised her back in Tennessee where she was born. Over the years Baird had been giving her extra baked goods to neighbors and friends, who raved about them. Now, out of necessity, she decided to bake her pies, cakes, and bread for sale. At this time her cooking was done in a wood-burning stove; trying to produce in quantity was laborious. In addition, "not only was it hot during the summer (a roaring fire had to be kept constantly blazing to keep the oven temperature as even as possible) but . . . wood needed to be chopped by hand and then loaded into the stove. Starting the fire was also a challenge. The stove's damper was small and didn't create much draft to get the fire started or to keep it going" (Mrs. Baird's Bakeries, 1998). Baird could only make four loaves at a time with this oven; as soon as the batches were done, her sons hand-carried the baked goods to their customers.

Baird's husband died from diabetes just a few years after her fledgling bakery business began. The children worked either with their mother or in jobs outside the home so that the family could survive. The business soon started to thrive in their Fort Worth, Texas, hometown. By 1915 Baird bought her first commercial oven for seventy-five dollars through an interesting financial arrangement: She paid cash of twenty-five dollars and the rest in baked goods. Another cash-flow strategy was giving customers the opportunity to pay in advance for their bread. They could buy tickets, twenty-four for a dollar, with each ticket exchangeable for a one-pound loaf of bread. Baird also reviewed the ledgers carefully to make sure that records were accurate.

By 1917 Baird was able to purchase a motorized vehicle so that she no longer had to use the horse and buggy to distribute her baked goods. "A panel body was built for it, the passenger seats were taken out and the truck was painted a cream color. The words, 'Eat More Mrs. Baird's Bread' were written on each side" (Mrs. Baird's Bakeries, 1998). At about this time the Bairds started to acquire wholesale accounts. By 1918 Mrs. Baird had purchased a new facility and a new oven in which four hundred loaves of bread could be baked at one time. Ten years later a plant in Dallas was added, but a year after this acquisition, the Great Depression hit the United States, with banks failing and businesses closing their doors. Fortunately, Mrs. Baird's was one of the survivors. Bess Hornbeck, a cashier at the bakery, recalled that "one time we had a million dollars in the vault at the plant. You couldn't put it in the bank and neither could anybody else. The different grocery stores around town would come to the bakery to get money—we sort of became an unofficial bank" (Mrs. Baird's Bakeries, 1998).

By 1938 Mrs. Baird had plants in Houston, Dallas, and Fort Worth. When World War II broke out just a short time later, the challenges that faced the company were mainly shortages—of both ingredients and employees. This caused the Bairds to narrow the variety of baked goods they were offering and led to what became a strategic change in their core business; they now focused on breads. Baird also had a consistent emphasis on total quality long before "TQM" (Total Quality Management) came into vogue. When other bakery businesses were using chemicals to speed up the dough-rising process, Ninnie Baird insisted on using the slower yeast process. She inculcated the theme of quality, freshness, and service into the value system of her organization. Baird had modeled these concepts from the early days when "she would break eggs one at a time so she could inspect each one before mixing it in the dough. 'She would look at the coloring of the egg and would smell it to make sure each one was good enough to put in the mix,' " recalled her grandson Arthur. "She was very precise and wanted everything done exactly right" (Mrs. Baird's Bakeries, 1998).

Throughout her lifetime, Ninnie Baird kept a tight rein on the company. When she died in 1961 at ninety-two years of age, "the Texas Legislature passed a resolution honoring Ninnie that declared, 'Mrs. Baird was a living example for mothers, wives, business executives, Christians, and people the world over' " (Thorpe, 1996: 54). The business she had started continued to thrive, run by family members, and in 1992 the family was inducted into the Texas Business Hall of Fame. Mrs. Baird's became the largest such business in the United States, operating twelve plants in the state of Texas; by 1995, the company was one of the top five revenue producers in the bakery business. Then a scandal hit; the Bairds were found guilty of price-fixing. The subsequent pursuit by former large customers led to a bankruptcy filing to move the plaintiffs into a willingness-to-negotiate posture. A reorganization of the company followed, and the company was subsequently sold in 1998 to Grupo Industrial Bimbo, Mexico's leading baking company (Hassell, 1998).

From her kitchen in a rented house at 511 Hemphill in Fort Worth, Texas, Ninnie Baird initiated a baking empire that eventually employed over three thousand people, had twelve plants throughout Texas, offered more than two hundred products, and had over $300 million in sales.

SOURCES: Hassell, G. (1998), "Mexican Firm Buying Mrs. Baird/Few Changes Seen under New Owner," *Houston Chronicle*, March 25; Hoover's Company Capsules (1998), Hoover's Company Profiles, *http://www.pathfinder.com/money/hoovers/corpdirectory/* (accessed July 17); Mrs. Baird's Bakeries (1998), *http://www.mrsbairds.com/* (accessed July 17); Thorpe, H. (1996), "Bad News, Baird's," *Texas Monthly*, August.

KAVELLE BAJAJ (1950–)

"I knew I had made it when I was able to hire my husband." (Kavelle Bajaj, Founder, I-Net)

For a female child born in India, the future was programmed. Her profession was to be a housewife and mother. "My parents were very typical," Kavelle Bajaj stated. "They thought you should endow a girl with whatever you can so that she can be a good wife and mother, and then you marry her off. My father sent me to a Catholic school even though we were Sikhs because it was well-known for its high educational standards" (Enkelis & Olsen, 1995: 116). Kavelle went to college and earned an appropriate home economics degree from Delhi University. In 1974, she agreed to a family-arranged marriage with Ken Bajaj, Ph.D., a computer science professor teaching in the engineering department of Wayne State University in Detroit, Michigan. They had met only a few times, and she had concerns because he was so quiet, but her father quipped, "You won't give him a chance to talk anyway!" (116). This marriage, though not unusual, would change her life's direction, slowly at first but exponentially in the decade to follow.

The Bajajs had two sons, Sunny and Rueben, but motherhood did not suppress Kavelle's restless spirit. She wanted to work and became an Avon lady but found selling cosmetics wasn't fulfilling her real basic need. "I felt that being a wife and mother was a thankless job. For most of us, we do it because we love the people we do it for, but there were days when I would thirst for intellectual stimulation" (Enkelis & Olsen, 1995: 117). In the meantime, as Ken had taken a new position with the Electronic Data Systems Corporation in 1982, the family moved to Washington, DC. Kavelle went back to school and took some computing courses. To keep his wife occupied while he was working longer and longer hours, Ken suggested she put what she was learning in the classroom to good use. He loaned her $5,000 to buy some word-processing equipment for a business in the basement of their home. "I had to overcome some cultural barriers," she recalled, because "I came from a very protected environment where you live in a shell. For me, the concept of going out and networking to establish business contacts was difficult, but I realized it was a necessity" (Estrada, 1994: F9).

As she was beginning to service other businesses, Kavelle made a critical observation about what was occurring in offices around the country at this early point in the personal computer industry. "There were no common standards so it was almost impossible to make all the computers 'talk' to each other. It was a nightmare. People really needed help coming up with solutions for this problem. . . . It just seemed like someone ought to be putting all these things together" (Enkelis & Olsen, 1995: 115). Bajaj followed her "gut," focusing on systems integration, particularly the problem of local-area networks in offices, and appropriately named her new company I-Net. She brought in the technical talent to carry out her vision and then, in 1985, landed her first six-figure contract as a minority-owned business with a federal agency, the National Oceanic and Atmospheric Administration. "The job turned into an $800,000, four-year contract for I-Net, Inc." (Horwitt, 1991: 69). Being nontechnical in a highly technical field was actually an advantage, Bajaj pointed out. "You are more likely to focus on the big picture, and you don't get bogged down in too many details. Your analysis of a customer's problem is much more accurate. And when you recognize problems, you can find solutions" (Enkelis & Olsen, 1995: 118).

Like other early comers to the computing revolution who started out in the 1980s, Kavelle Bajaj's rise to business success was meteoric. Revenues nearly doubled every year: For example, in less than three years from the initiation of I-Net, annual revenues were $8 million; by 1990, $30 million; 1992, $95 million; 1993, $147 million; 1994, $235 million; 1995, $327 million. At this point, I-Net had over 2,700 employees in the United States, England, Kuwait, Austria, Colombia, and Singapore.

In 1988 Kavelle convinced her husband to join I-Net as executive vice president. This wife/husband team had specific strengths, and they had carefully divided the responsibilities accordingly—Kavelle dealing with contracts and the financial affairs of the business; Ken, with operations and development. With all this success, however, has come a toll on family relationships. Kavelle admitted that she and her husband argue and debate, "It does get a little violent from time to time. I think it bothers the kids [but] people need to vent" (McMenamin, 1993: 344).

By 1996 Kavell Bajaj had sold I-Net to Wang Laboratories for $167 million. One observation she made about her family/work experience was that "keeping a good balance is so hard, but so important. When all is said and done, none of us can survive as an island unto ourselves; ultimately, what is truly valuable is to have a good family life" (Enkelis & Olsen, 1995: 123).

SOURCES: Corcoran, E. (1996), "Wang Laboratories to Buy I-Net of Bethesda," *Washington Post* [Online], July 25: D15 (available: Lexis-Nexis, accessed August 5, 1999); Enkelis, L., & Olsen, K. (1995), *On Our Own Terms* (San Francisco, CA: Berrett-Koehler Publishers); Estess, P. (1990), "Honey, You're Hired," *Entrepreneurial Woman*, December: 18–19; Estrada, L. (1994), "Recognizing an Emerging Market: Early Move into Computer Networking Boosts I-Net to Prominence," *Washington Post* [Online], May 4: F9 (available: Lexis-Nexis, accessed August 5, 1999); Horwitt, E. (1991), "I-Net Soars by Capturing Fledgling Niches," *Computerworld* [Online], September 9: 69 (available: Lexis-Nexis, accessed August 5, 1999); Meer, A. (1991), "I-Net's Bajaj Built Company from Basement Up," *Washington Post*, October 21 (available: Lexis-Nexis, accessed August 5, 1999); McMenamin, B. (1993), "Yes, Dear," *Forbes* [Online], November 8: 344 (available: Proquest, accessed August 5, 1999); Melwani, L. (1996), "I-Net Calling," *Asia, Inc.*, April: 70.

CLARA BARTON (1821–1912)

"Were you in my place you would feel it too, and wish and pine and fret in your cage as I do, and, if the very gentlemen who have the power

could only know for one twenty-four hours all that oppresses and gnaws at my peace . . . but they will never know. . . . I am naturally businesslike and habit has made me just as much so as a man." (Clara Barton, Founder of the American Red Cross)

Clarissa "Clara" Barton was the Christmas present to her family when she was born on December 25, 1821. Her parents, Stephen and Sarah Barton, already had four children ranging in age from eleven to seventeen in their North Oxford, Massachusetts, home. "Tot," as she was nicknamed by her older siblings, became a novelty. She also quickly became the shining star to her father, who not only was a successful businessman but also was captain of the local militia; she adored him in return. Clara was a tomboy who had a quick mind and a deep curiosity. As a young girl she became a very good equestrian, a talent that served her well later when she traveled and worked to save the lives of soldiers during the Civil War.

The education of Clara started when she was only three years old; surrounded by older siblings who taught from time to time, she was already able to read and spell. In fact, her oldest brother, Stephen, tutored her in arithmetic and David, in sports; sister Sally instilled in the little girl a love of literature. Since doing well in school was one way Clara could get attention from her family, she quickly became a high achiever, and as early as sixteen was herself a teacher. Barton was very good at both controlling students, even the young men, and imparting basic academic knowledge, a talent that made her a much-sought-after and popular teacher for more than ten years. During this time, she declared, "I may sometimes be willing to teach for nothing . . . but if paid at all, I shall never do a man's work for less than a man's pay" (Pryor, 1987: 23). In 1852 she started a free school in Bordontown, New Jersey. Since so many students were enrolling, she convinced the locals to build a new school the following year, supervising the construction herself. This school quickly became successful, so much so that they put a man in charge. This was the ultimate affront to Barton, and she left teaching.

In 1854, Barton went to Washington, DC, because a friend, Charles Mason, arranged for her to get a job in the Patent Office. She became the first female clerk in the federal government, a position that paid a salary of $1,400 a year. But just one year later, she and the other women who joined her in this office were sent home because Secretary McClelland felt strongly that women shouldn't be taking jobs away from men. Barton managed to continue to do work for the Patent Office for another year from home, but she then was forced to resign in 1857 because of "her strong anti-slavery stance [which] put her at odds with the new pro-slavery president, James Buchanan" (Straub, 1992: 60). Some rumors about Barton's sexual conduct were also circulating around town because, as author Elizabeth Pryor pointed out, "A woman who was not married—who chose not to be married—was already suspect; a woman who enjoyed men's company and forged brazenly into their fields of occupation was due for reproach" (Pryor, 1987: 61).

Clara Barton was to forge even more deeply into men's territory. The tensions between North and South were escalating over the issue of slavery. As Barton watched the soldiers of the Sixth Massachusetts Regiment marching off to war, she recognized almost forty of them as her former pupils (Pryor, 1987: 78). This added to her heightening sense that she had to do something to help. Barton started collecting clothing, food, medicine, even tobacco. Rapidly, she became the focal point for a massive collection effort, the first ever of this magnitude.

It was during these early days of the Civil War that Clara Barton's beloved father, as he lay on his deathbed, gave his daughter the rationale for aggressive action. Captain Barton was the one who "had frequently urged her to become part of the fight, dismissing talk that such behavior was unbecoming a woman. . . . [Reassuring his daughter, he said to her] 'I know soldiers and they will always respect you and your errand. . . . '[Then he reminded her that she was] 'the daughter of an accepted Mason' and on that account she must 'seek and comfort the afflicted everywhere' " (Burton, 1995: 31). Clara Barton now had a mission to fulfill, and she would spend every day of the rest of her life keeping this commitment regardless of the consequences to her reputation, health, finances, or spirit.

Fiercely determined to succeed, Barton set out to join her "boys" on the battlefield. Though she faced rejection initially because it was unheard of for a woman to be in the middle of war, that soon changed. It was clear that she had gathered an immense volume of supplies for the troops, something no one else had offered to provide. Once on the battlefield, Barton faced the horrible reality of war head on. "I saw many things that I did not wish to see and I pray God may never see again . . . [but] while our soldiers can stand and fight, I can stand and feed and nurse them" (Straub, 1992: 61). Her life was in constant danger. Once, when "she was giving a wounded man water to drink, a bullet passed the sleeve of her dress and struck the soldier dead" (Burton, 1995: 39). Not only did Barton serve on the front, but she also traveled around the country speaking about her experiences so that she could raise money for the many projects she had initiated. This never-ending, morbid, frenetic, stressful existence took its toll, and she almost suffered a nervous breakdown at age fifty-seven. Hoping to regain her health so that she could continue her work, Barton went to Switzerland for the cure. What she gained was her new life direction.

In Geneva, Barton met Dr. Louis Appia, a medical professional who had ministered on battlefields. He introduced her to the relatively new concept of the Red Cross, an organization started by banker and industrialist Jean Henri Dunant. Barton immediately took to this new method of serving and, once she was able, returned to America to lobby for the United States to sign the Treaty of Geneva, which incorporated the Red Cross. Barton was successful in her political maneuvering. In 1881, at age sixty, she started the American Association of the Red Cross, renamed in 1893 the American National Red Cross. In just a few short years, the need for such an agency became clear. For example, from 1885 to 1900, the Red Cross assisted in helping victims of major catastrophes such as a famine in Texas, an earthquake in Virginia, a yellow fever epidemic in Florida, and the Spanish American War. Barton herself remained active at the relief fields until her late seventies (Burton, 1995: 113).

Over her lifetime, Clara Barton achieved international celebrity for her courage and service on the battlefields and for establishing the Red Cross, an organization that thrives today with the same mission identified by its founding mother. She died of pneumonia in 1912 on another Christian holiday like the day on which she was born; this time it was a solemn day of mourning, Good Friday. Many of the surviving soldiers, though now old and gray, whom Clara Barton had served long and faithfully on so many military battlefields came to pay her their last respects. They and the nation would always remember this "Angel of the Battlefield."

SOURCES: Burton, D. (1995), *Clara Barton: In the Service of Humanity* (Westport, CT: Greenwood Press); "More to Clara Barton Than Nursing," (1997), *News Times*, November 28: A9; Pryor, E. (1987), *Clara Barton: Professional Angel* (Philadelphia, PA: University of Pennsylvania Press); Straub, D. (1992), "Clara Barton," in Christian Barnard, ed., *Contemporary Heroes and Heroines* (Detroit, MI: Gale Research), 59–63.

BEATRICE BEHRMAN (1895–1990)

"I made dolls for children to play with and learn [about] life and art."
(Beatrice Behrman, Founder, Alexander Doll Company)

Beatrice Alexander was the daughter of a New York City toymaker who had emigrated from Russia in the early part of the twentieth century. They had a loving, cooperative, and supportive relationship. With him, she learned the skills that would enable her to became an internationally famous personality as the designer and manufacturer of Madame Alexander dolls, making dolls that have been treasured as toys and as collector items for over seventy-five years. Her father was one of the first business owners to operate a "doll hospital" in the United States. It was his need for her help with replacing doll parts that shaped her story into a literal rags-to-riches one. "Bertha," as he called her, started by making heads for the rag dolls her father wanted to sell, the most famous being the World War I Red Cross Nurse rag doll. With the knowledge she gained from this experience, she started her own company in 1923. Before she sold the Alexander Doll Company in 1988, her dolls, ranging in price from $40 to many thousands of dollars, were grossing around $20 million in sales for her company.

Beatrice Alexander Behrman got off to a good start in her business with the added help of her husband, Philip Behrman. She located her doll-manufacturing company in the section of New York known as Harlem. This diminutive white woman eventually became the largest manufacturer in that predominantly black community, giving steady employment to many local residents. The company is still located there today. Her early rag dolls had distinctive handpainted features, and by the 1930s, Behrman was making eyes with eyelids that closed and hair that could be shaped. She even added knuckles to the fingers so that they would be more lifelike (Narvaez, 1990). As was her tradition, Behrman made dolls fashioned after famous people or characters in books. Her business was not seriously hurt by the Great Depression because of this decision. In 1934, she had wisely contracted to make dolls of the very popular Dionne quintuplets, and sales from these dolls alone kept her company afloat.

The next period of uncertainty was during World War II, when production of nonessential items was suspended to preserve the supplies needed in the military effort. However, once the war was over, doll manufacturing was resumed, this time using the now-popular vinyl, with hair that could actually be styled. The quality of the Madame Alexander dolls led to Behrman receiving the coveted Fashion Academy Gold Medal for costume excellence. In 1953, Behrman was also commissioned by the British government to make special dolls for the coronation of Queen Elizabeth II. She designed not only a doll for the queen but also dolls for the queen's mother, her sister, Princess Margaret, and thirty-five others; many of these Madame Alexander dolls were later given to the Brooklyn Children's Museum (Narvaez, 1990: D19).

During the early 1960s Behrman began a series of dolls in native costume that represented over forty nations of the world. Because of this, Arthur Goldberg, the U.S. ambassador to the United Nations, formally honored her in 1965. She also made black dolls, which was almost unheard of in the still largely segregated nation.

More than 5,000 dolls had been created by the Alexander Doll Company by 1990, when Beatrice Behrman died, at age ninety-five. They were made to represent such famous people as Lucille Ball and Billie Holiday and characters like Alice in Wonderland, Scarlett O'Hara, Mother Goose, Red Riding Hood, Charles Dickens' characters, and the sisters in *Little Women*.

Many thousands of enthusiastic Madame Alexander Doll collectors exist around the world. The art appreciation she wanted to share with others continues.

SOURCES: "Beatrice A. Behrman: Doll Designer," (1990) *Los Angeles Times* [Online], October 6: A28 (available: Lexis-Nexis, accessed July 15, 1998); Narvaez, A. (1990), "Beatrice Behrman, 95, Doll Maker Known as Madame Alexander," *New York Times* [Online], October 5: D19 (available: Lexis-Nexis, accessed July 15, 1998).

ANNE BEILER (1949–   )

"It's easy to dream. I thought that 'I can teach anyone to roll a pretzel and operate a business,' but to dream is one thing—to bring that dream to fruition, takes an awful lot of hard work, perseverance, patience, and discipline—all the things that don't come easy for most of us."
(Anne Beiler, Founder, Auntie Anne's Hand-Rolled Soft Pretzels)

"It's all part of the miracle!" That's how Anne Smucker Beiler would describe her astronomical rise to entrepreneurial fame as owner of a business that started in 1988 with a small booth at a farmer's market and, in just eleven years, had almost 600 stores in forty-two states and five countries, with sales of more than $167 million. The miracle description is easy to believe considering that all this success came from a most humble product—a pretzel.

Anne was the third of eight children born to the Pennsylvania Amish-Mennonite family of Eli and Amanda Smucker. As was the tradition in this religious culture, Anne left formal schooling after the eighth grade, when she was twelve. She began to help support the family in many practical ventures, such as baking sometimes as many as seventy pies and cakes in a day to be sold at local farmers' markets. Her parents were entrepreneurial role models; her mother had a quilt-making business; her father sold wood-burning stoves and had a stone masonry business. Anne recalled that "my dad taught me how to work [and that] it's fun to work. My mom taught me the social skills . . . [plus] giving, not being selfish with what you have" (Gates, 1994: D1). Her values were traditional; Anne wanted to get married and have children. When she was nineteen, she married Jonas Beiler. They had three daughters; one died at nineteen months of age, and the Beilers established and named a foundation for her—the Angela Foundation—to support missionary work.

After almost nineteen years of marriage, Jonas Beiler began to have problems with his auto-repair business. Anne went to work part time at a booth in the local farmer's market. Her boss sold pizza and pretzels. "With a streak of showmanship, [Anne] hand-rolled [the pretzels] in front of customers . . . her entertaining presentation was a hit" (Rohland, 1997: 3). She also keenly observed that the pretzels were outselling all other products. When the opportunity arose to purchase a booth for herself in a farmer's market in Downingtown, Pennsylvania, she borrowed $6,000 from her father-in-law and set up shop in 1988 as Auntie Anne's, the name she was called by her many nieces and nephews. Though Beiler worked to improve her pretzel recipe, she had a bad setback when one of her suppliers shipped her the wrong ingredients, resulting in an unsatisfactory pretzel. Her husband, wanting to help and convinced he knew what would make a tasty product because he had been the baker in his family as he was growing up, talked his wife into trying his "secret ingredient." It worked. People loved the new taste, and the business took off. They opened seven stores in 1989 and started receiving requests from others to buy into this enterprise. In no time, Auntie Anne's became a franchised business.

With growth and expansion came a need for more money. However, because Beiler was giving so much of the profits derived from the business to charities, the local banks were unwilling to provide loans to her. Yet, Beiler was adamant; she was not in business to get rich. She and her husband had always wanted to set up a counseling center in which he would work to help families, a place that would be free to those who could not afford such services and on a sliding fee scale for others. Beiler declared, "My business is a mission. The more money I make, the more I can help other people" (Rohland, 1997: 5). This Family Information Center was opened in 1992 in Gap, Pennsylvania. "Money is not everything in life . . . but the use of it is. Without it, you can't do anything, she pointed out" (Larson, 1997: 5). Beiler was able to get the needed financial resources for her ever-expanding business because she found what is commonly referred to in the entrepreneurial sphere as an "angel"—someone who would loan her the money she needed. He was a local, wealthy chicken farmer who believed in her product and in how she wanted to run Auntie Anne's (*Small Business 2000*, 1998).

Beiler later discovered that there was a religious connection to the very product she was making and selling. Pretzels were the seventh-century concoction of an Italian monk who had rolled scraps of leftover bread dough into the crossed-arm pattern of his students when they were praying and gave them out as "little rewards"—in Italian, "pretiolas," which, translated into English, became "pretzels" (Rohland, 1997: 2). Each of the three circles in the twisted bread represented the three elements of the Christian God—Father, Son, and Holy Spirit. To Beiler this was another message that she was on the right track. "I firmly believe that God is guiding and directing me. . . . As humans, we run out of ideas, but there's no end to God's ideas so we need to tune into [them]" (Gray, 1997: B2).

Even with the responsibilities inherent in her success, Beiler makes time for enjoyable activities such as motorcycling with her husband because she believes in maintaining balance in her life. She has come up with the basic ingredients not only for a tasty pretzel but for success, too: "Having a business is hard work that takes a lot of commitment. It takes all of your waking and most of your sleeping hours so the business should start with a purpose. You should treat others as you want to be treated. Put others first, yourself last. Seek to understand, then to be understood. Take love into the workplace . . . it works; it's basic and maybe old-fashioned, but it works. This will give you a sense of satisfaction and achievement" (*Small Business 2000*, 1998). Since Anne Beiler practices what she preaches, she draws employees, franchisees, and customers into her ever-expanding family.

SOURCES: Auntie Anne's (1998), *http://www.auntieannes.com* (accessed July 8, 1999); Gates, M. (1994), "Her Own Nook: The 'Producer of Auntie Anne' Makes Her Dough in Quilts," *Lancaster New Era*, October 6: D1; Gray, H. (1997), "By Applying Biblical Principles, Speakers Find Success in Business," *Kansas City Star*, November 7 (available: Lexis-Nexis, accessed July 8, 1999); Larson, G. (1997), "Auntie Anne's Soft Pretzels Puts a Twist on Snack Food Industry," *Entrepreneurial Edge Magazine* [Online], 1–5, *http://www.edgeline.com/main/edgemag/archives/beiler.htm* (accessed July 14, 1998; Patton, C. (1999), "Working Women 500," *Working Women Magazine*, June, 43–44; Rohland, P. (1997), "Rolling in Dough," *Income Opportunities* [Online], February 1: 1–6, *http://www.incomeops.com/online/content9608/pretzels/pretzels.html* (accessed March 12, 1997); *Small Business 2000: Auntie Anne's* [Videorecording], (1998), Flying Leap Productions.

RACHEL BELL (1974–)
SARA SUTTON (1974–)

"Everyone thinks we make so much money, but we still don't get paid even what an entry level professional would. We get stock in the company. Founders live lean, and it's better to be in debt when you're young." (Rachel Bell, Co-founder, JobDirect.com)

JobDirect.com is an Internet-based job search company that was started in 1995 by two lifelong friends, both of whom were then only twenty-one years old, with no computing skills and no business training. Yet they had conceptualized the idea for this business as they approached their senior year of college. Their goal was to enable college students seeking entry-level professional positions to find jobs easily and for employers to more effectively and efficiently utilize their recruitment resources to make the best entry-level hires. Within months, Rachel Bell and co-founder Sara Sutton convinced their parents to let them leave school, developed a business plan, found sufficient financial support, established a Web site–based business, hired a small but highly qualified staff, established an unusual but very effective marketing strategy, and hit the road—literally. In less than two years revenues exceeded $1.3 million with expectations for 1998 surpassing the $3 million mark. How was this possible?

Bell and Sutton had developed their strong friendship ties as children growing up in Pittsburgh, Pennsylvania. They physically separated in high school when Bell's family moved to Connecticut, but these young women never lost touch. For college Bell chose Hobart and William Smith in Geneva, New York, where she developed a self-declared major in socio-political diversity of minorities; Sutton went to the University of California at Berkeley where she majored in international relations. Though on two separate coasts much of the year, they had regular "conversations" via e-mail, which was a free service to college students. During the summer 1995 college break, they got together in Boston. Their story is now becoming legend. While in a taxicab, they were lamenting about how hard it was to find internships, which often led to full-time jobs. They started brainstorming and came up with the idea that ultimately led to JobDirect.com. "We couldn't eat; we couldn't sleep," Rachel recalled. "All we were doing was writing down ideas for our business" (Oppedisano, 1998; all direct quotes are from this source unless otherwise cited). They had found a unique market niche, but they realized that given the escalating competition for this concept, the window of opportunity was very small. They decided they had to leave college; they had to take advantage of the moment.

"We started talking to every friend of our families we could find; to Human Resource people, asking them would they need something like this; to our friends about the job search process, which was so very hard to navigate at the time," explained Rachel. Her father, Drummand Bell, himself a corporate executive, had been the one to encourage his daughter to be entrepreneurial. When he heard about the business they wanted to start, he quickly cautioned them to be discreet about those with whom they discussed the idea so that it wouldn't be stolen out from under them. Rachel's grandfather was their first investor; he gave them $20,000 to get started. "We thought all we'd need was a total of $60,000 because to us, at age 21, that was a lot of money. Then we met with CN Communications, a company that builds websites. When they threw out the cost to design and construct what we envisioned, it seemed so huge! But we decided to find a

way to do whatever we had to do," Bell emphasized. "You have to go with
your gut and follow your passion." They have now raised several million
dollars in venture capital funding and moved their company headquarters
to Stamford, Connecticut.

In a novel marketing decision, Bell and Sutton actually started visiting
college campuses in a 32-foot Recreational Vehicle (RV) equipped with
fifteen computers on board; students could enter their resumes, and all
could see how the system worked. Another unique idea of the Job-
Direct.com team was to have the RV painted with its Web site icons by
graffiti artists from New York City. "We couldn't even telephone these
artists; they had pagers only," Rachel laughed as she recalled the artists
commenting on how they now get paid a lot of money for doing what they
used to be thrown in jail for. But the day the vehicle was supposed to be
painted, it was pouring rain. They tried to use an airplane hangar but were
thrown out immediately once the owners saw the spray paint cans. Eventually they found a way to get the job done in time for the ABC news
media to videotape the kickoff. "The trick is overcoming obstacles," Rachel
advised. "The artists did a wonderful job—all free hand with spray cans—
they're so talented, and the event was highly successful." So was the impact
of this large, brightly painted vehicle, fully equipped with sleeping quarters,
a kitchen, and computer terminals, as it traveled across country and arrived
on various college campuses. Rachel herself was one of the staff who lived
on the bus for the first few months. The company added two similar vehicles to their program and have been able to do face-to-face marketing on
over three hundred campuses.

Another marketing strategy was to hire college students as interns who
promoted the program on their own campuses. Students enter resumes into
the JobDirect.com database for free, and they are encouraged by the company to do so as early as their freshman year. "Students can simply update
it each year. This way they'll learn about internships, summer jobs, etc.,
and when they get close to graduating, they'll be all set." If positions become available that match the interests of the students, they are notified by
e-mail within twenty-four hours; this was a competitive edge for the company. Employers pay a fee based on how many jobs they're posting, how
many databases they're accessing, and so on. These fees can range from
$500 a month to thousands. Employers who have taken part in this pro-
gram include the Peace Corps, Bankers Trust, Price Waterhouse, Sun Mi-
crosystems, Digital Equipment Corporation, Publishers' Clearing House,
Electronic Data Systems, Teach for America, IBM, Random House, and
Systems and Computer Technology Corporation.

Though young to have started such a phenomenal venture, considering
their technical limitations, these two entrepreneurs were wise enough to
admit how little they knew, to seek the advice of others, and to hire highly
talented and experienced executives. In December 1997, the company was

awarded the Spirit of Entrepreneurship award in *Inc. Magazine*'s 1997 Marketing Masters Awards. Bell pointed out that "we got this for making a company that is so small [only twelve people at the time] appear huge!" A year later, JobDirect.com was voted the top-ranked Web site for online searches in a 1998 survey of college students conducted by Memolink, Inc.

When asked how much control they had to give up to obtain the expertise they needed, Rachel said, "A lot. There are the investors, and we started an Employee Stock Option Program [ESOP] so our employees could own a part of the company. It's a great way to bring quality people in when you can't afford to pay them much. I guess we each have about seven percent, but it's a small slice of a very large pie, which is a lot better than having a large slice of a small pie."

SOURCES: Adler, C. (1998), "Have Resumes, Will Travel," *Business Week*, May 25: 18; D'Addio, D. (1998), "Site for Seeing: Two Students Dropped Out When They Founded the Answer to Their Job Search," *Pittsburgh Post Gazette*, July 15: C1; Fredericks, L. (1998), interview of Rachel Bell, February 15: Oppedisano, J. (1998), videotaped interview of Rachel Bell and Sara Sutton, July 22.

MARY McLEOD BETHUNE (1875–1955)

"The great need for uniting the effort of our women kept weighing upon my mind. I could not free myself from the sense of loss—of wasted strength—sustained by the national community through failure to harness the great power of women into a force for constructive action. I could not rest until our women had met this challenge of the times." (Mary McLeod Bethune, Founder of the Daytona Literary and Industrial Training School for Negro Girls; Bethune-Cookman College)

The name of Mary Jane McLeod Bethune is familiar to many persons in America for her extensive contributions to the education of children and adults of color. Few, however, are aware of her wide-ranging business activities, such as initiating the publication *Aframerican Women's Journal*; building the McLeod Hospital and Training School for Nurses; co-founding the Central Life Insurance Company of Tampa, Florida—at which, in 1951, her presidency made her the only woman leading a life insurance company in the United States; holding "interest in the Welricha Motel at the Bethune Volusia Beach, Inc.—a resort purchased in 1943 to provide recreational facilities for black Daytonians" (Flemming, 1998); and owning much real estate. The life of this African American woman, the fifteenth child in a family of seventeen and the first born after her parents were freed from slavery, is nothing short of phenomenal.

Mary's mother, Patsy McIntosh McLeod, an enslaved descendant of an African ruling family, had said a special prayer during that particular pregnancy. She told her husband, Samuel, "I asked the Master to send us a child who would show us the way out. Of course, I expected He would bless us with a boy. But His will be done" (Holt, 1964: 1). When this strong woman was finally freed, she continued to work for her former owner, saved money to purchase a five-acre farm near Mayesville, South Carolina, and managed to bring her previously sold children back together under the same roof. As Mary was growing up, Patsy McLeod provided an ethical structure that included generosity of spirit and freedom from fear. As an example, in an impoverished post–Civil War South, "poor blacks and whites knocked on the door to ask if the McLeods could spare a little food. Mary then followed her mother to where the winter provisions were stored and watched her distribute food she had been saving for the family. Mary was taught at an early age it was better to give than to keep everything for oneself" (Halasa, 1989: 22).

This strength of spirit was also reinforced when white boys would taunt the little girl of color as she tried to get to and from school, sending their dog after her to tear at her clothes while they shouted out, "Naked Nigger." Mary threw rocks for protection. But "her mother instructed her that, thereafter, she should always stand and fight back, not with her fists but with reasoning. Otherwise, she would be running forever" (Holt, 1964: 22). As a bright child, she became the favorite of a teacher who recommended her for a scholarship to the Scotia Seminary offered by Miss Mary Chrissman, a Quaker from Denver, Colorado. Her grades were so good there, too, that Miss Chrissman provided her with the opportunity to attend the Moody Bible Institute in Chicago. Mary couldn't have been happier, even though she found herself the only black among a thousand students, since her long-held dream was to be a missionary in Africa. When she completed her studies, Mary applied to the Mission Board of the Presbyterian Church, saying that she was willing to go anywhere in Africa. However, she was given the extremely disillusioning news that there were no openings for a black missionary.

McLeod returned east and taught for one year with Lucy Croft Laney, the founder of the Haines Normal and Industrial Institute in Atlanta, Georgia, a typical name for schools at the time. Laney, one of the early forerunners of education for blacks, became Mary's mentor and role model, since she had started not only this school but a hospital as well. Shortly thereafter, Mary met a former teacher, now a haberdasher, Albertus Bethune, who proposed to her. They were married in 1898 and the following year had a son, Albertus McLeod Bethune, Jr. However, being just a homemaker did not satisfy Mary McLeod Bethune; she still had her missionary goal. When Reverend Pratt spoke to her of the serious need for someone with her fervor and talents in Daytona, Florida, because of the large number of uneducated black children and adults, Bethune took her son and relocated, much to the chagrin of her husband.

When she got there, the need was evident. Bethune, with only $1.50 in her pocket, wanted to rent a building that went for eleven dollars a month. She convinced the landlord to let her pay the balance in four weeks, and she started cleaning and furnishing the place. "She used pieces of charred wood for chalk. Mattresses for the boarders were made from corn sacks that were sewn together and stuffed with Spanish moss that had been boiled and dried in the Florida sun. Ink was made from elderberries. According to Bethune, 'I begged strangers for a broom, a lamp, a bit of cretonne [a strong cotton cloth] to put around the packing case which served as my desk. I haunted the city dump and trash piles behind hotels, retrieving discarded linen, and kitchenware, cracked dishes, broken chairs, pieces of old lumber. Everything was scoured and mended' " (Halasa, 1989: 40). By October 4, 1904, the doors of the Daytona Literary and Industrial School for Training Negro Girls were opened, and the first five students (plus Bethune's son) began instruction.

For most of her life, Bethune would be asking for support for her school, her students, and later, her hospital, but from private sources, not the government. To go after government funding at that time, she would have had to follow the segregationist laws of the land, which she refused to do. As a black leader in a white-controlled society, she faced many hardships and even physical threats. There were days when she wasn't sure she'd be able to feed the children or keep them warm. Fortuitously, she met Thomas White, from Cleveland, Ohio, who was president of the White Sewing Machine Company and who also manufactured the White Steamer automobiles. He became her greatest single benefactor, providing blankets, construction assistance, food, and sewing machines. Along with another generous supporter of Bethune's work, Mr. Gamble of the Procter and Gamble Company, White also provided her with a small house near the school.

Such generosity could not protect Bethune or her students from bigotry. One night, one hundred members of the Ku Klux Klan (KKK) decided to march. "About ten o'clock one starlit night, they heard the tramp of horse hoofs and the sound of a trumpet and saw the hooded figures marching down Second Avenue . . . behind an upborne cross. The politically powerful KKK had turned off all the street lamps for its demonstration parade, designed to intimidate the entire Negro section and frighten its potential voters away from the polls. But, it could not control the lights of the school. Mrs. Bethune ordered that all lights within Faith Hall be turned off, and all the outdoor ones on the campus be turned full on. In that luminous blaze the ordered ranks of the men in white, men with distorted minds, could be seen and their actions observed and predicted" (Holt, 1964: 120–121). They turned around and left. Bethune was following her mother's message of so many years ago—to stand and fight.

By 1923 her school, which was offering an expanded educational curriculum, was merged with the Cookman Institute of Jacksonville, Florida, and was renamed the Bethune-Cookman College. Over the ensuing years, Mary McLeod Bethune was awarded more than eleven honorary academic degrees, became the national advisor on minority affairs for President Franklin Delano Roosevelt, and started the National Council of Negro Women, Inc. (NCNW). She worked until 1955, when she died of a heart attack, just before she would have turned eighty years old.

In Bethune's last will and testament she wrote of her legacy:

I LEAVE YOU LOVE. . . . Loving your neighbor means being interracial, interreligious, and international.

I LEAVE YOU HOPE. . . . Today we direct our economic and political strength toward winning a more abundant and secure life. . . .

I LEAVE YOU A THIRST FOR EDUCATION. . . .

I LEAVE YOU FAITH. . . . Without faith, nothing is possible. With it, nothing is impossible. . . .

I LEAVE YOU RACIAL DIGNITY. . . .

I LEAVE YOU A DESIRE TO LIVE HARMONIOUSLY WITH YOUR FELLOW MEN. . . . We must learn to deal with people positively and on an individual basis. . . .

I LEAVE YOU FINALLY A RESPONSIBILITY TO OUR YOUNG PEOPLE. Our children must never lose their zeal for building a better world. They must not be discouraged from aspiring toward greatness, for they are to be leaders of tomorrow. (Holt, 1964: 288–289)

SOURCES: Daniel, S. (1931), *Women Builders* (Washington, DC: Associated Publishers); Flemming, S. (1998), Bethune-Cookman College 1904–1994: The Answered Prayer to a Dream (excerpts), *http://www.bethune.cookman.edu/mmb2.html* (accessed August 12, 1998); Halasa, M. (1989), *Mary McLeod Bethune* (New York: Chelsea House Publishers); Holt, R. (1964), *Mary McLeod Bethune: A Biography* (Garden City, NY: Doubleday & Company); Mary McLeod Bethune (1998), *http://www.ncnw.com/about/bethunebio.html* (accessed August 12, 1998); Smith, E. (1993), "Mary McLeod Bethune," in Smith, J., ed., *Epic Lives: One Hundred Black Women Who Have Made a Difference* (Detroit, MI: Visible Ink Press); Straub, D. (1992), *Contemporary Heroes and Heroines* (Detroit, MI: Gale Research).

PATRICIA BILLINGS (1926–   )

"At my age, I don't know how much money you could spend. . . . I think we will probably sell the company at an offer of from between $80 and $100 million." (Patricia Billings, Inventor of Geobond, Co-founder of Earth Products Limited)

Over fifty years ago, Patricia Billings took a chemistry course in junior college. She never could have guessed back then how one day her application of that very basic knowledge would make her a millionaire. She was born in Clinton, Missouri, married twenty-one years later, had one daughter, and was divorced in 1964. Though she attended Amarillo College in Texas, where she studied art and sculpture, Billings didn't complete the program. She took a job with a hospital in 1946. As she humorously explained to *Wall Street Journal* reporter Alam Kumar Naj, "Honey, back in those days, when women wore button shoes, they didn't need a degree to be a medical technician" (Naj, 1996: 12). During the 1960s, Billings became head of tuberculosis research efforts at the hospital, but finally left to become a sculptor for a craft store, practicing the art form that is her first love.

Then, in the late 1970s, an accident changed her focus for the next sixteen years. Billings had just finished making a beautiful swan sculpture. "It was a gorgeous statue, if I do say so myself. It fell and broke into hundreds of pieces. I had spent four months to make it, and I was mad" (Naj, 1996: 12). She recalled that the great masters of the Renaissance like Michelangelo and Botticelli had successfully used plaster of Paris in famous works that have lasted for centuries, and she began to investigate just how they achieved this result. "The key was the catalyst—[it had already been done]. It's just that people have forgotten it" (12).

For the next eight years, Billings experimented in the basement of her house, adding chemicals to a mixture of gypsum and concrete. "Having tunnel vision is paramount to the success of a product," she pointed out (Bedford, 1996: F10). When she finally found the formula for an indestructible product, using it on one of her sculptures, she sent a sample statue to her friend Heinz Poppendiek, an expert in geoscience research. He recognized that this compound was very resistant to heat and suggested ways to make it even more "fireproof." She went back to perfecting her product, an endeavor that took another eight years. The result was "Geobond," a fire-resistant chemical product that has failed to ignite even at temperatures of over 6,000 degrees Fahrenheit in Air Force tests conducted at the Edwards Air Force Base in California (Naj, 1996: 12).

Because fires are annually responsible for around 5,000 Americans losing their lives, firefighters have been cautiously, yet enthusiastically, testing Billings' invention in burn exercises with insulation and other construction materials. Fire marshals have helped with demonstrations at conventions and even with Billings' appearances on national news programs. In one 1998 segment of *48 Hours* on CBS, reporter Bernard Goldberg saw one test building burn down completely in just a few minutes while he was able to place his hand on the outside of another building made of Geobond, even though the contents inside were completely in flames. When asked how it works, Billings smilingly responds, "It may sound crazy, but I really can't explain what theories apply to my work. . . . This old lady just used common sense" (Naj, 1996: 12).

Billings noted that such a technology venture is "not a business for someone with no capital. That's why most inventors don't get much for their inventions because they can't afford to take it to the marketplace" (Bedford, 1996: F10). Initially, Billings used the savings she had acquired from real estate ventures, past employment, and some small investor capital to do her testing, which ultimately cost over $400,000. Billings is board chair and director of technology of her company, GeoBond International, Inc.; in the latter part of 1992, she also formed the partnership Earth Products Limited. Her product has been successfully tested and/or used by such organizations as the Underwriters' Laboratory, Habitat for Humanity, the National Aeronautics and Space Administration, the U.S. Air Force, and construction contractors in Dallas, Texas.

Many suspect that Billings' invention will revolutionize the construction industry, which is personally important to her. "I want to be remembered as the person who made safe homes for everybody . . . at my age, that's more important than money—*maybe*," she smilingly adds (Goldberg, 1999).

SOURCES: Bedford, M. (1996), "Partnership Pays Off for Area Inventor: Patricia Billings and Investors Financed Firm Selling Geobond, *Kansas City Star*" [Online], January 21: F10 (available: Lexis-Nexis, accessed August 29, 1999); Goldberg, B. (1999), "Strike It Rich," *48 Hours*, CBS News (April 12); Naj, A. (1996), "Inventor's Fireproof Material Ignites into Hot Commodity," *Houston Chronicle* [Online], September 29: 12 (available: Lexis-Nexis, accessed August 29, 1999); Patricia Billings: Inventor of the Week, *http://web.mit.edu/invent/www.billings.html*.

ELIZABETH BLACKWELL (1821–1910)

"There's something in me that likes to start things anew. I guess I was born to be a pioneer." (Elizabeth Blackwell, First female medical doctor in the United States, Co-founder of the New York Infirmary for Women and Children and the London School of Medicine for Women)

Elizabeth Blackwell was born in Bristol, England, in 1821, one of four daughters in the privileged family of Samuel Blackwell, owner of a sugar refinery. A series of unusual incidents would guide her to become the forerunner of women in the medical profession in the United States and, ultimately, around the world, beginning with the fact that her father's industry was connected to slavery for its profits. In contrast, Samuel Blackwell was an abolitionist. From the time she was a child, Bessy, as her family called her, met many antislavery activists in their home and participated in the cause. This early planting of a humanitarian seed would blossom when she became a doctor. Her father encouraged her participation because he also believed in gender equality. "My daughters have as good minds as my sons, and I see no reason why they should not be taught to use them in the same way. As to what use they will put them in later life, that will be for them to decide" (Wilson, 1970: 27; all direct quotes are from this source unless otherwise cited). Needless to say, young Bessy felt a keen bond with her father, who gave her a self-esteem not often felt by young women of her time.

What brought the Blackwell family to America was the misfortune of fires in the sugar refinery and riots in the streets of Bristol. These took their toll on the family's finances and on Samuel Blackwell's health. Reluctantly, the Blackwells, with their daughters and two sons, left their homeland in 1832 and headed for New York. While their father was reestablishing his work as a sugar refiner, his daughters started a small school for children of color—a violation of the laws of the land at the time. In just a few short years, their father died, leaving them in debt. The boys had to find jobs, and the women of the family started a boarding school in their house. Though Elizabeth hated teaching, she practiced this profession for a number of years, as well as "kept accounts, budgeted and spent the slender income, planned the meals and often shopped for provisions for the increasing number of boarding pupils" (92).

Always wanting to help others, Elizabeth went to visit Mary Donaldson, a friend of the family who was dying of cancer. Donaldson's words in 1845 would redirect Blackwell's life. "It's a terrible thing, Elizabeth, to die a slow death like this. I hope none of my friends will ever experience it. But for me there is one thing that would have made the suffering so much easier. If only I didn't have to be examined and treated by a man. . . . You're young and strong, my dear. You have a keen mind and like to study. You have health and leisure. Why don't you try to become a doctor?" (119). Physiology was a subject that Blackwell had hated in school, yet she promised to consider entering this field.

As she began to peruse medical books, Elizabeth Blackwell stumbled across an astonishing fact: Even if she were successful at becoming a medical doctor, she would not be the first Elizabeth Blackwell to do so. In the annals of female medicine she discovered that a namesake had lived in the mid-1700s, "a Scotswoman who had studied medicine with her doctor husband. When he had been thrown into jail for debt, she had continued to practice as a midwife and published a book on herbs which had become a classic in medical libraries" (140). Blackwell was now clear on her direction though, at the time, it would have been impossible for her to understand the trials she would face in becoming the first woman in the United States to receive a medical degree. Much later she wrote: "A blank wall of social and professional antagonism faces the woman physician and forms a situation of singular and painful loneliness, leaving her without support, respect, or professional counsel" (281).

Rejection after rejection answered Blackwell's many tries at getting into medical school. Some even suggested that if she dressed as a man, they might consider her. Her response was an adamant "No, sir. . . . What I am doing is not only for myself, but for other women as well. Therefore, I will undertake the task as a woman or give it up" (208). Then, in 1847, the faculty of Geneva Medical College in Geneva, New York, decided that they didn't want to reject a female applicant. They turned the decision over to the all-male student body, convinced that they would reject her. Comments flew around the meeting room where the vote was to be taken: "Let us at her! . . . What a break! One woman to a hundred-fifty men! If she sticks the course out, that will be just about one day for each of us. . . . Wait until we get her in dissection!" (8). But when they realized how they were being used, not only did they unanimously vote to admit her, but they pledged "that no conduct of ours shall cause her to regret her attendance at this institution" (10)—an unheard-of opportunity and commitment for mid-nineteenth-century America, a time when women were still the property of men and couldn't vote or have control over their bodies, children, or earnings.

Blackwell's next hurdle was to find a place to live in this small town. Rumors had already spread that she was either a bad woman or insane. Finally, a Miss Walker rented her a room. Within two years, Elizabeth

Blackwell was the second woman to become a naturalized citizen of the United States and the first female to receive a medical degree. Following graduation, she went to Paris because she was told there were more opportunities there to follow her dream of becoming a surgeon. Blackwell accepted a residency at La Maternite. She wrote that in this facility, she experienced "the utter absence of privacy, poor air and food, and really hard work when sleep was lost on the average every fifth night, yet the medical experience was invaluable" (Blackwell, 1895: 154). It was here that she developed an eye disease from a young patient who had purulent ophthalmia; this seeming disaster would redirect her medical career. She asked for permission to leave the hospital until the eye had healed, but this request was denied. Shortly thereafter, Blackwell lost her sight in one eye and faced the reality that she could never be a surgeon.

Returning to New York, Dr. Blackwell tried to obtain a position at the City Dispensary in the early part of 1853. They rejected her, saying "It would not promote the harmonious working of the institution. . . . If you want to work in a dispensary, start one of your own"—to which she replied, "Thank you. . . . I will do just that" (294). With the help of some Quaker friends and Mrs. Cornelia Hussey, she found a room on Seventh Street and announced in March that she would treat patients three afternoons a week for free. She was soon joined by her sister Emily, who had just graduated from the medical school of Western Reserve University at the top of her class. The following year, Dr. Marie Zakrzewska from Germany showed up at their door, offering to work for almost nothing as the sisters were doing, just to be able to practice medicine.

Having chosen not to marry, Elizabeth Blackwell still wanted to have a family. She adopted a young Irish orphan, Katherine "Kitty" Barry, who was around seven years old at the time. Kitty became her adopted mother's caretaker for life. By 1857, Drs. Blackwell and Zakrzewska opened up the New York Infirmary for Indigent Women and Children in the Roosevelt house on Bleecker Street with the help of some philanthropists and income from fundraising events. They also established the first U.S. training school for nurses and the service of "sanitary visitors"—the forerunner of public health services. One of the women who worked with them in this capacity was Dr. Rebecca Cole, the first black woman to earn a medical degree from the Women's Medical College, and the second African American woman physician.

In spite of her lifelong devotion to the medical profession, Dr. Elizabeth Blackwell was known to advise her friends and family to avoid drugs and doctors. She lived for more than eighty-nine years and published many educational works such as *How to Keep a Household in Health, The Religion of Health, The Purchase of Women,* and *The Human Element in Sex,* in addition to helping establish many health-related organizations in the United States and Europe. Blackwell noted, "How good work is—work that has a soul in it. . . . I cannot conceive that anything can supply its want to a woman . . . true work is perfect freedom and full satisfaction" (378–379).

SOURCES: Blackwell, E. (1895), *Pioneer Work in Opening the Medical Profession to Women* (London: Longmans, Green, & Company); Wilson, S. (1970), *Lone Woman: The Story of Elizabeth Blackwell, the First Woman Doctor* (Boston, MA: Little, Brown, & Company).

AMELIA BLOOMER (1818–1894)

"I hold, not only that the exclusion of woman from the ballot-box is grossly unjust, but that it is her duty—so soon as she is permitted to do so—to go to it and cast her vote . . . until she shall do so, we can never expect to have a perfectly just and upright government under which the rights of the people—of all the people—are respected and secured." (Amelia Bloomer, Publisher and editor, *The Lily* newspaper)

What is often heard about Amelia Jenks Bloomer is that she catapulted a major change in the dress of the day for women with the "bloomer"—a loose-fitting pantaloon—which was named after her. But this is a minimal point when juxtaposed to all that she contributed to the women's movement of her day. Bloomer is credited with being the first woman in the United States to own and edit a newspaper; she began *The Lily* in Seneca Falls, New York. Publication started in 1849. From the start, the mission of the paper was to promote temperance. On its masthead was the slogan, or what would today be referred to as the "vision" statement: "The emancipation of women from Intemperance, Injustice, Prejudice and Bigotry."

As with many women of her day, Bloomer's professional career started out in teaching. She followed this by becoming a governess. A few years later, however, her husband, Dexter Bloomer, an editor and co-proprietor of the Seneca County *Courier*, convinced her to try her hand at writing articles (Thorp, 1949). Her passion for pertinent issues of the day and her commitment, perseverance, and determination to accomplish her goals were the characteristics that led her into the role of a publishing entrepreneur. Bloomer was a member of the Seneca Falls Ladies Temperance League. This group of women wanted a publication to promote their ideals, but once they understood the full ramifications of such a venture, "they then grew frightened and decided to cancel the whole plan" (113). But Bloomer felt that such an effort was necessary and took on the project herself.

Amelia Jenks Bloomer was one of the early advocates of the women's rights movement of the 1800s, along with such notables as Elizabeth Cady Stanton, Susan B. Anthony, and Mary Ann McClintock. They fought to permit married women to own property and for all women to have the right to wear less restrictive clothing, to divorce a drunken husband, to be educated, to vote. This led some people to suggest that *The Lily* had come under the negative control of others. In response, Bloomer wrote: "Some of our gentlemen readers are a little troubled lest we should injure ourself and our paper by saying too much in behalf of the rights and interests of our own sex . . . we wish to give them no uneasiness on our account, as we feel perfectly competent to manage our own affairs." (Thorp, 1949: 119).

When the Bloomers moved west to Ohio in 1854, Mr. Dexter bought an interest in the *Western Home Visitor*, while Amelia brought *The Lily* business with her. At this point, she had a newspaper circulation of six thousand. This didn't prevent her, however, from also being an assistant editor and contributing writer for her husband's publication. In fact, Amelia Bloomer introduced a female typesetter into her husband's business, at which point the male printers went on strike. The strategy the Bloomers decided upon was to fire all their printers; they then hired four women as typesetters and "three enlightened males" for the heavier tasks (Thorp, 1949: 134).

The Bloomers once again moved, this time to a town in Iowa that was three hundred miles from the railroad, making it difficult to circulate the newspaper regularly. Amelia Bloomer sold *The Lily* to Mary Birdsall in 1854. Unfortunately, the paper folded a year later. Amelia Jenks Bloomer continued to be an outspoken advocate of women's rights up to her death in 1894 at age 76; one hundred years later she was inducted into the Women's Hall of Fame.

SOURCES: Bloomer, D. (1895), *Life and Writings of Amelia Bloomer* (Boston, MA: Arena Publishing Co.); Kleinberg, S. (1975), *Life and Writings of Amelia Bloomer* (New York: Schocken Books); Thorp, M. (1949), *Female Persuasion: Six Strong-Minded Women* (New Haven, CT: Yale University Press).

BOBBI BROWN (1957–)

"I get bored. I have a very short attention span so I need to do something different every day." (Bobbi Brown, Co-founder of Bobbi Brown Essentials)

Bobbi Brown was a creative child, lucky enough to have understanding parents. When she experimented with her mother's makeup at the age of five, applying it to whatever was around—herself, her sister, the walls, the sink—her parents, James and Sandra Brown, didn't try to stop her. Instead, they gave her her own (though used) lipsticks and brushes. Her father laughingly recalled, "Bobbi went at it with the heaviest of hands—it was not a pretty sight" (Brown & Iverson, 1997: 1).

Brown was born in a suburb of Chicago, Illinois, the oldest of three children. Her father is a lawyer, her mother a housewife who, in Brown's mind, was the epitome of glamour—something this girl felt was unattainable for herself. However, admiration of her mother certainly contributed to Brown's desire to "create" images using cosmetics. For example, on family vacations, according to her father, Bobbi "would enlist her brothers as models for her theatrical makeup. Jeff would be made to look like an old woman. Paul would be made to look like an old man while Michael came out looking like the loser in the prizefight of the century" (Brown & Iverson, 1997: 2–3). This talent wasn't lost on her mother; she later encouraged her daughter to attend Emerson College in Boston, where she majored in theatrical makeup. Her father, in his naturally humorous style, would tease his daughter about how well she "would hold up under the stress of a mascara final!"

Where she was to become really stressed was in New York City, where she knew she had to go after getting her degree to be in the right setting for her craft. Brown didn't know anyone, and she had little money. "If it wasn't for my dad sending me my rent, I would have been in trouble," she recalled (Gregory & Nguyen, 1997: 92). While she freelanced in her chosen field, Brown took jobs waiting on tables to make ends meet. She later summarized this experience succinctly: "I think everyone should be a waiter or waitress before they are allowed to eat in a restaurant" (Moisio, 1999).

Both her talent and her persistence led to Brown's first assignments for *Glamour* and *Vogue* magazines and then for movie companies as her reputation for being a fine makeup artist spread quickly. In providing her talents, Brown became increasingly aware that, while her makeup kit became filled with expensive products, there still seemed to be few options in colors and a limited range in quality. On top of this, Brown began to have back problems carrying her ever-heavier case from job to job. As she started to narrow down the number of products in her kit, Brown came to an important concept that led to the premise for her business: "A woman only needs her essential things" (Moisio, 1999). Keeping both simplicity and her love of lipstick as her focus, Brown became determined to develop a line of lipstick colors that were more natural than those on the market. In 1990, she found a chemist who helped her do this. Before long, they had come up with ten new colors. Recognizing that her products would be popular, the prestigious Bergdorf Goodman store provided an accessory table for her. With this exposure and ever more clients asking for her lipsticks, Brown soon was finding it difficult to keep up with the requests. She then convinced her friend, Rosalind Landis, a vice president of a public relations firm, to help her start a company.

With both putting up $5,000, Bobbi Brown Essentials was born. As Brown's husband, Steven Plofker, was then in law school, she worked from her home and cared for their first son, Dylan. Landis was also working at the company part time. Brown confessed, "We were not very solvent at that time" (Moisio, 1999). What they were was in demand! Brown was translating fashion trends into wearable makeup. Her father summarized her basic beliefs in his introduction to her latest publication, *Bobbi Brown Beauty*: "[She believes that] you cannot create beauty. That is God's domain. You can only enhance the beauty that emanates from within. If the body is healthy, the face will glow. Then, with makeup, it's just the touch-up, the fill-in. Bobbi practices what she preaches. She works out constantly, eats healthful foods, and tries to make the rest of us do the same" (Brown & Iverson, 1997: 4).

This wholesome and healthy image has also played well on television. Brown has appeared on many programs, such as the *Oprah Winfrey Show* and *Today*. In the short span of five years, Bobbi Brown Essentials was bringing in over $40 million in sales and was bought out by the Estee Lauder Company. Brown continues to run her company, but spends a great deal of her time at her home in New Jersey. She has two other sons in addition to Dylan—Dakota and Duke. Being a mother is very important to Brown, which has led to another line of safe care products for babies, including massage oil and talc-free powder. She pointed out, "Mothers should enjoy every special minute of grooming and touching their baby. Everything with infants is a phase that passes so quickly and then is gone forever. My top advice to new moms . . . is to treasure this time—including the diaper changing and bathing and hair washing" (Astley, 1999: 346).

Brown is also committed to several community projects. Once a month, she takes her makeup artists to a women's shelter in New York City to teach its residents about makeup and hair techniques. The company does not receive or want press attention for this project. "We really do it for us," Brown said (Moisio, 1999). Brown also uses her resources and influence to support the expansion of a home for unwed mothers in Montclair, New Jersey, including activities such as an auction to raise money for additional beds. She serves as "class mom" at her children's school. Unlike many who have attained her level of international prominence, Bobbi Brown is approachable and has succeeded in creating a work/family balance. For her, "Personal success is about happiness. It is about visualizing who you want to be and being that person" (Moisio, 1999).

SOURCES: Astley, A. (1999), "Beauty Shop: Baby Love," *Vogue*, March: 346; Bobbi Brown Essentials, *http://www.bobbibrowncosmetics.com* (accessed May 22, 1999); Brown, B., & Iverson, A. (1997), *Bobbi Brown Beauty: The Ultimate Beauty Resource* (London: HarperPerennial); Gregory, S., & Nguyen, L. (1997), "Powder Broker: Cosmetics Queen Bobbi Brown's Success Is More Than Skin Deep," *People*, August 14: 91–92; Moisio, A. (1999), personal interview of Bobbi Brown, March 11.

CLARA BROWN (1803–1885)

"It seems like white folks are never gonna learn how to tell one person from another if their skin isn't white. They aren't able to tell one colored man from another . . . or one Indian from another, either. Maybe colored and Indians think all whites have the same face too—only they don't. Do you suppose the time will ever come that folks will just see each other as plain human beings?" (Attributed to Aunt Clara Brown, Proprietor of laundry business and co-owner of mining enterprises, by K. Bruyn, 1970)

It seems to strain credibility to say a woman who had been a slave in the southeastern part of this country would be linked to gold mines in the West, but the story of Clara Brown is a case where truth is definitely stranger than fiction. Brown was born a slave in 1803. She had four children by her slave husband, Richard: daughters, Margaret and twins Paulina and Eliza Jane; and one son, Richard. Paulina drowned by accident as a young child. The remaining three children were sold off separately as slaves—an all-too-familiar saga in the history of black people in this country. Brown worked hard, was well respected by the family who owned her, and at the age of fifty-seven was freed.

Brown knew there was no hope of ever finding two of her children, Margaret and Richard, but she never lost the belief that somehow she might find 'Liza Jane. She knew this would take money, and when Brown learned of the gold mines in Colorado, she set her sights west. She negotiated her way there by cooking for a wagon train; nonwhites couldn't buy train seats. When she arrived in Aurora, Colorado, she opened a laundry business, washing and ironing for the miners, which became profitable enough that she could invest in the mines themselves. Clara eventually opened a similar business in Gregory Point (renamed Central City) that added to her net wealth; she ended up staying there for twenty years.

Although Clara Brown had known nothing about mining methods, she made shrewd investments that produced enough income for a respectable savings account balance and permitted her to acquire a number of properties. These holdings included land in Denver and several mining properties, among them "one fourth of all the gulch claims owned by James N. Williams [which included] a share in Williams' cabin, derrick, tools, and miscellaneous equipment" (Bruyn, 1970: 101). But there were always serious risks from both nature and humans when you lived in the West. In 1863 not only was there a fire that destroyed her buildings in Denver, but a flood destroyed City Hall and, along with many other landowners, she lost the deed to her property in Denver. It was during this time, too, that a number of miners and their families were massacred by Indians. As if all this weren't enough devastation, in 1860 (and again in 1875), millions of grasshoppers invaded Colorado, Kansas, and Nebraska.

But Clara Brown never lost hope; she continually built and rebuilt her savings through land acquisitions and investing in mining ventures. It wasn't her goal to become rich; she just wanted to be able to help her daughter should she ever find her. In 1866 she decided that it was time to go back to Kentucky to try to find 'Liza Jane. The great risk in doing so was that, even though she was free, there were "nigger traders" who would abduct freed blacks, steal their papers, take them into slave states, and resell them as runaways.

Brown did not find 'Liza Jane on this trip, but what she did find was a calling that came through a spiritual experience:

[H]er mind seemed to go blank. She had gone down on her knees and prayed with her whole soul, beseeching Him to show her the way. After what seemed a very long time, a voice came out of nowhere, reminding her that *all* men were her brothers. It was in Clara's power to help folk unable to help themselves. She had money enough to pay the fare of fifteen or sixteen colored people from Kentucky to Colorado, and she was sure she could help all of them find work once they got there. Until they did, she estimated that she owned enough property in the area to provide temporary shelter. (Bruyn, 1970: 115)

While making the arrangements for this caravan, Brown was robbed of $4,000. Her lawyer told her: "The fact that you're a colored person and a woman, with no standing whatsoever in the courts, and that this scoundrel, whoever he is, lives in another state means just one thing: we are helpless. And to make things just as bad as possible, that state has to be Kansas. I need not tell you how much chance any colored person would have of obtaining justice in a case like this, where the defendant would be a white man" (Bruyn, 1970: 116).

Brown concentrated instead on helping "her" colored refugees find work and shelter. Helping others was not new to her; she had been invaluable to the miners and their families over the years. They, in turn, now helped her in this new work. According to one estimate of that time, there were eventually as many as 5,000 such freed-slave refugees. Clara continued her other philanthropic work, too. She donated time and money to various churches even when she wasn't a member. She was one of a "little group of Negro women who occupied a place in the town unlike that accorded them almost anywhere else in the world" (Baker, 1927: 1095). This was the result of both her philanthropies and her business successes. The *Denver News* of September 19, 1880, demonstrated that she had become so important that even her trips to the area were news: "Aunt Clara Brown, the colored woman who has a state, if not a national reputation as a successful miner and philanthropist, is now in the camp looking after some of her property here" (*Denver News*, 1880: 7). In 1881 Aunt Clara Brown (elderly blacks were given the title of aunt or uncle as a sign of respect) was elected a member of the Colorado Pioneer Association, one of the first blacks to receive this honor.

Then in February of 1882, fate stepped in through Clara's friend, Becky Johnson. Becky had joined the Negro Methodist Church in Council Bluffs and met a middle-aged woman named Mrs. Brewer, to whom she took an immediate liking. As they talked, she found out that Mrs. Brewer was a widow with two children and that her name was Eliza Jane. As Becky had heard Clara's life story many times, she began to ask questions about Eliza Jane's family. "[Eliza] recalled with agonizing clarity being placed on the auction block together with her parents, a brother and sister. [H]er twin had died as a child [drowned]" (Bruyn, 1970: 175). Clara's long-lost daughter, 'Liza Jane, had been found! This was a joyous time but short lived for Clara; she died in 1885 of congestive heart failure, but it would have been a very happy heart, indeed.

SOURCES: Baker, J., ed. (1927), *History of Colorado* (Denver, CO: Linderman Co.); Bruyn, K. (1970), *"aunt" clara brown: Story of a Black Pioneer* (Boulder, CO: Pruett Publishing Company); *Denver News* (1880), September 19: 7; Savage, W. (1976), *Blacks in the West* (Westport, CT: Greenwood Press).

DOROTHY STIMSON BULLITT
(1892–1989)

"I couldn't have been in business without the help of men who told me what to do next. Those men would never have helped a male competitor in the same way, and they kept me in business." (Dorothy Stimson Bullitt, Founder of King Broadcasting)

Radio and television are industries of the twentieth century. Certainly to be one of the first in either medium would be a major accomplishment, but to be a woman in both in the first half of the 1900s is phenomenal. This is the story of Dorothy Stimson Bullitt. She was born into an affluent family in Seattle, Washington; her father was the founder, owner, and operator of lumber mills; her mother was a former music teacher who founded the Seattle Symphony Orchestra Society and the Children's Orthopedic Hospital. From them she learned "that a person of wealth could put people to work, make a building rise from the ground and transform the landscape . . . that a person with taste and connections could bring Mozart to the frontier . . . they taught her to take risks, size up needs and possibilities, and to start things that were good for the city" (Corr, 1996: 12). At sixteen she was sent east to boarding school; she followed this by studying music in New York City, then returned to Seattle.

In 1918 she married a true blue blood, lawyer Scott Bullitt, who was fifteen years older than she. Both her beloved father and her husband died within a three-year period. When her husband died of cancer in 1932, she was forty years old and had three children to support and family business holdings to run that were financially troubled, like so many organizations, because of the Great Depression. Dorothy had no business background (Haley, 1995). But what she did have was the memory of her father's lessons about "the strategies of earning and keeping every penny and the value of patience in negotiations" (Haley, 1995: 45). Within seven years she turned the business around and was looking for additional avenues in which to invest her time and money. "Maybe I paid more attention than I knew because so many times years later when I wanted to do something that looked impossible or I had a hard problem, I'd think, 'Well now, how am I going to solve this? What would Father do?' He'd always say, 'Well, if you want it, go after it.' So I'd get up off my desk chair and go downtown and talk to someone" (45).

In the late 1930s radio was a new field; this excited Bullitt and challenged her. To enter this arena a license from the Federal Communications Commission was required. Bullitt would have filed for her license in 1940, but her efforts were delayed by the start of World War II, during which the issuance of licenses was suspended. Persevering, in 1946 she received her license to start radio broadcasting on both AM and FM frequencies; she named the company King after the county in which it was established. As soon as Bullitt acquired the necessary approvals, she initiated operations and began a meteoric rise in the communications industry that ended in ownership of the six radio stations: KING-FM/Seattle, KING-AM/Seattle, KING-FM/Portland, KGW-AM/Portland, KSFO-AM/San Francisco, KYA-FM/San Francisco. In television she ended up owning KING-TV/Seattle, KGW-TV/Portland, KREM-TV/Spokane, KTUB-TV/Boise, K38AS-TV/Twin Falls, and KHNL-TV/Honolulu. The corporation also had cable holdings in Idaho, California, and Minnesota. In addition, King owned North-west Mobile Television, reputed to be the largest mobile production company in television (Keene, 1990; Yang, 1990). Being a risk taker, Bullitt was one of the first television station owners to produce documentaries and to permit subjects such as gay rights and race relations to be raised through editorials and commentaries.

Bullitt served as president of her company until 1961, then as chair of the board until 1967. She remained a member of the board until the day she died. But Bullitt didn't focus only on owning radio and television busi-nesses; it was also important to her to follow in the philanthropic footsteps of her parents. One of her major efforts was the establishment in 1952 of the Bullitt foundation, an organization dedicated to supporting improve-ment of the environment. The first year's distribution was $150,000; by 1990, the moneys given to charities surpassed $6 million (Morrow, 1990).

At the time of her death, Bullitt's empire was estimated to be worth over $500 million (Keene, 1990). In addition, the Bullitt Foundation had an estimated value of more than $100 million. After their mother's death, Harriet Stimson Bullitt and Priscilla Bullitt Collins began dismantling King Broadcasting, selling the television properties to Providence Journal Com-pany, a number of the radio stations to a Mormon Church holding com-pany, Bonneville International, and turning King-FM into a nonprofit entity. The total revenues from the sales have been estimated at $600 mil-lion. Following in their mother's footsteps, they decided that most of their share of the money will go to the family foundation after their deaths (Yang, 1990).

SOURCES: Chasan, D. J. (1996), *On the Air: The King Broadcasting Story* (Seattle, WA: Island Publishers); Corr, C. (1996), *The Bullitts of Seattle and Their Com-munication Empire* (Seattle: University of Washington Press); Haley, D. (1995), *Dorothy Stimson Bullitt: An Uncommon Life* (Seattle, WA: Sasquatch Books); Keene, L. (1990), "King Broadcasting to Be Sold: Owners Will Devote Wealth to Environmental Issues," *Seattle Times*, August 21: A1; Morrow, T. (1990), "Wind-fall—The Bullitt Foundation's Padded Purse Should Boost Its Power of Conser-vancy," *Seattle Times*, November 11: 14; Yang, D. J. (1990), "From Owning King Broadcasting to Saving King Salmon," *Business Week*, September 10: 100–102.

FRIEDA CAPLAN (1923–   )

"To be a successful marketer of any kind, you have to be totally open to weird new concepts. . . . Just because something hasn't been done

before doesn't mean you shouldn't do it." (Frieda Caplan, Founder, Frieda's, Inc.)

Frieda Rapoport Caplan has been labeled the "VIP of Veggies," a "vegetable visionary," and the "queen of kiwifruit." While she herself attributed some of her food business success to recipes, it would surprise many people to learn that she doesn't even know how to cook. She even openly admitted that she is allergic to kiwifruit because she ate so many in her early years of promoting this produce item! Yet, when it comes to marketing these food products, Caplan is known as an amazing entrepreneur who has made a significant contribution to the economy. This was summed up in the description given about her when she received the very first *Working Woman* magazine's Harriet Alger Award for Entrepreneurship: "[Frieda Caplan is a] marketing genius who galvanized the California farm industry and almost single-handedly created fruit and vegetable trends" ("Frieda Caplan Wins Award," 1986: 31).

Born to Russian immigrants, Solomon and Rose Rapoport, in Los Angeles, Frieda and her sister, Ruth, early on learned the value of hard work and an education. Frieda attended the University of California at Los Angeles and graduated with a degree in political science and economics. For the next few years she worked for a nylon thread company as the production manager. By 1956 she was married to Al Caplan, a labor relations professional, had her first daughter, Karen, and wanted a job that permitted more flexible hours so that she could spend more time with her child. A series of opportune events followed that catapulted Frieda Caplan to a stunning entrepreneurial record of success.

These opportunities began when an aunt and uncle of Caplan's husband needed someone to manage the books for their produce business and hired her. She soon learned that she loved the actual selling of produce. Caplan's naiveté led to the next stroke of luck. She was asked by a buyer if she would be able to supply enough mushrooms for a special Thanksgiving ad campaign of a large grocery chain. She quickly responded in the affirmative, not knowing that this was the peak season for mushrooms and supplies would be very limited. "In the produce business, verbal commitments are as firm as written contracts—produce dies too quickly and prices change too rapidly for buyers and wholesalers to waste time signing and delivering written documents. Frieda hustled, pleaded, and cajoled to secure adequate supplies from growers. In some instances, she loaded her new baby, Karen, into her station wagon, drove to the mushroom farms, helped pack the mushrooms, then delivered them herself" (Larson, 1989: 4).

Because she was so good at selling and had visibly demonstrated her commitment to customer service, Caplan was approached by the owner of the Southern Pacific Railroad who also owned the wholesale market on

Seventh Street. He offered her three spaces, referred to as "doors." Her good luck continued when her father agreed to lend her $10,000. "I had ten days to go into business," Caplan explained (Balsey, 1987: 26). The first step was to get signs for the doors painted right away. "It turned out that purple was the only paint that the painter had enough of in his garage at the time. It was a stroke of luck," she pointed out (26). Purple became the signature color for all of Caplan's endeavors.

The next stroke of luck occurred when a Safeway grocery chain buyer asked her if she had heard of a fruit called the Chinese gooseberry. Caplan hadn't, but six months later she was offered the chance to buy some cases of this item, which at the time was an unknown fruit in the United States. In what was to become a master marketing strategy, Caplan convinced the New Zealand growers to change the name to kiwifruit, after the New Zealand bird and the country from which the fruit was being imported. Then she convinced a popular local restaurant to feature a pastry using the fruit and supplied posters to be displayed in produce sections of grocery stores explaining what the fruit was and how to use it. Her next move was to convince California growers to include kiwifruit as part of their crops. By 1971 Caplan could boast of the first domestic kiwifruit and can be credited with initiating this industry in this country. The demand for this fruit grew significantly—as it had with mushrooms in her original venture—and with this increased consumer demand, the competition also grew. As Caplan observed, "We breed our own competition. We know if something takes off, we'll only have the franchise on that business for a limited period of time" (Larson, 1989: 5).

Frieda's, Inc., has been a leader in introducing many innovative produce items to the American consumer—from kiwifruit to spaghetti squash, alfalfa sprouts to blood oranges and coquitos—over 400 different fruits, vegetables, herbs, grains and related items in the various product lines, with forty-five new items introduced in 1997 alone. "This is where I get turned on. . . . I get my excitement from innovation. [When Caplan believes a product will be a success] I feel it in my elbow," she explained. Quality and service are hallmarks of this company. A quality assurance manager tests what is stored in the warehouse to assure quality, customer letters are answered, and refunds are given to any shopper with a complaint. This family-owned and -operated wholesale produce company is the first of its kind in the United States to have been started by a woman. It has an almost all female sales staff and annual sales that exceed $27 million. A great joy to Frieda Caplan is her legacy. "Knowing that I've passed the company on to my daughters, Karen and Jackie, is the most gratifying aspect of the business for me," she pointed out (Konrad, 1986: 62).

SOURCES: Balsey, B. (1987), "Behind the Purple Door: After 25 Years as the Grand Dame of Unusual Produce, Frieda Caplan Introduces Three More Vegetables to Los Angeles," *Los Angeles Times* [Online], March 29 (available: Lexis-Nexis, accessed August 31, 1998); "Frieda Caplan Wins Award (1986), *Los Angeles Times*, November 13: Part 8, 31; Frieda's Press Room [Online], *http://friedas.com/ scripts* (accessed August 31, 1998); Konrad, W. (1986), "The Visionary of Vegetables: Frieda Caplan, Frieda's Finest Produce Specialties, Inc., *Working Woman* [Online], 11 (November): 62 (available: Lexis-Nexis, accessed August 31, 1998); Larson, E. (1989), "How Frieda's Finest Established Itself as a Major Marketer of Exotic Fruits and Vegetables," *Inc., Online*, November (available: *http:// www.inc.com/incmagazine/archives/11890801.html*, accessed August 31, 1998); Silver, D. (1994), *Enterprising Women: Lessons from 100 of the Greatest Entrepreneurs of Our Day* (New York: AMACOM).

SHARON CARLSON (1959–)
ELEANOR MacDONALD (1932–)

"Working together is great. If it were only me, I'd probably give the store away but Mom keeps track of things—her strengths are with accounting and taxes. My strong points are knowing what to buy because of what will sell and being good with customers." Sharon Carlson, Co-Founder, Geppetto's Toys)

They are on opposite sides of the spectrum when it comes to their interests in toys and their strengths in business, yet Sharon MacDonald Carlson and her mother, Eleanor MacDonald, have been running the successful shop, Geppetto's Toys, in Woodbury, Connecticut, for more than ten years. Sharon, educated in recreation therapy at Southern Connecticut State University, went to work for Danbury Hospital. There she developed their Recreation Therapy department, becoming keenly aware of the benefit of play and observing which toys were beneficial for which ages. Her mother, on the other hand, "hated" buying toys for her two children. As Sharon recalled, "We didn't have toys like Play Doh or paint" (Brophy, 1998). What Eleanor did have, though, was the ability to keep good financial records, a skill honed from her years working in a doctor's office. However, it was the death of Sharon's maternal grandmother that became the stimulus for the actual start-up. This loss brought both mother and daughter to the decision to do something different in their lives.

While Sharon was still working at the hospital, she and Rick Carlson, a physical therapist, fell in love and were married. After several years, both were getting frustrated with the regulatory pressures that imposed so many restrictions on hospitals in order to get reimbursement. Rick decided to open his own physical therapy business, and Sharon joined him part time because they now had a daughter, Nicole. After three years, she felt that "[i]t was too difficult to work with Rick and then come home and be in the different roles of husband and wife." Her mother had also gotten bored with the office routine of her job. When Sharon suggested they open a toy business, Eleanor was far from jumping on the bandwagon, though she did agree to travel to a specialty shop in Vermont to see how such a business operated. The small, intimate setting and the friendly, cooperative owner helped to convince her to become a partner with her daughter in this new venture.

At the suggestion of her father, "Mac," Sharon and her mother both took an adult education course where they learned three important guidelines to starting a small business: "It's a high risk since nine out of ten start-ups close in the first five years. You have to be knowledgeable about what you're selling, and like both what you sell and the clientele it draws. Do promotions in a big way so that people feel as if they are really getting something special." Though the men in the family were against the way they were going about it, Sharon and Eleanor decided to start the store as if it were a hobby—though they each put in $10,000, with Sharon having control of fifty-five percent of the partnership and Eleanor, forty-five percent. They used their pooled resources to rent 900 square feet of space, get necessary fixtures, and buy their first toy supplies.

The mother-daughter team soon realized that they needed not only more footage but also a more visible location, so they moved to a shop with 1,800 square feet. In 1994, they expanded once again with the help of a bank loan for $15,000 and now have a shop that covers 3,600 square feet. In the beginning, neither partner was concerned with competition, but then a toy-store franchisee moved nearby. That forced them, for the first time, to look at how a competitor handled their kind of business. "This motivated us to put out a newsletter that made community announcements, explained new products, and contained coupons. We also started a mailing list to keep track of our customers. The competition turned out to be good for us. We worked harder, became more appropriately focused, and gave better attention to our customers," Sharon pointed out.

Except for holidays, Sharon and Eleanor do not usually work together in the store; as they cover different times, "the only drawback to being partners is that we're always discussing the business when we do get together." At special events, holidays, or sales the whole family pitches in to help. Rick and Mac become part of the sales force, daughter Nicole covers the cash register and wraps gifts, nine-year-old Ben serves popcorn; and five-year-old Matthew tests the toys. The store is operated with the old-fashioned values depicted in one of Sharon's favorite movies, *Miracle on 34th Street*. "If Geppetto's doesn't have something, and any of our staff know that someone down the street does, the customer should be told that because people will remember that we were honest and considerate." Sharon added that "if savings are passed on to Geppetto's from manufacturers, the customer benefits as well. We do not raise prices just to make a larger profit."

As for future plans, Eleanor might be up for expansion, but Sharon's priority right now is her family. "I'm open to opportunities as long as it doesn't take away from them," she explained.

SOURCE: Brophy, S. (1998), interview of Sharon Carlson on March 27, in Woodbury, Connecticut.

MARILYNN COOPER (1929–)

"You may be tired at the end of the day, but you look forward to the project being finished and meeting the people who will live in it." (Marilynn Cooper, Founder and President of a construction company in Albuquerque, New Mexico)

From the time she was a little girl, Marilynn Wayne Cooper knew she wanted to build. "I had a tricycle with a tool box on it. I built *more* tree houses than I can remember! I'm a natural love-to-build person," she recalled (Oppedisano, 1997). Cooper was born in Birmingham, Alabama, the oldest of the three children in the Cooper family. Cooper's value system was soundly developed by the behavior she observed in her parents. "My mother pioneered the first milk program in Alabama. She was a creative person; everything in the house was beautiful. My father was a builder and realtor." Cooper recalled a specific incident quite vividly. "My father was developing a subdivision and sold a lot to a member of his congregation— we were Methodists—and the guy skunked him! I was a young girl when this happened, but I'll never forget what he said to my mother: 'I'm not going through life distrusting people.' " Her father, Lanios Cooper, was an enlightened parent for a female child born in the late 1920s. As he felt that his daughter could do anything, Marilynn grew up believing she could achieve in whatever venues she chose.

Marilynn attended Birmingham Southern College, where she worked on the school newspaper and was elected to the honor society. After she earned her bachelor's degree, she married Melvin Jaschke. They moved to Texas and then to New Mexico, where her husband worked for the state government. At age thirty, she decided to start her first business, a remodeling firm that she still has. "I needed survival money because I was raising five children. I started in 1959 buying up houses, assuming loans, fixing up and renting. I was an independent—no company name—I worked out of the house." Cooper's next business was "homes by marilynn," which was incorporated in 1965. An architect advised her against using this particular name for her business because he thought it would be hard for her to get accepted as a female contractor; she followed her instincts and stayed with the name. "There are aspects to this business in which women are naturals; our love of shopping, comparing prices are a real help to work like this. I've always tried to hire women for jobs like tile setting and other trades; we're good at these skills," she explained.

Cooper wrote the actual state legislation for authorization to build condominiums in New Mexico and then built the first fifteen of these structures in the state. She has been responsible for the construction of over three hundred custom homes in the Southwest and takes great pride in creating nice atmospheres in which people can live and work. As described in a company brochure, custom "homes by marilynn" are in "a mode that blends historical experience as expressed in Pueblo Indian and Latin American villages, in space-conscious European cities, and in the towns of an earlier period of our own history." But "it hasn't always been easy. There were some tight squeezes—many a night I paced the floor wondering how I'd make payroll," she recalled. Cooper has also been known to fight with subcontractors who don't do quality work. "I won't put up with that. My reputation is that I'm tough to tangle with. I've done sheet rock, etc. so I know what it takes to miter good framing or do a good paint job; I know what it should be," she pointed out.

Cooper's commitment to the history and ecology of her surroundings is evident both in the designs she chooses and in her third business, Southwest Sun Systems, started in 1976 with two partners. Her solar business distributes the Revere Solar Systems, a residential active solar water system developed under a federal Housing and Urban Development Department (HUD) grant. By 1978, Cooper had diversified into land development, beginning with a $4.5 million clustered apartment and townhouse development.

However, during the administration of President Jimmy Carter, when the interest rates soared from twelve to eighteen percent, Cooper thought she was going to fail. "It nearly bankrupted me but I managed to struggle through it. Then after that, we had experienced the worst winter weather ever here—a serious blow to a builder. I remember that I boasted to my father that I had learned everything there was to learn in the construction business after these experiences. He chided me: 'Sister, you will *never* learn all the lessons in this business; there's a new one to know every day.' "

By 1981 her company had grown to the point where Cooper decided to build a $1 million office complex. In response to the question of how she dealt with competition, Cooper explained, "We don't have any. We do very little advertising. Our reputation is spread by word of mouth." After more than thirty years in the industry and over three hundred custom homes to her credit, she still retains responsibility for the management of rental properties and an office complex but has been considering divesting the rental management so that she could have more time with her children, grandchildren, and community service activities. An example of her community involvement is with a program at the Technical Vocational Institute (TVI), which builds and sells Habitat for Humanity houses so that more can be built, thus giving additional students the opportunity to learn about construction. Cooper also serves on the Board of Trustees for the World Population Explosion and for St. John's Methodist Church. She is the past president of the United Nations Association in Albuquerque, a program that includes student participation in a mock U.N. meeting while spending three days at the state capital with their legislators.

Cooper has tried to encourage local Hispanic women to consider purchasing a duplex; they could then use the potential income from the second apartment to demonstrate to a lending bank that they can afford the mortgage. This would increase the likelihood of their application getting approved, but she's meeting some resistance. "I try to convince them that they can handle the responsibility, but it's hard for them to overcome their cultural conditioning that it's the man who does such things." This is hard to accept for a woman who has been decisive her entire life and more than willing to take risks—including those involved in her multimillion-dollar business ventures. In fact, when people ask Cooper why she's still building houses and not retired after a total of forty years in the construction business, she retorts, "Why should I quit? I'm having a good time!"

SOURCE: Oppedisano, J. (1997), interviews with Marilynn Cooper, August 21 and 30.

MARTHA COSTON (1826–   )

"[I] recount my life . . . in the honest desire to encourage those of my own sex who, stranded upon the world with little ones looking to them for bread, may feel not despair but courage rise in their hearts; confident that with integrity, energy, and perseverance they need no extraordinary talents to gain success and a place among the world's

breadwinners." (Martha Coston, Inventor and Founder of the Coston Supply Company)

Her widowed mother nicknamed her "Sunbeam"—perhaps a foreshadowing of the critically important light source that Martha Coston eventually was to supply to the navies of the world. Her mother also moved her family from their native Baltimore to Philadelphia when Martha was a young girl, believing this city could provide better educational opportunities for her children. This move was to be providential for Martha. When she was fourteen, she attended a picnic where she met and fell in love with a nineteen-year-old Philadelphia inventor, Benjamin Franklin Coston. He evidently felt the same way because he began to find socially acceptable excuses for making frequent visits to their home. After a couple of years of this informal courting, Coston was given the position of head of the laboratory in the Washington Navy Yard and assigned to be part of a two-year science expedition. Faced with separation for the first time, they secretly married, expecting to go through a formal ceremony when she turned eighteen. They had been seen, though, at the minister's, so the secret didn't last long. With the marriage openly known, Martha and B. Franklin Coston moved to Washington, DC, to start their new life together.

Children came swiftly to the young couple, as did success and prominence to Coston because of his scientific genius. While still in his teens, he had invented the submarine boat that could stay underwater for eight hours; by 1846 he was working on rockets in a federal pyrotechnic laboratory. When the Costons were later transferred to Boston, their fourth son was born. Then one tragedy after another befell Martha Coston. On a trip back to Washington, her husband became sick; it seemed like a simple cold, but then progressed into a severely high fever. She rushed to care for him, but within three months, the man she had loved since she was fourteen was dead. When her mother pleaded with her to return to the family household, Martha Coston did so. Shortly afterward, her son Edward became sick and died. Then the mother whom she adored also died. Coston recalled: "When she passed away, I felt that I was indeed adrift. I had lost both my anchor and my pilot, and was at the mercy of unknown seas" (Coston, 1886: 37).

As a result of all this tragedy, Coston, at the age of twenty-one, found herself the single parent of three small boys and penniless. "I had not demanded, as I should have done, more accurate accounts of the men who were in business with my husband; nor had I realized the enormous expense illness and death had entailed, and which my husband's business associates insisted had swallowed up the ready capital" (Coston, 1886: 37). But as if he were reaching from the grave to help her, Coston recalled her husband telling her of a box of valuable papers. When she searched through the materials, she found the blueprint for what was to be her initial contribution to naval safety, plans for color-coded signals to be used at sea.

However, in 1847, getting someone to listen to her, a woman, was another matter. When Coston approached the captain of the Washington Navy Yard, he simply ignored her. She was persistent; he refused to take her calls. Eventually she appealed to the secretary of the navy, and with the assistance of family friend, Admiral Charles Stewart, Coston had a receptive audience, and the trials of the signals began. While she was awaiting the results of this invention, tragedy struck again; illness claimed the life of another son. Then she received the news that the signals had failed. The Navy Yard brass did offer to permit her to use their laboratory and staff should she want to try to get the signals to work. However, the man in charge of the laboratory stalled the process. She recalled, "The men I employed and dismissed, the experiments I made myself, the frauds that were practiced upon me, almost disheartened me; but despair I would not, and eagerly I treasured up each little step that was made in the right direction," (Coston, 1886: 43–44). Though facing penury, Coston looked elsewhere for someone with whom she could work, sometimes using a man's name to eliminate gender issues. She herself then worked long hours with a manufacturer and pyrotechnist to perfect what she knew was essential to the success of the signals—clear, intense, vivid red, white, and green colors that were long lasting. This time the Coston Night Signals were successful in the Navy trials, and her business began.

By 1859, Coston had a $6,000 order from the Navy for signals that would be used by the North and South Atlantic, the North and South Pacific, and the African fleets. She then submitted patents to cover foreign countries as well and, with her surviving sons, Harry and Will, set off for Europe. During this time Coston obtained patents for her signals in England, France, Holland, Austria, Denmark, Italy, and Sweden. She also faced regular reminders of the international restrictions women had to endure—especially those women who dared to enter the male domain of military supplier.

The United States government eventually bought the signal patent from Martha Coston for $20,000 with the understanding that she would continue to manufacture them for the military. Though this may sound like a lucrative deal, circumstances greatly diminished what she actually received. For example, one captain refused to compensate her, saying, "Mrs. Coston, you are making too much money on those signals. I have nothing but my pay, and my wife is obliged to make her own dresses and bonnets." To which Coston replied: "I can hardly see the connection between the Coston Signals and Mrs. Wise's millinery" (Coston, 1886: 95).

The value of the ship-to-ship and ship-to-shore Coston Signals during the Civil War is well documented. Coston went on to supply her devices to shippers, yacht clubs, and maritime insurers; after almost 150 years, they are still in use today. Her commitment was clear: "I had . . . the intense desire to accomplish something for the good of humanity; in some way to lighten the load of watching and responsibility that rests on the shoulders of the brave mariner and to place in his hands the means of saving not only property but precious human life; to prevent perhaps other women from becoming widows like myself, other children from growing into manhood with no other Father than the wise and all-merciful One above us" (Coston, 1886: 4–5).

SOURCES: Coston, M. (1886), *Signal Success: The Work and Travels of Mrs. Martha J. Coston* (Philadelphia, PA: J. B. Lippincott Company); Fitzroy, N. (1999), "It's Time to Recognize the Contributions of Women Inventors," *U.S.A. Today* 127: 66–68 [Online: Proquest] (accessed May 31, 1999); U.S. Department of Transportation (1998), *Women in Transportation: Changing America's History* (Washington, DC: Federal Highway Administration).

RITA D'ANGELO (1954–)
MARISA IOCCO (1957–)

"We had no investors, no corporation, only ourselves. Everything was split down the middle fifty-fifty." (Rita D'Angelo, Co-founder of Galleria Italiana, La Bettola, and Ciao Chow Catering)

Though born three years apart in the small town of Orsogna, Italy, Rita D'Angelo and Marisa Iocco developed strong friendship ties that would defy distance, custom, and language barriers. When Rita was a teenager, her family emigrated to the United States, where she attended a private all-girls school. In Italy, when Marisa was only thirteen, her mother died, and in response, the teenager threw herself into art studies in her Italian school. "My father wasn't there for me but I have great brothers, one in particular who encouraged me to do what I truly love to do," she explained, adding, "I have a small but special family." She went on to attend the Villa Santa Maria cooking school in Abruzzi, Italy.

Then, fortunately for the two faithful friends, the D'Angelo family returned to their native land; Rita and Marisa quickly renewed their ties. It was a difficult period economically in Italy at the time, and the young women faced severely limiting work opportunities. But an unplanned happening changed the destiny of these two friends. In 1982, Rita gave birth to a daughter, Amanda, and decided that this child was going to be raised in the United States. It was this circumstance that led two friends to travel across the ocean to start anew in Boston, Massachusetts—even though Rita was a single parent and Marisa spoke no English.

Intimidated, perhaps, but undaunted, Marisa Iocco began to acquire an outstanding reputation as a chef in her newly adopted country. She explained, "I love to cook. . . . I used to cook for my friends and family. Through food I express my self, my feelings." Rita D'Angelo soon joined Iocco and worked the "front of the house" since her forte was the people end of the business. They soon found that they were often at odds with the owners about how the business should be run. After a year, D'Angelo and Iocco made the decision to create their own special place, discussing, "Why should we work for others when we can do it ourselves?" Their dilemma was finding a location they could afford. It was Iocco who found a piece of property in what was then called the "combat zone" of Boston— now the Boston Common. D'Angelo was wary and wondered if they could attract customers to such a questionable neighborhood. Yet, the artist in Iocco could only see the potential and convinced her friend and now business partner to take the risk.

With $10,000 each from personal savings and some small loans, they purchased the building, cleaned away the dirt and grime, decorated the space in memorabilia from Italy, and in 1990 opened their doors to customers for breakfast and lunch. D'Angelo reminisced: "We found ourselves alone in this country with only each other as our support system, our team. What we did was turn our employees, suppliers, and customers into our family. We wanted to create someplace special—a home away from home—that would remind us of Italy, the home we love, and connect these memories to our new home in America."

Three years later, they were offering dinner as well as breakfast and lunch at their first restaurant named the Galleria Italiana. Fifteen-hour days became the norm, the business, their life. How do they deal with this level of pressure? According to D'Angelo, "This business is a great rush; it's the instant gratification that keeps you going." For Iocco, this fits her life pattern: "I've always wanted to do something different every day since I was a little girl." Both entrepreneurs were quick to point out that, thanks to the pioneering women chefs Julia Childs and Lydia Shire, the doors for other women chefs to be accepted and recognized were open.

Though only in its first decade, the Galleria Italiana has consistently been critiqued very favorably over the years and has received much recognition including "Top Italian Dining" from the 1998 Zagat Boston Survey, "One of Boston's Best Restaurants" by *Yankee Magazine*, and the 1998 DiRona Award. In 1997 D'Angelo and Iocco opened a second restaurant, La Bettola, in a different area of Boston. The following year they started a catering business, too, Ciao Chow Catering. In this enterprise they offer a more international cuisine rather than their traditional Italian menu. Their com-

mitment to being international has also been apparent in the week-long
Celebratory Dinners series that they initiated at the Galleria Italiana in
recognition of International Women's Day. Speakers at these events have
included women chefs such as Ana Sulton, Rebecca Esty, and Corinna
Mozzo; Barbara Lee, founder of the White House Project; and artist Cheryl
Warrick. Proceeds from these dinners go to organizations like the YWCA
of Boston, the Dimock Community Health Center, and the Institute of
Contemporary Art.

Another of D'Angelo and Iocco's commitments to supporting women is
their involvement with the Women's Lunch Place, a safe daytime refuge for
poor and homeless women and children that maintains a "no questions
asked" policy. D'Angelo and Iocco not only give of their time, but these
two lifelong friends often bring their famous bread pudding, pastas, breads,
and flowers to share with the women and children in this environment.
"Those at the shelter teach us far more than they gain from us," these
friends pointed out.

Though both are shy by nature and, in their own word, "vulnerable"
because of not wanting to be lonely, D'Angelo and Iocco confront these
perceived weaknesses, forcing themselves to do what it takes to be successful, to be part of a community. "We define success as creating new
dishes, running the businesses smoothly, and not breaking any dishes,
plates, or wine glasses in the process," they laughingly concluded (Ruff,
1999).

SOURCE: Ruff, E. (1999), interview with Rita D'Angelo and Marisa Iocco on
March 31.

DOROTHY DAY (1897–1980)

*"If you feed the poor, you're a saint. If you ask why they are poor,
you are a communist."* (Dorothy Day, Founder, *Catholic Worker*
newspaper)

If ever the early history of a person didn't fit her later passion and accomplishments, that person would be Dorothy Day. How could it happen that
a sometimes wild woman of the early twentieth century who believed in
free love, had an abortion, and was a left-wing socialist is today being
proposed for sainthood in the Catholic Church?

Dorothy Day was born in Brooklyn, New York, on November 8, 1897, one of five children. Her father, John Day, a sports journalist, "was a distant and disapproving figure" (Shoemaker & Breen, 1996: 92). Luckily, this little girl had a loving relationship with her mother, Grace Day. When Dorothy was six years old, her family moved to Oakland, California, because her father had the opportunity to be sports editor for a newspaper there. Then the San Francisco earthquake hit and the newspaper plant burned down; he, like so many others, became unemployed. The family then moved to Chicago, where they lived in relative poverty until Mr. Day got another job as a sports editor with the *Inter Ocean* newspaper.

Day entered the University of Illinois at Urbana in 1914 at the age of sixteen, having won a Hearst scholarship. However, as she was quickly bored, she only attended classes that held her interest, leaving school after one year. However, she found writing stimulating and took a job with a local newspaper in Urbana. Not long afterward, she went to work for the *Chicago Examiner*. Day's next writing position was with a socialist newspaper, the *Call*. This didn't last long either, because "after being criticized by a fellow reporter for slapping an anarchist who accosted her at a dance," she left (Shoemaker & Breen, 1996: 95). Her life was in turmoil now, especially as she found out she was pregnant. She loved the man responsible, but he convinced her that the way to save their relationship was to end the pregnancy. She found someone who did backstreet abortions and went through this alone. The man she loved abandoned her. In these dark times, Day is alleged to have tried suicide twice. She continued her involvement and identification with various socialist activities, worked at left-wing newspapers, and in 1924 published a book, *The Eleventh Virgin*. By selling her rights to this work, she received enough money to move back east, where she bought a cottage on Staten Island.

During these years of struggle, Day was drinking and smoking heavily. In 1924, she got involved with another man, Forster Batterham, an Englishman, who moved in with her. When she became pregnant by him, their relationship became unstable and rocky. Five years later, Day ended it. However, giving birth to her daughter, Tamar Teresa, in 1927 changed everything for Dorothy Day. She said of her daughter, "I knew I was not going to have her floundering through many years as I had done . . . doubting and hesitating, undisciplined and amoral" (Hendrickson, 1997: 8). Day was now deeply searching her soul and found herself drawn to religion. She converted to Catholicism. Her spirituality was decidedly practical and social, and she was more and more drawn to helping the poor.

Having Tamar was a triggering event for Day to change her life for God's people and so was meeting Peter Maurin, a man committed to living in abject poverty to serve the poor. Dorothy Day started the *Catholic Worker* newspaper, encouraged by Peter Maurin, and together they started the Catholic Worker movement. As writer Rosalie Riegle explained, the movement is "a lay community of women and men dedicated to living the social dimension of the Gospel in a radical way by serving the poor, struggling for social and economic justice, and working for peace" (Riegle, 1997). Today, this organization is still very much alive and serving many thousands of people a year.

The Catholic Worker movement set up Catholic Houses, which, according to historian Charles Chatfield, started out in Day's New York city flat and expanded quickly. "Here was lodging for some and meals for many (about 800 'discarded people' a day were fed at the New York house alone in 1937). No questions asked, no forms to fill out; just open hands identifying with the victims of social misfortune" (Chatfield, 1997: 3). Twenty years after her death, more than 130 Catholic Worker houses and farming communes are still operating in the United States, England, Mexico, The Netherlands, New Zealand, Australia, and Germany; and the newspaper has a circulation of 89,000. Day's values about the caring community continue to be espoused. She reminded us, "We cannot love God unless we love each other. . . . We have all known the long loneliness; we have learned that the only solution is love and that love comes with community" (Eichenberg, 1992: 84).

Through the newspaper, Day created a "voice and hands within the Church for her fellow workers and for the poor." It's been estimated that by 1936—just three years after the paper was initiated—150,000 copies were being printed and distributed; it was and is printed on the cheapest stock around, newsprint, and sold for a penny originally and for only a quarter today. One of the most significant impacts that Day had through this newspaper was on a particular Catholic tradition. She suggested an alternative to the "just war" concept supported by the Church; that alternative was pacifism. Chatfield explained her communication strategy for such a potentially volatile position: "She insisted that war is sin, that peace is of intrinsic, absolute, spiritual value. There was a penitential quality in her pacifism that was comparable to the personalist ethic from which the faithful were invited to take on themselves the social injustice of poverty" (Chatfield, 1997: 5).

Day was willing to risk incarceration for the beliefs she held. The first time she was locked away was for demonstrating in support of women's suffrage. Her family so disapproved that none of them would visit her in jail. Later, came a series of arrests—in 1956, 1957, 1959—each in protest of nuclear arms proliferation. Her last arrest occurred in 1973 at the age of seventy-five, when she participated in a picket line for farm workers. In spite of all of this notoriety, her daughter, Tamar, appears to have led a reasonably "normal" life in terms of her relationship with her always active and sometimes distracted mother. She married a man she loved, they had five children, and she chose to live near her mother so that Day could enjoy her grandchildren.

Dorothy Day died in 1980 at the age of 83 without leaving even enough money for her burial; the costs were covered by the archdiocese of New York. Reporter Paul Hendrickson asked Jesuit activist Daniel Berrigan to describe this self-sacrificing, courageous woman: "Dorothy Day? Where do you begin. . . . She's just like Merton. They were both tumultuous, crazy people in their youth. Sexually rampant. Spectacular sinners. . . . [I] used to be warned off Dorothy Day by Jesuit wise-heads. It was merely the way the chauvinist church viewed her, demeaned her. After all, she was a woman" (Hendrickson, 1997: 7). Today, some are suggesting that the process for canonizing Dorothy Day as a saint may be starting soon in this very same Catholic Church.

SOURCES: Chatfield, C. (1997), "Dorothy Day, the Catholic Worker, and American Pacifism," *Fellowship Magazine, http://www.nonviolence.org/for/fellowship/fel1197–01.htm*; Day, D. (1952), *The Long Loneliness: The Autobiography of Dorothy Day* (San Francisco, CA: Harper & Row); Eichenberg, F. (1992), *Works of Mercy* (MaryKnoll, NY: Orbis Books); *Entertaining Angels: The Dorothy Day Story* (1997), [Videorecording] (Mahwah, NJ: Paulist Press); Hendrickson, P. (1997), "Sinner and Reluctant Saint: A Century After Dorothy Day's Birth, Her Work Still Helps the Helpless," *Washington Post, http://www.washingtonpost.com/wp-srv/Wplate/1997/11/12/0841–111297-idz.html*; Riegle, R. (1997), "Mystery and Myth: Dorothy Day, the Catholic Worker and the Peace Movement," *Fellowship Magazine, http://www.nonviolence.org/for/fellowship/fel1197.htm* (accessed February 2, 1998); Shoemaker, P., & Breen, M. (1996), "Dorothy Day (1897–1980)," in N. Signorielli, ed., *Women in Communication: A Biographical Sourcebook* (Westport, CT: Greenwood Press).

HENRIETTE DELILLE (1813–1862)

> *"We are poor, it is true, but look at how many are so much poorer than we. Never refuse them. Perhaps we can teach them to desire the Bread that gives life to their souls."* (Henriette Delille, Founder, Order of the Sisters of the Holy Family)

Henriette Delille was a child of mixed blood. Being the offspring of miscegenation was not, in itself, unusual, but being a female of French and Negro blood and born in New Orleans, Louisiana, added expectations that did not exist elsewhere in the United States. Under these circumstances, Henriette was raised with the anticipation that she would be the mistress of some wealthy white man and bear his children. Their offspring would not be considered illegitimate even by the Catholic Church, but instead would be referred to as "natural" in this quadroon society. Although she was basically uncomfortable with this arrangement, Delille might have followed that path if she had not come under the guiding influence of Sister Marthe Fontier. It was Fontier who started the first school for free girls of color in New Orleans, Louisiana; Delille became a teaching assistant there while she was still in her teens.

Henriette was named after her maternal grandmother, Henriette Labeau, a free quadroon; her maternal grandfather was Don Joseph Dias, a wealthy merchant. Henriette's father was Jean Baptiste Delille-Sarpy and her mother, Marie Joseph Dias. Their daughters were educated in French language and literature, music, dance, and nursing. However, by 1835, because of her mother's failing health, Delille was declared legally an adult, and, as such, was able to access her inheritance money and property. She was only twenty-two, but she made the decision to sell all of her property and begin the process of establishing a religious community for women of color. In 1842, along with Sister Juliette Gaudin, Delille established the Sisters of the Holy Family. This work that Henriette Delille chose was filled with risks—physical, psychological, and financial. For example, free persons of color who were teaching those still enslaved had to be very careful to observe the law when interacting with people still bonded; if not, they endangered themselves and their families. Before long, Delille was disowned by all of her relatives because of her activities; they especially considered it a blight on their family honor for her to work with black girls and women. None of this caused her to retreat from her goal of educating young girls of color. Delille gave her all, personally and financially. She and those who followed her "were ridiculed and laughed at. [T]heir own wealth had been spent on the unfortunate. [T]here were times when they gave their own meals to a poor widow and her children and simply drank a glass of 'sweetened water' before bedtime" (Detiege, 1976: 35).

There were also political obstacles that had to be overcome. The Louisiana legislature deemed it necessary to "incorporate" organizations such as religious groups, but such an association needed to have six members or be dissolved; the Sisters of the Holy Family only had three members at the time. What Delille did have were advocates. These people established the Association for the Holy Family and became active supporters of the work, which enabled the Sisters to be incorporated. With the help of the association's members, Delille was able to eventually build a home for the sick, aged, and poor—the Hospice of the Holy Family; to establish a convent to house the growing number of nuns; to build an annex to the Charity Hospital to expand their ability to nurse the sick; and to open the Asylum of the Children of the Holy Family where orphans of color could be housed and educated.

This seemingly indomitable woman suffered from pleurisy throughout her life, which she kept secret from most people. The disease, coupled with the stress of the work she had chosen, took a serious toll on her health. Delille died in 1862 at the age of fifty. In 1988, the Sisters of the Holy Family initiated the Catholic process of canonization for Henriette Delille in recognition of this woman's great achievement. Today the Sisters not only continue the work of "Mere Henriette" in Louisiana but also minister in California; Oklahoma; Texas; and Belize, Central America.

SOURCES: Clarke, P. (1992), *The Greatest Gift of All: A Pictorial Biography of Mother Henriette DeLille* (New Orleans: Heritage of America Foundation Press); Detiege, A. (1976), *Henriette DeLille, Free Woman of Color: Foundress of the Sisters of the Holy Family* (New Orleans: Sisters of the Holy Family); Davis, C., O.S.B. (1990), *The History of the Black Catholics in the United States* (New York: Crossroads); Estes-Hicks, O. (1995), "Henriette Delille: Free Woman of Color, Candidate for Roman Catholic Sainthood, Early Womanist," in Jacquelyn Grant, ed., *Perspectives on Womanist Theology* (Atlanta, GA: ITC Press); Hart, M. (1976), *Violets in the King's Garden: A History of the Sisters of the Holy Family of New Orleans* (New Orleans: Sisters of the Holy Family); King, G. (1895), *New Orleans: The Place and the People* (New York: Macmillan & Company).

ELSIE DE WOLFE (1865–1950)

"I can't paint, I can't write, I can't sing, but I can decorate a house, and light it, and heat it, and have it like a living thing, and so right that it will be the envy of the world, the standard of perfect hospitality." (Elsie de Wolfe, Creator of the concept of interior design and the First Lady of American design)

Ella Anderson (Elsie) de Wolfe, born on December 20, 1865, in New York City, was one of five children from a middle-class family. Her father was a doctor, but it was her mother's relatives in Scotland who exposed her to a way of living that was to change the direction of her life. While still a teen, Elsie was sent abroad to live with her mother's relatives and be educated there. She became exposed to what wealth and high society looked and felt like. While visiting London, Elsie was even presented to Queen Victoria. She returned to the United States with the desire to acquire money and status, but not as most young women of her era did—through marriage. Elsie would ultimately become wealthy and internationally famous as an interior designer.

The first entrepreneurial venture for de Wolfe was not in this field, however. In 1901 she formed her own theater company. She had been a professional actress since 1890. This venture lasted four years, during which time her reputation as a set designer also became established. De Wolfe left acting in 1905 to work as a designer at the suggestion of her friends Elisabeth Marbury and Sara Cooper Hewitt. She sent out cards with the logo of a wolf with a flower in its mouth to announce herself as an interior decorator. Her first major commission was decorating the Colony Club, America's first exclusive private women's club. According to authors Tapert and Edkins, "When Stanford White, the Club's architect, was consulted about this choice, he replied: 'Give the job to Elsie, and let the girl alone. She knows more than any of us' " (Tapert & Edkins, 1994: 100).

However, the offer that expanded her reputation and ultimately made de Wolfe a wealthy woman was a request from steel magnate Henry Clay Frick that she decorate his Fifth Avenue mansion. At this time he was America's leading art and antiques collector. For this project, de Wolfe only received a small percentage as compensation for her work—ten percent— but since this project was for a very visible, wealthy man, it led to many more professional opportunities for clients such as the Duke and Duchess of Windsor, the Morgans, the Astors, and the Vanderbilts and for famous actors such as Sarah Bernhardt and Oscar Wilde. In time, her interior design projects would be found in major cities of the world including Hollywood, Chicago, New York, London, and Paris. And though she had achieved status, wealth, and influence, de Wolfe was willing to risk her life during World War I. She performed hospital relief work in France, most notably with gas-burn victims, for which she earned the Croix de Guerre and the Legion of Honor.

Elsie de Wolfe was also an inventor; she patented an armchair that pulled out to make a bed, she designed a vanity dressing table that opened in front to reveal drawers, and she created the profession called interior decorating by simply declaring herself to be one (Owens, 1992). De Wolfe established new concepts of what was acceptable in interior decoration. "I believe in optimism and plenty of white paint," she pointed out. In contrast, however, she became known for her brightly colored rooms, particularly those with green and yellow, and for the use of the shiny cotton floral print called chintz she introduced that earned her the nickname "The Chintz Lady."

Elsie de Wolfe was a nontraditionalist in other ways as well. Her diet was vegetarian—a practice less common then than today; she practiced yoga; she was the first celebrity woman to wear kid gloves; she didn't marry until she was 61 years of age, and only then because she hadn't done it yet; and when her hair grayed, she was the first to dye it blue. "Long before I could understand why," de Wolfe wrote in her memoirs, "I reacted against the dull rigidity of the [Victorian] era" (Tapert & Edkins, 1994).

In 1926 Elsie de Wolfe married Sir Charles Mendl, shocking her wealthy companion of forty years, Elizabeth "Bessie" Marbury. The Mendls were living in Paris, but World War II caused them to move to California, where they became a social focal point with the rich and famous of the movie industry. However, a few years before her death in 1950, Elsie de Wolfe returned to Villa Trianon in France, a place she greatly loved and had shared with Marbury. De Wolfe was weak and confined to a wheelchair by this time, but she was also a living legend. Lady Mendl left her fortune to the Elsie de Wolfe Foundation, a charitable organization that sponsors scholarships for artists and students of design and also funds museum exhibitions and public facilities for the arts.

SOURCES: De Wolfe, E. (1935), *After All* (New York: Arno Press); Owens, M. (1992), "Echoes of Elsie," *Metropolitan Home* 24 (November): 44; Tapert, A., & Edkins, D. (1994), "Thank Elsie," *House Beautiful* 136 (November): 100.

PILAR DEXTER (1954–   )

"When I first started, they [the general contractors] wanted me not because of my experience, not because of the quality of my work but because I was a woman and a minority. But now we get calls automatically, regardless of whether they have [EEO] goals or not." (Pilar Dexter, President, StraightLine Industries)

Pilar Gemeinhardt Dexter has two important memories of her childhood in Selkirk, New York. One was feeling upset because of the discriminatory way people dealt with her mother simply because she was Mexican and spoke with an accent. But the other was how her father, a railroad engineer at the Conrail Railroad Yard, taught her how to turn a negative into a positive. "My father would point out how lucky we were that *our* mother spoke two languages while the mothers of the other children didn't," she recalled (Oppedisano, 1999; all direct quotes are from this source unless otherwise cited). Because of this positive spin on life experiences, she had a happy childhood, did well in school, and learned never to let others diminish her.

Her family expected her to go to college and Gemeinhardt did, attending Georgetown University in Washington, DC. She graduated from the foreign service program, then worked in the office of a congressional representative for a year and a half. She was turned off, however, by the national political scene. Realizing she had impressive language skills, as she was proficient in Spanish, Portuguese, German, and English, Gemeinhardt decided to go to New York City to work with the United Nations' Latin American division. For three years she was an assistant to a Bolivian and to a Russian representative. Unfortunately this position was also a turnoff. "I thought politics was bad at the national level, but quickly learned that it was much, much, much worse at the international level," she explained.

Leaving the political field behind, Gemeinhardt enrolled at New York University, going on to earn a masters' degree in public administration. Her Bolivian contact helped her to become a personal assistant at Channing Weinberg, a firm that did consulting in the health care industry, along with marketing and business studies for the pharmaceutical industry. "They were relatively new; I was their eleventh employee. And their revenues were about $250,000." At the same time, she met William Dexter, a musician; they were married a year later. When the company later was bought by the Wilkerson Group, she worked directly for L. John Wilkerson for thirteen years. "I did all the hiring and firing for this company." When she left, the corporate revenues had grown to $18 million, and the company had 100 employees. "This is where I learned about business," Dexter pointed out.

During these years, the Dexters had become parents of a son, Adam. Not wanting to raise him in New York City, they moved to Albany, New York. Pilar spent four years commuting up and down the Hudson River highways. She would have preferred finding work in her field closer to home, but "found that the Capital District was rather closed especially for women. It's an old boys network—old families, old money." Once again she turned to education; this time she took a Dale Carnegie course to improve her interpersonal skills and reaffirm her positive attitude. Rick Fremont, the operations manager for the Albany County Airport at the time, also had a striping business on the side. He asked her to be his operations manager. She wanted to become his partner, but he didn't want a female partner, which initially made her dislike him. He suggested to Dexter that instead she should "Go start your own business. There are good opportunities through the NYS Department of Transportation for women. I will help you with contacts." He kept this promise.

What Dexter discovered was the importance of timing. With affirmative action programs requiring diversity efforts, companies now needed to do business with women and minority-owned businesses to get construction contracts from the state. Using funds from her retirement account, she started up as a distributor for Adco solar road signs and had a profitable first year. This opportunity was followed by another; a woman-owned business in Syracuse was going out of business, and Dexter was asked if she wanted to buy the equipment. "I didn't know if I could get the financing but was willing to try. John Wilkerson taught me that if you don't take a chance, nothing will happen." Dexter made an offer, put together a business plan, got a loan from TrustCo bank for $200,000, and bought five trucks.

With her business underway, she now got into the striping business through Rick Fremont, establishing StraightLine Industries as a distributor of solar road signs and as a company that could do all kinds of striping. By 1999 Dexter had thirty-two employees—four women and twenty-eight men. "I learned the business through listening, on-the-job experience, and taking a chance." First-year revenues were $340,000; in just seven years, by 1998, they had grown to $5.3 million. In a twist of fate, Rick Fremont now works for Dexter. "I saw in him a very unique talent; he was an extremely bright individual. My soul was not in the striping business; his was." And then getting personal, Dexter added, "He was there for me when I needed a job to support my family." They are close friends now; while she owns the company, she also considers him her "silent partner."

Dexter pointed out that finding financial resources is one of the difficulties entrepreneurial women have almost always faced. She believes that women don't take advantage of the opportunities that are available. "You have to have a feasible business plan. It's a Catch 22 with financing because you have to prove that you can do it before you'll get the money so you have to start small and prove yourself. A lot of women are afraid to go into banks and ask for money. They go into the bank with hat in hand, saying 'Please Mr. Banker, will you give me some money.' I didn't do that. I needed some heavy financing because my business uses large equipment. I knew I couldn't go in as a meek and humble woman because that's how they would treat me." Dexter noted that local banks were more willing to look at a small, woman-owned business than were large banks. She advises that women shouldn't take "no" at face value.

As StraightLine Industries has a seasonal workflow, in the off-season Dexter handles bids, estimates, phone inquiries, hiring, background checks, training (hazardous materials, safety on the highways), and planning. However, in the heavy work season, which runs from June to December, her day starts at 4:00 A.M. with the phone ringing and ends at 10 P.M. "It's a juggling act." But on weekends, her husband turns off the home phone. "Do I spend as much time with my son as I would like to? No! No working mother can ever say that she gives her children 'enough' time. But I'm lucky because my husband is a stay-at-home father. If you have a good support system, I think your children are not worse for wear." While the plans of this forty-five-year-old entrepreneur are to keep the business going and add new elements, she concluded by saying, "Someday I'd like to sell the business. I don't want to die 'there.' "

SOURCE: Kellogg, A. (1999), interview with Pilar Dexter in Waterford, NY, March 1; Oppedisano, J. (1999), interview with Pilar Dexter in Saratoga, NY, March 11.

MARY DONOHO (1807–1880)

"This well known Hotel which has been kept by the present Proprietress for the last seventeen years, has been lately rebuilt and enlarged, until it is now one of the largest and most commodious in the State . . . [with] ample accommodations for all who may patronize it. It is pleasantly situated on the public square, and is especially a comfortable house." (Mary Donoho, Proprietress, the Donoho Hotel, Clarksville, Texas)

Mary Dodson Donoho learned to be an adventurer from her parents, James and Lucy. Her father, though born in Virginia, was raised in Tennessee, becoming both a doctor and the owner of a gristmill. After he married Lucy in 1804, the couple moved to Missouri. Their daughter, Mary, grew to be a beautiful young woman with striking red hair, who caught the attention of Kentuckian William Donoho. They fell in love and married in 1831. Shortly after their daughter, Mary Ann, was born, they then left Missouri with a wagon train of over three hundred people, headed for New Mexico. Mary, her husband, their nine-month-old daughter, and three slaves Mary had inherited from her father made their way across a thousand miles, along the treacherous Santa Fe Trail, arriving in Santa Fe in 1833, one family among the 150 pioneers who had survived this trip. When Mary Donoho, who had been one of the first five white women to successfully make this journey, gave birth to another daughter in 1885, Harriet became the first "white" child to be born in this state. Their son, James, was born two years later, and three more children followed.

The Donohos opened a hotel in Santa Fe, and even though Mary had three little children under five at this time, in a truly frontier setting, she was also helping with cooking for guests and running the business. However, after four years, they decided to leave New Mexico, which had become life-threatening for "Anglos" living there. White women, in particular, were being captured and enslaved by both Mexicans and Indians, who murdered their children and men. When he heard that three white women had been captured by the Comanche Indians, William, deeply concerned, negotiated their release for $900. One of them, Rachael Plummer, later wrote of her feelings for the Donohos: "I hope that every American who reads this narrative may duly appreciate this amiable man, to whom under the providence of God, I owe my release. I have no language to express my gratitude to Mrs. Donoho. I found in her a mother, a sister to console with me in my misfortune . . . the best of friends . . . one who was continually pouring the sweet oil of consolation into my wounded and trembling soul" (Meyer, 1991: 67, 69).

The Donohos then decided to move to Clarksville, Texas, where in 1842 they opened the Donoho Hotel. Shortly afterward, Mary's beloved husband, who was only forty-seven, died, leaving her at age thirty-eight to raise five children—one had died—and run a business that she had to make successful if her family was to remain in the rugged West. Then more blows came, and she was left struggling to survive spiritually as well as physically. Mary's seven-year-old daughter, Lucy, died, presumably from some childhood disease. As her husband had died without a will, Mary had to go through court battles for the next six years to regain what should have been theirs all along.

Yet, Mary Donoho never capitulated to life's blows. Her commanding spirit and high energy enabled her to stay strong and never give up. In 1851 the court battle ended, with Mary getting half of her husband's estate and her children getting the other fifty percent. She not only survived but gained fame as the force behind a well-respected hotel. In fact, the 1860 census listed her as a "hotel keeper, head of the household with a financial worth of $41,000, about triple the amount she inherited from the estate" (Meyer, 1991: 96). The Donoho Hotel, itself, existed for more than fifty years. It was even used as the Clarksville stagecoach stand during the Civil War. From 1861 to 1865, there were "31 stage lines in Confederate Texas [hauling] mail, soldiers, civilians" (79). As for her personal life, Mary Donoho was to continue to experience tragic loss. Three of her daughters and one daughter-in-law died in childbirth, an experience all too common before the twentieth century. This mother outlived all of her female children.

In the recorded history of Clarksville, Texas, Pat Clark, grandson of the town founder, described the Donoho Hotel operation: "If any case of conduct did not measure up to the standard of the hotel, this guest was never accommodated in the future. . . . A long bell was mounted in front . . . which was rung 15 minutes in advance of a meal. . . . The parties and balls given at the Donoho Hotel were among the greatest pleasure events in the history of the grand old town" (Meyer, 1991: 80). However, Mr. Clark has rewritten history because, instead of acknowledging Mary Donoho's exceptional business acumen, he has credited the successful management of this establishment to Mary's son, James, who was only eight years old at the time.

SOURCE: Meyer, M. (1991), *Mary Donoho: New First Lady of the Santa Fe Trail* (Santa Fe, NM: Ancient City Press).

KATHARINE DREXEL (1858–1955)
ELIZABETH DREXEL SMITH (1855–1890)
LOUISE DREXEL MORRELL (1863–1943)

> *"It is the thought of why I am here . . . to prepare me for a future of responsibility . . . a life which is most apt to be one of opposition, trial and subjection to criticism, even of the Church . . . seems enormous . . . my heart goes down in sorrow when I think of it. . . . New orders always . . . have to pass through the baptism of the cross!"* (Mother Katharine Drexel, Founder, Sisters of the Blessed Sacrament for Indians and Colored People)

Entrepreneurship is often thought of as initiating organizations to create wealth. For the three Drexel sisters—Elizabeth, Katharine, and Louise—it was the opposite. They initiated organizations to distribute their wealth. Their father was Francis Anthony Drexel, one of the famous Drexel men who made a fortune in banking. Hannah Langstroth Drexel died giving birth to Katharine; Elizabeth was three years old at the time. Within a year, their father married Emma Bouvier, and they had their only child, a daughter, Louise. Emma continued the Drexel family tradition of charity, which was strongly influenced by their Roman Catholic religious background. "Three afternoons weekly the doors of her Walnut Street home [in Philadelphia] were thrown open to the poor in need of help. Clothing, medicine, rent money, amounting to some twenty thousand dollars a year were generously distributed. . . . [The daughters learned early on] that wealth was entrusted to them by God as a means of helping those in need" (Duffy, 1977: 27).

As they grew, the Drexel sisters became well educated and religiously grounded; they were raised with all of the creature comforts money could buy, including travel both in the developing United States and Europe. In each of the family homes, they were able to pray in their own private chapels. "Prayer was like breathing . . . there was no compulsion, no obligation . . . it was natural to pray," Katharine wrote (Baldwin, 1988: 14). But wealth could not save the lives of those they loved most. In 1883, Emma Bouvier Drexel died of inoperable cancer. To help them move through their grief, their father took them on a cross-country trip by private railroad car into the Northwest. This was the first trip into Indian country for the three young women, but they were so influenced by what they saw happening to the Indians and their traditions that they became committed to helping educate this disenfranchised population.

Two years after returning from this excursion, their father died of pleurisy. The sisters were devastated. Their father was as charitable in his death as he was in his life, and as protective of his daughters, too. His 1885 estate was valued at over fifteen million dollars. He gave ten percent, about $1.5 million, to specific charities. "The remainder of his estate, some $14 million dollars, was placed in a trust fund. He wished to be certain that, no matter what happened, [his daughters] could not fall victim to fortune hunters" (Baldwin, 1988: 29). This was very unusual for a Victorian era father; women were considered property, and few women owned it. Another restriction of the document was that, if the daughters died without offspring to inherit their estates, what was left would revert back to the original charities designated in Mr. Drexel's will.

In honor of her father's special interest in and support of Catholic orphanages for boys, Elizabeth Drexel had a trade school, the St. Francis de Sales Industrial School, built on 200 acres in Eddington, Pennsylvania, for the older boys from these establishments. On opening day in 1888, the school enrolled two hundred boys, "all dressed in clothing supplied by the Drexel sisters" (Baldwin, 1988: 35). Previously, Elizabeth "had founded and taught at a Sunday school for Negro children at Old St. Joseph's . . . [which] later became St. Peter Claver, Philadelphia's first Black Catholic parish" (36). The "All Three"—as they had nicknamed themselves—gave $50,000 to the Catholic University of America in Washington, DC, to establish the Francis A. Drexel Chair in Moral Theology. Louise gave $59,000 in 1888 to begin the Epiphany College in Baltimore to serve poor blacks. Six years later, she and her husband, Colonel Edward Morrell, founded a military academy near Richmond, Virginia, for young black men, naming it the St. Emma's Industrial and Agricultural Institute. For Katharine Drexel, the sister who was to become the most famous of the All Three, Native American Indians and children of color were to be the dominant life focus—but through a religious structure.

For a number of years, Katharine Drexel had been struggling with her desire to become a nun, which conflicted with the counsel of her religious advisors, archbishops of the Roman Catholic Church. They wanted her to stay a layperson and do charity "in the world." These men understood that, since religious orders required that all money and property be turned over to the particular religious order that Katharine would enter, they would no longer be able to have influence over or access to the kind of financial Drexel gifts they had become accustomed to receiving over many decades. But since she was adamant about wanting to be part of a religious group of women, the Church's final suggestion was for her to start her own religious order. Though living in poverty as required by the "rules," she would still retain control over the distribution of her great wealth. For her initiation into and study of the religious life, Katharine went to the Convent of St. Mary in 1889, entering as a postulant of the Sisters of Mercy.

The following year, Elizabeth Drexel married childhood friend Walter George. Nine months later, she died attempting to give birth to a stillborn child. In great grief, the surviving sisters determined that Elizabeth's endowment of the St. Francis Industrial School would be completed in her memory. They "jointly donated $120,000 a year for a period of eight years to complete this endowment, and Louise took upon herself the direct supervision of the school" (Baldwin, 1988: 44).

With thirteen women, Katharine Drexel founded her own community-based religious order in 1891, the Sisters of the Blessed Sacrament for Indians and Colored People, now known simply as the Sisters of the Blessed Sacrament. From the beginning, these women risked their lives to keep the significant commitment to social change initiated by their founder. They crossed the nation on horseback, covered wagons, or early railroad trains to begin or revive missions and schools in the West. Over time, Mother Drexel was responsible for the establishment of more than fifty missions and schools in fifteen states or territories. In the South, the Sisters risked bombings to enable blacks to receive an education. Mother Drexel also established five schools in Harlem, New York. She always felt that she was doing God's work and thus was protected. Indeed, this might seem to be the case, as this one example illustrates. After being on a train all day, Mother Drexel and another sister arrived in Richmond, Virginia, late at night only to learn that they wouldn't be able to get their next train until the following day. On top of this, the station closed at night, so they had no place to stay. Suddenly, "an elderly gentleman came up to them. . . . 'Are you the ladies which the Sisters in Duval St. sent me to meet?' Mother Katharine was surprised by this since she had made no plans for staying anywhere. . . . [Nonetheless, they went with him] to St. Joseph's Convent. . . . [He] deposited their bags on the porch, rang the bell, and bid them good evening" (Baldwin, 1988: 60). The Franciscan Sisters who lived there were awakened and welcomed these two religious comrades, but they had not "sent a driver for anyone. . . . Mother Katharine was of the opinion that St. Joseph had intervened for their protection" (61).

In 1945, Mother Katharine's youngest sister, Louise, died, but not before she had sold many of her personal belongings to support her soup kitchen, clothing the poor, and, with Katharine, giving large sums to the Catholic Interracial Movement of the New York Jesuit Rev. John La Farge. By the time of Katharine Drexel's own death in 1955, she had over five hundred members in her religious order, with more than fifty convents and almost as many schools. She had established the first Black Catholic University in the United States, Xavier University in Louisiana, and had given more than $12 million in her philanthropic work. In 1988 she was beatified by the Roman Catholic Church, the first step in the canonization process for sainthood. The significant generosity of the All Three Drexel sisters should be heralded. Their message continues to ring true today through the words of Katharine: "Don't deprive the children of bread and meat so as to weaken them. Keep the children happy. If they love school . . . you will have done much . . . God wants it" (Baldwin, 1988: 77).

SOURCES: Baldwin, L. (1988), *A Call to Sanctity: The Formation and Life of Mother Katharine Drexel* (Philadelphia, PA: Catholic Standard & Times); Butler, A. (1997), "Mother Katharine Drexel: Spiritual Visionary for the West," in G. Riley & R. Etulain, eds., *By Grit and Grace: Eleven Women Who Shaped the American West* (Golden, CO: Fulcrum Publishing); Duffy, C. (1977), *Katharine Drexel: A Biography* (Cornwells Heights, PA: Sisters of the Blessed Sacrament).

ABIGAIL DUNIWAY (1834–1915)

"If we formulate laws to shut away from the child the tree of knowledge of good and evil, he grows to maturity as a moral weakling. . . . [For a mother) to transmit character-building to her children, she must first, herself, be free and independent of all restrictive influences and laws opposed to the God-given right of individual liberty." (Abigail Duniway, Founder, Publisher, and Editor of the *New Northwest* newspaper)

To most historians, Abigail Scott Duniway is the mother of the suffrage movement in the Pacific Northwest. Few recognize that she funded these women's rights efforts, supported her own family, and gave work to many women who needed to support their own families. She did this by initiating and managing two simultaneous entrepreneurial enterprises—a millinery shop and a newspaper. From the time she was just a small child, Abigail had a clear understanding of what it meant to be female in the mid-nineteenth century. Born in Groveland, Illinois, she was the third child of twelve in the family of Tucker and Anne Roelofson Scott. Abigail wrote, "I remember that my mother informed me on my tenth birthday that her sorrow over my sex was almost too grievous to be borne" (Duniway, 1914: 3). By this age, Abigail and other female pioneering children were expected to be chopping wood, churning butter, tending chickens, helping watch the smaller children, tapping maple sugar, picking wool, and spinning fabric. Most females married young and died young giving birth, as did Abigail's mother.

When Abigail was seventeen, her father faced two crises—the murder of

his brother and a bankruptcy that ensued when he paid his deceased
brother's debts. This led him to the decision to go west to Oregon to seek
his fortune. Abigail described this 2,400-mile expedition of 1852: "[My
adventurous father] started with his invalid wife and the nine surviving
children . . . to travel with ox teams and covered wagons across the plains"
(Duniway, 1914: 3). Her mother died on the trail giving birth to her twelfth
child, who also died. Abigail's father had assigned the job of journal writing
to her. It was common practice for people going west to send back east
documentation of the trip for others to use should they decide to follow
suit. However, Abigail also added narrative and stories; later in her life the
journal was turned into the book *Captain Gray's Company, or Crossing
the Plains and Living in Oregon*, the first novel to be commercially published in Oregon (Moynihan, 1997).

After almost six months, the Scotts reached Oregon, and Abigail, with
less than a year of formal education herself, began teaching in the small
village of Cincinnati, Oregon. Here she met a handsome rancher, Ben Duniway. After a short courtship, they were married and quickly had two children in rapid succession, Clara and Willis. Abigail, who had suffered with
rheumatoid arthritis since childhood, described this juncture in her life: "I,
if not washing, scrubbing, churning, or nursing the baby, was preparing
their meals in our lean-to kitchen. To bear two children in two and a half
years from my marriage day, to make thousands of pounds of butter every
year for market, not including what was used in our free hotel at home;
to sew and cook, and wash and iron; to bake and clean and stew and fry;
to be, in short, a general pioneer drudge, with never a penny of my own"
(Duniway, 1914: 10). She began to submit her narratives to local papers
like the *Argus* and the *Oregon Farmer*; many were accepted, and Duniway
soon established herself as a regular contributor.

But then the tables turned quite suddenly for the Duniways. Generous but
not wise, her husband had signed notes for an acquaintance who then failed
to pay the loans. This was followed by crops failing, and the Duniways were
forced to sell their house to pay the debt. Ben Duniway went to work on a
farm, but he was severely injured when a runaway team of horses with the
wagon they were dragging ran over him; he was never able to do farm work
again. Now Abigail Duniway had to figure out ways to support her family
alone. At first she opened a private boarding school in the upper portion of
their small dwelling. Her day was long and complicated: "I would arise from
my bed at 3 o'clock [A.M.] . . . do a day's work before school time . . . [teach]
often hearing recitations from text books I had never studied, over which, so
keyed to thought was I from sheer necessity, that I caught the inspiration of
every problem as I came to it, and never . . . let my pupils see that it was new
to me . . . until 4 o'clock [P.M.], before taking up my household duties again"
(Duniway, 1914: 16–17). Yet, this grueling schedule actually brought a renewed life energy into Duniway. She added, "My work was rest for both

mind and body. Health improved and hope revived." Her husband became the caretaker of the children while she worked.

Once Duniway had earned enough money from teaching to open a business, she started a millinery and notions store in Albany, Oregon. Unfortunately, the place required extensive remodeling, and after paying all of these costs, she had just thirty dollars left to buy stock. Then she met what today is referred to in entrepreneurial parlance as an "angel." Jacob Mayer, a local wholesaler, believed in what she was trying to accomplish and provided her with $1,200 worth of stock. "I was back in three weeks," she later proudly wrote, "and paid the debt in full. My next account was for three thousand dollars; and from that day to this, I have not known extreme poverty. . . . I have earned and expended over forty-two thousand dollars in my long drawn struggle for Equal Rights for Women, which if I had used in trade, or invested in real estate, would have made me several times a millionaire" (Duniway, 1914: 19–20).

Once her millinery business was flourishing, Duniway turned her attention to the fight for women's equality, moving her family to the city of Portland and initiating a newspaper called the *New Northwest* in 1871. At this time in U.S. history, women had no legal rights to their children or property, nor did they have voting privileges. It was her husband who explained to Duniway, "It will never be any better for women until they vote. Some day a woman will start something" (Richey, 1975: 75). And so his wife did. The goal of her publication was vividly clear to Duniway. This newspaper would be not just a "Woman's Rights, but a Human Rights organ, devoted to whatever policy may be necessary to secure the greatest good to the greatest number . . . fastened upon the rock of Eternal Liberty, Universal Emancipation and Untrammeled Progression" (Moynihan, 1997: 182).

Duniway traveled throughout the northwest region of the country for the next sixteen years speaking for women's rights—sometimes dodging rotten eggs and overly ripened fruit—while still editing the paper, writing articles and serialized novels, and getting the material back on time through the postal service. Her sons were the printers, one of her sisters became associate editor, and correspondents from "Washington, New York, and Europe were hired to furnish weekly news" (Capell, 1934: 49).

Then in 1886, Clara Belle, Duniway's only daughter of her now six children, died of consumption. Her mother wanted to die with her, but Clara's deathbed whisper was, "You must finish your work, Ma" (Duniway, 1914: 72). Duniway and all her family, emotionally traumatized, decided to find a place of refuge. She sold the newspaper, and they moved to a ranch in Idaho purchased by money from the sale. However, Duniway, who had long been independent, soon became restless. She returned to Portland and became a strong focal point for the women's suffrage movement in Oregon. She occasionally traveled back to the ranch to be with her sons and her husband, who died in 1896. Abigail Duniway lived to see the state suffrage struggle become successful, and in 1914 she became the first Oregon woman to vote. She died the following year. Her life story gives evidence to this Duniway observation: "Success will seldom come in the ways that one has planned for it; but come it will, sooner or later, to all who are faithful" (Duniway, 1914: 13).

SOURCES: Capell, L. (1934), "A Biography of Abigail Scott Duniway," unpublished thesis, University of Oregon; Duniway, A. (1914), *Path Breaking: An Autobiographical History of the Equal Suffrage Movement in Pacific Coast States*, reprinted in 1971 (New York: Schocken Books); Moynihan, R. (1997), "Abigail Scott Duniway: Mother of Woman Suffrage in the Pacific Northwest," in G. Riley & R. Etulain, eds., *By Grit and Grace: Eleven Women Who Shaped the American West* (Golden, CO: Fulcrum Publishing); Richey, E. (1975), "The Unsinkable Abigail," *American Heritage: The Magazine of History* 26, no. 2 (February): 72–89.

VERA DUSS (1910–   )

"When all the various qualities of each woman's voice are heard in unison, you get the sound of something 'being right,' the sound of people being at peace." (Lady Abbess, Mother Vera Duss, Founder of the Abbey of Regina Laudis, speaking about women in chant)

Vera Duss was born in Pennsylvania; however, she expected to live out her days in France where she had lived as a child and been educated. In June 1936, Duss received a medical degree in Paris. Although this was the avenue her mother wanted her to pursue, it was not what Duss felt was her real calling. That same week, she joined the Benedictine Order at the Abbey of Jouarre and eventually was given the name "Mother Benedict." What changed her life and brought her back to the United States is the stuff of which movies are made, and one was. In 1949, Twentieth Century Fox put out *Come to the Stable*, with Loretta Young in the role of a fictionalized Mother Benedict Duss.

History now records that the late 1930s and early 1940s were a time of calamity, with World War II raging in Europe. For a while, Mother Benedict was able to continue practicing medicine for the nuns and local residents of Jouarre; but once the Germans occupied Paris and most of France, she became a Gestapo target simply because she was an American and, therefore, an enemy. She had to go into hiding in the Abbey. For a long period, the only diversions that Mother Benedict had were some books, music, and mundane tasks like mending the worn-out napkins used by the nuns in the Abbey.

Then all of this changed for her on August 27, 1944. The sirens started up again, the church bells started ringing—the American soldiers were liberating France. Seeing the Americans with the white star on their vehicles coming through the village was "an absolutely astounding experience for me. It shook my foundations, if you will. I realized how much blood had been shed for this liberation, and I had to ask myself, how was I going to match this gift?" (Bosco, 1997). It was then that she decided to start an organization that would offer a cloistered, monastic life in America—the first of its kind there—"to extend the life-giving work" of the Americans in Europe. To fulfill such a dream would require papal approval, other people who would want to join such a community, travel to the states, the support of a local bishop, and moneys to purchase property and support the fledgling organization. The question was how she could accomplish all of this when she was sworn to poverty, but this did not deter her.

Within two years Mother Benedict got the approval of both her Abbess and Rome to travel to the United States to explore the feasibility of her vision. To do this, she had to acquire the necessary visas, get commitments from other nuns who wanted to join her here, and receive enough contributions to cover her travel. Through a wealthy Frenchwoman, Duss was told of two artists, Lauren Ford and Frances Delehanty, who might have a place for her to stay in America. These two women lived in a small rural town in Connecticut called Bethlehem. The religious significance of the town name and its relationship to the star she had seen on the military jeeps was not lost on Mother Benedict. But by the time she arrived at the farm, she literally had only three cents left to her name. And that was just the beginning of her problems. The local bishop was refusing to see her, and without his support, her mission would fail. The message he eventually conveyed indirectly to her was that if she had some land given to her, then he would see her. Again, a benefactor was there for Duss. Lauren Ford introduced her to a neighbor, Robert Leather, who listened to the plight of Mother Benedict. Moved by her vision, he said to her, "I have a beautiful hill . . . too beautiful for one family to own, and too beautiful to be divided up for development. I want it to be a place where many people come to worship. I give it to you for your monastery . . . [it's] the best fifty acres in Bethlehem" (Bosco, 1990). Thus, in 1946, the foundation that would one day become the Abbey of Regina Laudis was begun.

By the end of the twentieth century, the monastery consisted of about four hundred acres with several old buildings, including a refurbished factory that serves as living quarters for the nuns, a rustic chapel, and a new monastery church designed by the nuns themselves. "The guiding principle [had been] to make a contemplative foundation, which was very difficult in America . . . because the country was not at that point of maturity and resources . . . [at that time] women were pulled out to teach or to work in hospitals," explained Lady Abbess (Tuhus, 1998: 1). The nuns of the Abbey of Regina Laudis constitute a unique group of approximately forty women who, before making this religious commitment, were doctors, social workers, actors, lawyers, farmers, sculptors, politicians, blacksmiths, artists, horticulturists—one even a grandmother; they live according to the Benedictine rule, in an enclosure, yet still remain attuned to their respective fields. They support themselves in part by making and selling handcrafts, bread, butter, cheese, and artwork like pottery. Their goals are simple by today's standards, which makes them all the more unusual: Practice common sense, be self-sufficient as much as possible, "see the beauty in creation and having a reverence for all created things. Work with a carefree heart . . . deal with a problem without fuss and quietly proceed to the next matter" (Bosco, 1990: 17).

The nuns of the Abbey continue to offer hospitality to all regardless of why they come to the door. According to Sister Monica, the grandmother: "Each one who comes is received warmly and no questions [are] asked. They don't have to be Catholic. Just come" (Bosco, 1990: 17). There is also a group of *oblates*—laypeople who maintain their own working lives and/or businesses but who want to include the way of St. Benedictine into each day; they take an active part in what goes on at the Abbey. The nuns also maintain a land program that is designed to teach young people how to farm and revere nature.

Many people have given witness to the impact that even a simple visit to the Abbey can have. Writer Simon Montefiore wanted to interview Mother Delores, the former movie star Delores Hart. Instead, he spent a day helping with the harvest and getting only a short time with his intended subject. From working with the nuns and experiencing the land, he "discovered a warm and neglected part of myself. I did not become religious. No one tried to convert me to anything. Looking back, I realized that when I left, I took something with me and left something behind" (Montefiore, 1993: 24). The legacy of Lady Abbess's initiative will be its impact on the lives of so many—those who visited, those who stayed to work, and those who entered.

SOURCES: Bosco, A. (1990), "The Abbey of Regina Laudis," *Litchfield County Times*, November 16: 15–18; Engerl, S. (1995), *Come to the Stable* [Videorecording], Fox Video; Pomposello, T. (1997), *Women in Chant* [CD], Sounds True; Montefiore, S. (1993), "A Cloistered Life: Visit to the Abbey of Regina Laudis in Bethlehem, Connecticut, *Psychology Today* [Online], November: 24 (available: Lexis-Nexis); Tuhus, M. (1998), "Women Devoted to Chant, Serving as Stewards of the Land," *New York Times* [Online], March 15: 1 (available: Lexis-Nexis).

JOYCE EDDY (1929–   )

> *"We always joked about making the same mistakes twice to make sure that we were wrong the first time. But we know that this company would not exist if it weren't for God. . . . The disappointments and failures all fall by the wayside. I always looked at them positively as a challenge and opportunity, a new chance to start over again and work toward other successes."* (Joyce Eddy, Founder, Habersham Plantation Furniture)

In 1929, the year the world was feeling the consequences of the stock market crash, Cora Mae and Bill Cash became parents for the third time, with the daughter they named Joyce. To make it financially, Mr. Cash worked for the railroad by day and then labored on the family farm in Ravenna, Ohio, in the evenings. Over the years four more children were born, each actively participating in the life of a Midwestern farm family. As Joyce later explained, "We were poor; we had very little money, but we never knew it" (Williamson, 1985: 41). What they did know was that religion was an important component of their daily lives, with Sunday being the day set aside for formal worship. This deep spiritual base served as the anchor for Joyce's life and is a part of the mission statement of the furniture company she subsequently founded: "To conduct our business with the highest level of integrity and respect for our customers, associates, and vendors [and] to honor God in all that we do" (Habersham Plantation, 1999).

One has to ask how a young girl raised on a farm in Ohio became the founder of a multimillion-dollar manufacturer of fine furniture in the state of Georgia, especially since she started out as a young bride, marrying her teen sweetheart, Craig Eddy, right after completing high school. Seven years later, while she was pregnant with their second child, her husband had a nervous breakdown with no likelihood that he would ever be able to make a living again. His doctor suggested to Joyce Eddy that she get a divorce, not a common avenue for women of the 1950s. However, she did follow this advice and went to work to support her family. Her parents, who had moved to Toccoa Falls, Georgia, after her father had a heart attack, came back to visit. When they saw how difficult life was now for Eddy and her family, "[they] got me, my two sons, and all of my possessions and moved us back to Toccoa Falls" (Williamson, 1985: 46).

By 1967 Eddy had again married, this time to a musician. Her husband also had an antique store in an old laundry building in Clarksville, Georgia. She ended up taking care of the store while her husband pursued his career as a road musician. The marriage lasted only two years, and Eddy was able to keep the business. Then more trouble hit when she lost her home in a fire. Now, at age forty, Eddy found herself not only divorced for the second time, but without a place to live and barely eking out a living for herself and her family. To bring in more income, she started to use her handcrafting skills honed over the years in crocheting, knitting, and other hobbies to make and decorate small pocketbooks out of old wooden cigar boxes. Then she got the idea to use the discarded wooden spools from a nearby textile company to make candlesticks and towel racks. She bought 20,000 spools at two cents a piece. These creative Americana products were so successful that Eddy decided to branch out into small furniture made in the early American country style. Her brother, Ralph, agreed to work for her, as did a retired minister and friend of the family, Doyle Anderson. "They built the furniture in the basement from materials bought on credit from the local lumber yard and hardware store, and Joyce and [her son] Matthew painted, stained, waxed, and finished them . . . 'a piece at a time' " (Williamson, 1985: 50). Eddy named her company Habersham Plantation because they were located in Habersham County, a place known for its plantations.

However, it was the opportunity offered by two Gatlinburg, Tennessee, businessmen that changed the scope of Eddy's business. They understood the market interest in early American furniture and were so impressed with the quality of the Habersham products that they wanted to open a store featuring these pieces. This fortunate turn of events didn't mean that times were easy. "Between 1972 and 1975, Joyce's salary was $50 a week. Withdrawing only a minimum salary meant that she and Matthew would have to continue . . . to 'camp' above the store for another two and one-half years and that they would eat many tomato sandwiches and grits during that time" (Williamson, 1985: 61). This worked, and sales for the 1974 fiscal year hit $400,000. Eddy not only was able to build and finance a new facility for her business, but had bankers calling on her to offer money—just when her cash flow had been depleted. "Talk about answered prayers," she exclaimed.

In 1984 Joyce Eddy was named the Georgia Small Business Person of the Year and was honored by the president of the United States. The Habersham items were being sold in more than 250 stores in the United States and Canada, with sales reaching the $5 million mark a year later. By 1998, the more than four hundred handcrafted pieces of Habersham furniture also were being offered in Bermuda, Europe, and Japan; and the company had added a new line of hand-painted, signed, numbered, and limited editions of works of fine art. When Eddy looked back on these last three decades of her business, she said, "It just happened. We all worked very hard. None of us possessed a particular talent, but we believed in what we were doing" (Roots, 1987: 2).

SOURCES: Habersham Plantation (1999), *http://www.habershamplantation.com* (accessed May 2); Roots, G. (1987), "HOME," *Chicago Tribune*, September 13: 4C (available: Lexis-Nexis, accessed August 31, 1998); Wray, K. (1998), "Broad Strokes Habersham Refines Identity to Reflect Upscale Thrust," *HFN, The Weekly Newspaper*, 72, no. 13 (March 30): 29 (available: Lexis-Nexis, accessed August 31, 1998). Williamson, L. (1985), "Joyce Eddy: A Successful Female Entrepreneur," unpublished dissertation, University of Mississippi.

MARY BAKER EDDY (1821–1910)

"In natural law and in religion the right of woman to fill the highest measure of enlightened understanding and the highest places in government, is inalienable. . . . This is woman's hour, with all its sweet amenities and its moral and religious reforms." (Mary Baker Eddy, Founder of the Christian Science Association, 1887)

Born on July 16, 1821, into the Baker family in the small town of Bow, New Hampshire, Mary Morse Baker was ill from childhood. Because of this, even what limited education was available to girls at the time was difficult for her to access; however, she became self-educated through her reading and writing. At twenty-two she married George Clover, who died a few months later, leaving her pregnant with the only child she was to have, a son named after his father. As the pregnancy and birth had exacerbated her health problems, she did not raise the child herself.

Suffering from the consistent pain of a spinal disease led Mary Baker Eddy to seek out those who might provide her some relief. For two years she was able to get such help from Phineas P. Quimby, a holistic healer, but once he died, the illness returned. In 1866, her condition was complicated even further by a serious fall. At this point, Eddy turned to the New Testament of the Bible for hope. Meditating on a story of Jesus' healing in Matthew 9:2, she herself was cured. After this experience, she went into virtual seclusion for several years to construct, write, and teach to a selected few what she believed to be the system for healing through Christ. This was the beginning of a series of monumental accomplishments by Mary Baker Eddy.

At the age of fifty-four, Eddy put in place the foundation for the Christian Science Association by publishing *Science and Health with Key to the Scriptures*, a work that described her tenets of faith, and by holding public meetings in Massachusetts towns like Lynn and Roxbury. This was the beginning of a stream of entrepreneurial ventures that spanned more than three decades. In 1879 she founded the Church of Christ, Scientist; in 1881 she opened the Massachusetts Metaphysical College with a tuition fee of three hundred dollars for those wishing to learn her healing methods; in 1883 she founded the publication *Christian Science Journal*; in 1895 she published the first edition of the *Manual of the Mother Church*, which is the ruling authority for her organization and, as such, could not be amended—her followers considered it an inspired work; in 1898 she published the *Christian Science Weekly*, which was later called the *Christian Science Sentinel*; and in 1908 at the age of 88, she founded the international daily newspaper *Christian Science Monitor*. In fact, at her resolute direction, both the Christian Science Board and the trustees of the Christian Science Publishing Society "organized [this] newspaper, including purchasing all the printing equipment, building a new wing on the publishing house, and gathering a staff—all within just one hundred days (Goodrich, 1993: 9)!

At her death in 1910, Mary Baker Eddy left an estate estimated to be worth $2.5 million. Her organization and her publications continue today. Eddy's legacy includes a World Headquarters in Boston, Massachusetts; over two thousand branch churches in more than sixty countries; writings disseminated in seventeen languages; and sales of her original text, *Science and Health with Key to the Scriptures*, having exceeded nine million copies by the end of the 1990s—no small feat for anyone, much less a woman born in 1821 who was sick for the first half of her life.

SOURCES: Ellwood, R., & Partin, H. (1988), *Religious and Spiritual Groups in Modern America* (Englewood Cliffs, NJ: Prentice-Hall); Ferguson, M. (1995), *Women in Religion* (Englewood Cliffs, NJ: Prentice-Hall); Gillian, G. (1998), *Mary Baker Eddy* (Reading, MA: Perseus Books); Goodrich, L. (1993), "How It All Began," *Christian Science Monitor*, November 23: 9; Hudson, W., & Corrigan, J. (1992), *Religion in America: An Historical Account of the Development of American Religious Life* (New York: Macmillan); *Soul of a Woman: The Life and Times of Mary Baker Eddy* (1994) [Videorecording], New Hampshire Public Television (Durham, NH); Thomas, R. (1994), *"With Bleeding Footsteps": Mary Baker Eddy's Path to Religious Leadership* [Videorecording], Durham, NH.

FREDA EHMANN (1839–1932)

"In looking over these first pages of the history of our business, one might truthfully say that I did not realize the enormity of the task

which was before me." (Freda Ehmann, Founder of the Ehmann Olive
Company and "Mother" of the California Ripe Olive Industry)

Freda Loeber, born in 1839 in Germany, came to America as a teenager
with her mother after her father died. She later met and married Dr. Ernst
Ehmann, a physician-druggist, and they had three children—Mathilda, Edwin, and Emma. Life was good for Freda Ehmann until her daughter Mathilda died of typhoid fever at age nineteen. Shortly after this, her husband
became ill. He did not recover; his health progressively worsened, and he
died in 1892. At this time, her son, Edwin, convinced her to start anew by
moving to California where he was a salesman for Nathan-Dohrmann
china. He was also interested in the olive business. One of his customers,
Herman Juch, convinced Edwin to invest with him in Olive Hill Grove, an
1,800-acre ranch. Ehmann used the money from the sale of her home to
help him do just that.

Weather washed away this dream, literally. The winter of 1894–1895
had heavy rainfall, the fields were flooded, and all of Ehmann's money was
lost. However, Mr. Juch deeded a twenty-acre parcel to her to try to make
up for the loss. Edwin wanted to claim bankruptcy, but his mother
wouldn't hear of it. She reminded him that *this* family always paid its debts.

It wasn't until two years later that Ehmann's grove finally bore fruit. She
was now 58 years old. The caretaker of her grove gave her the idea of
trying to pickle the olives for sale. No grower had been successful yet with
such a venture because spoilage was so high. In fact, in New York city,
"ripe olives . . . spoiled and smelled so bad that the merchants had to sneak
them through the streets at night and dump them in the East River" (Bolles
& Bartley, 1979: 53). Nan Walker, a current olive grower, vividly painted
the picture of what faced Ehmann:

Olives were picked green in October and November for the ripe olive. The acid
content of the olives make them impossible to eat off the tree. . . . The lye process
for making olives edible was known at the time, but it was not standardized or
formalized. One batch of home-cured olives would be wonderful; the next batch
would not be fit for pigs! It takes enormous patience, water and salt for the brine
[to cure the olives]. The lye has to soak to the olive pit. Removed too soon and the
olive is bitter; removed from the lye too late and the olive is mushy. (Walker, 1994)

Ehmann sought help for finding a way to preserve the olives from Professor Eugene Hilgard of the Agriculture Department at the University of
California, Berkeley. He gave her a basic recipe, but she had to put together
the equipment. Her son-in-law, Charles Bolles, got old wine barrels and
made vats for her, and her experimenting began. Because there wasn't any
piping for water to the back porch where she was working, Freda had to
hand-carry the water necessary for processing—an estimated two hundred
gallons that first year! At the crack of dawn she'd be up checking what

was going on, and based on what she found, adapting the recipe. Finally the hard work and persistence paid off. Professor Hilgard thought her product was the best he had ever tasted, and one of the largest local grocers ordered her entire output.

The following year Freda Ehmann began the adventure that would make another strong mark on the economy of California. She decided to go to the East Coast, to New York and Pennsylvania specifically, to market her processed olives. Prior to this, olives were distributed near where they were grown. Ehmann came back from this trip with contracts for 10,000 gallons of olives. Her son wasn't the only salesperson in the family! Freda knew she could only produce a thousand gallons; she simply purchased the entire crop of another grower, leased a pickling plant, took a nearby room, and started to go to work.

In 1898 the Ehmann Olive Company was incorporated, and by 1904 it had national distribution. It was a family business. Her son, Edwin, handled marketing and sales, and her son-in-law, Charles, was in charge of plant and construction; Ehmann herself watched over production. "Every piece of equipment, every method of handling fruit from tree to finished product had to have her approval. For instance, no olive that was not at least a cherry red color was allowed to enter the plant" (Bolles & Bartley, 1979: 53). This was consistent with her slogan: "[It's] not how much nor how inexpensive but how *good* a product we can produce" (52). Up until she reached her mid-seventies, she actively supervised the packing operation.

Not only was Ehmann a determined person, but she was also a concerned employer and a philanthropic community member. At a time when many in this country would not hire Asian immigrants or pay them fairly, Freda Ehmann offered them employment at the same wages she paid American workers. She had a barracks built for them to stay in rather than the yard they had been in before; even a dining hall was provided. However, at the end of World War I, this hiring policy ended because the company was getting threatening notes from anonymous anti-Japanese harassers. The female employees also were watched over very carefully by Ehmann. They had their own dining room, where tea was served with lunch. Ehmann would join them each day no matter how busy her schedule, but the men were not allowed in this dining room.

Not only did she help her own employees, but Freda found informal ways to help others who needed work. "Christmas bonuses were unfailingly given to all employees and Mother Ehmann always found an unobtrusive way to help employees in need . . . [and] friends from town often received gifts of lovely embroidery work and sets of monogrammed sheets and napkins from Mrs. Ehmann, gifts Freda had employed needy women to make for her" (Bolles & Bartley, 1979: 66).

Ehmann supported the suffrage movement and was friends with Susan B. Anthony and Carrie Chapman Catt. In addition, her advocacy for the industry she loved was very strong. Even at the age of 92 she wrote a letter to American women urging them to purchase what was grown in this country, thereby supporting the employment of U.S. workers.

Freda Ehmann is credited with creating a demand for a product that didn't exist and for giving birth to a new industry—all this, started by a person with no background in the industry, no training in the process, and at an age when she was already past the normal life expectancy of her female contemporaries. Few would argue that Freda Ehmann took incredible risks, had no certainty of income from the endeavor, impacted the economy, and possessed the internal characteristics of being intelligent, decisive, and persuasive; of having integrity, a need for independence, and a need for achievement. She truly was an entrepreneur.

SOURCES: *All About Ripe Olives* (1993), California Olive Industry brochure; Bolles, W., & Bartley, G. (1979), "Freda Ehmann," *Butte County Historical Society: DIGGIN'S* 23, nos. 3 & 4: 47–71; "Freda Ehmann" (1994), upublished correspondence of Nan Walker, August.

LINDA ELLERBEE (1944–   )

"In the last few years [before 1991] I quit a salaried job; started a company; renovated an old house; saw my mother die; saw my children grow up, move out, move back in, move out; watched my weight go up, down, up; and underwent other, sometimes more difficult changes, for the better, I hope." (Linda Ellerbee, Co-founder and CEO, Lucky Duck Productions)

By age thirty-one, Linda Jane Smith Ellerbee had been married four times, had two children, and had started writing professionally, exposing a talent that ultimately led to a career climb in network news. She was born in Bryan, Texas, the only child of Lonnie and Hallie Smith. Her mother joked that Linda was "going to keep getting married until she gets it right" (Ellerbee, 1991: 90). From her father's perspective, she could have walked away from the decision to marry. He pointed out, "Linda Jane, there are two doors here. One will take us down the aisle and one will take us out the door. We can go either way, and either way you decide to go, I'll be with you. Love is too important to be taken too seriously" (96). Ellerbee had always had a close relationship with her father. They especially shared a love of words from before she was five years old, when he already had taught her to recite poems. She later realized that they also shared the disease of alcoholism. She never questioned his love of her, a fact reinforced when Ellerbee discovered after his death that her father had saved every single letter she had ever sent him.

After a short-lived first marriage, Ellerbee married Van Veselka, the father of her children Vanessa and Joshua, who were born only a year apart in 1969 and 1970. The following year, her husband moved the family to Alaska so that he could work for the Model Cities Program. The job didn't last. He was fired, and Linda faced the reality that, if her children were going to eat, it was she who would have to put the food on the table. She recalled her predicament at the time. "I swore that I would never allow myself to become helpless again" (Gross, 1986: 32). She explained in her typically self-deprecating humor, "I was begging for work, not knowing how to do anything but talk and scribble" (Ellerbee, 1991: 230). She got a job at a local radio station, KNJO, in Juneau. Then she faced a new crisis—an unfaithful husband who brazenly justified his acts by saying that the 1970s were a "new age."

Ellerbee decided to return to Texas in 1972, and now with radio experience as a media credential, got a job with the Associated Press (AP). This employment was short because she made a critical mistake—Ellerbee accidentally sent out a personal letter that criticized many politicians and some of the management of the AP; she was summarily fired. However, since the letter was written in what was to become her special and acerbic yet humorous style, it caught the attention of a news director in Houston, who upgraded her to an on-air reporter. A year later she was hired by WCBS in New York City; that job was followed by a position with the National Broadcasting Company (NBC). Within a few years, Ellerbee was co-anchoring and directing the NBC *News Overnight* program. After eleven years at NBC, she switched networks and became co-anchor for the American Broadcasting Company (ABC) program *Our World*. She wrote her first book, *And So It Goes: Adventures in Television*, the same year.

By 1987 Ellerbee had decided to quit ABC to pursue a long-held dream. "For years I'd said I wanted to leave the networks and start an independent television production company. However small . . . it would be mine. It's one of those all-American dreams, and I was one of the all-American dreamers" (Ellerbee, 1991: 152). She and her life partner, Rolfe Tessem, a cinematographer, pulled together several hundred thousand dollars from savings and started Lucky Duck Productions, with offices in the basement of their townhouse. The original goal was to specialize in nonfiction film, "some good television." As their programming became more popular, particularly the news and documentary programs targeted toward children, contracts were established with the Nickelodeon, Lifetime, HBO, FOX, and MTV cable networks. One program that Ellerbee herself moderates is the syndicated Nick News series. "The core audience is children roughly 9 to

11," Ellerbee says, "but I know it skews down to 5 or 6 and up to 80—
we also have an adult cult" (Cawley, 1995: 8E). The quality of the Lucky
Duck Productions programming has attracted many awards, including two
Peabodys, an Emmy, a Dupont, and three CableAces.

However, two years after founding her company, Ellerbee came face to
face with the serious consequences of her long-term destructive alcoholic
behavior. "In the summer of 1989, I turned to my son and said please hold
my hand, I think I'm in terrible trouble. I'm going to phone the Betty Ford
Center. I don't know where else to call and if I take the time to find out,
I'll chicken out" (Ellerbee, 1991: 221). Though it was frightening, she
worked with the program and restarted her life. In 1991, Ellerbee wrote
her second book, *Moving On: Adventures in the Real World*. Then a year
later, her next, almost tragic blow hit. Ellerbee was told she had breast
cancer. She chose to undergo a double mastectomy and chemotherapy and
followed this by an ABC special program in 1993, *The Other Epidemic:
What Every Woman Needs to Know About Breast Cancer*. Her company
continued to be successful. After only six years in business, Lucky Duck
Productions had moved to a large facility in Greenwich Village in New
York, had over thirty employees, and was grossing about three million
dollars; the following year it topped four million, and seven million the
next. Ellerbee pointed out that, "The wonderful thing about impossible
dreams is that they don't know they're impossible! Which is another way
of saying fools rush in where fools belong" (121).

After the roller coaster ride of her life story so far, what observations
does Ellerbee share? "I've learned to do things my own way, even if I'm
wrong, which often I am, but only dead fish swim with the stream . . . that
if you don't want to get old, don't mellow . . . always to set a place in life
for the unexpected guest. And be content with questions. . . . Most of all,
I've learned that a good time to laugh is any time you can" (Ellerbee, 1991:
266). She has also come to appreciate nature in a much more powerful
way. "I don't know whether it came from the cancer or just from getting
older, she said, but I am clearly aware of a need for beauty in my life. The
snowflakes looking like powdered sugar on the dead leaves in November
or the smell of grass up on the hills in April—I need this, it's a physical
need" (Kaplan, 1997: C1:2).

SOURCES: Cawley, J. (1995), "Ellerbee's Lucky Duck Helps Her Cope," *Cleveland
Plain Dealer*, March 21: 8E; Ellerbee, L. (1991), *Move On: Adventures in the Real
World* (New York: G. P. Putnam's Sons); Goodman, M. (1993), "Life Force: Linda
Ellerbee Beat Breast Cancer with Calculated Ferocity," *People Magazine*, September
20: 59; Gross, K. (1986), "Facing a Pay Squeeze at NBC, Linda Ellerbee Takes a
Half-Million-Dollar Hike to ABC," *People Magazine*, July 28: 32; Kaplan, F.
(1997), "Linda Ellerbee: Life's Just Ducky," *Boston Globe* [Online], April 22: C1:2
(available: Proquest, accessed March 28).

MARY EMERY (1845–1927)

"And the children? Do you feel safer about them? Are their faces a bit ruddier? Are their legs a little sturdier? Do they play and laugh a lot louder in Mariemont? Then I am content." (Mary Emery, Founder, village of Mariemont, Ohio)

Early in the twentieth century, Mary Muhlenberg Emery had a vision of what she believed could be a living tribute to her deceased husband, Thomas J. Emery, keeping his memory alive. She loved and respected him enough to conceive an unheard of idea—designing and financing the creation of a town that would encompass almost four hundred acres of land with over fifty acres of parks as a tribute to him. It took several decades for her project to go from dream to reality, but even major intervening events like World War I and the Great Depression could not halt her grand design.

To build what would one day become the Village of Mariemont, Ohio, Mary Muhlenberg used her inheritance from her husband's estate. Authorizing five million dollars in capital, she hired her son Sheldon's best friend, engineer Charles Livingood, and the best architects money could buy. "She engaged [Grosvenor] Atterbury and [Robert] McGoodmwin as well as Paul Cret, Edmund Gilchrist, and Wilson Eyre. . . . [Later] Gilchrist chaired President Hoover's Conference on Home Building and Home Ownership; Eyre was the founder of *House and Garden*" (Rybczynski, 1997: 78). Mary Emery sponsored three years of Livingood's travel in Europe to study various housing there. During the construction phase, he had some buildings he had located in England disassembled, brought to Mariemont, and reassembled. One example is the Community Church.

The Emery Project was begun in 1910. As land was being acquired, Mary Muhlenberg Emery, referred to by some as "Lady Bountiful," had a dream. She wanted to create a community of from 9,000 to 20,000 people that was close enough to jobs to keep its residents employed, that was clean of the smog of the early industrial neighboring city of Cincinnati, that would permit residents to either rent or buy their homes, that sponsored all denominations in religious worship, and most especially, that was a desirable place for children to live. A 1924 demographic picture of Cincinnati puts this huge cultural and construction commitment into perspective. The population of this city was over 400,000, with more than one-third living in tenements because of the housing shortage and low wages; some 2,239 factories employed about 70,000 workers, and there was a high death rate from typhoid fever (*Mariemont: The New Town*, 1925). Mary Emery had a different vision of what life should be like for families.

Mariemont was clearly a real estate development project, but "a limit [was] put on the profit to the owner to give force to the idea that the maximum return should not be extracted from the man who earnestly desires a home for his own use. . . . [It] is to furnish to Cincinnati a more pleasant place to live than in the crowded downtown districts" (*Mariemont: The New Town*, 1925). The project encompassed over $2 million for its infrastructure of roads, sewage facilities, a central heating plant, water, and electricity. More than twenty-six architects were involved, as well as over three hundred employees on the payroll, from construction workers to skilled crafters to gardeners. The very first building was the nondenominational Mariemont Community Church. The houses were deliberately different in design, unlike the later suburban neighborhoods of the 1950s in which each building was a carbon copy of the one next door. By 1924, the first residents were moving in. Most significant, the children here could walk to all that they needed or wanted to reach. They didn't have to be driven by parents or use trains or buses unless someone wanted to go into the city.

Mariemont was not conceptualized as a Utopia by Emery but rather as a very practical example for others to follow. She wanted residents to share a community that enabled its families to have a good social life with access to schools, free recreational facilities, a library, a museum, a bank, and so on—all in a bucolic setting. Mariemont "was to be a National Exemplar. Once demonstrated as an object lesson, [she] believed that this plan would not rest with one lesson . . . [it] would spread through the country, bringing benefits wherever it took root" (*Mariemont*, 1925: 39). Indeed, that has been the case, according to the 1999 story of ABC television network reporter Erin Hayes: "The Congress for the New Urbanism, which promotes neighborhood principles in suburbs as well as in cities, says that more than 200 projects based on the Mariemont model are in the works around the country" (Hayes, 1999).

Mary Muhlenberg Emery died in 1927, before her project was completed, but she had made arrangements not only for the plans to go forward through the Mariemont Company, later called the Thomas J. Emery Memorial, but for support to continue as the community matured. "[Certain] pieces of property were to be held in perpetuity, maintained and operated for the benefit of all the residents of the community" (Sexton, 1966: 33). The Village of Mariemont was incorporated in 1942 and put on the National Historic Register in 1979.

SOURCES: Hayes, E. (1999), "Hi Hopes for Hemp," ABCNews.com, *http://www.abcnews.go.com/onair/dailynews/wnt990809_hayes_story.html*; *Mariemont:*

The New Town, "A National Exemplar" (1925) (Cincinnati, OH: Mariemont Company); Rybczynski, W. (1997), "Housing Without Architects," *Architecture* [Online], August: 78–81 (available: Lexis-Nexis, accessed August 28); Sexton, P. (1966), *Mariemont: A Brief Chronicle of Its Origin and Development* (Mariemont, OH: Village of Mariemont).

MARY ENGELBREIT (1952–   )

"There's always a reason not to do things. It's too expensive, or it's not the best time . . . but I believe there are wonderful opportunities constantly sailing by, and you have to be ready to grab them. Even if you can't really see to the end of it, you have to be willing to jump in." (Mary Engelbreit, Founder, Mary Engelbreit Companies)

The entrepreneurial spirit in Mary Engelbreit became apparent when she was just twelve years old. Her father had built a playhouse for Mary and her sister, Alexa, in their backyard in the hometown of St. Louis, Missouri, where she still resides. Mary painted it colorfully, one of her trademark characteristics even today, and opened a store selling various items to the neighborhood children. As her mother recalled, "She decided to have a store, and come hell or high water, she was going to have a store. . . . Mary was relentless" (Regan, 1996: 24).

This pattern of following her own "different drummer" was, and is, the way that Engelbreit has fashioned her life and business. During high school her friends would ask her to draw cards for special occasions; it didn't pay much but helped her become confident in her ability to understand her customer. These cards led her to approach the owners of a local gift shop, Froelich's, to see if they would be willing to buy her cards. "I was very nervous, but I was so happy when they said they'd put them in their shop. And they sold them all! I couldn't make them fast enough," Engelbreit recalled (Regan, 1996: 27). At first she earned twenty-five cents per card, then fifty cents. Her success led her to consider going to design school, but a nun in her Catholic high school tried to dissuade her by labeling Engelbreit's drawings "too bohemian" and suggesting she become a teacher (Chandler, 1996). Instead she went to work for a small ad agency, Hot Buttered Graphics. "It was great because the owner taught me everything about the *business* of art . . . how much to charge, how to bill, and how to work fast so you can make enough money. . . . I learned more there in eighteen months than I would have in four years at an art school" (Regan, 1996: 34).

By 1977 Engelbreit had decided to go to New York City to find a children's book company that would hire her to illustrate their stories. Not one was interested. But within the four short days that Engelbreit spent in this first marketing trip to the big city, she received two invaluable pieces of advice from two different art directors. The first was to approach greeting-card companies with her artwork; the second was to add more characters and movement to her drawings. Engelbreit returned to St. Louis and did just that. She contracted with Portal Publications, a greeting-card company that paid her fifty dollars a card but retained the original drawings. This same year she married Phil Delano, the man who, several years earlier, had encouraged her to follow her dreams.

"After a period of free-lance work and fantasy art . . . Engelbreit turned her attention to portraying the real-life experiences of children. She credits this change to the birth of her son, Evan, in 1980" (Mary Engelbreit Home Page, 1998). In 1984, though her son was now three years old and she was expecting her second child, Engelbreit teamed up with a venture capitalist to fulfill her new dream of having her own company. He negotiated for fifty-five percent of the business—the first and last time Engelbreit would be so naive about her contributions as the creative artist. However, within just two years, revenues exceeded $1 million, and she bought out her partner. At this time she convinced her husband to leave his position as a St. Louis juvenile court social worker to become her business manager. By 1988 Mary Engelbreit's business was experiencing exponential growth, with card sales alone having quadrupled; ten years later, fourteen million cards were being sold annually. "At the beginning, the business end of it scared me . . . but when I learned to trust my instincts, I discovered I liked it. Running a business takes creativity, too" (Jarvis, 1997: 16).

Among the strategic decisions that have contributed to Engelbreit's financial success were finding people with the business skills she lacked, retaining legal and artistic control, copyrighting her designs, retaining the right to product approval before distribution, keeping licenses short so that negotiations could reflect her market value, and licensing the same design to more than one company but for different products (Chandler, 1996; Jarvis, 1997). She has licenses with over fifty companies worldwide, and her annual sales revenues are running $80–100 million; she received $4 million in royalties in 1997 alone.

Engelbreit openly admits to having made some mistakes along the way. One of the early ones was sending a potential customer her portfolio of original drawings without retaining copies; she never saw them again. A product that Engelbreit thought was going to be a big seller was a doll house, but only two were sold because they were so expensive. Another initiative was a mail-order catalogue, but this effort was abandoned when expectations weren't met. One of her retail stores, the St. Louis Union Station location, didn't meet sales goals and was closed. However, Engelbreit learned from each situation. "I can hardly think of a disappointment that you can't turn around into a good situation. It sets you off on a different track, and there's nothing wrong with that. It just makes you look at things differently" (Regan, 1996: 41).

Her other boutiques have done quite well. Located in Denver, Chicago, Dallas, Atlanta, and St. Louis, these stores brought in $4.6 million in 1997 sales, and her plans are to expand to sites in all of the major metropolitan cities (Stout, 1998: 1). In 1996, she started the magazine *Mary Engelbreit's Home Companion* in a new venture, Universal-Engelbreit Communications. Within two years, the magazine's circulation had hit 450,000. She has published over thirty books, has a syndicated newspaper column, and in 1998 launched her Web site, *http:www.maryengelbreit.com*. For all this success, she maintains that all she "ever wanted to do was make a living as an artist . . . drawing what I wanted to draw" (Jarvis, 1997: 16).

At her Mary Engelbreit Studios in a St. Louis suburb, she has more than eighty employees, mostly women. Her customers are approximately ninety-nine percent white, somewhat affluent females ranging in age from ten to eighty-five. She also employs six artists who transfer the designs to the product and a writer who produces her column. "Engelbreit maintains rigid control of the business. She signs off on every level of product development and every page of the magazine. . . . She [draws] . . . usually at home and in the middle of the night" (Stout, 1998: 2).

Engelbreit has drawn over two thousand images; these appear not only on cards but also on books, calendars, ornaments, gift wrap, kitchen accessories, baby furnishings, T-shirts, watches, and wall hangings. "People say, 'Don't you want to quit? Don't you want to just travel? Don't you want to do this or that?' No! I never want to quit! I don't think I really have a choice. What else would I do? I'd go crazy if I didn't draw," Engelbreit explained (Regan, 1996: 95).

SOURCES: Chandler, S. (1996), "The Martha Stewart for Real People," *Business Week* (available: Lexis-Nexis, accessed February 8, 1999); Jarvis, C. (1997), "The Art of Branching Out," *Nation's Business* (available: Lexis-Nexis, accessed February 8, 1999); Mary Engelbreit Homepage (1998), *http:www.maryengelbreit.com* (accessed February 12, 1999); Regan, P., with Engelbreit, M. (1996), *Mary Engelbreit: The Art and the Artist* (Kansas City, MO: Andrews and McMeel); Stout, H. (1998), "The Home Front: An Artist Builds an Empire of Cute," *Wall Street Journal* (available: Lexis-Nexis, accessed February 8, 1999).

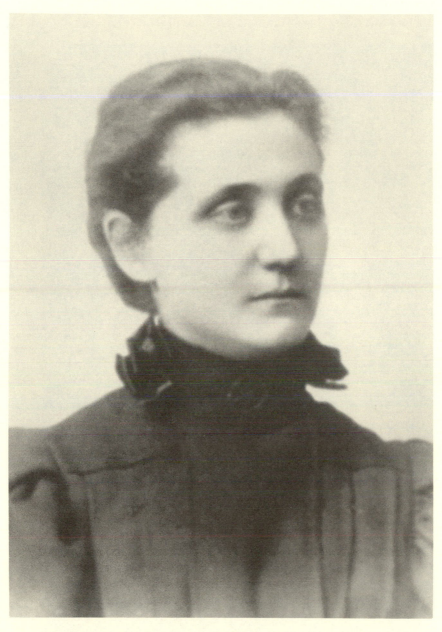

Jane Addams. Photograph courtesy of Wallace Kirkland Papers, Jane Addams
Memorial Collection, Special Collections, The University Library, The University
of Illinois at Chicago.

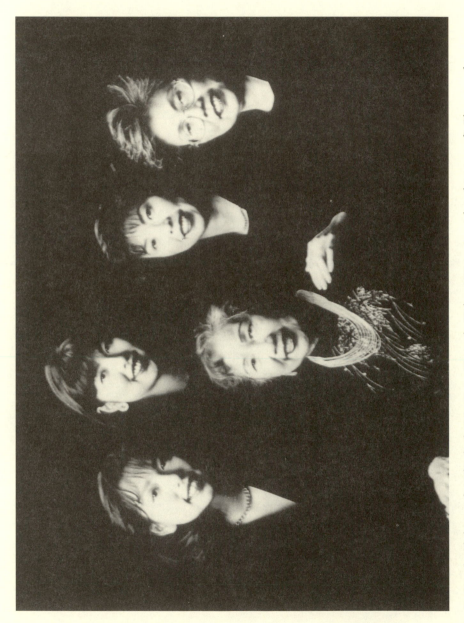

An Family: (*left to right*) Elizabeth, Monique, Hannah, Helene, Diane (grandmother; *seated*). Photograph courtesy of Elaine Sense, S.N.E.

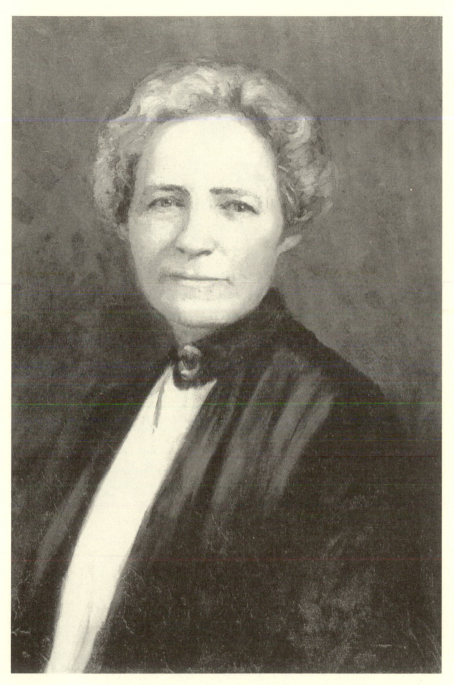

Ninnie Baird. Copyright Mrs. Baird's Bakeries. Photograph courtesy of Mrs. Baird's Bakeries.

Freda Ehmann. Photograph courtesy of Butte County Historical Society.

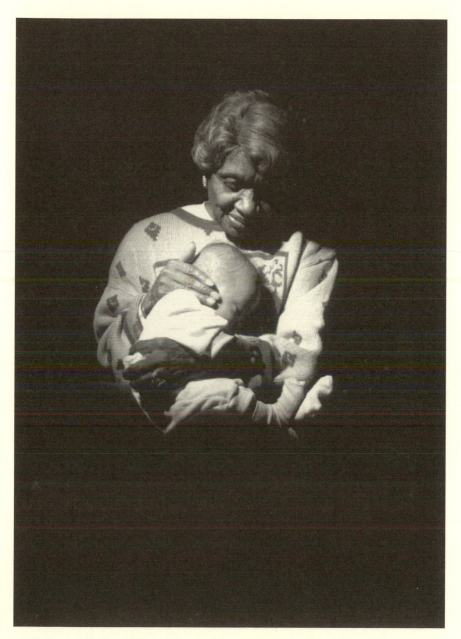

Clara Hale. Photograph courtesy of Hale House.

Catherine Hinds. Photograph courtesy of Catherine Hinds Institute, reproduced with permission by Catherine Hinds.

Carrie Jones. Photograph courtesy of Sparkle Cleaning Associates, Inc., reproduced with permission by Carrie Jones.

Nancy Mueller. Photograph courtesy of Nancy's Specialty Foods, reproduced with permission by Nancy Mueller.

Lucy Scribner. Photograph courtesy of Special Collections, Skidmore College.
Lucy Scribner Collection.

Maggie Walker. Photograph courtesy of the United States Department of the Interior, National Park Service.

Terrie Williams. Photograph courtesy of Terrie Williams Agency, reproduced with permission by Terrie Williams.

ADA EVERLEIGH (1875–1960)
MINNA EVERLEIGH (1878–1948)

"Real men, we found, would rather gamble any day than gamble with women . . . men prefer dice, cards or a wheel of fortune to a frolic with a charmer. I have watched men, embraced in the arms of the most bewitching sirens in our club, dump their feminine flesh from their laps for a roll of the dice." (Minna Everleigh, Co-owner, the Everleigh Club)

While only in their mid-thirties, Ada and Minna Everleigh were faced with the strategic decision of whether or not to continue operating their very profitable business, the Everleigh Club on South Dearborn Street in Chicago. According to a report of the mayoral vice commission, this establishment was "probably the most famous and luxurious house of its kind in the country" (Washburn, 1974: 110). Yet these sisters were very politically astute—the "protection" costs were getting too high, and they were sensitive to an upcoming wave of corruption cleansing. Ada and Minna assessed their worth: over a million dollars in cash, approximately a quarter of a million dollars in jewelry, at least $150,000 in art works and furnishings, and $25,000 in IOUs due to them (Johnson & Sautter, 1994; Washburn, 1974). Most of this was acquired during the years 1900 to 1911. They decided to retire and lived out the rest of their lives in relative obscurity.

The intriguing questions are: How did two sisters from Kentucky who were raised in comfort and privilege in the home of their attorney father choose to set up an establishment in the "oldest profession" to acquire their wealth? Why would they make that decision, and why would they select Chicago for their business? According to biographer Charles Washburn, the sisters had married two brothers who turned out to both be spouse abusers. For example, to demonstrate his authority over her, Minna's husband allegedly choked her on her wedding night and each day afterward until she left him. The sisters decided together to leave their husbands, never telling their parents the truth; instead, Ada and Minna led their parents to believe they were pursuing theatrical careers.

As the sisters had about $35,000 from savings and inheritance money, they did some traveling and then headed for Omaha, Nebraska, because the 1898 Trans-Mississippi Exposition was being held there. It was a casual remark from an actress friend that first put the idea of a bordello into the minds of the sisters: "My mother would be angry if she knew I was on the stage. She thinks I'm in a den of iniquity" (Washburn, 1974: 16). From this triggering comment, the Everleighs opened their first establishment near the Exposition site; the prices for the services of the women they employed were higher than at other bordellos because the Everleighs incorporated the fine surroundings and deportment of their upbringing. In less than two years their $35,000 was parlayed into $70,000.

The sisters then decided to move to Chicago, where they opened their famous Everleigh Club in a mansion built in 1890 for $125,000. The establishment had six parlors named, furnished, and perfumed after flowers such as the rose, the sunflower, and the lily (Masters, 1944). Other rooms included the Silver, Copper, and Gold Rooms and the Chinese Room, where the male guests could shoot off firecrackers if they so desired (Kiernan in Swanson, 1997). There were thirty boudoirs—some with mirrored ceilings, marble-inlaid brass beds, or gold bathtubs—and each year the rooms were redecorated (Johnson & Sautter, 1994). As with other high-class houses of assignation, the Everleigh Club was also known for its fine food; dinner started at $50, and that was without a female "companion." The sisters had hired a Cordon Bleu chef and, when needed, there were as many as twenty-five cooks in the kitchen, which was operated around the clock (Foxworth, 1997).

In the short span of eleven years of operation, an estimated 600 women were hired to serve clients. They were groomed and dressed by personal maids (Masters, 1944) and trained by the sisters to be sophisticated. Minna would remind them, "You have a whole night before you . . . and one $50 client is more desirable than five $10 ones. Less wear and tear . . . be polite and forget what you are here for. Stay respectable by all means; I want you girls to be proud that you are in the Everleigh Club" (Johnson & Sautter, 1994: 79). If they didn't act like ladies, they were fired. These young women were also permitted to keep half of the amount customers were charged; a man usually spent between $150 and $1,000 a visit. Reporters were very much welcomed; one of them, Jack Lait, remarked: "Minna and Ada Everleigh are to pleasure what Christ was to Christianity" (Washburn, 1974: 28). Their guests included the rich and powerful of Chicago and beyond as well as "an entire U.S. congressional committee" (Johnson & Sautter, 1994: 77). As there was no income tax at this time, the sisters were able to net approximately $10,000 a month, or $120,000 annually.

The Everleighs were also known for their love of butterflies. These colorful creatures could be seen adorning their vases, jewelry, and some furnishings. On occasion, they would also unleash boxes of live butterflies in the club so that they could fly throughout the establishment. One rival remarked: "No man for sure is going to forget he got his balls fanned by a butterfly at the Everleigh Club" (Johnson & Sautter, 1994: 76). Customers were carefully screened, and word of mouth was sufficient to bring in the appropriate clientele, but the sisters weren't willing to rely on that marketing alone. "Several times a week the sisters would call their carriage, drawn by two splendid dappled gray horses, and sally forth into the great open spaces of Chicago. There was a richly garbed coachman. And sitting with the sisters was always one of the beauties out of a choice of thirty. They didn't need a band nor cages of wild animals to attract attention" (Washburn, 1974: 62). It was another marketing device that finally brought down the sisters in 1911. They circulated a brochure describing their services; it also contained pictures. When this was brought to the attention of Chicago's mayor, Carter Harrison, Jr., he was so outraged by this "audacity" that he issued an immediate order that they be closed down. Rather than fight this decision, they simply retired to New York City and lived there until Ada died at the age of 70; Minna then moved to Virginia, where she resided until her death at age 85.

Certainly there were high risks for the Everleigh sisters in establishing a venture such as a house of prostitution. These ranged from the consequences of the protection racket to the possibility of hiring girls under age eighteen or being set up by rivals for allegations of murder and/or drug dealing. But the sisters did whatever it took to stay above the more typical criminal element of their industry, from strict adherence to a no drugs policy on the premises to not serving hard liquor, and were very successful in their efforts (Johnson & Sautter, 1994). They were also wise enough to know when to call it quits. At the end, Minna, known to be the more eloquent of the two sisters, ordered champagne and toasted: "The ship has sunk. . . . She was a good one. Let's give her a hurrah" (79). And when asked in 1911 why they weren't willing to "play ball" like the rest of the Chicago madams and stay on, Minna replied: "I'll go my way and the rest can go hang" (80).

SOURCES: Foxworth, J. (1997), *The Bordello Cookbook* (Wakefield, RI: Moyer Bell); Johnson, C., & Sautter, R. (1994), *Wicked City Chicago* (Highland Park, IL: December Press); Masters, E. (1944), "The Everleigh Club," *Town & Country Magazine* 99: 70–71, 109–111; Swanson, S. (1997), *150 Defining Moments in the Life of a Great City* (Wheaton, IL: Cantigny First Division Foundation); Washburn, C. (1974), *Come into My Parlor* (New York: Arno Press).

SUSAN FENIGER (1953–   )
MARY SUE MILLIKEN (1958–   )

"We're very good at developing ways to use each other as a big support which makes being in a partnership really lovely, really fun. I can't

imagine working any other way." (Mary Sue Milliken, Co-founder, Border Grill)

They appear to be opposites—one tall, one short; one blonde, the other brunette. Even their personality preferences have them focusing on different aspects of their businesses. Yet, after nineteen years as a team, Susan Feniger and Mary Sue Milliken are so bonded and work so well together that they complete each other's sentences and seem more like sisters than business partners. Feniger, an Ohio native, and Milliken, from Michigan, met in 1979 at Le Perroquet, a top-rated restaurant in Chicago. Feniger wanted to work at this establishment so badly that she accepted the job of onion peeler even though she had been educated at the Culinary Institute of America. This type of initiation experience was not atypical in the culinary field. Milliken, who trained at the Washburn Trade School Chefs Program, described hers: "I was a rounds person, for banquets, and [I] would [be told to] make sixty quarts of hollandaise by hand. . . . I thought my arm would come off . . . that my arm was just going to die. . . . [I kept telling myself], 'These guys are not going to get to me!' " (Cooper, 1998: 95).

This dogged determination was instrumental in the journey to phenomenal success that Feniger and Milliken were to achieve. After their initial job experience together in Chicago, they both went to work for different restaurants in France in 1980, once again meeting fortuitously there. Feniger laughingly recalled, "One evening, we decided after a second bottle of wine to be partners someday, and we shook on it" (*Dining in Style*, 1998). Then she went on to her next cooking position in California. Within a year, Feniger contacted Milliken and encouraged her to come to the West Coast to partner with Feniger and several of her friends in a tiny restaurant called the City Cafe in Los Angeles. They could only seat fourteen in the cafe, and for cooking surfaces these chefs had just a hot plate in the 12 × 13 foot kitchen and a hibachi in the parking lot. Feniger remembered: "The night before we opened, Mary Sue and I slept . . . for about twenty minutes. . . . Opening night was a nightmare. It was horrible! We were so busy. It was August, in Los Angeles I think it was literally 112 degrees . . . the fans didn't work. . . . We just made the same food over and over again. . . . At the very end . . . we collapsed in a corner . . . we're sweating and crying and sweating!" (Cooper, 1998: 98). They persevered. Word about the quality of their food spread quickly, and long lines outside the establishment became the norm.

By 1985, they opened a second and larger City Restaurant, where they had 125 seats and were able to serve 400 dinners each night. This same year the first restaurant became Border Grill, and a second establishment with this name was also started in 1990 in Santa Monica, California. Within a couple of years, an economic downturn had struck, and the original partnership ended. In the subsequent distribution of the businesses, Feniger and Milliken retained the City Restaurant and the Santa Monica Border Grill. These were difficult times for those in the restaurant business, and all suffered a sharp decrease in customers. By 1994 the City Restaurant site was closed. Then a guest spot on the fledgling cable television Food Network in 1995 catapulted them to national fame and resulted in their own television show, named "Too Hot Tamales." They travel back and forth to New York City for the videotaping of their program doing as many as 350 shows a year. Feniger pointed out, "That means 1,300 recipes we had to test and develop all by ourselves" (Ramirez, 1996: F1).

Their accomplishments continued to accrue. Feniger and Milliken wrote four cookbooks; hosted a weekly radio show; opened a Border Grill at the Mandalay Bay Resort and Casino in Las Vegas, Nevada; and designed a product line of dishware and peppermills. They are still hands-on managers at Border Grill four to five days out of the week when they're in California. For balance, Feniger likes walking her dog and going to the ocean. "It's amazingly relaxing to me. There's a different freedom there that gives me this whole sense of peacefulness," she explained. Milliken learned how better to manage her personal and professional time by being more focused once her son, Declan was born. She is married to Josh Schweitzer, the lifelong friend and ex-husband of her partner. Milliken pointed out that she is "working less hours and working smarter. That comes with age, I think" (Cooper, 1998: 114).

How "fewer hours" would be defined by these two entrepreneurs is a curiosity considering their organizational expansion and celebrity demand; however, their passion for food and their commitment to each other is unquestionably solid. Feniger and Milliken attribute their longstanding relationship to talking to each other and not taking each other for granted. Milliken added, "We definitely complement each other in terms of strengths and weaknesses. We're both pretty adult, and we both get a lot out of [the relationship]. If we didn't get a lot out of being partners, we wouldn't stick together. Regardless of whether there are hills or valleys, success or failures, it's more fun to go through it with somebody" ("A Perfect Pair," 1992: 34).

SOURCES: "A Perfect Pair: Chefs Susan Feniger and Mary Sue Milliken Discuss the Contents of Their Refrigerators" (1992), *Restaurant Hospitality* [Online], December: 34 (available: Lexis-Nexis, accessed June 2, 1999); Bios: The Chefs Story, *http://www.bordergrill.com/abbg/msmsf/bio/body_bio.htm* (accessed June 2, 1999); Cooper, A. (1998), *A Woman's Place Is in the Kitchen: The Evolution of Women Chefs* (New York: Van Nostrand Reinhold); *Dining in Style* (1998), E-Entertainment Television, Style Network; Ramirez, O. (1996), "Two Hot," *The Press-Enterprise* [Online], November 7: F1 (available: Lexis-Nexis); Sahgal, A. (1997), "With a TV Show, Radio Gig, Four Cookbooks, a Busy Restaurant and Plans for More, Susan Feniger and Mary Sue Milliken Aren't Just Chefs, They're an Emerging Industry," *Los Angeles Times* [Online], October 26: 10 (available: Lexis-Nexis).

DEBBI FIELDS (1956–   )

"I never accepted the system and continually tested it to see what I could get away with. I discovered that the best way to stay out of real trouble was to make people laugh. Funny, but that's what I learned in school—how to get into trouble and how to get out of it. I learned about how the rules say you can't do this and you can't do that, yet the rules seem to make room if you test them a little. I learned to depend on myself." (Debbi Fields, Founder of Mrs. Fields Chocolate Chip Cookies Company)

Debra (Debbi) Sivyer was the youngest of five daughters, a tomboy, who was teasingly referred to by her older sisters as the "dumb one." She grew up believing this label and spent many years trying to gain acceptance and recognition from people both inside and outside her family. However, she has loving memories of those early years in their hometown of East Oakland, California. "If we were poor, we sure didn't know it. We were one of those big, tightly-knit Catholic families of the late fifties" (Fields, 1987: 15). As a youngster, Debbi also learned her father's golden rule. He would remind his daughters that "My wealth has never been in money—it's been found in my family and friends" (16). From their mother, the five sisters absorbed what was expected of female children born in the 1950s. "My mom took good care of her husband and her girls, and we were expected to do the same when our turn came. College just wasn't in the picture for any of us" (18), Debbi explained.

Like other teens of her generation, Debbi wanted to buy "nice things" so she went looking for work at age thirteen. Almost immediately she was successful, being chosen as one of the first foul-line ball girls for the Oakland A's baseball team. Significantly, during this experience she observed a negative behavior that disturbed her and later would influence her professional value system. "Those guys who wouldn't take a minute to sign an autograph would never know it, but they taught me a lesson that lies at the foundation of my business: There is no such thing as an insignificant human being. To treat people that way is a kind of sin, and there's no reason for it, none," she declared (Fields, 1987: 30).

As a teenager, Debbi was also the cookie baker in the family. At first she had to use margarine in the batter because that's all her family could afford, but once she had some money of her own, she started using butter. The taste was notably better. "I discovered that the secret of the cookie lay more in the quality of its original ingredients than in any variation of the formula" (Fields, 1987: 54). Debbi committed herself to using only the best ingredients when she baked—a hallmark of her future chocolate chip cookie company. After graduating from high school, Debbi held a number of positions, including being governess for five children. Most of the money she earned was spent traveling to participate in her favorite sport, downhill skiing. On one of these trips, she was in an airport when she was spotted by Randy Fields, a rising star economist. He became determined to make her acquaintance even though he was ten years older. After an on-and-off courtship they were married in 1976.

At first, Fields was happy in the role of the wife baking cookies for her husband's clients. But then she had an unfortunate experience at a social gathering that brought back all of her childhood feelings of inadequacy and of being "the dumb one." She used the word "orientated" instead of "oriented" and was publicly humiliated by the host for using a word that didn't exist. After much soul searching, Fields decided to no longer be what she considered an appendage of her husband; she was going to find a niche of her own. It was as if her father were whispering in her ear what he had said so many times before—"Do something you love." She knew that was baking cookies. Fields then asked her husband's clients what they thought of the idea; even though they loved her chocolate chip cookies and repeatedly had asked her for more, when it came to her turning this into a business, they all said it would fail. Her husband and family weren't encouraging either. But Fields was dogged in the pursuit once she had determined the goal. She baked cookies and went to the banks to demonstrate her product so that she could get the $50,000 needed to start up. Again, they loved her cookies but rejected her request. She persevered and, with her husband's less than enthusiastic support, was ultimately successful in getting the loan.

In 1977 she opened her first store, Mrs. Fields Chocolate Chippery. She was just twenty years old, had no formal business training, and no management experience, but what she did have was a skill for and a passion about her product. She found she had another talent besides baking, too. "I have a very keen taste sensitivity, especially to chocolate, and I've found I can detect all sorts of shades of flavor that seem to elude other people" (Fields, 1987: 75). However, on Field's first day of business, no one was coming into the store. Since her husband had bet her that she wouldn't make $50 that day, her competitive spirit kicked in. She took a tray of her cookies into the shopping mall and offered them to passersby. "The more we gave away, the more we sold" (95). The sales that day were $75; by year's end, her little business had sales of $250,000. Her goals quickly became "best cookies, best locations, best price" (98).

By 1984 the company was generating sales of over $40 million in three hundred cookie stores in the United States, Australia, and Asia—all from word-of-mouth advertising (Richman, 1984). Fields explained her dilemma: "We had to open new stores. In both the physical and the business sense, growing isn't something you do when you feel like it. It happens to you" (Fields, 1987: 101). As Fields had large commercial loans at twenty-two percent interest rates when the country went into a recession, her financial difficulties became overwhelming. She was forced to swap equity for debt reduction. "It was the worst, most devastating experience of my life because it was like putting my child up for adoption" (Dobbs, 1996). Yet, the business then thrived, and by 1990 the company had 488 stores in forty-nine countries. A few years later, she sold the now $100 million company to an investment group. Fields remained on the board and as a consultant to the company (Hofman, 1998).

During all of the years that Debbi Fields was growing an international business, she was also giving birth to and raising her own five daughters, now ranging in age from nineteen down to seven. "I'm teaching them that the moment you believe the glass ceiling exists, it becomes your barrier," she noted (Naiman, 1999: E6). In 1996 she and Randy Fields were divorced, sharing custody of their children. Debbi Fields has since married Michael Rose, a retired executive. In just over twenty years, the company she started with a simple chocolate chip cookie was grossing over $425 million annually in the global marketplace.

SOURCES: Dobbs, L. (1996), *CNN Managing with Lou Dobbs*, Cable News Network, November 23, transcript #96112301V33; Fields, D. (1987), *One Smart Cookie* (New York: Simon & Schuster); Hofman, M. (1998), "Famous Splits," *Inc. Magazine*, September: 89; Mincer, J. (1999), "Sweet Ambitions: Founder of Mrs. Fields Cookies Gives Her Recipe for Success," *Kansas City Star* [Online], April 21: C1 (available: Lexis-Nexis, accessed July 25, 1999); Naiman, S. (1999), "Debbi Fields Is One Smart Cookie," *Toronto Star* [Online], January 18: E6 (available: Lexis-Nexis, accessed January 30, 1999); Richman, T. (1984), "A Tale of Two Companies," *Inc.* [Online], July: 38 (available: Lexis-Nexis, accessed July 25, 1999).

LINDSAY FRUCCI (1952–   )

"I am a brownieholic. I love thick, fudgey, chewy brownies. I hate fat. In my food and on my hips, fat is something I like to live without. . . .

Were brownies without guilt a possibility?" (Lindsay Frucci, Founder, No Pudge! Foods, Inc.)

To some, the story of the beginnings of the No Pudge brownie company might sound like a marketing scheme. Yet, Lindsay Frucci was trying to alter an already available, packaged, no-fat brownie mix to taste good enough to be acceptable to her husband and children. When all attempts failed, she decided to experiment with her own various ingredients, using as her more-than-willing testers two construction workers who were remodeling her home in New Hampshire. These men were eager to eat brownies as often as she baked them, but they also gave her excellent feedback on the taste and texture of what she was concocting. By the time the remodeling was done, Frucci also had her recipe.

However, she had no training in the business field; her father had been an art teacher and her mother worked whatever odd jobs would help put food on the table. Lindsay was the first in her family to go to college. She attended the Dartmouth-Hitchcock School of Nursing in Hanover, New Hampshire, graduating in 1972. Then she accepted a position at the Children's Hospital in Boston while studying for an additional degree in pediatric nursing. Within a few years, Lindsay burned out from the physical and emotional toil of this responsibility; she then went to work for a computer firm in the customer service division. While there, she met, fell in love with, and married Adam Frucci. They decided to return to New Hampshire to raise their family.

In 1983, their first son, Adam, was born, followed two years later by their second, A. J. As Lindsay explained, "I was very fortunate to be able to have a family situation that permitted me to stay home with my boys." But when A. J. was in the first grade, she decided that she would try her hand at selling real estate. She stayed in this field for the four years preceding her entry into the food business.

Once Frucci had her product, she next needed a business to get it to the customers. She had read articles in *Inc.* magazine that had been a valuable resource, but now she needed some advice from experts in the food industry specifically. Frucci turned to the local Small Business Administration office and learned about the S.C.O.R.E. (Service Corps of Retired Executives) program, which would enable her to have the assistance of retired executives who had volunteered to help entrepreneurs just like her. "Without the help of these two men," Frucci stated, "No Pudge wouldn't exist. They were excellent, highly skilled in the food industry, and very supportive" (Shea, 1998).

The next question was how to fund the start-up. As Frucci and her husband had already decided that no family savings would be risked, she continued to sell real estate just long enough to put together the $20,000 she needed. Then, in January 1995, No Pudge! Foods, Inc., was born. Her original brownie mix first became available that August through a few stores in New Hampshire and Massachusetts. Quickly, the sales volume reached 6,000 bags of brownie mix. Within two years, more than 250,000 bags were sold, distribution had spread to both the East and West Coasts, and she had set up a mail-order business to handle orders both in the United States and in Germany. Then, in 1998, Frucci received a stroke of immense luck. Her No Pudge brownies were one of the twenty New Hampshire products selected to be offered on the QVC home shopping channel.

Frucci has expanded her line of all-natural brownie mixes to four flavors. She added additional retail items like an apron and a shirt with the company logo to her product line. Recently, a Web page was designed and set up for the No Pudge company to provide direct interaction with its growing customer base. But Frucci is wise enough to know her limitations. "I can only take the business so far. It would be unhealthy to try to run it past my comfort level. . . . It's fine to run a small company on instinct, but to grow past a certain point takes the knowledge of someone who has studied business." Frucci would like to make enough profit from the eventual sale of the company to pay for her children's education and to have a comfortable retirement. "I will consider myself successful if my children are happy. Oh, and that's important for me, too!" she smiled.

SOURCES: No Pudge (1999), *http://www.nopudge.com*; Shea, J. (1998), interview of Lindsay Frucci in Elkins, New Hampshire, on April 18.

JOLINE GODFREY (1950–   )

"Looking back I can say that I had been entrepreneurial since I was five years old. I was someone who always fixed things, always initiated things, was always 'thinking outside the box,' but I didn't understand myself in that language. I was resourceful, feisty, a little strange maybe, but never did I have the vocabulary placed on me that would have helped me label myself, that would help me see myself as entrepreneurial." (Joline Godfrey, Co-founder, Independent Means, Inc.)

As a young girl growing up in rural Maine, Joline Dudley Godfrey had two strong female role models—Margaret Chase Smith, the renowned senator from her home state, and her grandmother, Hazel Dudley—both of whom helped to establish Joline's bias toward action. Dudley's grandparents had started a small commercial dairy farm where, from a young age, she had helped load the delivery trucks. "We were not wealthy," she recalled, "but my brother and I developed wonderfully solid roots in that small town." They grew up with an understanding that work was what they were expected to do and that being in business implied that they were to be a contributing member of the community. "I was in my late twenties before I heard about 'social responsibility.' I grew up to respect everybody, that everyone was important—these values were simply understood."

After graduating from the University of Maine in 1972, Dudley married David Godfrey, whom she had met through a friend shortly after high school. Several years later, Joline Godfrey moved to Boston, Massachusetts, to get her master's degree in social work at Boston University. Her life now took on a new path, as her marriage ended in 1977 and a job was offered to her by the Polaroid Corporation in Cambridge, Massachusetts. She held several positions over the next ten years.

At Polaroid, Godfrey got to work closely with Jerry Sudbey, who was to become her mentor and a contributing force in her subsequent ventures. He invited her to be a part of a new project team. "They wanted to shift from technology driven to a market-driven focus. Sudbey told me to 'do whatever it is you do.' They were techies and I was a psychologist. . . . I got to see the highest levels of the organization go from the start-up of a product to market," she explained (Oppedisano, 1998). Godfrey greatly enjoyed what she did. She was working on a "world-class stage" where excellence was expected; she was encouraged to ask questions and utilize her nontraditional perspective. However, it eventually became clear that the project was outside the core business of the company, and Godfrey was given the choice of returning to a more traditional role or spinning off the ideas into a new company. Sudbey suggested that she live with ambiguity and see what came up. "This was still the time of the corporate glass ceiling so there was no way I was going to get to the senior ranks of the company," she pointed out.

Godfrey took a trip to Mexico. After only forty-eight hours in this colorful country, she had a brainstorm. "The company had been obsessed with the widget. I was interested in the process—in how do people see. So I went back to Cambridge, and told Jerry that I wanted to teach people how to see, to develop a service industry." She asked him to give her six months, a secretary, and her salary, for a promise that she would come back with "something." He agreed. However, the full responsibility of her suggestion then hit her. "I would go home to my 'perfect' condo in Harvard Square, drink scotch, and cry—asking myself why I was considering such a project? We would be trying something that hadn't been market tested yet. Why wasn't I playing it safe?"

She snapped out of this quandary quickly, and the outcome was the establishment of a new company. In 1986, she began Odysseum, Inc., with partner Jane Lytle and seed money from Polaroid as a minority stakeholder. Their business was to provide training seminars for Fortune 500 companies on creating innovation within their companies. Their clients included American Airlines, General Electric, and American Express. In 1989, the company had sales of $500,000 with twelve employees. Commenting on this success, Godfrey pointed out that "You cannot do it all by yourself. There needs to be a foundation of people who share your values." Lytle was that person for her. "Jane had an MBA from Yale and was such a remarkable, amazing person, a great working partner," Godfrey recalled—with sadness, because Lytle was killed in an automobile accident in the mid-1990s.

Unexpectedly, an article in the January 1990 issue of *Inc.* magazine resulted from a challenging "Letter to the Editor" sent in by Godfrey. "I was a regular reader of the magazine. Then they did this special tenth anniversary issue in 1990, and there was such a noticeable absence of women among what they were calling their entrepreneurial visionaries that I became infuriated" (Oppedisano, 1999). She wrote to the editors: "You cite statistics showing we're out there in the millions, but very few of us show up in the pages of *Inc.* When we do, we're usually in the sidebars and short items. We're almost never the heroes or the role models. So what gives, guys? Are we invisible? Or are you wearing blinders?" ("Face-to-Face," 1990: 31). The editors asked to meet with her. The result was a dream assignment; she got to travel around the country gathering the stories of women entrepreneurs for the magazine. This offer couldn't have come at a more opportune time. Godfrey's Odysseum company had lost a lot of business as a consequence of the 1987 market "crash." She sold it in 1990.

Not only did that letter stimulate a writing opportunity for the magazine, but it resulted in Godfrey publishing her first book in 1992, *Our Wildest Dreams: Women Entrepreneurs Making Money, Having Fun, and Doing Good.* Then her next professional shift occurred. "While I was writing the last chapter, I realized that I couldn't spend any more time on adult women because what I was hearing from my colleagues was that the obstacles they faced related to things we hadn't gotten as girls. I had an epiphany. I wanted to help girls across race and class become economically independent and to be excellent in whatever they chose to do." She started the nonprofit organization "An Income of Her Own" (AIOHO) to teach teen girls about entrepreneurship—the only supplier of such programs at the time. In 1994, her second book was published, *No More Frogs to Kiss: 99 Ways to Give Economic Power to Girls.*

By 1996, Godfrey began buying back the AIOHO assets because "it seemed hypocritical to be teaching girls to be entrepreneurial out of a not-for-profit model." The organization was renamed Independent Means, and it began seeking working capital from sources such as Investors Circle, a group focused on socially responsible organizations. Within just a few years, the programs from Independent Means were being offered in sites across the country, a Web site had been created, and Godfrey was working on her third book. In describing her life path to date, she concluded: "It's like when you're sailing—the wind sends you on another track—in ways and places you can't ever anticipate." And she added reflectively, "I do think there's a power that sends you on your path."

SOURCES: "Face-to-Face" (1990), *Inc.*, January 31 (available: Lexis-Nexis, accessed December 14, 1999); Godfrey, J. (1993), "The Player," *Inc.* magazine [Online], November: 23 (available: Lexis-Nexis, accessed June 2, 1999); Oppedisano, J. (1998), personal interview of Joline Godfrey, March 19.

BETTE NESMITH GRAHAM (1924–1980)

"I went to the library and found the formula for a type of tempera paint. . . . A chemistry teacher from Michael's [her son] school helped me a bit. I learned how to grind and mix paint from a man at a paint manufacturing company." (Bette Nesmith, Graham, Founder, Liquid Paper Company)

From an early age, Bette Claire McMurray was a strong-willed individualist. That inability to conform caused problems in school, where she was labeled a discipline problem. In 1941, when she was seventeen, she dropped out of high school and went job hunting, knowing she had few skills that were marketable. What this Texas native demonstrated, though, was that she had an ability to talk herself into opportunities. McMurray proved this when she went on an interview for a secretarial position in a local law firm. She was so impressive that not only was she hired, but they also sent her to night school so that she could learn to type and finish her high school education.

A year later, McMurray married Warren Nesmith, her high school sweetheart. World War II was raging, and her husband went into the military; she was thus alone when their son, Michael, was born. The war and the marriage ended at about the same time. Bette Nesmith remained a single parent during the years her son was growing up. Her secretarial skills continually improved, and she moved up the ranks, finally securing a job as an executive secretary for the Texas Bank and Trust Company.

Her nemesis, however, was the newly introduced carbon ribbon of the electric typewriter. When she tried to erase a mistake, it would smudge. Then Nesmith made an important observation. "I remembered trying to make a little extra money by helping design the holiday windows at the bank. With lettering, an artist never corrects by erasing but always paints over the error. So I decided to use what artists use. I put some tempera waterbase paint in a bottle and took my watercolor brush to the office. And I used that to correct my typing mistakes" (Vare & Ptacek, 1988: 39). For more than a few years this was her personal secret. However, in time, other secretaries asked her to share her concoction with them, too. Because of this rise in demand, Nesmith started making batches of what she labeled "Mistake Out" in her kitchen. Soon she was being encouraged to get a patent for her invention.

Nesmith was a secretary by day and a researcher by night. As her son remembered it, "We were very poor. . . . She was a single working woman in Texas with a small child. It was very hard for her" (Morgenthaler, 1994: 1). But Nesmith doggedly pursued her dream and worked at perfecting her product. She then offered it to IBM, but it was rejected; however, her belief in this *liquid paper*, as she now referred to it, was strong. Nesmith made the decision to go it alone. While she mixed ingredients in an electric mixer in the kitchen, her son and his friends filled bottles with the fluid in the garage. In 1957, just a year after she had begun, a hundred bottles a month were being sold, and she expanded into a small trailer in the backyard. Then the big break came. A national office supply magazine carried an article about the product, and sales started to climb. With her business doing well and her son grown, Nesmith made a critical personal decision; in 1964 she married Robert Graham, the man who would become a co-conspirator against her in later years.

By 1968, Nesmith-Graham's Liquid Paper Company had a million dollars in gross income. In the next decade that figure jumped to $38 million, and the product was being distributed in more than thirty countries. Then came the betrayal. In 1975, her now ex-husband, Robert Graham, gained control of the management of her company. Her response strategy was to sell the company a few years later to the Gillette Corporation. The price for the Liquid Paper Corporation was $47.5 million in cash, and Nesmith Graham was to receive royalties on per-bottle sales for the next twenty years. She also retained almost half of the shares in the company. Nesmith Graham alleged that "the two [conspirators] . . . changed the product's formula in order to deprive her of the royalties. But Gillette plans to bring in new management and bring back the old recipe. Said Nesmith Graham: 'I'm thrilled. Everybody has gotten what they wanted. The other stockholders got their money—and my baby is in good hands' " (Tracy et al., 1979: 32).

Bette Nesmith Graham died the following year when she was only fifty-six years old. She left half of her $50 million estate to her son, who by now was more known as one of the famous entertainers on *The Monkees* television show. The other half of her fortune was assigned to her favorite charities and to the Gihon Foundation, which she had established just a few years before her death. The foundation has over $3 million in assets and is located in New Mexico, where Michael Nesmith chose to live. Nesmith Graham's vision for this organization was to enable entrepreneurial philanthropy. It is also the home of a permanent "Works by Women" art collection that she had begun. Artists in the collection include Mary Cassatt, Georgia O'Keeffe, and Louise Nevelson.

According to Patricia Hill, Nesmith Graham's former attorney and a trustee of her foundation, "Bette was a very visionary person. . . . She was in the forefront of women's rights. But more than that, she had a sense of the gestalt of the world" (Morgenthaler, 1994: 2). Nesmith Graham's perception of possibilities, stimulated in part by watching artists at work, led to the creation of a multimillion-dollar firm with international distribution of her product.

SOURCES: Morgenthaler, E. (1994), "At Council on Ideas, It Is Helpful to Be a Daydream Believer—Michael Nesmith Administers His Mother's Foundation with a Monkish Gravity," *Wall Street Journal* [Online], July 29 (available: Proquest); Tracy, E., Meyer, H., Morrison, A., Leggett, R., & Curran, J. (1979), "Liquid Gold," *Fortune* [Online], November 5 (available: Lexis-Nexis); Vare, E., & Ptacek, G. (1988), *Mothers of Invention: From the Bra to the Bomb: Forgotten Women & Their Unforgettable Ideas* (New York: William Morrow and Company).

MARTHA GRAHAM (1894–1991)

"I believe we learn by practice. Whether it means to learn to dance by practicing dancing or to learn to live by practicing living, the principles are the same. In each it is the performance of a dedicated, precise set of acts, physical or intellectual, from which comes shapes of achievement, a sense of one's being, a satisfaction of spirit. One becomes in some area an athlete of God—practice means to perform, over and over again in the face of all obstacles, some act of vision, of faith, of desires. Practice is a means of inviting the perfection desired." (Martha Graham, Founder, Martha Graham School of Contemporary Dance in the United States and the Batsheva Dance Company in Israel)

Martha Graham lived ninety-seven years. She was an internationally renowned dancer, choreographer, and costume designer who premiered her last of over 180 dance pieces, *Maple Leaf Rag*, when she was ninety-six. Much has been written about this phenomenal woman but little about the entrepreneurial drive that was necessary for her to accomplish her dreams.

Graham was born in Allegheny County, Pennsylvania, the first child of four born to George and Jane Beers Graham. Her father was a psychologist who impressed upon her that people couldn't really lie because their bodies would reveal the truth. It was a lesson that made the young girl focus her attention on body movements. This ultimately became the base of an entirely new dance form that became her signature creation.

Because her sister Mary had chronic asthma, the family moved to Santa Barbara, California, in 1909. Graham attended the Cumnock School in drama and elocution after she finished high school, but the pivotal experience that redirected her life was attending a dance performance by Ruth St. Denis. Young Martha was so impressed that she enrolled in St. Denis's school. After her beloved father died in 1914, Martha had to provide the early family support; she went on the road as a dancer with St. Denis's dance troupe, the Denishawn Company. This led her back to the East Coast and, ultimately, to her independence from St. Denis.

By 1926 Graham had opened her own first studio in New York City and within a year produced twenty-nine dances, started a school—the Martha Graham School of Contemporary Dance—and initiated a theater within which she could have her creative works performed by herself and her students. But in those days, money was always difficult to come by. Organizations like the National Endownment for the Arts didn't exist yet. Martha Graham encountered a further problem because she was "stretching the envelope" in her dance form, literally creating the Modern Dance Movement—an evolution being rejected by those who might normally support a struggling artist. In fact, at times, much of the audience would simply walk out during a performance. This didn't stop either Martha or her students because they instinctively knew they were in the forefront of creating something important and innovative. One of Graham's dancers, Bessie Schonberg, recalled, "[Martha] was constantly in search of money. She would ask one of the dancers to take out a bank loan so she could open the studios and get to work. She had on—day in, day out, year in, year out—the same camel-hair coat and blue French beret. She looked as if she didn't have a nickel for the subway. . . . [E]verybody was very poor, but we really didn't care—nothing mattered except that we worked every day, that we were at the studio every day, and that there was Martha" (Mazo, 1991: 39).

Graham was mentored by composer and conductor Louis Horst, who became her lover, though he made it clear he would not divorce his wife. Although they remained a creative team until his death in 1964, their intimate relationship ended in the 1940s when Graham fell in love with Erick Hawkins, a dancer trained in ballet, whom she met while teaching at a college summer program. She made many changes in her dance company to accommodate Hawkins, the most significant being that she allowed a man to enter what had been a completely female company. He became a pivotal focus of her work, but over time, Hawkins wanted more and more control. They were together more than eight years before they married in 1948. But they were divorced a year later, split over the issue of who was to be in charge of Martha and her now internationally renowned enterprises.

It wasn't until 1965 that Graham received her first government grant of $10,000 from the National Endowment for the Arts. Every penny counted since expenses were so high—especially considering the cost of such a labor-intensive business. According to biographer and Graham dancer Agnes de Mille, "Martha was now in command of a big industry. The funds that passed through her hands amounted to hundreds of thousands of dollars—even, on occasion, a million or over. Her payroll was complicated, with a sizable roster of employees. . . . [It] was Martha's presence . . . that procured funds, and this meant constant interviewing, consultations, examinations with corporation presidents, foundation heads" (de Mille, 1991: 402).

Flushed with success and trying to cope with the increasing organizational demands, Graham's response was to drink heavily. Fortunately, she still managed to maintain her creativity and capacity to manage multiple organizations. By 1984 the grant from the National Endowment for the Arts had risen to a quarter of a million dollars. Graham was also being recognized by honorary degrees from such educational institutions as Harvard and Yale and was receiving international recognition with such awards as the Italian Golden Florin, the Knight of the French Legion of Honor, the Swedish Carina Ari Medal, the Japanese Order of the Precious Butterfly with Diamond, and the National Medal of Arts from the United States. In fact, then President Gerald Ford officially called Graham a national treasure when he presented her with the Medal of Freedom.

Graham is credited with creating "the first codified vocabulary to offer an alternative to classical ballet," structuring a unique system of training that involved breathing, strength, endurance, and a different organization of time (Hardy, 1991: 18). She initiated what is now the oldest continuously performing dance company in the United States. Graham herself performed until she was seventy-six. By the late 1990s her school had three studios conducting more than fifty classes a week by over twenty-five faculty (Dekle, 1991). She also had initiated a school in Israel and was responsible for having encouraged many other entrepreneurs to start their own dance schools or companies. In her own words, "If you are going to grow, you have to absorb life. . . . Talent is the ability to experience life, and to communicate the experience to others. . . . You have to look for the truth. You eat the truth in your mouth. Sometimes it is bitter and sometimes it is sweet, but you have to eat life. . . . We exist in space—that is the energy of the world, and each of us is a recipient of that energy, if he so wills" (Mazo, 1991: 45).

SOURCES: Dekle, N. (1991), "Martha's Missionaries," *Dance Magazine*, July: 32–33; de Mille, A. (1991), *Martha: The Life and Work of Martha Graham* (New York: Random House); Hardy, C. (1991), "Martha Graham, American Pioneer, May 11, 1894–April 1, 1991," *Dance Magazine*, July: 18–19; Lewis, A., & Woodworth, C. (1972), *Miss Elizabeth Arden* (New York: Coward, McCann, & Geoghegan); Mazo, J. (1991), "Martha Remembered," *Dance Magazine*, July: 34–45; Shuker, N. (1989), *Elizabeth Arden: Cosmetics Entrepreneur* (Englewood Cliffs, NJ: Silver Burdette Press).

CLARA HALE (1905–1992)

"All children are born with something special. And you can bring it out and make them good people. But they need the right start. They need love." (Clara Hale, Founder of Hale House)

At age sixty-five, when most people choose to retire, Clara McBride Hale was faced with a dilemma. At the suggestion of Hale's daughter, Dr. Lorraine Hale, a drug-addicted infant was literally left at her door by the child's addicted mother. Clara called her daughter for an explanation. "She was not pleased," remembered Dr. Hale, who went on to explain simply, "Mother, the baby needs you." Clara Hale's response was, "Then you'd better take a second job to help me pay for her" (Hale, 1998: 20). Within just two months, the number of such afflicted infants being cared for by "Mother Hale" rose to twenty-two. With little more than a rocking chair, but with an unending supply of hugs and words of love, Clara Hale—in 1969—initiated what was to become Hale House, and she became mother to hundreds upon hundreds of troubled babies and their drug-addicted or AIDS-afflicted mothers.

Hardship was not new to Clara Hale. Her father had been murdered when she was still quite small. Her mother took in boarders and ran a lunchroom for longshoremen to support her family, but she died when Clara was only sixteen, leaving her an orphan. In spite of this, Clara finished high school and then married Thomas Hale, who owned a floor waxing business. To supplement her husband's income, Clara cleaned Loew's theaters (Lambert, 1992). They had two children, Lorraine and Nathan, when tragedy struck again. Thomas Hale died of cancer, leaving Clara widowed at age 27. Because she wanted to be with her children, Hale became a foster mother, taking in seven to eight children at a time, caring for them in a small five-room apartment. During the next thirty years of this "home business," about forty children and their families benefited from her loving care. She informally "adopted" a child, Kenneth, and raised him as her own son.

Once Hale took in that first drug-addicted baby, word spread quickly that there was a woman in Harlem who would take in addicted children between the ages of ten days and four years. Mothers, police, clergy, and community workers all sought out the help of Mother Hale. Shortly after she began this work in 1969, Percy Sutton, president of the Borough of New York City, demonstrated his backing of the effort by providing some much-needed funding (Holley, 1993). At first the Hales leased a building, but later a church congregation gave them a facility on West 122nd Street. News of her work spread, and by the 1980s Hale became well-known outside the New York area. "Her program especially drew attention in the 1980's when so-called boarder babies languished for months in municipal hospitals, at a cost of several hundred dollars a day for each one. No one else wanted them, and the city's social-services agency was ill-prepared to place them (Lambert, 1992: 50).

By 1984 the Hale House operating budget had grown to $147,000 with almost eighty-five percent coming from city funding sources; city restrictions, however, permitted only fifteen children to be admitted. Yet, Mother Hale had great difficulty in turning needy children away. "Sometimes we have 30 or 40. . . . When city inspectors pop in . . . we hide them. They say, 'Oh, Mother Hale, don't you give us any trouble.' I say, 'Not if I can help it' " (Beyette, 1990: 4).

In 1986 Hale received federal funding of $1.1 million; by 1989, the annual city funding had risen to $370,000, and the same year, she received a $2 million housing development grant to build a facility with thirty-five apartments, the Hale House Homeward Bound program. This effort provided apartments and a safe environment for women who were trying to change their lives after they had completed drug rehabilitation. "The residence offers counseling, exercise classes, massages, and child care to tenants who need a break" (Cunningham, 1997: 3). The message Hale was giving to these women was that "America's a rich country . . . and you have to work to become a part of that richness. Nobody's going to hand it to you" (Hale, 1998: 19).

The goal of Hale House efforts always has been to help the children through drug or alcohol withdrawal and return them to a responsible family member or to their mother, if and only if she has successfully completed drug rehabilitation. When this was not possible, the children would be up for adoption; however, the potential parents had to pass the scrutiny of

Mother Hale. "We arrange [the adoption] through the Children's Aid Society," Hale explained. "But they have to bring the parents here, and I have to OK them. They don't just take my children anyplace" (Italia, 1993: 11). Hale House also became the first residential facility to care for infants infected with AIDS. Mother Hale now had many supporters, including entertainers. For example, Spike Jones contributed $100,000, and the John Lennon Foundation provided $20,000 annually, a generous practice started by the singer himself just a short time before he was murdered.

Mother Hale became widely recognized for her work. In 1985 she received an honorary Doctorate of Humane Letters from John Jay College of Criminal Justice; in 1989, the Truman Award for Public Service; in 1990, both the Candace Award for being an outstanding Black American and the Booth Community Service Award, the Salvation Army's highest award; and on more than one occasion, then-President Ronald Reagan referred to her as an American Hero.

Clara McBride Hale was determined to remain active in the care of her special children until she died. 'When I get to heaven, I'm going to rest,' she said. 'God put me down here to work' " (Beyette, 1990: 3). Hale kept this commitment until her death at the age of 87, always focused on the needs of the children. Hale even left very clear instructions about how her funeral arrangements were to be conducted. "There was . . . [to be] just a plain pine box . . . [and] a joyous celebration . . . [with] songs sung . . . by the Addicts Rehabilitation Center Gospel Choir, the Harlem School of the Arts Concert Chorale and Stephanie Mills. Mother Hale said any money that would have been spent for an expensive funeral should be used instead to take care of her babies" (Baye, 1992: 9A). Interspersed among the celebrities in attendance at her funeral service were many of the formerly downtrodden whom she had helped—prostitutes, drug dealers, and thieves.

Dr. Lorraine Hale, Executive Director and CEO of Hale House, continues the work she and her mother initiated thirty years ago; as of 1998, more than 3,000 children had been helped. In addition, she and her staff also assist those from other countries such as Japan, Brazil, Kenya, and Uganda who want to learn how to implement such programs. Clara McBride Hale was clear as to why this work was and remains so important: "If we don't take care of these children, we've lost a generation" (Beyette, 1990: 3).

SOURCES: Baye, B. (1992), "The Remarkable Mother Hale," *Courier Journal*, December 31: 9A (available: Lexis-Nexis, accessed August 23, 1998); Beyette, B. (1990), "Mother Hale's Solution; Children: Love Is What Clara McBride Hale Recommends for Drug- and AIDS-Afflicted Babies. She Should Know; She's Taken Care of Hundreds," *Los Angeles Times*, March 8: (available: Lexis-Nexis, accessed August 23, 1998); Cunningham, A. (1997), "Loving the Unloved Children: Following Her Mother's Example, Dr. Lorraine Hale Brings Hope to the Neediest Kids," *Ladies Home Journal*, November: 206 (available: Lexis-Nexis, accessed November

20, 1997); Hale, L. (1998), "Other People's Children," *Guideposts*, December: 18–21; Holley, M. (1993), "Clara Hale," in J. C. Smith, ed., *Epic Lives: One Hundred Black Women Who Made a Difference* (Detroit, MI: Visible Ink); Italia, B. (1993), *Clara Hale: Mother to Those Who Needed One* (Edina, MN: Abdo & Daughters); Lambert, B. (1992), "Clara Hale, 87, Who Aided Addicts' Babies, Dies," *New York Times*, December 20: 50 (available: Lexis-Nexis, accessed October 13, 1998).

MOLLY HALEY (1942–   )

"My father started influencing me really early. He used to knock out walls and remodel our small house on weekends. Since he didn't have a son, I was building with him from the time I was very little. One of my favorite photographs is of me standing with my foot on a sawhorse, hammer in hand, next to my father, both of us radiating with our similar smiles. I've felt him by my side all these years even though he died in 1975." (Molly Haley, Co-founder, Marblehead Handprints, Inc.)

Molly Brister Haley's first entrepreneurial venture began when she was fifteen years old. She and her sister, Meg, who was eighteen months older, started a summer day camp for youngsters of families in the neighboring community of their farmhouse in Weston, Connecticut. "We took them swimming and had arts and crafts classes. This was the beginning of my artistic and teaching careers, I guess" (Oppedisano, 1999; all direct quotes are from this source unless otherwise cited). Molly's family had moved to Connecticut from Orange, New Jersey because her father, J. Edward Brister, an engineer with Union Carbide, felt that it would be an easier commute to New York City, where his job was based. The family lived on a seven-acre farm for twenty-five years, a setting and lifestyle that Molly remembers as idyllic. "My father was always around, and we had wonderful times together as a family. Maybe it was too good," she smilingly recalled, since life got much more complicated as Molly grew older. Artistic accomplishment started early for her. She won her first prize in grammar school for a drawing she called "Hen on a Hill." She pointed out that as this was the time of no television, "I was always being creative; we made our own fun then."

Writing as meaningful work was exemplified by Molly's mother, Margaret Palmer Brister. "She was also a very strong influence on me. She was the editor of the *Weston Town Crier* newspaper. She got the news, she wrote the news, she did everything. She was also politically active and elected Justice of the Peace in our town. Both my sister and I later followed in her journalistic footsteps. We became editors of our school newspapers." Molly went on to Skidmore College, and during her college years she met Douglas Haley, a law student at Boston University (BU). They were married a week after she graduated with a degree in art. To help support them both, Molly became a dorm mother at BU. She also not only took courses to earn her teaching certification, but also completed classes in silk screening, the art form that would soon become her entrepreneurial focus.

The couple moved to Marblehead, Massachusetts, when Doug found a position there. Molly Haley got a job teaching art at Marblehead High School, and at the young age of twenty-six, she became the head of the art department. "I was a sabbatical replacement who didn't know what I was doing and since I was the only art teacher in the school, I couldn't consult with anyone else. It was here that I developed the 'why not?' philosophy that has since permeated my career and life choices." In 1967, Haley became pregnant with her first daughter, Maggie; she had to leave teaching because, in those years, women weren't allowed to work in front of students when "with child."

Haley's disappointment at leaving high school teaching was lessened when she was asked by a colleague at the school if she would like to teach a course in silk screening for the Marblehead Arts Association. Even though she had taken only a few courses in the subject, Haley followed her "why not?" philosophy and accepted the opportunity. This was the professional turning point for her. "My initial course was for silk screening on paper. It was here that I met the woman who would become my business partner, Kathy Walters, then a psychiatric social worker. We were both young, married women with small children. It was Kathy who convinced me to teach another course because she wanted to learn how to do silk screening on fabric." Then, in 1970, both women experienced tragedy. Molly Haley had a stillbirth, and Kathy Walters lost her seven-month-old baby. In their grief, these two women bonded and started printing fabric together as a therapeutic release. At first, they worked together only one day a week, creating silk-screened fabrics in the kitchen of Haley's house, drying them on the dining room table, and heat treating the fabric in the oven. They made baby bibs, quilts, ties, and pillows from these originally designed fabrics—at first for their own children and other family members. "We were only printing for about a month when people began noticing us and wanting to buy what we were making. We sort of 'backed' into the business." Both of the women put in $50 to buy supplies. "We'd buy discounted fabric, print it, sell it, and go back and buy more." Within six months, the business had grown to the point where they needed more space, so they rented a small shop in town for $100 a month. "We put the same amount of money in, and we took the same amount of money out.

We didn't try to figure out who put in more hours one week than the other. This worked really well for us. We had the same value system."

Local newspapers wrote stories and carried pictures of the two moms with their babies close by safely behind baby gates. They were the business owners, but they were not referred to by their own names, only as Mrs. Douglas Haley and Mrs. Frederick McDonald. However, few knew the marital problems both women were experiencing. The McDonalds separated and divorced; and after ten years of marriage, Molly Haley's husband simply left her and their two daughters, Maggie and Melissa. "I had no child support. I had to make my business grow."

The man who was still there for Molly was her father. Early on in her business career, she recalled that "my father kept me 'captive' one weekend . . . to teach me business practices and principles. He told me that it's what jingles in your pocket that counts." The two partners also instinctively discovered a special marketing technique; they did their printing in the window of their shop to get customer attention. "It wasn't as if we worked out a business strategy," Haley pointed out. "It was a natural progression." In short order, these two artists/business owners/moms were getting special design orders from the Museum of Fine Arts in Boston, the Boston Symphony, American Heritage, and four of the Rockefeller Resort hotels. By 1972 they needed to move to a larger space because of the increased demand for their bright, rainbow-colored fabric and products. By now, they had hired stitchers, who worked either at home or in the shop, and had taken on as a partner Nancy Foster, who stayed until 1983.

Marblehead Handprints was in its second year of business when the partners got their first order from Saks Fifth Avenue. Saks was so pleased with customer response that they ordered more product for all of their twenty-two stores. "We took the order to the bank and got the money to finance it," said Haley. "I tell entrepreneurs that you must be prepared for sudden growth and be able to deliver. You don't have to spend a lot of money doing it. Make your product well, get it produced, and get it to them on time." The following year Marblehead Handprints had a second store, this one in Nantucket; and during the next three years, additional shops were opened in Harvard Square, Cambridge, and Faneuil Hall. A mail order catalog was also started, and the first franchise of the business was initiated. The unique two color, simple, repetitive designs now appeared on a number of products, including mugs, canvas bags, clothing, paper, and glass. Between 1978 and 1988, Marblehead Handprints established eighteen distributorships in Maryland, Rhode Island, Florida, California, Missouri, New Jersey, Indiana, and Texas.

In 1981 Molly Haley married Edward Freitag, then a senior corporate counsel for mergers and acquisitions with MCI in Maryland. She continued with the business as a long-distance partner, with responsibilities divided up as appropriate. "I learned a lot of things about myself when I had to work alone. I missed having my business and partner around to bounce things off. Kathy and I had a synergistic energy that almost sparked off us when we were working together. I found that I needed other people to work with. This was an important lesson."

After ten years, the distance and separation became wearying for both partners so they faced a very difficult decision—to sell their business or close it down. Quality assurance and reputation were the pivotal decision criteria. "Maintaining our name and reputation was more important than money," so the partners dissolved Marblehead Handprints, Inc., in 1993. "We didn't have planned obsolescence so I still see our products all over the place," Haley observed with much satisfaction, concluding, "I miss doing it, but life moves on and there are cycles for everything. We did all we wanted to do. We're very proud of that and of our business."

SOURCE: Oppedisano, J. (1999), interview of Molly Haley on August 16, in Saratoga Springs, New York.

CATHY HAMILTON (1957–   )
GLORIA GRISKOWITZ (1965–   )

"I never, ever said I wanted to have my own business while I was growing up. My original intention was to go to college, study biology, and get into a pre-med program." (Gloria Griskowitz, Co-owner, Hamilton Company and the Putnam Street Market)

The Hamilton sisters, Cathy and Gloria, two of eight siblings, grew up in a large and entrepreneurial family in West Chester, Pennsylvania. Their father, James, was in real estate and had a masonry business; their mother, Gloria, had started her own Scandinavian furniture stores, now run by three of her sons and grossing over $4 million annually. For Cathy Hamilton, though, the strongest influence was her maternal grandmother, who was a serious antiques collector. She remembered, "My grandmother was so articulate and knowledgeable that she would give public lectures on the subject. She was such a 'modern' woman for her time" (Earle, 1998). For Gloria, it was her older sister: "Cathy has always been my role model. She was great in sports; I wanted to be like Cathy. She was the valedictorian; I wanted to be like Cathy. She was the world traveler. I wanted to be just like Cathy" (Quigley, 1999). All eight of the Hamilton offspring are high achievers and in their own businesses. Gloria's twin brother is an industrial designer; other siblings, besides those in the furniture stores, are in hydro-geology and professional training.

Both Hamilton sisters earned college degrees having international components that helped them develop a broad cultural understanding, a skill that would facilitate their purchasing decisions later on. After receiving her bachelor's degree in chemistry, Cathy got her master's in business administration (MBA) from the London Business School, where she met the man she would later marry. Gloria gave up the idea of pre-med and ended up majoring in international business, studying one summer in Germany and her senior year in Copenhagen, Denmark. The Hamilton sisters followed their formal education with employment in two major U.S. industrial companies. Cathy worked at General Electric (GE) for twelve years, ultimately being promoted to general manager of sales and marketing for the Silicone Division in Waterford, New York. Gloria went with Bristol Myers-Squibb for seven years, first in the sales division, working in various locations in the Northeast and, later, to corporate headquarters, working on national accounts for the Clairol division.

In her heart of hearts, Cathy Hamilton always knew she was not going to retire from GE; she also found that she really loved the upstate New York area near her Waterford assignment and she began to look around for opportunities. She learned that there were no specialty food stores in Saratoga, New York, an upscale summer resort at the foot of the Adirondack Mountains. She began to explore the possibility of opening up such a business and approached her sister, Gloria, with the idea of a partnership.

Their business training served them well. They wrote up a business plan, Cathy cashed in her GE stock options, both sisters combined some savings and inheritance money, and they initiated the Hamilton Company. Cathy was the majority owner with sixty percent; Gloria had forty percent. They then found and renovated a warehouse at 63 Putnam Street in downtown Saratoga and opened their doors in June 1995 as the Putnam Street Market, a retail operation with both national and imported products, deli sandwiches, soups, baked goods, and wines. "No one in our family has ever worked in a restaurant or in a food environment," Gloria noted, "so we were starting totally from scratch. We like food, we grew up with a mother who was always exposing us to new foods . . . so it's been quite a learning experience for us" (Quigley, 1999). Since opening the store, Cathy "has become a wine, cheese, and chocolate connoisseur" studying both food and the chemistry that relates to it—in a throwback to her undergraduate studies (Earle, 1998).

In just three years, the Putnam Street Market was grossing over a million dollars, and they hit the breakeven point. The Hamilton sisters openly talk about roadblocks they encountered along the way, particularly with renting out space to others. They've been "burned" three times because these small companies went out of business, leaving them bills amounting to many

thousands of dollars. Cathy summed up these negative experiences by saying, "Nothing ever happens the way you think it will" (Earle, 1998). The
sisters attribute their rapid success to their strong business experience, being
numbers oriented, and having complementary skills. Cathy described herself as being able to take a complex business concept and making it simple;
she is the "macro" partner, the one with the vision. "We want to be the
premier specialty food store between Montreal, Canada and New York
City," she declared (Oppedisano, 1998). Gloria, on the other hand, is the
"micro" partner. "My strength is merchandising and operations, the day
in, day out supervision. . . . I see the leaf on the floor, the crumbs. I'm the
worrisome person" (Quigley, 1999).

After just four years, the Hamilton sisters have branched out into whole-
saling and catering. For example, just one of their products, the home-
baked biscotti, is wholesaled out to a thirty-store chain located throughout
the Northeast. Since the Putnam Street Market is open seven days a week,
the sisters try to make sure that one of them is present during all hours of
operation. This has been difficult because each has had a baby since the
store first opened. However, they are exuberant mothers and sometimes
bring the babies to the store to meet and greet customers, too. It's all part
of the "fun" experience they wish to create within their establishment. After
all, Cathy points out humorously, "No one needs what we sell" (Earle,
1998). As for their future plans, they project that the Putnam Street Market
will plateau at between $5 and $6 million annually. They are planning a
Web site, expanding their catering business to include weddings, and developing a product catalog. As Gloria explained, "We were raised with the
expectation that we *would* excel."

SOURCES: Earle, M. (1998), interview of Cathy Hamilton on February 18, in
Saratoga, New York; Oppedisano, J. (1998), interview of Cathy Hamilton on
March 5, in Saratoga, New York; Quigley, R. (1999), interview of Gloria Gris-
kowitz on February 25, in Saratoga, New York.

LISA HAMMOND (1967–   )

> *"My strength is my vision, my ability to draw on my creative intuition
> and manifest my dreams. My commitment to my passion for women's
> issues is also a strength. Without that motivation, I wouldn't have had
> the courage to start this business."* (Lisa Hammond, Founder, Femail
> Creations, Inc.)

Lisa and Jeff Hammond were only teenagers when they got married but wise beyond their years. They were determined to be equal partners in whatever lay ahead. Not surprising, today they are co-owners of a successful construction company, and Lisa is the founder and sole owner of a mail-order catalogue business, Femail Creations. Hammond asserts that her marriage has been truly egalitarian from the beginning. She is not shy about saying she is lucky, especially when she sees how difficult it is for most women who have children and, in actuality, find themselves raising them alone whether married or single.

Hammond's awareness of how difficult a mother's lot could be was rooted in her childhood in Utah. Her father was a schoolteacher but didn't earn enough money to support his wife and six children. Her mother had to take a lot of different jobs to fill in the income gap. But "she was a 'doormat,' " Hammond recalled. "I remember thinking, 'How could anyone tolerate what she put up with?' " (Oppedisano, 1999). Hammond became determined to seek out as behavioral models women trailblazers who had bulldozed the way before her. "Women of spirit like Rosa Parks, or Sojourner Truth, or Amelia Earhart became my role models."

By the mid-1990s, Hammond was working full time managing the construction business along with raising her daughter, Harlie, and son, Bridger. But she was still feeling restless. She kept a list of what she would do next "if only." One possibility that appealed to her was starting a catalogue business. "As a mother and a businesswoman, I relied heavily on the convenience of home shopping and home delivery. Being a catalogue fiend, I often wished for a woman-owned catalog that I could support with my shopping dollars" (Femail Creations, 1999).

By 1996, in spite of having absolutely no experience in this business, Hammond initiated a catalogue to "make a difference in the lives of women. I searched a long time for work that would be meaningful and, to me, that meant empowering and inspiring women and honoring our creative souls. I wanted to build a business that would help women be economically independent." She set up the company using about $30,000 in savings, and with the help of her family, friends, and a few local services got her first catalogue designed, written, printed, and distributed. While her first publication was attractive and well received, it was not profitable. "I was so naive. In my mind having a distribution of about 30,000 seemed huge to me. Today I know that I need at least a million names on my list to make my dreams a reality. I knew nothing about cataloging, printing, drumscans, film output, photo shoots, circulation plans, phone systems, call centers, shipping and fulfillment, websites, pagination, graphic arts . . . *but I've learned*," she declared.

Though financial risks have been significant, Hammond remains determined to see her business grow, encouraged by the strong early response.

The first issue of the Femail Creations catalogue was mailed in April 1997. Sales the first year were $221,000, in 1998 they were $1.7 million, and the projected sales for 1999 were approximately $5 million. To get this far, she had to use the family savings, credit cards, and mortgage the house— all with her husband's support—for her labor of love. "We had some consultants come in who, after analyzing our business, told me that we shouldn't be the success we are by any conventional catalogue standards. We've done everything wrong, but it was working so we were advised to keep doing what we were doing." These same consultants pointed out that it usually takes five years before such an effort sees a profit, if it survives at all.

In addition to offering products targeted to and for women, Hammond is giving outlet opportunities to many women-owned businesses because most of the products are made by women. "I know all too well how hard it can be to get a company off the ground. I want to support women all over the world who are doing or who have done that," noted Hammond, who also has a commitment to what she describes as "focus charities." Each issue of the catalogue has a product offered whose revenues go to a charity such as the National Women's History Project, LAAW—Helping Women and Children Rebuild their Lives, and Rainbow Socks—handknit products by refugee women in war-torn Bosnia-Herzegovina and Croatia. "Whenever I feel overwhelmed or tired, I think of the entire village of women in Croatia who think of me as 'the good woman' for helping them make money through their knitting skills. This is how I know it is all worth it." The winter 1999 issue carried the "Healing Heart Pillow," with sales proceeds going to the Women's Development Center, an organization dedicated to bridging the gap for women in transition. Hammond's ultimate goal in creating a successful business with Femail Creations is to set up a foundation so that she can be even more effective for helping women in transition. "Making a difference is success to me. I feel it is imperative for our daughters to see their mothers follow their dreams if we want them to believe they can follow their own. The world needs our talents, our intelligence, and our passions. This is how we can build a better future."

SOURCES: Femail Crations (1999), *http://www.femailcreations.com* (accessed February 12); Oppedisano, J. (1999), personal interview of Lisa Hammond, March 28.

KIMBERLY HARBOUR (1964–   )

"I started on my own too early. I had no plan, no contacts. I learned by making mistakes and just hoped that I wouldn't make them again."

(Kimberly Harbour, Founder and President, Harbour Media Relations, Inc.)

Until recently, Kimberly Harbour thought of herself as a "reluctant entrepreneur." Then, as she reviewed her life experiences and choices, she realized that she had started down this path back in the third grade. "I began to crochet caps and matching purses for students for fifty cents—remember that this was around 1970. When my mother found out, she was furious with me because she felt I could have sold them for three to five dollars. I then was commissioned by ladies in our church to make the sets for their children and grandchildren," Harbour recalled (Oppedisano, 1999; all direct quotes are from this source unless otherwise cited). She began to equate creative output with selling and that with personal worth.

Harbour was born in an upstate New York suburb; she was the oldest of Alice and William Harbour's three children. Her mother had earned a secretarial degree and worked until the children came. Her father put himself through Rensselaer Polytechnic Institute, the oldest engineering university in the United States. While Harbour thinks highly of her parents, she still rates their parenting as far less than an "A." In fact, as she was growing up, she wished she had been an only child, because she didn't feel that she was permitted to have an individual personality. "If I wanted to take ballet lessons or learn how to ride horses, my mother would have my little sister do the same, too. She even had us dressing alike. She must have thought it was cute, but it wasn't to me. I wanted to be my own person and be recognized for that."

When Harbour was a preteen, her father became a partner in his company, often bringing work home with him at night, making it difficult for her to spend time with him. Something good came from this, she noted, because "the only way I could get his attention was to develop an interest in something that interested him. I was good at math and science so we could talk about that." Harbour thinks of those years as a time where she was a loner and a bit of an introvert, finding solace only in arts and crafts.

While Harbour was attending a private all-girls high school, she was given a vocational psychological screening and told that she had the necessary ability to become, among other careers, an airplane pilot. Harbour's mother had an emotional response to this idea, telling her daughter that this was a man's job, that there had to be something wrong with the test, and that she should consider becoming an airline stewardess. That negative message was followed by another, this time from a professor. As a business major at Skidmore College, she, like the other students, was told that the core of that program was changing and was given the option of choosing the old or the new. Because she was finishing her junior year, Harbour decided to stay with the old core curriculum. This professor told her that she would probably never be an entrepreneur because Harour's decision-making skills demonstrated that she didn't like taking risks. Certainly the years that followed would point out the error of that judgment.

After she graduated, Harbour found work in Bloomingdale's Retail Management Trainee Program in New York City. Here she discovered she was not comfortable in a bureaucratic environment and with taking orders from someone else. She left and then took a job in a computer manufacturing company, leaving that one to join a small public relations firm, which she liked. Though she learned the marketing and public relations work, Harbour realized that she had to be in a position where she had the opportunity to be heard, so again she left. "I was kind of lost at this time in my life. But I believe that you pick yourself up by the boot straps so I decided to see what I could do. I 'worked it'—hit the phones, called everyone I knew, and told them I was out on my own and did they have any work for me. It was a mean-and-lean time. I was working PR in the day, telemarketing in the evenings, and spritzing perfume at Bloomingdale's on weekends just to make ends meet," she explained. In 1990 Harbour took the plunge, becoming the sole proprietor of her own company. "Money totally drives me and I'm not ashamed to admit it. But, when you're the sole proprietor, your income is capped since you're the only one producing."

Harbour began to get small contracts but being young and considered inexperienced by sophisticated New Yorkers, she kept hitting setbacks. To show her seriousness and ability, she, at times, would even work for free saying, "If you think I'm doing a good job, then pay me." This risk actually contributed to her success. "I went to interview for a contract and was asked if I knew how to book a satellite media tour. I convinced them that I could though I didn't even know what it was. I thought I'd have time to learn before the job actually started, but they wanted me the very next day." Harbour found that she was very good at "winging it" and that media relations came naturally to her. "I had a talent for it and I liked it, plus I enjoyed the freedom that this type of work permitted."

Harbour was twenty-eight and on her way when her parents told her they were divorcing. When she heard that it was because her father wanted to marry his secretary, her very foundation was shaken. He was the parent she had placed on a pedestal. "He was my model of what principles and ethics were supposed to be. Since I held what he did in such high disregard, what did his choice now mean to my core values?" On reflection, Harbour realized that this became a healthy experience "because it caused me to break out of my mold. My parents no longer would be there for my financial security; the only person I could rely on was myself." Harbour decided to move her business to Albany so that she could help her mother sell her house and adjust to her new life style. Coming back to this area also permitted Harbour to have an actual office rather than use her apartment as she had in New York, since the cost of doing business was so much less expensive than in Manhattan.

The slogan of Harbour's business, Harbour Media Relations, Inc., is "Unleashing the power of television news." She and her employees develop video clips and news releases for companies, ad agencies, and individual clients, then market these television spots to news program producers such as those of CNN, NBC, ABC, and CBS. With a database of over eight hundred stations, network affiliates, and independent stations located in the larger markets, she has many clients, among them multimillionaire Steve Forbes, Amazon.com, and Fabio, a model for romance paperback novels. As with many production companies, the videos are recorded in rented studios in New York City. The services are priced per package and can range up to $25,000.

Today, Harbour sees herself as a manager of her company, which is now growing steadily. But "I miss the booking, pitching to TV producers—it was incredibly and immediately satisfying." Her goal is to grow her company to between $3 and $5 million and then sell it. While she has no plans to have a family of her own, she does have another goal, wanting to start a bed-and-breakfast before she reaches forty-three years of age. Although her client base is national and much of her competitors' work is generated by being located in New York City, she is proud of choosing to keep her business in upstate New York because she wants to have a better work environment for herself and her employees. Harbour has followed her intuition and instincts and is happy with the decisions she's made. After all, she concluded, "Success is having no regrets."

SOURCES: Oppedisano, J. (1999), personal interview of Kimberly Harbour, March 23, in Saratoga, New York; Harbour Media Relations, Inc. (1999) [Online], *http://www.harbourmedia.com* (accessed March 24).

LORE HARP (1944–   )

"To succeed you have to do it for yourself and not because somebody else is telling you to. We come into the world alone and the decisions we make, we make ourselves. Entrepreneurial companies are in a continual state of change. . . . [We] are automating, decentralizing, restructuring, reshaping, and re-evaluating our market position, programs, products, and personnel . . . however, we must not change the basic character of the company. We must remain true to our convictions

[and] stick to what we know." (Lore Harp, Co-founder of Vector
Graphics, Inc., and Founder of Aplex Corporation)

In 1966, at the age of twenty, Lore Harp made the decision to leave her
family and her homeland of Germany to explore the United States. Her life
had been good, but she was a "fidget," restless to be active, to explore, to
learn, admitting that "I was always tremendously strong-willed" (Collins,
1982: 140). She chose the West Coast because she had friends there and
took odd jobs to try to support herself. "At one point I was down to $20,
but . . . somehow I always made it" (140). Four years later, in 1968, Lore
married Bob Harp, a senior researcher with Hughes Research Laboratories.
By 1972 they had two children and were living in suburbia, a prototypical
American family life. But Lore was restless and bored once again. Having
two daughters, a husband, and a home to run were not enough. "I cannot
stand being at home," she declared. "It absolutely drives me crazy" (140).
She tried going back to school, but that wasn't the answer. Then her husband came up with an idea. Frustrated by not getting a company to market
a computer memory board he had designed, he threw a challenge out to
his wife. "If you're really that antsy, how would you like to market it?"
She jumped at the chance, and the rest is entrepreneurial history—but with
a dramatic twist.

Harp got her friend Carole Ely to join her. With $6,000, the power of
persuasion, natural marketing instincts, and much chutzpah, they initiated
Vector Graphics in 1976, from Harp's kitchen table. These two women
attended trade shows, separated the small component parts into kitchen
bowls, packed boxes, answered phones, and even had the children helping
as the orders started rolling in. Harp humorously recalled, "After a while,
salesmen started coming to the house, too. I think our neighbors must have
thought we had some sort of brothel going because the salesmen would
stay for half an hour and leave" (Harp, 1985: 8).

Vector Graphics became one of the fastest-growing manufacturers of
small business computers because according to Harp, "Most people were
flabbergasted by the attention they got . . . dealers were overwhelmed by
the support we gave. We were troubleshooting over the phone and servicing
right from the start" (Harp, 1985: 8). In 1977, they had $400,000 in sales.
In short order, the company was doing so well that Bob Harp left his job
at Hughes and joined the fledgling business full time. By 1978, sales were
$2 million; the next year, almost $5 million; and by 1980, they made $11.9
million (Akst, 1985). The following year, the company had over $25 mil-
lion in sales and profits of $2.6 million. Lore Harp took her Vector Graph-
ics company public in 1981, and the founders became millionaires. In 1983,
sales climbed to what was to be the company's peak number, $36.2 million,
with profits of $2.4 million. But now they were operating in the decade of
the 1980s, and within just a few years, all of this would change.

The same year the company went public the Harps were divorced, and Bob left Vector Graphics to start a new venture; co-founder Carole Ely married another Vector executive, Robert Wickham, and they both left; Lore Harp was on her own. International Business Machines (IBM) had also entered the personal computer market, knocking out many competitors; for Vector Graphics the first sign of trouble was a drop in income in 1982. Depending upon the analysts, the other reasons for Vector's rapid downslide besides IBM entering this segment of the marketplace included a fight for control between Harp and her husband, departure of senior management, few new products, a fixed keyboard design that never caught on, and an announcement of the Vector 4 machine before it was ready for shipping. Further compounding the problem was the fact that the company still had millions tied up in the inventory of Vector 3 machines, Bob Harp's refusal to adopt the industry standard of a 16-bit computer, and the global economic recession.

Lore Harp decided to bring in new corporate leadership, Fred Snow of Honeywell. She married publishing executive Patrick McGovern and "didn't meddle [with Vector] for nine months," as she pointed out. As the company got worse, not better, Harp fired Snow and returned to run Vector Graphics personally once again. She let one hundred managers and other employees go, restructured her organization, and tried desperately to help the company survive. "These are difficult and serious steps that must be taken to preserve cash flow," declared Lore Harp (*The Squeeze*, 1983: 91). After three years, Vector Graphics had almost $20 million in losses, and in 1985 the corporation filed for bankruptcy. "It was a very, very frustrating feeling. A lot of stupid things happened," Lore Harp remembered. "But I do not go backwards. I look forward. I'm trying to build a new business" (Stavro, 1987: 9A).

In her roller-coaster adventure with Vector Graphics, Lore Harp learned an important fact about herself. "What I really enjoy is growing the company, growing people within the company, accepting the challenge of being out there, competing against other companies and making an impact. Power may have something to do with it as well. I won't deny that" (Akst, 1985: 5A).

SOURCES: Akst, D. (1985), "The Rise and Decline of Vector Graphic; Management Mistakes and IBM Crush Couple's Computer Venture," *Los Angeles Times* [Online], August 20: 5A (available: Lexis-Nexis, accessed July 29, 1999); Collins, E. (1982), "The Entrepreneur Sees Herself as Manager: An Interview with Lore Harp," *Harvard Business Review* [Online], July/August: 140 (available: Lexis-Nexis, accessed July 22, 1999); Harp, L. (1985), "An Exception to the Rule," in R. Guiles & D. Peelle, eds., *Starting a High-Tech Company: An Insider's View of Entrepreneurship* (Ann Arbor: University of Michigan); Hyatt, Joshua (1984), "Lore Harp: Better to Give than to Receive," *Inc.* [Online], October 21 (available: Lexis-Nexis, accessed July 29, 1999); "The Squeeze Begins in Personal Computers,"

(1983), *Business Week* [Online] May 30: 91 (available: Lexis-Nexis, accessed July 29, 1999); Stavro, B. (1987), "Firm with Storybook Start Has Sad Ending: Vector's Assets Are Liquidated," *Los Angeles Times* [Online], October 20: 9A (available: Lexis-Nexis, accessed July 29, 1999).

CATHERINE HINDS (1934–)

"One's personal life has to be in balance especially for a woman. And, if you have children, there are days when the family has to come first and days when the business has to come first. Surround yourself with people who understand this." (Catherine Hinds, Founder, Catherine Hinds Institute of Esthetics and the C. E. Hinds Manufacturing Company)

The label *pioneer* certainly fits Catherine Hinds when we note just several of her many accomplishments: She opened the first accredited esthetics school in the United States, the first exclusive skin-care salon in New England; and the first spa therapy program in the United States; in 1998, she established a medical esthetics program, one of only a few in the country at the time. She is the president and CEO of one of the oldest woman-owned businesses in the state of Massachusetts, the Catherine Hinds Corporation—all this from a woman who was supposed to be the typical *good wife* of the 1950s, a "real asset to a man" as her father described her.

Hinds was born in 1934 in the rural community of Sandy Creek, New York. Her grammar school teachers were women who had graduated from the Normal Schools as educational institutions were called in their day. There were no other girls in Hinds' age group at the school, and since she was not close to her older brother, she spent most of her time with adults. "I was lonesome as a child so I became a voracious reader and resourceful; I loved being the entertainer. I was nine-going-on-thirty. These experiences also helped me become a people-reader" (Oppedisano, 1998).

While a student at Skidmore College majoring in philosophy and religion, Hinds met and married her first husband, Walter Bird, a Williams College graduate who was by this time in the military. "Women of my generation were supposed to be in college to get a husband. What was unusual was that I was the first student permitted to attend class while pregnant." Hinds graduated in 1956, second in her class, and moved to Framingham, Massachusetts, when her husband returned from military duty. After six years of marriage and the birth of two children, she and the children were deserted. "One day my husband drove down the driveway, and we never saw him again. Divorce was a disgrace back then; I felt guilty. I was alone and broke, ashamed and not assertive. I needed to figure out how to keep mind and soul together and to take care of my children who were only two and five years old."

Because she so desperately needed a job, Hinds lied about her experience and was hired by Jordan Marsh, a national upscale clothing retailer. "You need a little luck. They put me in the cosmetics department for $85 a week/ six days a week, and I became enamored of the beauty business." This employment didn't last too long, though, because Hinds was a self-described troublemaker. "I was a labor-leader, a rebel. I couldn't really take direction from anyone." Through this experience, Hinds realized that she wouldn't be happy working for someone else in the long run.

Then luck came her way. "My ex-husband's grandfather had taken a liking to me even though we had only met briefly. When he died, he left me $10,000 which was sufficient for me to rent a shop on Newberry Street in Boston and to open my first business, a facial salon. Newberry Street was a 'village'—a community in itself in the early days. We learned a lot from one another; we were a bunch of entrepreneurs." It was here that Hinds met Mildred Albert, the owner of a modeling agency. She was a role model for Hinds in that she loved life and put fun into work, philosophies incorporated by Hinds in her own management style. Albert was also the only woman Hinds knew who had her own business.

It was through this new venture that Hinds met the man who would become her second husband, Joseph Grady, a cosmetics salesperson. He turned out to be a womanizer and an abuser, yet she stayed in the marriage until her stepdaughter, Betsy, was old enough to leave home. The divorce was bitter and very public; in the end, she was forced to leave the space and clientele she had worked so long to establish. In 1974 Grady got the space and the business and put his daughter's name on it. "He owned me— the house, the car, the children's trust funds." But, in retrospect, Hinds realized that all of this pain and suffering made her the person she was now because she had the strength to survive. "He couldn't take my knowledge about skin away from me. This fact empowered me." But her ex-husband problems didn't end with the divorce. "If I opened a salon, he would open one nearby, sometimes across the street. He knew how to 'push my buttons.' " Instead of continuing in this personal/professional battle, Hinds decided to open a school about skin. "By 1979, I had seven salons. So what I did was regroup my assets and started the school in the basement of one of my salons." This initially small effort resulted in the graduation of more than 1,500 students by 1999; over this same period, Hinds has encouraged more than three hundred women to become entrepreneurs by starting their own spas and salons.

Also in 1974, Hinds had established the C. E. Hinds Manufacturing

Company in order to have her own laboratory and chemist conducting research and development for her skin-care products. Initially she offered a proprietary line of about twelve products, including cleansers, toners, moisturizers, and exfoliators. By 1998 almost ninety products were offered, mirroring the change in curriculum: for example, aromatherapy, plant essences, the spa line "Catherine Hinds Tree of Life," and "Catherine Hinds Classics."

The academic program offered at the Catherine Hinds Institute for Esthetics emphasizes the maintenance of skin throughout the entire body. "It's all about 'brushing,' like with teeth," Hinds explained. Students can take advantage of training at four distinct levels. The program provides education in such subjects as makeup artistry, American or European facial treatments, the science of tissue and metabolism, pathological skin disorders, nutrition, skin health and aging factors, circulation, the nervous system and body response, and clinical training. This course of study enables students to pass state licensing exams. Hinds has always been a leader in her industry. "My most recent direction has been in the development of a Medical Esthetics Program to bridge the gap between the medical and esthetic fields and to solidify a holistic approach to skin care treatment."

As she approached the year 2000, Hinds began to address the transitioning of her business into the hands of others. She had finally achieved contentment in her personal life, with her third husband, Milton Kanser being a significant contributor to this. "At the age of sixty, I gave myself a party. I realized I couldn't keep up the pace; I didn't have the desire to do it the same way. Yet, I wanted the business and school to go on. I didn't want to sell it. There's a whole group of alumni and a spirit to it that's different than a money machine. I wanted to save the Institute for future generations." With this in mind, Hinds began the succession planning process.

SOURCE: Oppedisano, J. (1998), personal interviews of Catherine Hinds conducted July 21 in Woburn, Massachusetts.

DEBORAH HOLLINGWORTH (1946–   )

"I started the business because I had to—I had to produce an income. I guess you have a sense when somebody is going to walk out on you. I had no money for a car, no wardrobe, and I had three little kids to support." (Deborah Hollingworth, Founder and Former Proprietor of Quiltworks, Ltd.)

Deborah Hollingworth's story is more about the triumph of the human spirit than about long-term success in the turbulent world of business. It was, in fact, her difficult life as a young wife and mother that brought her to discover her talents and her strengths. While a college student at the University of Massachusetts in the 1960s, Deborah Hollingworth met and married a faculty member who was leaving the campus. They decided to move to New York City, renting a small apartment in what today is the popular Soho district. Life was difficult for them. "I had never lived in a city, had never been on a subway. We had no jobs, no money so at first I took a lot of 'pick up' jobs" (Donovan, 1998). Hollingworth did some babysitting and started to sew clothing for the children, even though she had not been trained in this skill. However, she found she had a real talent for sewing and also was attracted to how sewing machines worked. Then, because she was able to sew well, a local furrier suggested she make up some business cards, and he would refer customers to her who needed their furs altered. When some of these referrals were for coat alterations for movie contracts, Hollingworth had her first homebased business.

Getting into the business of making children's clothing, however, happened by circumstance. Her firstborn son, Mica, refused to keep anything on his feet, and as a concerned mother, she used some sheepskin to make him what she later called chuck-a-boots. Hollingworth got the idea to approach a baby boutique in the neighborhood called Small Business. When the boots became a hit in this cold, northeastern area of the country, she began to make other items like quilts and baby buntings—all from her own designs. As the owner of this baby boutique wanted to go into the antiques business, she suggested that Hollingworth buy the store, which was then grossing about $6,000 a year. Hollingworth bought the business, and when she sold it three years later, sales had quadrupled. By that time, the Soho area of the city was being "discovered" by female tourists.

Hollingworth sold Small Business because she wanted to raise her children in what she felt was a more child-friendly location. When her son, Mica, was three, the couple adopted another small boy, Marco, even though Hollingworth knew she was pregnant with her third child, Jeremy. The family moved to Chester, Massachusetts, the kind of small-town environment in which Hollingworth had been raised. She continued to make items for the new owner of the New York baby boutique, but soon requests began to roll in from different children's boutiques, and she responded. Within three years, Hollingworth's work was bringing in $55,000 annually. "It started getting serious, and I couldn't make enough to keep up with the demand from different boutiques so I had to start getting some help." She hired local women as stitchers who would pick up a kit she made and get paid on delivery of the finished goods. The Hollingworth household became a factory. "Every room in the house was filled with wall-to-wall boxes of

quilts and vests except for the kitchen and bathroom," she laughingly recalled, and Hollingworth's new company, Quiltworks, was born.

Hollingworth felt additional pressure to be successful because she had a
crumbling marriage. Her husband was chronically out of work and alcoholic, and he "finally left home." At first she tried to use only her own
resources to grow the business. "If I made a dollar, I would use fifty cents
to put food on the table and invest the other fifty cents back into the
business." However, when the business grew to 110 accounts, Hollingworth approached a local banker with a fully detailed business plan asking
only for $20,000. He told her, "You're a woman, and we don't loan to
women," but since she had done such an impressive job on the business
plan, he was willing to take "a big chance" on her and loan her this paltry
amount; most small business loans from that bank were for around
$200,000. Hollingworth still recalls her anger that day: "I remember leav-
ing feeling like a second-class citizen! It never occurred to me that they
would think I would fail because I was a woman. It was my livelihood. It
was how I was paying my bills. I had to make this business work. I was
more motivated than most guys who would walk in there. This was my
business; I felt like it was my baby. I was invested in it emotionally. I was
highly motivated!"

Around this same time, the first baby boutique trades show was held in
New York City. Hollingworth went down with two of her workers and set
up a booth. Before this, her business had two dozen accounts; after the
first day of the trade show, she had written $150,000 worth of new busi-
ness. "We were the hottest thing there. It was amazing!" Quiltworks products would now be in boutiques in major cities across the country, and
Hollingworth had to figure out how to meet these commitments. "The
following year we maxed out at 225 accounts," she pointed out. "We
couldn't make the items fast enough; 1978 to 1980 were the 'gold rush'
years." The business was growing very fast and grossing over $200,000
annually; Hollingworth had thirty-six stitchers working for her. The largest
single order shipped from Quiltworks was a thousand vests for Neiman
Marcus.

By 1981 Hollingworth moved her business to a large warehouse in Chester. As the past tenant had disappeared and the bank was left with a run-
down piece of property, she convinced them to let her renovate the
building. She had it repaired, put in space on the first floor for a local day-
care center that was looking for another location, and used the top floor
for Quiltworks. This was an interesting time for her at first. "You never
knew what you were going to deal with from one week to the next," Hollingworth explained. "We could be trying to get a variance for a septic
system, or the plumber would hit granite and, instead of the few inches he
had estimated, it turned out to be four foot wide blocks, and the cost
estimates would jump." In spite of these obstacles, Hollingworth was able

to maintain her accounts until the mid-1980s. Then a confluence of factors led her to make a very difficult decision.

Recession hit the national economy in the early 1980s, and interest rates had begun to soar during the Reagan presidency. Like other small business owners, Hollingworth had become dependent on commercial lenders to whom she was now paying interest at 22.5 percent. "My loans were up to $100,000 so I was paying $22,500 every year. This was more than I was paying myself!" Her accounts were also disappearing because boutiques, too, were in financial trouble and she wasn't being paid for orders she had shipped. For three years in a row, Hollingworth missed the breakeven point, even though she had gross sales of around $200,000. With sadness, she knew she had to choose bankruptcy or liquidation. She shut her doors in 1986 and paid off all of her bills. "Nobody got stiffed. I could have made out very well by closing that business and not paying my debts, but I wasn't cut out to do that. This may not have been the smart thing to do, but it was the right thing," she concluded.

Hollingworth returned to college and earned a degree in social work, the field in which she is now employed. She also has remarried. She may make and sell quilts again someday, but this time to interior designers and decorators. She mused, "Maybe someday I'll write a book on quiltmaking and owning my own business."

SOURCE: Donovan, K. (1998), interview with Deborah Hollingworth in Chester, Massachusetts, on February 2.

MARIA IBANEZ (1955–   )

"My father was good for me; he always pushed my education. In my mind it was never an issue that I was a woman. . . . [Besides] since I started programming, people did not have a choice; I was the only one who could do it so they could not discriminate against me. It was me or nobody else." (Maria Ibanez, Founder, International High Technology, Inc.)

From the time she was a little girl in Barranquilla, Columbia, Maria Elena Ibanez rebelled against anyone who tried to squeeze her into a traditional mold—even the nuns who were her teachers. "I remember when I was eight years old, I was very sure of myself. The nuns always wanted me to go to church to pray. I hated it. So one day, I [said], 'Listen, nun, I don't think that we should pray the rosary and repeat the same prayer fifty times to the Virgin. If the Virgin is smart, she will hear me the first time' " (Silver, 1994: 148).

Though very young, Ibanez was already an entrepreneur. Her father, a producer and exporter of fruit juices, had told her she could have all the fruit that came from two trees in their backyard to sell. This is when she first learned the power of "cold calls"—she gave her telephone sales pitch to the mothers of all of her friends and made her own money. Even more important, her father taught her to keep appropriate business records. "I even had to show my father an income statement" (Voss, 1992: 68). When Ibanez was later suspended from high school, her father again stepped in, having her work in the accounting department of his company and take a seminar in the subject. What she gained from that program was a jubilant interest in the new computing technology of the 1970s. Recognizing that Columbia needed an accounting software package in Spanish, Ibanez translated one from a U.S. company, charging as much as $5,000 each. From this profitable experience, she determined that she had found her calling.

With no knowledge of English, Maria Elena Ibanez took the money she earned and came to Miami, Florida, to take more courses in computing at Florida International University. Being a whiz in math, she calculated that if "I could . . . learn all the verbs in the present tense, I could learn 900 verbs instead of 300 in all three tenses. And if I just added 'ed,' I hit 80 percent of the time. That was good enough for me" (Silver, 1994: 149). She earned her degree in computer science, and with $15,000 from her earlier venture, she started her second business, Micro Systems, in 1979. She had chosen to become a computer distributor and was savvy enough to convince the Apple and Altos computer companies to permit her to have an exclusive contract with them in South America for nine months—just long enough for her "baby" to be fully gestated and successfully launched into the computing industry. Ibanez sold this business to Micro America in 1988 for "several million dollars" (Voss, 1992: 68).

Convinced that she would now start to take it easy, Ibanez even gave all of her business suits away to a friend, but her entrepreneurial spirit wouldn't let her rest. Since she had a noncompete clause for South America in the sale, Ibanez started looking for new territories and determined that Africa and the Middle East were just the regions for her enterprise, mainly because of the political, religious, and economic turmoil in third-world countries and because big companies were not yet making noticeable inroads there. Ibanez felt that a small computing business could enter these markets early and get a strong foothold. She approached computer vendors at the annual convention in Las Vegas with her idea. She described their reaction: "I was the joke of the show. . . . They said, 'Sure, go ahead, but there isn't any business in Africa—It's all in Europe' " (Voss, 1992: 68). Again, her instincts were correct. In 1991, she launched her next business, International High Technology, Inc., based in Miami, and within just two years, gross revenues had reached $15 million. "When I went to Africa, I gave educational seminars. I pitched my talk to the technical departments, to the trainers. I gained their trust by answering questions about all products, not just my own. They trusted me because I showed I knew what I was talking about, and I could help them," she explained (68).

Admitting that she has never written a business plan, Ibanez offered to small business owners the following pointers that helped her achieve her success: Use the regular telephone book as a type of database since it contains a wealth of information on potential clients/customers, including products and services. Since big companies are less flexible, go where they don't want to or can't go, including, as she did, third-world countries. Use technology as an extra pair of hands. The marketing department of Ibanez's firm consisted of only two of her thirty employees in 1994, yet they "could send information to customers around the world in five languages through a computerized system that organizes and directs faxes. The around-the-clock system is programmed to send the faxes at the most affordable time. If the call doesn't go through, it reschedules it" (Blackford, 1994: 3). Ibanez also cautioned entrepreneurs to become very knowledgeable about the different cultures where they plan to do business. "In Nigeria . . . it can take 25 times to get a call through. . . . In Peru, they throw the mail away if they are behind" (3).

Ibanez explained that she got her self-confidence from the way her mother responded to her pleadings. "Don't complain," her mother always said. "Fix it yourself. Crying will not do you any good; no one will fix it for you" (Silver, 1994: 149–150). Never forgetting that, Ibanez has been a technological "fixer" for more than twenty years. She strongly espouses that anyone can choose to be a success. "If you can read, you can learn" is one of the important messages Maria Elena Ibanez gives (150).

SOURCES: Blackford, D. (1994), "Use Common Sense in Foreign Markets," *Columbus Dispatch* [Online], October 9: 3 (available: Lexis-Nexis, accessed August 30, 1999); Silver, A. (1994), *Enterprising Women: Lessons from 100 of the Greatest Entrepreneurs of Our Day* (New York: AMACOM); Voss, B. (1992), "Against All Odds: Women in Business," *Sales and Marketing Management* [Online], July: 68 (available: Proquest, accessed July 30, 1998).

AMANDA JONES (1835–1914)

"This is a woman's industry. No man will vote our stock, transact our business, pronounce on women's wages, supervise factories. Give men whatever work is suitable, but keep the governing power." (Amanda

Jones, Founder, United States Women's Pure Food Vacuum Preserving
Company)

Amanda Theodosia Jones was born in East Bloomfield, New York, one of
twelve children of Quakers, Henry Alma, a weaver, and Mary Mott. A
precocious child, she was educated in the public schools of Buffalo, going
on to graduate early from the Aurora Academy normal school. By the age
of fifteen, Amanda Theodosia Jones was a teacher in her hometown of East
Bloomfield. She quickly became a published author, most notably of poetry,
including, *A Prairie Idyl and Other Poems*; *Ulan and Other Poems*; *Atlantis
and Other Poems*; *Flowers and a Weed*; *Rubaiyat of Solomon and Other
Poems*—many inspired by the Civil War. Jones served in editorial capacities
for such periodicals as the *Universe*, the *Bright Side*, and the *Western Rural*
(Willard, 1893). In addition, she wrote music—Civil War songs. This focus
on patriotism had been indelibly inscribed on the hearts of the Jones children by their Quaker parents. "Love of country characterized our parents
equally. Our father read aloud to us the history of the long struggle [re-
ferring to the fall of Richmond] with as much evidence of emotion as he
exhibited . . . in his fervid church meetings. Our mother sang and recited
to us innumerable revolutionary ballads," recalled Jones (Jones, 1980: 14).

Yet, while she was writing her poetry and her music and in spite of ill
health caused by tuberculosis when she was twenty-nine, Jones was con-
ceiving her invention—a mechanism to improve the preservation of foods.
She went to Albany, New York, to seek out the help of Professor L. C.
Cooley, her brother-in-law's cousin. Cooley's first response was to warn
her, "If this one flask should fail . . . I see no more to do." Jones responded,
"If there is nothing more to do, it will not fail, for God has promised me"
(Jones, 1980: 344). By Christmas day they knew that the process worked.
"And so I took away from Albany next day a pretty lot of samples; and it
was evident that I must learn to be a business woman," declared Jones
(346).

By the age of thirty-eight, Amanda Theodosia Jones held six patents. She
was not the first woman to receive a patent—that was Mrs. Samuel Slater,
in 1792—but at the time she was unique in the number of patents she held.
Jones invented lug, flange, and bar designs on what she called "my fruit
jar"—a type of glass container used for canning—a design still in use today.
Another innovation of hers was the vacuum process of food preservation.
This is how she explained the process in the patent filing: "[T]he fluid will
boil vigorously in the vacuum created . . . and thereby the tissues of the
fruit be softened and the air expelled from its cells without subjecting such
fruit to the chemical change called cooking" (Jones, 1873). Jones was also
instrumental in the creation of a device for burning liquid fuel that was
used in manufacturing and for the generation of steam.

Jones was a spiritualist as well, traveling around the country giving se-ances for wealthy clients. She decided to settle in Chicago and became an entrepreneur, even though she had "no mercantile forbears. They fought or preached or farmed, built bridges, manufactured cloth. . . . But now I learned respect for bargainers—little admired before" (Jones, 1980: 295). In 1890, with the help of her friend Mary Allen West, Jones, who was now fifty-five years old, put together $100,000 in capital stock and $1,800 in cash. She started her own company, the "United States Women's Pure Food Vacuum Preserving Company," where rice, tapioca pudding, and luncheon meats were preserved. All officers, employees, and stockholders were to be women. As a result of her efforts, "Jones at one point [was] operating canning plants in Illinois and Wisconsin. . . . [H]er 'Jones exhauster' (Patent Nos. 139,547; 139,580; and 140,247) canning machine was a break-through in food preservation. She was the first to preserve fresh food safely in quantity without first cooking all the flavor out of it" (Vare & Ptacek, 1988: 106).

When she expanded into meat canning, that business made Jones an almost overnight success with sales quickly reaching approximately four hundred cans a day, all that was being produced. She wisely sent a sample to the Thurber-Whyland Company in New York, and they responded by ordering 600,000 cans. Sales were profitable, and within three months, her company had paid all its bills. This exponential success drew the attention of a group of businessmen who initiated a takeover strategy. Sadly, Jones learned that the company was being stolen out from under her because she was being sabotaged by her own female board members. "Men had slith-ered in; their names were on the books" (Jones, 1980: 417). Pressures mounted; eventually she knew she had to sell her business and did so a few years later to a meatpacking company that continued operations until 1923. In spite of these disappointments, Jones went on to invent and patent a liquid fuel burner as well as three other patents in this field.

Jones never married; she was committed to her relationship with Jane Kendall. "We had begun to love each in 1859 . . . we never stopped; and I suppose throughout eternity, we two shall call across as many worlds as Heaven may interpose, and answer each to each. But now . . . we bide our time" (Jones, 1980: 339). In spite of recurring bouts of ill-health, Jones lived to be seventy-eight years of age. Her words summarize her own per-sonal life's journey:

Spirits may clear away the mists before us;—it is our eyes that see! Spirits may point the way; it is our feet that walk! Spirits may scatter thoughts like meadow-flowers; our hands must gather them. Whatever spirits know, they have no right to tell us—they have no *power* to tell us—unless we have the necessary mind and brain development, enabling us to fully apprehend. *Then* we can meet as equals—not before. And so this golden blossom dropped beside me,—so I picked it up. (339)

SOURCES: Jones, A. (1980). *A Psychic Autobiography* (Reprint) (New York: Arno Press); Jones, A. (1873), U.S. Patents 139,580 (Washington, DC: U.S. Patent Office); Vare, E., & Ptacek, G. (1988), *Mothers of Invention: From the Bra to the Bomb: Forgotten Women & Their Unforgettable Ideas* (New York: William Morrow and Company).

CARRIE JONES (1952–)

"I didn't start out with a full investigation of what it took to be successful in this business so it was very stressful. I was learning everything." (Carrie Jones, Co-founder, Sparkle Cleaning Associates, Inc.)

In 1985, Carrie Jones found herself a single parent needing to support two boys. Though she had no funds, she began to think of ways to start a business that wouldn't require any investment. Remembering her mother Muriel Clements Johnson's favorite saying, "Where's there's a will, there's a way," Jones, her sister, and a close friend brainstormed and came up with the idea of a cleaning business. It was doable because they had vacuum cleaners as well as the basic supplies, and Jones wouldn't have to hire a babysitter. The women were lucky enough to receive their first contract from another woman-owned business, Faith Casler Associates in South Natick, Massachusetts, near where Jones lived in Framingham. At the same time, Jones was also completing a master's degree in Media Management from Northeastern University, hoping to land a job in the management of newspapers, where there were few minorities. Now in the cleaning business, she was on a far different path than the original career in journalism she had envisioned for herself.

Jones, born and raised in Framingham, married her high school sweetheart. They had a son, Derron, but the marriage did not work out so she went to the West Coast to earn a degree in journalism from California State University. Once there, she met the man who became her second husband and fathered her son, Qion. Jones worked briefly during this time with both the *Los Angeles Times* and the Central News Wave Publications. She then took up the challenge of becoming the public relations director for the Community Youth Gang Services. When her second marriage failed, she returned to Massachusetts, "with no money I might add!" (Oppedisand, 1998). Luckily, she and her children were able to get into subsidized housing, and she eventually found a man with whom she could have a long-term relationship. Though they had a son, Taylor, together, Jones was determined not to marry again. Since she had experience with media in California, she was hired by the *Middlesex News*, as their first black reporter. Following this job, she was employed by the *Worcester Telegram and Gazette*, but there she began to work so many hours to support her family that she burned out.

"This is when we started Sparkle Cleaning," Jones explained, "and I got the money to go back to school." She went to classes by day, worked as a secretary from time to time to keep afloat financially, and cleaned offices at night for the new enterprise they had started. "Owning your own business gives you a lot of independence," she explained, "and a lot of control. It let me be home with my kids when I needed to be" (Oppedisano, 1998).

That first cleaning contract for Casler led to more business in the same building, but bringing in enough income to make ends meet was not easy. Jones explained, "We funded our company, Sparkle Cleaning, month to month. We'd get money for the work we did and buy the supplies. There was little to live on. It was hard. I was the only one making money in my house. I had to feed my kids." After three years, the strain of finding customers, bringing in sufficient business, and doing the cleaning themselves was too much for her two partners, and they left the business. Jones was faced with the decision of whether to follow suit or go it alone. "It was either relocating elsewhere to get a job using my degree—but I didn't have the money to do that—or stay with the business" (Bunker, 1997: 27).

Jones chose to stay with Sparkle Cleaning and, in time, this proved to be a wise and lucrative choice for her. She conducted a door-to-door effort to find new clients and joined organizations and groups in the community for networking. The task was difficult because, as Jones learned, although cleaning is often thought of as women's work, "commercial cleaning was a man's business that used the good old boys network and [she] was a woman and a minority" (Oppedisano, 1998). Yet, by 1990, her training, determination, hard work, and staff of seven employees resulted in sales passing the $120,000 mark. Jones knew that for her business to grow any larger, she would need a full partner again.

Her friend Denise Rhone shared many of Jones' interests—media, family, and a desire for a lucrative challenge. Rhone had started her career in the film and broadcasting industry as a production assistant, associate producer, and writer with the Education Development Center in Newton, Massachusetts, and with WGBH-TV in Boston. Like Jones, she left to have more time with her three children and went to work as the business manager of her husband's company. However, when Jones offered her the opportunity to become a partner in Sparkle Cleaning Associates in 1990, Rhone accepted. Together, they joined the New England Minority Purchasing Council and received certification by "the City of Boston and the International Executive Housekeepers Association—important qualifications that helped them land contracts to clean medical facilities and government offices" (Bunker, 1997: 27).

In the beginning of their expansion efforts, they faced employee turnover issues since they could not pay well; getting people to show up and to be on time was a regular concern. Jones talked of the lesson she learned: "We put in a training program for employees conveying to them how important they are to the image of the companies we service. If the facility doesn't look clean, there will be a negative impact on business" (Oppedisano, 1998). By 1993, they had over fifty employees, three government contracts, and corporate clients that included Polaroid, New England Telephone, and Harvard University. Sparkle Cleaning sales passed the million-dollar mark.

"Denise and I have different strengths," Jones emphasized. "She is great in operations management, and I'm good at administration, marketing, and networking. We also have a rule—we can argue, debate, disagree, and be angry at one another, but once we've left for the day and come back the next day, we have to move on because you can't run a business if you're not talking to one another. You get twenty-four hours to get over it!" Their commitment to each other and the business continued to pay off. They received the Vendor of the Year Award from the New England Minority Purchasing Council in 1990. Then, in 1993, they were named the Small Business Persons of the Year by the United States Small Business Administration. By 1998, the Sparkle Cleaning company had 160 employees, was operating in four neighboring states, and sales had passed the $3 million mark. Jones credits some fundamental strategies. "We listen to our clients. Supervisors visit them on a regular basis to get feedback. We also can give higher wages to our employees now that we're bigger which has helped cut down on turnover," she pointed out. "Our philosophy is that it's cheaper to pay better than to have to hire, train, and start all over again with new employees."

When asked if her sons wanted to follow her in the cleaning business, Jones laughed, recalling that they worked with her during their youth and knew how to strip and wax floors by the time they were twelve. "My oldest son wants nothing to do with the business. He's paid his dues. My middle son is in college, and the youngest says he wants to own his own business like I do," but not necessarily the cleaning business. "They hate cleaning like I do," she added. As for corporate expansion plans in the future, Jones expressed hesitation, since "both partners have families. We want to go home at five o'clock and be home on weekends. I'm happy if I can send my kids to college and have my own comfortable home." A recent joyful event was celebrated by the Jones family. On July 3, 1999, Carrie Jones married Tony Johnson, and her family of four happily expanded to seven.

SOURCES: Bunker, P. (1997), "Sparkle Cleaning Cleans Up on Contracts," *Boston Herald* (available: Lexis-Nexis, accessed October 25, 1998); Oppedisano, J. (1998), interview with Carrie Jones, July 22, in Wellesley, Massachusetts; Shao, M. (1993), "Start-up Cleaning Company Doing a Sparkling Business," *Boston Globe* (available: Lexis-Nexis, accessed October 25, 1998).

ELIZABETH KECKLEY (1818–1907)

"With my needle I kept bread in the mouths of seventeen persons for two years and five months [while just a girl]." (Elizabeth Keckley, Dressmaker)

From slave in central Virginia to dressmaker of President Abraham Lincoln's wife—how was this transition possible? Elizabeth "Lizzie" Hobbs was born to Agnes Hobbs, a slave on the plantation of Colonel Burwell, the man who she learned later in life was her father. Her early experiences were similar to the horror stories of other female slaves; she was beaten and raped whenever some white person felt she deserved it; her only son was conceived from a four-year period of sexual abuse by a neighboring plantation owner, Alexander Kirkland. Around 1840 she was sent to live with another family, the Garlands, but without her son, who had to stay on the Burwell plantation. Hobbs' consolation was that at least he was being watched over by her mother. At the death of Colonel Burwell four years later, the three were reunited and moved with the Garlands to St. Louis, Missouri—a move prompted by the desperate financial straits in which the Garland family members found themselves after losing their savings in poor real estate investments and bad loans.

As every resource had to be used, Garland decided to hire out Hobbs' elderly mother as a dressmaker. "The idea was shocking to me. Every gray hair in her old head was dear to me, and I could not bear the thought of her going to work for strangers. . . . I would rather work my fingers to the bone, bend over my sewing till the film of blindness gathered in my eyes" (Keckley, 1988: 44–45). Hobbs begged their owner to permit her to go instead. Garland agreed to substituting Elizabeth for her mother but only on the condition that she bring in enough money to provide for the family. In just a short time, Hobbs was supporting all seventeen members of the household through her sewing skills. During this time also, Lizzie got permission from her owners to marry James Keckley, a man of color who led her to believe he had been freed when this wasn't the case. "Let me speak kindly of his faults," Keckley wrote. "[He was] dissipated and a burden instead of a helpmate" (Garrett, 1993: 314). They separated after eight years.

Lizzie Hobbs Keckley never wavered from her dream. After repeatedly asking her owner to let her know how much it would take for her and her son, George, to purchase their freedom, he finally set the price at $1,200. But no matter how hard she worked, she was not able to put together the total amount. It was the kindness of one of her patrons, Mrs. Le Bourgois, that made achieving the dream possible. Le Bourgois decided to raise the money, but Hobbs would only permit this largesse if it were a loan that she would then repay. The bargain was struck, freedom was purchased, and her fateful journey to becoming dressmaker to the First Lady of the nation began.

As she traveled, Keckley was able to establish dressmaking businesses to support herself and her son. New York, Baltimore, and Washington, DC were among the cities. The nation's capital was where Lizzie Keckley was most successful. She began in two small rooms in the rear of the Walker Lewis boardinghouse. As her skill at making the difficult mantuas—the complicated dress of the day—was greatly valued, according to author Becky Rutberg, Keckley became the most popular dressmaker in the nation's capital. "The bodice of the dress fit snugly through pleats stitched in the back to the waist. . . . The skirt of the mantua draped over a cone-shaped understructure that ended in a hoop made from whalebone or metal. The circumference of the skirt could be as wide as eighteen feet and could require as many as twenty-five yards of material" (Rutberg, 1986: 40)—and all of this was sewn by hand. Because Keckley was an artist with needle and thread, her clientele quickly grew. At the height of her fame, she employed over twenty assistants who were working in the large facility she now rented across from the boardinghouse.

This former slave also was a philanthropist. "If the white people can give festivals to raise funds for the relief of suffering soldiers, why should not the well-to-do colored people go to work to do something for the benefit of the suffering blacks?" she wrote (Keckley, 1988: 113). In just a few weeks, the Contraband Relief Association was organized, forty members joined, and Keckley became its president. She also helped found the Home for Destitute Women and Children.

Keckley became the dressmaker for Mary Todd Lincoln and, on occasion, even groomed the president. The friendship that developed between the First Lady and this woman of color caused much disapproval. A newspaper even depicted them in a cartoon that suggested their relationship encouraged miscegenation. However, Keckley became Mrs. Lincoln's confidante; when the president was assassinated, the only person Mrs. Lincoln wanted to have near her at this sorrowful time besides her sons was Lizzie Keckley. Keckley's deep commitment to Mrs. Lincoln ultimately led to the demise of this woman's reputation, business, and lifestyle.

Mrs. Lincoln was in need of money; with Keckley's help, she attempted to sell some of her belongings, but had only limited success. To help her friend, Keckley decided to do as other freed blacks were doing—write a book about her experiences. She was contracted by Carleton and Company to do so with the help of writer James Redpath. Historians now credit Keckley with providing a very valuable and accurate resource for Lincoln scholars in her *Behind the Scenes, or Thirty Years a Slave and Four Years in the White House*. But there was a terrible backlash for Keckley. Because Keckley publicly disclosed personal information about the First Family Mrs. Lincoln never had anything to do with her again. Keckley's business dried up seemingly overnight, blacks considered her a traitor to the much-loved Lincolns, and she had to leave town to find work.

Keckley's son, a soldier, was killed in the Civil War. He had attended Wilberforce University in Xenia, Ohio, before he entered the military. It was to this school that she returned to accept a teaching position in the Department of Sewing and Domestic Science Arts. After six years she returned to Washington and continued to sew until her eyesight became too poor. Keckley then retired to the very place she had helped to establish, the Home for Destitute Women and Children. Her pension of $12 a month as the mother of a dead Civil War soldier was what she lived on until her death in 1907 at the age of eighty-nine. In her book she wrote, "The labor of a lifetime has brought me nothing in a pecuniary way. I have worked hard, but fortune, fickle dame, has not smiled upon me. . . . Though poor in worldly goods, I am rich in friendships, and friends are a recompense for all the woes of the darkest pages of life" (Keckley, 1988: 330). The notoriety of her memoirs clouded the fact that a former slave, at the age of forty-two, established and ran a very successful dressmaking business in Washington, DC, provided regular employment to women during the tumultuous period that included the Civil War, and gave both her time and money to worthy charities.

SOURCES: Alexander, A. L. (1995), "White House Confidante of Mrs. Lincoln: Elizabeth Hobbs Keckley, Dressmaker," *American Visions*, February/March: 18; Garrett, M. (1993), "Elizabeth Keckley," in Jessie Smith, ed., *Epic Lives: One Hundred Black Women Who Made a Difference* (Detroit, MI: Visible Ink); Keckley, E. (1988), *Behind the Scenes, or Thirty Years a Slave and Four Years in the White House* (New York: Oxford University Press); Rutberg, B. (1986), *Mary Lincoln's Dressmaker: Elizabeth Keckley's Remarkable Rise from Slavery to White House Confidante* (New York: Walker and Company).

SUSAN LANDAU (1944–   )

*"I don't do taxes anymore—except my own, of course. . . . I prefer to
use the right side of my brain. It gives me much more pleasure."* (Susan
Landau, Founder, Susan Landau Designs)

Susan Landau, born in Aruba, was educated through high school in Switzerland and then, in 1964, chose to attend college in California. She earned
both her bachelor of arts degree and a master's in business administration
at UCLA. Her first job was as an accountant, and though she was professional and successful in this field, she felt a creative restlessness that left
her unsettled.

Eventually, she left the business of numbers and became a partner in an
art gallery. When it closed in 1991, Landau found herself in the position
of having to face another career decision. Her choice was to become a
sculptor, inspired by the very artists she had represented. Very soon, she
began studying the craft and the different materials that can be used in
sculpture. Landau found that she wanted to work with wired steel, and
even though "people think of steel as hard-edged and heavy, I like to make
it look like it's flowing, growing, organic. Poetic things happen for me in
steel" (Thornburg, 1995: 26).

Now, very serious about her new creative work, Landau felt she needed
more formal training and began to study welding with a steel fabricator.
"After three years of $55-an-hour sessions, the head welder told me I knew
enough to do it myself" (Thornburg, 1998: 28). Her first break came when
one of her tables was accepted for the Sergio Palazzetti furniture show-
room's Maverick collection. With this visibility and the resulting opportunities, her business, Susan Landau Designs, was now a reality.

That first piece was made of a glass tabletop on three bicycle wheels.
Other designs include her Bamboo Series, inspired by her mother. "My
mother mixed antique Chinese furniture with modern silver and stainless
pieces. . . . I've always loved Asian pieces, especially bamboo" (Thornburg,
1998: 28). Landau has had exhibitions of her work in the Neocon in Chicago, Illinois; the Jacob Javits Center in New York City; La Porte de Ver-
sailles in Paris; the Furniture Fair in Cologne, Germany; and the Seibu
Museum in Tokyo. Her light-box series has included pieces titled "crimson
crystals," "romeo gigli," "flower tendrils," and "holy blue light." She also
has more than thirty pieces in a collection of steel beds, tables, chairs, and

mirrors that include a flower bed, a "hostess walking table," and a "bicycle desk with drawer"—the last two are part of what she has labeled her "wheel series." Landau has also designed kitchenware, including ladles and serving spoons, in addition to sculptured pieces like flower vases and outdoor planters (Susan Landau Designs). Landau's sculptures are clearly both decorative and functional art. As she has described her work: "I love using a man-made process on an inorganic material to create an organic look. . . . It's nature tweaked" (Thornburg, 1998: 28).

SOURCES: Susan Landau Designs. Portfolio. Los Angeles, CA; Thornburg, B. (1995), "Spring Home Design: Steeling Home" [Online], April 23: 26 (available: Proquest, accessed August 30, 1999); Thornburg, B. (1998), "Silver Metalist: An Artist Turns Steel Tubing into Exotic Furnishings" [Online], May 17: 28 (available: Lexis-Nexis, accessed February 2, 1999).

LUCY LANEY (1854–1933)

"Nothing in the present century is more noticeable than the tendency of women to enter every hopeful field of wage-earning and philanthropy, and attempt to reach a place in every intellectual arena. . . . The educated Negro woman, the woman of character and culture, is needed in the schoolroom not only in the kindergarten, and in the primary and secondary school; but she is needed in high school, the academy, and the college. . . . Not alone in the schoolroom can the intelligent woman lend a lifting hand, but as a public lecturer she may give advice, helpful suggestions, and important knowledge that will change a whole community and start its people on its upward way."
(Lucy Laney, Founder, Haines Normal and Industrial Institute)

By the time Lucy Craft Laney was born, her parents, former slaves, had bought their way to freedom. Her father, David, as a slave in a South Carolina family, had become an expert carpenter and been permitted to earn money on the side. Eventually he was able to buy his freedom in the 1830s, moving then to Macon, Georgia. There he met and fell in love with Louisa, a thirteen-year-old slave of the Campbell family. Though he purchased her freedom and they were married, Louisa stayed on in paid service to her former masters. This proved to be invaluable to the Laney children, especially Lucy, since Miss Campbell taught her how to read and write by the time she was four years old.

Lucy was the seventh of the Laneys' ten children; she had four brothers and five sisters. From a very early age, the parental value system of kindness and generosity was clear. In fact, Lucy's father had become one of the first black ordained ministers of the Southern Presbyterian Church. "I have wondered since I have grown and know what responsibility is, how my mother and father ever did it. . . . But we always had enough to eat, we were always comfortable. . . . Pa always said there was enough to share with one more" (McCrorey in Cottingham, 1995: 10).

As a bright, articulate youngster, Lucy, who even became fluent in Latin by the time she was twelve, was able to successfully complete her initial education at a school supported by the Freedman's Bureau and the American Missionary Association. Because of her academic achievements, though only fifteen, she was chosen to attend the newly created Atlanta University in a class that was almost seventy percent male. Lucy completed her degree program and was a member of the first graduating class in 1873. She started teaching in schools in the surrounding area and then moved in 1876 to Augusta, Georgia, where she became one of the first black teachers to be hired by the educational system. After four years, she moved to Savannah planning to continue teaching, but then a particular newspaper story became the catalyst for a new direction to her life. "Laney was apparently inflamed by an article appearing in the *Savannah Daily News* which asserted that black women were not fit to nurse or care for white children. For this Laney 'resolved that day to devote her life to the training and uplift of her people' to prove that black women were as capable of caring for children of any color as were white women" (Kendall in Cottingham, 1995: 17). Her response was to start her own school for girls of color.

"Miss Lucy," as she was called, located available basement space in a Presbyterian Church, where she began a nursery school and day school in 1883. Her philosophy was salvation through education. However, in quick order, she had to leave that location because local white women complained about the noise the children made when they were playing. Fortunately, Laney found a white attorney who was willing to let her use an allegedly "haunted" two-story house he owned if she paid the property taxes. The local people helped her clean up and repair the place, and within the first year, seventy-five students had enrolled. This number almost tripled the following year. With minimal tuition and some fundraising activities, she managed to meet expenses.

The secondary curriculum Laney eventually developed was largely based on that of New England schools, and strict discipline was imposed in the classroom. "High school students were required to take four years of English, four years of Mathematics, and three years of history. More than half of the students took Latin [often taught by Laney herself]; others took French, German, or Greek. Students could also choose from electives in psychology, physics, physiology, chemistry, civics, and sociology" (Cottingham, 1995: 73). The manual training consisted of such programs as chair-caning for the girls and woodworking for the boys. "Each student [was] required to do his [or her] work independently and accurately, thus cultivating the habit of self-reliance, order, and accuracy, which is very important in the formation of character." Laney's excellent educational background and strong religious base were evident throughout the programs offered.

Though she now had her dream fulfilled in an educational institution of her own, life did not go smoothly for this young, single, poor black woman. Not only did Laney have to regularly thwart racism and sexism and use her own savings to help support the school, but she faced natural disasters as well. In 1888, the Savannah River flooded, trapping some of the children inside the building, and there was much damage to the school. Though no students died of the flood, a typhoid epidemic followed. Many in Augusta died. A personal tragedy for Miss Lucy was the loss of Cora Freeman, her assistant and friend. In sorrow, Laney turned her attention to financially shoring up her school with an all-out effort to get financial support from the Presbyterian Church.

With only a one-way ticket, Laney headed to Minneapolis, Minnesota, to speak to the General Assembly of the Presbyterian Church, which was convening. They only paid for her return ticket to Georgia. In fact, they later admitted, "We cannot claim the credit of having the foresight to assign her to the position she is filling so well, for she has simply made the position for herself by her courage, her ability, her self-denial" (Cowen in Cottingham, 1995: 43). However, it was at the church assembly that Laney met the first of a long line of Northern women who would become her backers in the political and financial efforts to follow.

Francina E. H. Haines from Elizabeth, New Jersey, was one of the founders and the president of the Women's Executive Committee of Home Missions. She helped Laney get her school chartered in 1886 and was influential in Laney's school receiving a $10,000 bequest from Thompson Bell because of his sister's interest in supporting women's education. Laney responded by naming her school after Francina—the Haines Normal and Industrial Institute. The first graduating class consisted of only five women, but the total enrollment had escalated to more than four hundred. In the following year, 1889, another $10,000 gift was given by a Mrs. Marshall, who had also been present at the Presbyterian Church assembly. In 1906, a gift of $15,000 was received from a Mrs. McGregor; and, in 1924, a $10,000 bequest from a Mrs. Wheeler. Laney pointed out that the way women could help lift the burdens of slavery was through "true culture and character, linked with that most substantial coupler, cash" (Cottingham, 1995: 67). These monies were used largely for construction of buildings as the student body and program grew. By 1931, more than 700 students were enrolled.

Lucy Laney was also responsible for other important endeavors. She initiated a choral group for fundraising, a technique later adopted by an early student of hers, Mary McCleod Bethune, who also believed in educating the head, the heart, and the hands. Miss Lucy established one of the first kindergartens for children in Augusta in 1890. She helped establish the Lamar Hospital, and she brought in a white Canadian nurse, Virginia Bowden, to train black nurses (Cottingham, 1995: 50). She was fond of saying, "I want to wear out, not rust out." Lucy Craft Laney lived a long, outstanding life, finally "wearing out" near her eightieth year. Miss Lucy was a woman of much integrity, self-confidence, perseverance, courage, and dedication—clear in her message for all of us: "I am as good as anybody else; God had no different dirt to make me out of than that used in making the first lady of the land" (in Cottingham, 1995: 82).

SOURCES: Cottingham, B., ed. (1995), "The Burden of the Educated Colored Woman: Lucy Laney and the Haines Institute, 1886–1933," unpublished Master's thesis, College of Arts and Sciences, Georgia State University; Lucy Craft Laney 1854–1933, *http://www.gawomen.org/honorees/long/laneyl_long.htm.*

ANN LEE (1736–1784)

"I know fresh scenes of trial and bitter persecutions await me in America, still my obedience to the call gives me power to comply." (Ann Lee, Founder of the Shakers)

It was inevitable that Ann Lee would be persecuted for her religious beliefs because they were contrary to those preached in the established Christian Church of the late 1700s in England, especially when she began preaching and gaining followers who, like herself, were expected to believe in Christ, to confess their sins, to be celibate, to work hard, and to be self-sufficient. Additionally, in spite of the prevailing norms of the time, their membership was open to whites *and* people of color. For being a woman of such disobedience to the religious norms of her time in England, she was openly derided. According to biographer Nardi Reeder Campion, "Once she was chased by an angry mob that knocked her down with clubs, kicked and reviled her. [A]nother time she escaped her pursuers by lying all night on the ice of a frozen pond. In another crisis, a friendly neighbor saved her from harm by hiding her beneath a pile of wool in an attic" (Campion, 1976: 35–36). As if this weren't enough humiliation and pain, Lee was beaten by one of her own brothers, who did not approve of her public behavior; she also was imprisoned in a rat-infested madhouse. Ann Lee and her small band of followers risked their lives on a condemned cargo ship and survived seventy-nine days at sea to acquire the right to worship as they chose. They first settled in the area now known as Niskayuna, New York, and established the United Society of Believers in Christ's Second Appearing, more commonly known as the Shakers because of their physical movements during worship.

Religious persecution in England had spurred Ann Lee and eight of her followers to come to America in 1774. Lee's persecution didn't end when she landed in America, "because everything she stood for was dangerous: the rejection of creeds, liturgies, sacraments, and priesthood; the refusal to take oaths or bear arms; promotion of communal living and common ownership of property; the insistence on . . . the fact that the gifts of preaching, teaching, and prophecy were available to women as well as to men . . . most threatening of all was her open animosity toward marriage (Campion, 1976: 92). Perhaps her distaste for sexual relations can be somewhat understood by the fact that Lee had borne four children one after the other; three died as babies, the fourth at age six.

Lee's American persecutors were no better than the English. To test their theory that she *had* to be a man in disguise, they tore her clothes and beat her across the chest—once in front of a judge in a court of law, and he didn't object. Her followers, however, believed in Lee, seeing her to be the "Second Appearing of Christ in female form" (Proctor-Smith, 1991: 3). They willingly participated in a communal form of life with strictly delineated roles for women and men. Women (sisters/deaconesses) were to take care of the household tasks, to teach the children, and to produce what was needed for sale so that the community could purchase what was needed including land. The men (brothers/deacons) handled the carpentry, the finances, and the property.

To maintain their independence, the Shakers produced a number of products, which were sold to the surrounding communities: baked beans; maple syrup and maple sugar cakes; honey from their beehives; butter, cheese and poultry; fruits from their orchards; vegetables, their first principal source of revenue from their fields; and cloth. They started making their world-famous furniture around 1780. Their stated ideals were: "Equality of the Sexes, in all departments of life. Equality in Labor, all working for each, and each for all. Equality in Property . . . Freedom of Speech, Toleration in Thought and Religion . . . Abolition of Slavery . . . Temperance in all things. Justice and Kindness to all living beings. Practical Benevolence . . . True Democracy" (Campion, 1976: 87).

The community Lee started grew eventually to over 6,000 members in twenty units with communal ownership of over 100,000 acres of land in the states of New York, Connecticut, Indiana, Kentucky, Maine, Massachusetts, New Hampshire, and Ohio. Although today the Shakers have only a few remaining members, their impact is still felt worldwide. The Shakers were known not only for their canned applesauce, pies, medicines, and cookbooks but also for their practical inventions, creating tools that would make them more efficient and effective. These included the apple corer, pea-splitter, cheese press, double rolling pin, revolving oven, splint, pill-making machine, wheelchair, metal pen nib, musical-staff pen, beeswax cakes for keeping needles rust free and strengthening thread, iron tailor's sheers, and a spiked wheel for planting (Lim, 1996). The Shakers are still world-renowned for their architecture, furniture, baskets, and over 8,000 songs. This was all started by "a woman rather below the common stature of women; thick set, but straight and other wise well proportioned and regular in form and features. Her complexion was light and fair, and her eyes were blue, but keen and penetrating. Her manners were plain, simple and easy; yet she possessed a certain dignity of appearance that inspired confidence and commanded respect" (Green & Wells, 1848). Though only forty-eight when she died, Ann Lee left an enormous legacy in her story of what a woman of courage can achieve.

SOURCES: Andrews, E. (1953), *The People Called Shakers: A Search for the Perfect Society* (New York: Dover); Campion, N. (1976), *Ann the Word: The Life of Mother Ann Lee, Founder of the Shakers* (Boston, MA: Little, Brown, and Company); Ellwood, R., & Partin, H. (1988), *Religious and Spiritual Groups in Modern America* (Englewood Cliffs, NJ: Prentice-Hall); Ferguson, M. (1995), *Women in Religion* (Englewood Cliffs, NJ: Prentice-Hall); Green, C., & Wells, S. (1848), *A Summary View of the Millennial Church, or United Society of Believers (Commonly Called Shakers) Comprising the Rise, Progress and Practical Order of the Society; Together with the General Principles of Their Faith and Testimony* (Albany, NY: Packard & Van Benthuysen); Hudson, W., & Corrigan, J. (1992), *Religion in America: An Historical Account of the Development of American Religious Life* (New York: Macmillan); Lim, S. (1996), Shaker Cooking, *http://www.ctdnet.acns. nwu.edu/sku/shaker/* (accessed February 8, 1997); Loengard, J. (1978), "The Shakers," in M. Edey & C. Sullivan, eds., *Great Photographic Essays from Life*, 257–267 (Boston, MA: New York Graphic Society); Procter-Smith, M. (1991), *Shakerism and Feminism: Reflections on Women's Religion and the Early Shakers* (Old Chatham, NY: Shaker Museum and Library); Tierney, H., ed., (1991), *Women's Studies Encyclopedia, Volume III: History, Philosophy, and Religion* (Westport, CT: Greenwood Press).

JULIETTE LOW (1860–1927)

"Only thyself, thyself can harm,
Forget it not—and full of peace.

Ignore the noise and world's alarm.
And wait till storm and tumult cease."
(Juliette Low, Founder, Girl Scouts of the U.S.A.)

Juliette Gordon, of Savannah, GA, was born into privilege and wealth, the second of six children of William Gordon, a Southern cotton broker, and Nellie Kinzie Gordon, a Yankee from the famous Chicago, Illinois, Kinzie family. Educated in private boarding schools, Juliette Gordon was bright, spunky, direct, artistic, and religiously grounded in the Bible. She had a facility with languages, which proved quite useful in her later world travels, and she loved sports like swimming, boating, and riding. However, at age twenty-five, Juliette Gordon made a critical error in judgment. She pressured her medical doctor to use an experimental treatment, nitrate of silver, for an ear infection. The consequence was not only intense pain but almost complete deafness in that ear. This incident didn't stop her from becoming Mrs. Willy Low in December of the same year, 1885, in a fairy-tale wedding ceremony—yet one that ended in a serious physical outcome for the bride. A kernel of rice thrown at the couple for good luck lodged in her healthy ear; it became inflamed, and she became totally deaf from the infection.

The Lows became part of the international jet set since he had residences in England and the United States. The fact that Juliette Gordon Low had married a wealthy playboy became quickly apparent to her. She lamented, "I see so little of Billow [his nickname] I feel there is no human affection for me except in the family" (Shultz & Lawrence, 1988: 233). By 1901 he was flagrantly flaunting his mistress, a widow named Mrs. Bateman, and he and Juliette began a long divorce struggle. In complete public humiliation of his wife who, by all accounts, simply loved him and did him no harm, he shut off her access to the family homes, limited her income, and named his mistress as his primary heir. Because of his heavy alcohol consumption, he died in 1905, and then the legal battles between Bateman and Low began over the will. Low was thrown into relative poverty until 1906, when a settlement was reached awarding her the equivalent of half a million dollars, she later used a large portion of this inheritance to fund the Girl Scouts. However, for seven years after the will was settled, she "shuttled aimlessly between Savannah, England and Scotland [the homeland of her mother's ancestors] feeling that she had wasted her best years" (Lyon, 1981: 103).

Then Low bought one of the early automobiles, learned how to drive, went to Europe to study sculpting, and then met a brother and sister in England who would change her life's direction. General Sir Robert Baden-Powell had started the Boy Scouts. Subsequently, his sister, Agnes, started the Girl Guides in response to the six thousand requests from young girls to be considered for the Boy Scouts, impossible at that time since "the first law was that they must not even speak to a Boy Scout if they saw him in uniform" (Schultz & Lawrence, 1988: 299). Such an overwhelming response by girls led Juliette Low to think about their situation in her ancestral Scotland, where poverty forced young children into cities to try to make a living. Since raising sheep was quite common in this land, Low got the idea to teach the girls how to card and spin wool, but first she had to learn the skill herself. Not only was she successful at training the girls in this work, but she also found a market for their output in London. She then started two Girl Guide troops in this city and decided to start a Girl Guides group back in her home town of Savannah, Georgia.

With her strong determination and energy, the transition from Girl Guides to Girl Scouts and the growth of national participation occurred rapidly, even though Low was contradicting the widely accepted social norms for girls and women of the day. Ironically, Low may have been so successful precisely because of this timing, since women were beginning to speak out for their rights and opportunities. As her niece Daisy, the first registered Girl Scout, recalled: "[We changed] into our enormous pleated gymnasium bloomers and wearing overcoats which reached nearly to our ankles, we would go to the lot across the street to play basketball. But before doffing our coats, we pulled together the huge canvas curtains, strung on wires . . . to shield our bloomered legs from the gaze of passers-by on the street" (Lawrence, October 1938: 32). Low started with eighteen girls and within a year had 565; the next year, the number was 1,000. America's participation in World War I gave the Girl Scouts even more visibility since the troops were volunteering their time wherever needed—from providing services in hospitals to selling bonds to growing vegetables. At least by 1920, there is a clear commitment to allow all girls to participate, regardless of color or ability. In fact, as early as 1917, there was a troop in New York City for physically disabled girls and, by 1921, a troop for Onondaga Indian girls.

Low died in 1927 from cancer at the age of sixty-seven. She had traveled around the country and around the world spreading the importance of the Girl Scouts and their credo, which includes the following: "A Girl Scout's honor is to be trusted . . . [her] duty is to be useful and to help others. (She should do at least one good turn to somebody every day); . . . a Girl Scout is a friend to all, and a sister to every other Girl Scout no matter to what social class she may belong—" (Schultz & Lawrence, 1988: 323–324). In just fifteen years under Low's leadership, membership had exceeded 100,000.

As the century progressed, the Girl Scouts had many campaigns. Among them were the National Youth Conference on Natural Beauty and Eco-Action, on environmental education and improvement. Current projects are in such areas as finance, computers, and other technologies. Author Nancy Lyon pointed out that "Juliette Low wanted young women to think big—to feel entitled to an education, career, *and* family if they wanted. Her conviction that girls should think of themselves as capable of becoming doctors, architects or pilots, able to survive in the wild . . . gave to many the beginnings of self-determination" (Lyon, 1981: 101). By the year 2000, the Girls Scouts of the U.S.A. was the largest organization for girls in the world with a membership of almost three million (one out of nine girls) in more than 220,000 troops, including those members who are U.S. citizens living abroad in about eighty countries. Estimates suggest that in the decades since this movement was begun by Juliette Gordon Low, over fifty million girls and women have been positively influenced by participation.

SOURCES: Girl Scouts of the U.S.A., *http://www.girlscouts.org* (accessed May 3, 1999); Lawrence, D. (1938), "Juliette Low Shortly After Her Marriage," *The American Girl*, October: 4–7, 32+; Lawrence, D. (1938), "Juliette Low's School Days," *The American Girl*, November: 8–11, 33+; Lawrence, D. (1938), "Juliette Low Grown-Up," *The American Girl*, December: 11–15, 39+; Lyon, N. (1981), "Juliette Low: The Eccentric Who Founded the Girl Scouts," *Ms.*, November: 101–105; Rhodes, D. (1986), "Juliette Low, Girl Scouts Founder, Led Rich Life," *Augusta Chronicle-Herald*, January 19; Schultz, G., & Lawrence, D. (1988), *Lady from Savannah: The Life of Juliette Low* (New York: Girl Scouts of the U.S.A.); Williams, L. (1996), *A Bridge to the Future: The History of Diversity in Girl Scouting* (New York: Girl Scouts of the U.S.A.).

REBECCA LUKENS (1794–1854)

"There was difficulty and danger on every side. Now I look back and wonder at my daring. I had built a very superior mill, though a plain one, and our character for making boiler plate stood first in the market, hence we had as much business as we could do." (Rebecca Lukens, CEO, Brandywine Mill and Lukens Steel)

At age thirty-one, Rebecca Pennock Lukens, who had recently lost her beloved father and a young son, found herself hurled into grief once more—now a widow—with four small children at her feet and pregnant with another. "Necessity is a stern mistress; and my every want gave me courage," she wrote (Miniter, 1997: 45). In spite of overwhelming financial, physical, and social constraints, she became the first woman in the history of the United States to run a major heavy industrial business—the oldest continuously operating steel mill in the country—one that eventually became "a Fortune 500 company with 3,600 employees and over $1 billion in sales" (45). Her story should be legend.

Rebecca Pennock was born in 1794, the oldest of the surviving children of a Pennsylvania couple, Isaac and Martha Pennock. Though the family members were Quakers, they practiced their religion in the less restrictive mode known as "Gay Friends." Rebecca's mother ruled over her daughter in typical Victorian fashion and trained her in the traditionally expected female skills of cooking, sewing, and spinning. However, her father would permit his daughter to ride horses and occasionally go with him to his very successful Federal Slitting Mill and to his later acquisition, the Brandywine Mill. In her early teens, Rebecca was sent to Wilmington, Delaware, to attend the Hilles Boarding School for Young Ladies. Here she discovered her love for chemistry and for reading. "She sometimes read secretly in her room until dawn" (Nulty, 1994: 118).

Fate took over through an illness that afflicted her father. His attending physician was Dr. Charles Lukens. Rebecca and Charles fell in love and were married in 1813. Her husband made the critical career decision to leave his medical practice to join Rebecca's father in the milling business. In just a few years, he leased the Brandywine Mill in Coatesville, Pennsylvania from his father-in-law so that he could put his own ideas into action. Charles led the transition to production of charcoal iron boilerplates from copper just as the steam engine was making its grand entrance on the transportation front. In fact, his was the first plant to roll boilerplate. Unfortunately, Charles did not remain focused and, instead, made too many changes in the business too quickly. He failed to attend to the necessary regular maintenance of the mill, leaving it in a state of disrepair and bringing the company to the brink of financial ruin and in disrepair. Then, suddenly, in 1825, Charles Lukens died. On his deathbed, he had extracted an unusual promise from his wife, already vastly overwhelmed and in the difficult position of being pregnant again, that she would take over the company.

Unfortunately, there was no last will and testament. When Rebecca Lukens tried to keep her promise, her own embittered, widowed mother filed a lawsuit to try to stop her daughter from transgressing the female norms of the times. The mill was in serious debt, in decrepit condition, and it "depended entirely on the unpredictable Brandywine River for water power, which meant that she had to shut the mill down when the river ran dry" (Steck, 1994: 48). But even under these circumstances, Lukens did not lay off her employees. She hired her brother-in-law, Solomon Lukens, to be operations manager, and she focused her attention on stabilizing her company. Instead of firing workers, she kept them busy on maintenance jobs so that the mill would remain in top condition and the employees could keep food on their families' tables—even if it meant paying them only with produce or dairy products from her farm (Miniter, 1997). "In the meantime, a number of her competitors began to build mills immediately upstream, siphoning off water power before it reached her location. And when she repaired her dam, one competitor even sued her for raising the water level" (Steck, 1994: 48). In spite of these challenges, in less than a decade, Lukens had rebuilt the mill, paid off the old debts, and had a very successful iron plate production business. "She is remembered for listening to customer needs, embracing new technology, reinvesting in her company in good times and bad, pursuing specialty markets, [and] maintaining profitability" (Yafie, 1995: 42).

Some might argue, however, that Lukens is not an entrepreneur because she didn't start the business—her father did—so we should note that while she was bringing the mill out of the ashes and building it into one of the premier steel manufacturing companies of the world, she also "opened a store, a warehouse, and a freight agency at the Coatesville depot, providing access to Philadelphia and Pittsburgh" (Yafie, 1995: 42). By the late 1840s, Lukens began to transition her enterprises over to her sons-in-law. She died in 1854, and the company was renamed in her honor as a tribute to this industrial giant. In 1998, Lukens, Inc. was merged with the Bethlehem Steel Corporation, and Rebecca Lukens had been inducted into *Fortune* magazine's "National Business Hall of Fame." As a young girl, she had been proud that she was "a favorite of my teachers and at the head of all my classes" (Steck, 1994: 43). Rebecca Lukens' life accomplishments demonstrate that she retained that lofty position—ahead of the class.

SOURCES: Earle, N. (1994), "O Pioneer. A Mother of Six Made a Killing in the Boilerplate Trade," *Wall Street Journal* [Online], January 6: B1 (available: Proquest, accessed July 28, 1999); Miniter, B. (1997), "Women in Business: The Prequel," *The American Enterprise* [Online], July/August: 45 (available: Proquest, accessed July 28, 1999); Nulty, P. (1994), "The National Business Hall of Fame," *Fortune* [Online], April 4: 118 (available: Proquest, accessed July 28, 1999); Steck, R. (1994), "Woman of Steel," *D&B Reports* 43 [Online], March/April: 48 (available: Proquest, accessed July 28, 1999); Whitmyre, R. (1993), "America's First Woman Industrialist Honored: January 6 Proclaimed Rebecca Lukens Day," *PR Newswire* [Online], December 29 (available: Lexis-Nexis, accessed July 28, 1999); Yafie, R. (1995), "R. W. Van Sant: Stepping Up to the Plate," *Journal of Business Strategy* [Online], September/October: 42 (available: Lexis-Nexis, accessed July 28, 1999).

MARIA MARTINEZ (1881–1980)

"Nicolasa, Martina, and my grandmother—they didn't teach. Nobody teaches. But in 1932 much later, someone took me to the government Indian school in Santa Fe and told me to teach. I said, no, I come and I work, and they can watch." (Maria Martinez, Mother of the Black Pottery industry of the San Ildefonso Pueblo)

The historical communal nature of the American Indian culture would not appear to be the kind of climate that would stimulate entrepreneurial endeavors—especially for female members of a tribe at the turn of the twentieth century. But this was exactly the case when an opportunity was presented to a young married potter, Maria Montoya Martinez. In 1907 Dr. Edgar Lee Hewitt, an archeologist working at an excavation on the Pajarito Plateau in New Mexico, found black shards from Tewa pottery. He wanted to find someone who could recreate these forms and designs. Martinez was recommended to him "as the one who could make the thinnest, roundest pots in the least time" (Peterson, 1989: 89; all direct quotes are from this source unless otherwise cited). She accepted the challenge and experimented until she was able, in effect, to clone the original from the piece that he gave her, and, with the help of her husband, turn the red clay pots to shiny black. At first she thought her work was not good and hid these efforts on a back shelf. As fate would have it, the researchers were visiting; when they spotted her pots, they were thrilled. This began a seventy-year pottery business "led" by Maria Montoya Martinez; there have now been five generations of such crafters in her family.

The process of making these artistic yet practical products was and is labor intensive. The artisans dug their own clay from the barren desert; they did not use potters' wheels, but hand-coiled the clay; the firing was done with sticks. Susan Peterson, a potter and educator who developed a television film series, "Wheels, Kilns, and Clay" explained the process: "The fire was covered with ash so that the flame did not heat and smoke was made. It was the fact that there was not access of much air that caused the pots to become black. It rather depended on the will of the wind and the will of the fire" (15). She continued, "To make thin-walled pots of perfect symmetry by coiling alone is a major accomplishment. The black-on-black ware, as it was eventually called, was made by painting designs in a refractory clay slip after the pot was polished and then smothering the fire with manure to carbonize the clay black" (98). Martinez used a stone for burnishing the hand-coiled pots; her husband painted them. Her reputation as a skilled artisan began to spread; even the rich and famous such as John D. Rockefeller came to the pueblo and purchased her works.

Since Indian pottery is created as a joint project for the most part, the other 475 members of the San Ildefonso Pueblo also benefited from Martinez's fame. She would often facilitate the sale of pots made by other women of the tribe because her objective was not to make a lot of money but to have a means of survival for her family and tribal members. She also carried on the Indian tradition of passing the pottery-making craft on to others as she had first been taught by her aunt.

In the isolation of pueblo life, for all who are part of it [observation-instruction is continuous]. It is real direct learning—learning by imitation, from demonstrations, by watching. . . . Indian daily life is organized so that it sets up sequences of repetitions that become frameworks for a subtle educative process. In this way, Maria and Julian continuously showed others in the pueblo their method of making black pottery, so that those others could make it for themselves and involve their own family members. (83)

Along with making her pottery, Martinez also ran a grocery store, which today is still open on the grounds of the pueblo. In this enterprise she helped not only her own people but the local Spaniards as well. "I used to have a little grocery store to feed the people," Martinez explained. "The Spanish people say I was good to them. They owe me money or something, I just forget it. I say I gave it to God" (85).

Maria Martinez was internationally recognized and rewarded. She received the Palmes Academique from France for her worldwide contributions to art and crafts, the Craftsmanship Medal of the American Institute of Architects, and two honorary doctorates. She was a welcome guest at the White House during both the Roosevelt and the Johnson administrations; the Rockefellers were early purchasers of her art. " 'For the big polychrome pots we used to make,' says Maria, putting her hand out flat, three feet above the floor, 'if I was lucky I got maybe $10.00. Pots like the one [to carry] on your head maybe $1.50, and they were all decorated. Now that I'm not making pottery like that, they cost a whole lot!' " (97). In fact, at a 1979 Smithsonian Institution exhibition of her work, Martinez's pottery already was selling for between $1,500 and $15,000. Maria Montoya Martinez died the following year, when she was over ninety years old.

Dr. Francis Harlow, who has researched American Indian pottery for more than thirty years and written many books on the subject, credits Maria and Julian Martinez with leading a rebirth in artistic pottery that revitalized the craft at villages throughout the Southwest. Martinez's personal risk in this venture was the challenge of whether or not she could recreate unique indigenous pottery under the difficult desert conditions where she lived. Her success in the early years of the twentieth century started a venture that continues today and can be enjoyed by visitors to the San Ildefonso Pueblo or to museums throughout the world. Maria Montoya Martinez could not have dreamed of the adventures she would experience as a result of her unique skills.

SOURCE: Peterson, S. (1989), *The Living Tradition of Maria Martinez* (New York: Kodansha America, Inc.).

SARA MILLER McCUNE (1941–)

"No one in my family would have dared to say I couldn't do some-thing—either because of my grandmother's influence or just because I was who I was . . . like my grandmother—tough and determined, shrewd and hardworking." (Sara Miller McCune, Founder, Sage Publications)

Sara Miller was a precocious child, born in New York City, the older of Rose and Nathan Miller's two children. By the time she was four she was reading, and by sixteen Miller had graduated from high school. As a student at Queen's College, she worked on the newspaper and yearbook staffs. During these late teen years, Miller's growing professional ability showed in the fundraising speeches she gave in the United States and Canada for her B'nai B'rith youth organization. "I have always been self-confident so that helped" (McCune, 1999).

After graduating from college in 1961 with a degree in political science, Miller went to work for Macmillan and Pergamon Press, Ltd. But after a few years, she had to face the reality of those times—that opportunities for women in publishing were limited. George McCune, a Macmillan executive, suggested she start her own company. This was coupled with the idea of initiating a social science journal, which came from her friend Professor Marilyn Gittell. "While I loved publishing, I found that I was very impatient with bureaucracy so that kind of pushed me into going out on my own," she explained (McCune, 1999).

Her decision to become a publisher at the young age of twenty-four took personal fortitude and an unwavering resolve, particularly since she had very limited capital. Yet, with only $500 of start-up money, Miller took the plunge and founded Sage Publications in September of 1965. "My dad and his three brothers all had their own business so all the time I was growing up, I was in the middle of a family where it seemed pretty normal to have a business of your own" (McCune, 1999). The title of her company, Sage, was a play on initials and words—a merging of the first two letters of Miller's first name and of the first name of her mentor and friend George McCune, with the actual word referring to wisdom.

Since Miller was the sole employee, she not only did all the editing and proofreading but also took consulting jobs on the side to support herself and her new company. By the end of 1965, however, she had acquired a second journal, the *American Behavioral Scientist*, and the company had sales of $12,000; within two years that number had increased eightfold. "I made lots of lists. And I worked 80 to 100 hours per week for quite a few years," she pointed out (McCune, 1999). In the fall of 1966, Miller married George McCune. He became a partner in the business, and she became stepmother to his four children. The struggle of being a working parent was difficult for Miller McCune: "I don't think it's possible to strike a balance. . . . I think all you can do is juggle and run very hard" (Lewis, 1996: 286).

Although the focus of the original publication was in the social sciences, Miller McCune branched out into other fields such as business, political science, religious studies, operations research, and engineering. The product mix included journals, textbooks, reference works, and eventually videos and electronic media. In 1971 the company began its international expansion by going into London, England. A decade later Sage Publications went into New Delhi, India, and subsequently into many other different countries. "The year I was on the road as Editorial Director and added up my days away from home [I] realized the total was 40% of the year . . . something had to give! I was married, and even though my husband and I were working together, I missed seeing him at home. I didn't sleep well on the road" (McCune, 1999). In addition, there were still cultural and gender-related issues, especially in foreign countries with which Miller McCune had to deal. "It is still hard to be taken seriously as a business woman in Japan, and I am not alone in feeling this way," she pointed out recently (McCune, 1999).

Initially, Miller McCune was the president and publisher of the company; however, in 1984 she became the chairperson, with her husband serving as president until his death in 1990, when she resumed that title. Before George's death, the couple founded the McCune Foundation to benefit higher education; Miller McCune serves as president. As of 1999 her publishing company had over 1,400 book titles with more than two hundred journals and offices on three continents. In thinking back over her accomplishments, Sara Miller McCune commented that what she considers a great achievement might be overlooked by some for its simplicity: "holding the first of anything that comes off the press. I love the smell of a book and the feel of a new journal. I love browsing in something new with the Sage imprint on it" (Lewis, 1996: 290).

SOURCES: Lewis, C. (1996), in N. Signorielli, ed., *Women in Communication: A Biographical Sourcebook* (Westport, CT: Greenwood Press); McCune, S. (1999), *http://www.independentmeans.com/ask/ask mccune.html* (accessed April 16); Sage Publications, Inc. (1998), *http://www.sagepub.com* (accessed February 7).

CARRIE McINDOE (1960–   )

"There's not much margin for error. People are waiting for me to fail so I need to work harder than the man next door." (Carrie McIndoe, Founder, Strategic Capital Resources, Inc.)

Though Carrie McIndoe was born in Mount Lebanon, Pennsylvania, she spent much of her early years relocating with her family to Kentucky, Illinois, and New Jersey. She survived this upheaval because of her father. "He was my role model. He taught me to be humble, ethical, and fair. I only wish that I had spent more time with him in these last few years before he died," she added sadly (Oppedisano, 1998). The values McIndoe learned at home were also reinforced through her participation in Girl Scouts, which she loved. It was in this organization, too, that she realized what a competitive nature she had. "I wanted to be the number one cookie salesperson. I took it on like a vengeance . . . me and my little red wagon . . . even brought my younger brother along, too. I saved my logs from the year before so that I had a base of customers and achieved my goal."

McIndoe worked all through high school and college. She attended Boston University (BU) part time while she worked for Kidder Peabody as a sales assistant. She graduated from BU with a bachelor's degree in business administration in 1986. Though McIndoe earned her Series 7 General Securities License and the Series 63 State Laws License, she soon discovered that a hidden quota was holding women back in the investment banking field during the 1980s. She continued working with companies such as Winthrop Securities Company, the Beacon Hill Capital Corporation, and the Harborside Capital Corporation but found herself becoming more and more restless with what she called the three evils of the male-dominated securities business—ego, power, and greed. "There was no room for emotion," she explained. "They were in and out for the kill."

In 1990, with credit-card funding, something that she doesn't recommend to others, McIndoe started her own company, Strategic Capital Resources, Inc. (SCR), in the heart of Boston's financial district. At the time, she had been involved in a long-term personal relationship with a man who couldn't understand why she wasn't holding a "paycheck" job. "He wouldn't accept me for who I was. He made me feel stupid because I wasn't doing things the 'normal' way." The relationship ended; McIndoe had learned that surrounding herself with positive people was critical to her personal and professional success.

Her company specializes in analyzing business plans, forming strategic alliances, performing due diligence, and assisting in the early stage development of companies, helping them obtain needed capital. Besides meeting with clients, McIndoe and her associates make three types of calls each day: new prospect calls, follow-up calls, and closing calls. She has learned that "most people say 'no' three times before they say 'yes.' " SCR growth has been steady and diverse with clients in the communications, entertainment, medical devices, biotechnology, and retail industries. Among these are Boston Duck Tours, Boston Chicken franchisees (now Boston Market), Blockbuster Videos, SJR Food Technologies, Immunetics, and the Marathon Technologies Corporation. "What we look for," explained McIndoe, "is a solid management team, a well-developed business plan, coupled with honesty and integrity."

For SCR services, McIndoe charges a small consulting fee and usually takes stock in the new company. "In essence, I'm sometimes waiting three, five, seven years to get paid," she added. She meets with eight to ten potential clients a year, but only adds one or two to those with whom she already works. One of her most interesting projects was for a gene-splicing, biotechnology firm that was researching how polar fish don't freeze and how this new knowledge could be applied to humans. "I love what I do!" McIndoe smilingly exclaimed.

With the goal of helping entrepreneurs write a business plan that would attract funding from private investors, McIndoe and her associates have developed a booklet titled *The Perfect Shell*. Her emphasis is on encouraging the pursuit of excellence, then, she pointed out, "money and success will follow."

McIndoe's personal and religious belief is that we must give back to the system; as she states it: "Remember the food chain!" She walks the talk. McIndoe is an active alumna of Boston University, has worked with such community efforts as Easter Seals, Trinity Church's Prison Ministry, Special Olympics, and the Starlight Foundation. Since McIndoe wishes she had asked for help with her business ideas sooner and that she had found a female mentor, she spends time mentoring college students and women in the industry. Some of the advice she shares with them includes "keeping balance. [She plays piano, flute, collects antiques, and keeps scrapbooks.] Write thank you notes; they have a bigger impact than most believe! Sign and date everything you do; documentation is critical. Find something good about each day, and laugh often!"

SOURCES: Oppedisano, J. (1998), interview of Carrie McIndoe, on February 23, in Saratoga Springs, New York; Strategic Capital Resources (1999), *http://Strategic-Capital.com*.

AIMEE SEMPLE McPHERSON (1890–1944)

"Who ever heard of a woman without earthly backing . . . undertaking the raising of funds and the erection of such a building?" (Aimee Semple McPherson, Founder of the International Church of the Foursquare Gospel)

As the year 2000 approached, leaders of the International Church of the Foursquare Gospel—the organization founded by Aimee Semple McPherson in 1915—reported impressive data demonstrating that the work initiated by this remarkable woman in the early part of the twentieth century was both lasting and significant. "As of December 31, 1998, the balance sheet shows a total fund balance (assets minus liabilities) of $461,301,818," with 2,863,232 members and adherents worshipping in 24,473 churches and meeting places in 99 countries (Williams, 1999).

Aimee Kennedy Semple McPherson was dedicated to the work of God even before she was conceived. Her mother, Minnie Pearce Kennedy, did not want to be childless. She prayed specifically for a girl and promised the Lord that if he answered her prayer, she would give her daughter "unreservedly into your service, that she may preach the word I should have preached, fill the place I should have filled, and live the life I should have lived in Thy service" (Epstein, 1993: 10). In 1890 her prayer was answered; she named her daughter Aimee Elizabeth.

This little girl had a childhood different from most of her peers at the time. She heard Bible stories read to her continuously by her mother. Aimee learned to tell these stories herself in ways that would draw a crowd even before she was five years old. As she approached her teens, she was known as a girl-preacher, was winning public speaking contests, and being asked to "entertain" at various church events. Her mother was the moving force behind her. While this was not a historic time for women's rights, Aimee's mother was a dedicated member of the evangelistic Salvation Army movement, which included gender equality as a basic premise (Blumhofer, 1993). She acted on that belief.

Then, at age eighteen, Aimee suddenly changed her life dramatically. She met, fell in love with, and married Robert Semple, an Irish revivalist, going with him to China to perform missionary work. They both contracted malaria and dysentery; he died in August of 1910, only two years after they were married; her first child, Roberta Star Semple, was born a month later in Hong Kong. A weakened and saddened Aimee Semple returned to the United States to recover from this succession of human trials. Two years later she married accountant Harold McPherson; their son, Rolf, was born in March 1913. It was at this time, according to Aimee, that God would not let her rest. "She heard the voice of God until she could not bear it anymore; it commanded her to do a thing no honorable wife and mother could do in the face of American society of 1914." Her internal conflict caused her to become seriously ill. She underwent many surgeries. "Each time she returned from the hospital a little worse, more nervous, more depressed . . . she begged God to let her die" (Epstein, 1993: 74).

But then something happened, perhaps a kind of subconscious revelation, and Aimee changed. Now she believed she was called by God for a special ministry. She left her husband to devote her life to spreading the Gospel. With the help of her mother, Aimee began her ministry in 1915 at a revival meeting in Mount Forest, Ontario. Within days, the crowds numbered over five hundred people. When her ministry began, Sister Aimee, as she was now called, had no assistants to help her set up. "In rain and snow and heavy winds, she would drive stakes until she developed a lumberjack's strength and the expertise of a circus roustabout, and until there was no tent on earth that would hold the crowds that followed her" (Epstein, 1993: 84). This vagabond life and the competition for his wife's time and attention was too much for her husband, Harold McPherson; in 1919 he returned to his home in Providence, Rhode Island, while Aimee continued her ministry.

Sister Aimee was not only preaching; she was laying her hands on people with illnesses and disabilities, and many of these people claimed to be healed. Word of Sister Aimee's powers spread throughout the land. Thousands upon thousands came to hear her speak, many hoping to receive the healing of her hands for themselves or for those they loved. Objective reporters covered the stories of her miracles for decades. Some became believers; others at least credited her with providing them with enough material to keep them working throughout their careers.

During this time, Sister Aimee and her inner circle developed a seven-year plan that included constructing a 5,300-seat church in Los Angeles, California. This Angelus Temple, which still stands, cost $250,000 to build and, at its completion, was valued at $1.5 million. This project was funded from the contributions garnered through the preachings of Sister Aimee in more than a hundred locations in her travels back and forth across the United States from 1917 to 1923. She and her mother faced many physical dangers in these excursions. First, there was the reality of these lone women with two small children driving on the early dirt roads with few, if any, service stations and tires that tended to blow out after less than sixty miles of travel. Then there was the consequence of trying to cover a hundred miles a day in the early auto. Sister Aimee's daughter, Roberta, recalled "that some nights her mother could not sleep because the steering wheel's vibration continued in her arms long after the engine had quit" (Epstein, 1993: 148).

Sister Aimee was the first woman to preach a radio sermon, and she became the first woman to receive a broadcasting license from the Federal Communications Commission in 1924. Her pioneering station, Radio KFSG, located on the third floor of the Angelus Temple, was the first U.S. religious broadcasting station. Aimee Semple McPherson was also the pioneer of religious theater. An important aspect of the way Sister Aimee conducted her services was that the door was open to all—regardless of color or economic status; thus, black and white, rich and poor sat together if they wanted to attend. Once again, she accepted great risk—human, physical, and financial—in making this decision.

The organizational structure of her International Church of the Foursquare Gospel, which was incorporated in 1927 in California, included Bible classes and a Bible College with early enrollments numbering nearly 1,000; a Sunday School; a music department with orchestras, bands, and choirs that played compositions ranging from a cappella to jazz; a training school for radio announcers; a magazine, *The Bridal Call*; a sewing-circle group that made clothes for the needy; a brotherhood that found jobs for the unemployed; nurseries so parents could attend services; a "prayer tower"—volunteers who prayed in shifts; and a telephone counseling service. These community service outreach efforts were critical during some of the nation's most notable crises: the Santa Barbara earthquake, the Great Depression, and World War II. When Sister Aimee put out an appeal on her radio station, truckloads of supplies and helpers would arrive wherever they were needed. "Everyone recalls that she kept tens of thousands of people from starving to death. . . . Angelus Temple was the only place anyone could get a meal, clothing, and blankets, no questions asked" (Epstein, 1993: 369). Her efforts included setting up soup kitchens that fed 80,000 people in the first month alone; a free medical clinic with physicians, dentists, and nurses; and a government-owned facility where 20,000 to 30,000 might be housed. She also "sold $150,000 worth of war bonds in one hour. . . . The Army made her an honorary colonel. For her fund-raising and her use of Radio KFSG to teach the public about rationing, air-raid blackouts, etc., the U.S. Treasury and the Office of War Information issued her special citations for her 'patriotic endeavors' " (427).

These accomplishments are all the more impressive in the context of Sister Aimee's consistent and significant health problems. In 1930 the toll of all of her extensive and exhausting work both here and abroad became evident. Sister Aimee had suffered insomnia all of her life; she now experienced her first nervous breakdown. Because she attempted to continue with her normal routine, there was a second breakdown in 1932, and she would never again be truly healthy for more than a few months at a time. Yet, during her last national tour in 1933–1934, she still managed to travel "15,000 miles, preaching in 21 states and 46 cities—336 sermons to more than two million people (which was about two percent of the population in 1934)—not counting the listeners reached by 45 radio stations" (Epstein, 1993: 388).

This is not a life story without controversy, however. Over the course of her lifetime, there were an estimated forty-five lawsuits filed against her ranging from breach of contract to adulterous affairs to hoax allegations. The saddest of these involved the cases between Aimee and her mother, Minnie, and then later with her daughter, Roberta. There was even a question raised about whether or not the barbiturate overdose that led to her death in 1944 was a suicide; the court ruled it accidental.

Sister Aimee had paid off the Temple's debts by 1939. At the time of her death, the organization's assets were estimated at $2.8 million with over four hundred churches in North America and two hundred mission sites. Over 60,000 people came to mourn her passing, people spent more than $50,000 on flowers alone, and there was a six hundred-car motorcade to the cemetery at Forest Lawn Memorial Park. The gospel of body, soul, spirit, and eternity preached by Aimee Semple McPherson had reached the masses.

SOURCES: Blumhofer, E. (1993), *Aimee Semple McPherson: Everybody's Sister* (Grand Rapids, MI: Eerdmans); Epstein, D. (1993), *Sister Aimee: The Life of Aimee Semple McPherson* (San Diego, CA: Harcourt Brace & Company); The International Church of the Foursquare Gospel (1998), "Official Statistics," *http://www.foursquare.org/statistis/html* (accessed December 21, 1998); Williams, R. (1999), Re: ATT: Ron Williams, e-mail, July 28, to J. Oppedisano.

FE MONDRAGON (1946–)

"Young women should maximize their potential, develop their brains as much as possible, and not be afraid to take risks to succeed." (Dr. Fe Mondragon, Founder of Fe A. Mondragon, M.D.)

Fe Mondragon was breaking the norms from the time she was born in the Philippines, the oldest child of Ligaya and Lapulapu Mondragon. As a female born in poverty and raised in the Catholic religion, she was expected to be submissive and follow the traditional paths of dutiful daughter, obedient wife, and devoted mother. However, as a girl, she was a tomboy who played with the boys and climbed trees. As a young woman, she was an exceptional student and overachiever. These personal characteristics shaped her destiny and led her far from her homeland.

When Mondragon wanted to attend the University of the Philippines for her education in the medical field, her parents objected. They had made sure that so far her education had been in the safe confines of an all-girl Catholic school system. If she were to go to the university, she would be in a coeducational environment far away from home. However, as she had received a full scholarship as part of her father's GI bill benefits, they eventually gave permission. In her typical hard-driving fashion, she was determined to finish college early. Along with taking the maximum number of credits each semester, Mondragon took courses in the summer, which allowed her to graduate a year ahead of her peers. She earned magna cum laude status as well. Mondragon went to medical school at the University of Santo Tomas, a Catholic university established in the Philippines by the Dominican Friars in 1611. Next, she went on to be trained as a specialist in obstetrics and gynecology (ob-gyn) at the same university and became a member of the faculty soon after graduating from the residency program. She married Amando Tu, a doctor like herself, in 1971.

Over the next six years, three children were born to the couple, and they moved to the United States to continue advanced medical training. Mondragon explained her predicament: "Amando wanted to be free of the responsibility of children. In a way, I resented him for choosing to complete his education and assuming that I would give up my schooling" (Phinitsovanna, 1999). By 1978 they were separated. Although he stayed in contact with the children, he paid "minuscule" child support.

Mondragon's next hurdle was finding a job. She inquired about an ob-gyn residency at Albany Medical Center in Albany, New York, and when she couldn't seem to get a reply, Mondragon took matters into her own hands. "I decided to do something about it. I really needed the position so I charmed the department chairman's secretary to get me an interview. I told him about my gyn experience in the Philippines and why I would be the best candidate for the job. He saw my confidence and qualifications and hired me," she recalled with a smile.

Mondragon finished her second residency at Albany Medical College but, in time, found that she really didn't like working for others. At thirty-five, she decided to set up her own private practice even though she didn't know anything about running a business. "I read a lot of books, talked with a lot of people, and started an office in Clifton Park, New York." This was done with small loans from local banks and some personal savings. She hired a secretary and an accountant, and by the end of the first year, with minimal advertising, she had acquired approximately six hundred patients, mostly from word of mouth. Mondragon's goal has been consistent: to maintain relationships with her patients as both their doctor and their partner for good health. "I'm not worried about competition," she explained, "because I know I can give better service. You also have to be very confident and honest about yourself because this is risky business. People have to feel that they are getting the best health care possible, and we continue to make that our daily goal" (Oppedisano, 1999).

In 1996 Dr. Mondragon opened a second office in Schenectady, New York, spending three days at one and a half day at the other. The rest of the week is spent either in the operating room or in the delivery room. By 1999 she had over 2,500 active patients, but she had no plans for further expansion. Mondragon balances her long days by playing the piano, cooking, and enjoying her family. "For me, success is being able to do that I want—something that makes me feel good, keeps me humble; it is not about monetary value," she pointed out.

SOURCES: Oppedisano, J. (1999), Re: Entrepreneurship of Dr. Fe Mondragon, e-mail, June 2, to Fe Mondragon; Phinitsovanna, S. (1999), personal interview of Fe Mondragon on March 1.

JULIA MORGAN (1872–1957)

"If it had been simply for the advantages of the Ecole [des Beaux Arts in Paris, France], I would not have kept on . . . but a mixture of dislike of giving up something attempted and the sense of its being a sort of test in a small way . . . made it seem a thing that really had to be won."
(Julia Morgan, Architect)

Julia Morgan was born in San Francisco, California, and raised by parents who provided a comfortable—and some might say privileged—lifestyle. They were somewhat overprotective of their daughter because she had had a childhood infection in the bones behind an ear, a most serious illness in those pre-antibiotic days. Yet Morgan was a feisty girl who learned how to play the violin, shoot a bow and arrow, and use her brothers' gym equipment to build up her physical capabilities. From a very early age, it was evident, too, that Morgan had a fascination and a talent with all things mechanical. Because of this, she was encouraged to pursue an engineering degree by Pierre LeBrun, the husband of one of her cousins and a noted architect.

Morgan went on to attend the Berkeley campus of the University of California and graduated with a degree in civil engineering. By then she knew she wanted to be an architect; she applied to the internationally renowned L'Ecole des Beaux Arts in Paris. Knowing she might not be taken seriously when school officials saw "Julia," Morgan applied using initials for her first and middle names. She was accepted, to the chagrin of school officials when they discovered that they had admitted a woman. Since they didn't want to just expel her, they made her sit outside the classrooms, hoping to discourage her enough so that she would just leave. The male students and teachers may have treated her politely, but they didn't take her seriously as an architect.

Morgan wrote Pierre LeBrun that one of her teachers "always seemed astonished if I do anything showing the least intelligence . . . as though that was the last thing expected" (James, 1990: 43). No doubt to the surprise and, perhaps, astonishment of the male establishment there, this petite but determined woman went on to win four medals for exceptional work in design and drawing while she was still a student. Indeed, Morgan was the first woman to receive a degree in architecture from the L'Ecole es Beaux Arts in Paris, and she did so at the age of thirty.

When Morgan returned to the United States, she took a job with John Galen Howard. He was the supervising architect for the Hearst Mining Building. Howard boasted: "[I have] the best and most talented designer, whom I have to pay almost nothing, as it is a woman" (James, 1990: 50). Morgan served as supervisor for Howard's next Hearst project, an amphitheater on the Berkeley campus. In 1904 she became the first woman architect to be registered in California yet she still had to deal with the frustration of not receiving recognition from her male colleagues. Because of this, Morgan decided to start her own business.

Her first independent commission was a bell tower and library for Mills College in San Francisco. She designed and supervised the construction of both. Her professional reputation was well established when they withstood the earthquake of 1906, which left few of San Francisco's buildings standing. She immediately received a contract to rebuild the earthquake-torn Fairmont Hotel in San Francisco, a project that secured her position as a gifted and competent architect. She was only thirty-four at the time.

When her business began to take off, Morgan hired as many women as she could find who were trained in this field. She thought of her employees as her family and was more a loyal and generous friend than a boss. "She took only enough of the firm's income to pay for the office's operating costs and her basic living expenses. What remained, she generously shared with her employees—she had no interest in accumulating personal wealth. . . . During the Great Depression of the 1930s, when work was scarce, she offered whatever financial help she could to her laid-off staff members until they could find other jobs" (James, 1990: 70).

Morgan was a dedicated perfectionist who worked long, hard hours, which left no time for a personal life. She never married. Some days she didn't even take time to eat, getting by on only Life Savers and black coffee. Her nephew, Morgan North, said of Morgan, a small slender woman just over five feet, that she had the constitution of an ox. When she was on construction sites, she would wear men's trousers under her long skirts to make it easier to climb around the projects and to avoid any embarrassing exposure of her legs. Morgan was known to have started to demolish the brickwork of a house chimney with her bare hands because it didn't meet her standards. However, she managed to maintain her sense of humor. A botched-up ear operation had altered the lines of her face so she attended few public functions explaining: "An architect should never appear unsymmetrical" (James, 1990: 101).

Examples of Morgan's architectural structures in California alone include the Hearst Castle Estate, San Simeon; St. John's Presbyterian Church, an architectural landmark in Berkeley; the California State Monument at Asilomar, originally a summer conference center for the YWCA where Morgan built seven of the buildings; the Mills College Campanile and Library; the YWCAs in Oakland, Berkeley, Palo Alto, San Jose, San Diego, Fresno, Pasadena, and Long Beach, California; the Studio Club in Hollywood; and the Berkeley Women's City Club.

Julia Morgan's professional philosophy was summed up in her own words: "Don't ever turn down a job. . . . The reason I tell you this is that one of the smallest jobs I ever had was a small two-room residence in Monterey. This was done when I first started in practice for myself. The lady for whom I did it was most pleased with the job and now the lady is the chairman [sic] of the YWCA. And from that comes all these fine, big jobs we have" (James, 1990: 59). Morgan retired in the 1950s after 46 years in business.

SOURCES: Boutelle, S. (1995), *Julia Morgan, Architect* (New York: Abbeville Press); James, C. (1990), *Julia Morgan* (New York: Chelsea House Publishers); Morgan, J. (1980), *Julia Morgan, 1872–1957* (Newport, RI: Budek Films & Slides); Rolka, G. M. (1994), *100 Women Who Shaped World History* (San Francisco: Bluewood Books); Rutz, M. E. (1992), *Women's Influence on Planning and Design in America* (East Lansing: Michigan State University); Torre, S. (1977), *Women in American Architecture: A Historic and Contemporary Perspective* (New York: Whitney Library of Design).

NANCY MUELLER (1943–   )

"In Silicon Valley, we are dreamers, innovators, and risk-takers. Entrepreneurs from all nationalities and venues are changing the very fab-

ric of society and industry." (Nancy Mueller, Founder and CEO of
Nancy's Specialty Foods)

Cooking was not at all appealing to young Nancy Sothern (Mueller), the
oldest of two daughters born in Mineola, New York, to Ruth and Jack
Sothern. In fact, "I was the oldest son [she joked]" (Fernandes, 1997: 14).
"My sister was the athletic one; I was the biologist and project daughter."
But in the 1960s, while working as a chemist for the Syntex Corporation
studying new drug delivery systems and drug absorption rates, Nancy lived
with three roommates, sharing cooking chores. These four women learned
to cook with Julia Child's *Mastering the French Art of Cooking*. She didn't
know then what was in her future—that with no formal business training,
she one day would become known as the "Queen of Quiche" and run a
food-processing company earning over $50 million annually.

Nancy Sothern (Mueller) attended Russell Sage College, a small private
women's college in upstate New York, where she earned a bachelor's degree in chemistry in 1965. While there, she met and fell in love with Glenn
Mueller, an electrical engineering student at nearby Rensselaer Polytechnic
Institute. Nancy followed Glenn to Palo Alto, California, after her graduation and typed his papers as he completed his MBA at Stanford University.
The Muellers were married in 1966; by 1970, Nancy Mueller decided to
leave her job at Syntex to become a full-time wife, mother, and homemaker.
Their two children, Gregory and Carin, were born three years apart.

During this time, Mueller also volunteered for a nonprofit restaurant
called the Bay Window, which donated proceeds to support the Palo Alto
Family Service Agency. Here she was the business manager "and, yes, the
restaurant served quiche," she added, but it was in her role as supportive
wife and hostess that the concept for her own business took root. "I knew
I didn't want to be a better tennis player in ten years. I wanted to build a
business and have something to show for my time" (Oppedisano, 1999).
Mueller explained, "It was all serendipity. Although I was eager to build
a business, yet I had no idea where it would lead. I was doing what interested me at the time" (Dennison, 1995: B1). Nancy's culinary skills were
especially noticed at the annual Christmas party she and her husband put
on for "200 of their closest friends." For this special yearly event, Nancy
would make over 3,000 hors d'oeuvres, freeze them, and train her baby
sitters to act as caterers. By 1977 the compliments she had been receiving
on her appetizers convinced her to try to sell them in local grocery stores
as a frozen food item. Nearby Draegers Market agreed to stock the products, which sold out quickly, and Nancy's Specialty Foods was born. There
was still much for her to learn since she had no training in marketing or
sales, much less manufacturing, and quiche was unfamiliar to Americans
at the time.

In those early days, Mueller hired a couple of part-time employees to make a few hundred quiches a day by hand. She delivered these "to grocery stores in the Bay Area in her station wagon. She did demonstrations at the stores to build trial and awareness of her products" (Newark Chamber of Commerce, 1999: 2). Glenn Mueller, a Silicon Valley venture capitalist, helped Nancy identify sources of financial capital. She borrowed $30,000 in the second year from the bank to equip a small factory. Her business grew slowly but steadily. Then, in 1983, the book *Real Men Don't Eat Quiche* became a best seller. In hindsight, Mueller said it was the best thing that could have happened. "At first I thought: 'This is terrible. Everybody is going to hate the idea of eating quiche.' [But I was] wrong. Everybody now knows what quiche is as a result of that book" (Dennison, 1995: B2).

Another factor responsible for the rapid growth of the Nancy's Quiche brand was the expansion of the club store industry in the early 1980s. By 1990, her company's annual sales had grown to fifteen million dollars and, within four years, sales had more than doubled. The company built a new production facility to support the growth and develop new products. Sadly, along with the good news, this year also brought tragedy with the unexpected death of her husband, Glenn. "I enjoyed running the company and was determined to carry on even though Glenn was gone. I know he would have been very proud of the company and what it is today" (Behnke, 1999).

By 1999, more than 50,000 pounds of Nancy's Quiche and Party Spirals were being made at the company's 80,000-square-foot frozen-food processing plant in Newark, California. Nancy's Specialty Foods had ninety-five percent of the quiche market, with her products being distributed not only in the United States but in Mexico, Canada, Japan, Turkey, Cyprus, and the Middle East as well. From Mueller's perspective, "the business has grown based on my commitment to making easy gourmet foods from fresh, natural ingredients—just like you would use at home" (Nancy's Specialty Foods, 1998). She added, "The company has attracted a first class management team who have carried on the core values as the organization has grown" (Oppedisano, 1999). Because of this, Nancy Mueller has been able to be active on several boards, including Rensselaer Polytechnic Institute and the San Francisco Opera. She is a member of the Committee of 200 and the Women's Forum West. Mueller was inducted into the San Jose Junior Achievement Hall of Fame in 1996, received the Women of Vision Award from the Career Action Center, and the Trendsetter Award from NAWBO, the National Association of Women Business Owners.

For fun and balance, Mueller swims, water skies, and sails. According to daughter Carin, her mom also is an eternal optimist and "is one of my best friends. She has boundless energy. . . . She is fit and active and loves to keep up with us younger people" (Fernandes, 1997: 3). For Mueller, it has been important for her to wake up every morning enjoying her job and running the company, especially during the high growth phases. She pointed out that "success is a process that has different meanings as one goes through the many stages in one's life. Since we only go through this lifetime once, we owe it to ourselves to enjoy the process and derive maximum benefit from our experiences" (Behnke, 1999).

In 1999, Nancy Mueller sold Nancy's Specialty Foods to United Signature Foods, a very high-growth food company. She has kept an interest in the new entity and is participating as a board member. In questioning Nancy as to her thinking behind this move, she said, "I have been committed to Nancy's Specialty Foods for twenty-two years. During this time, I have taken care of my family and my company. There are many things I want to do during my life while I am healthy and active, and I plan to devote my time to the new business entity, selected philanthropy, my passions, and my family" (Oppedisano, 1999).

SOURCES: Behnke, M. (1999), interview conducted with Nancy Mueller on June 16; Dennison, G. (1995), "The Queen of Quiche: Nancy Mueller's Frozen Products Rolling in Dough," *San Francisco Chronicle* [Online], May 4: B1 (available: Lexis-Nexis, accessed February 25, 1999); Fernandes, L. (1997), "A Recipe for Success; Nancy's Specialty Foods President, Nancy Mueller," *Business Journal* [Online], August 11: 14 (available: Lexis-Nexis); "Focus on Northern California" (1998), *Rensselaer Magazine* (available: *http:www.lib.rpi.edu/dept/NewsComm/Magazine/Dec98/n_california4.html*, accessed July 2, 1999); Nancy's Specialty Foods (1998) (available: *http://www.nancys.com/nancy/html*, accessed January 14, 1999); Newark Chamber of Commerce (1999), "Business News: Feature Article" (available: *http://www.newark-chamber.com/bnews/bn990307.html*, accessed July 2, 1999); Oppedisano, J. (1999), faxed correspondence from Nancy Mueller dated August 4.

JOSIE NATORI (1947–   )

"My grandmother was my real mentor.... Grandma was a truly liberated woman and matriarch who said that a woman should never ask her husband for anything and should earn things herself through making her own money." (Josie Natori, Founder, The Natori Company)

For her fiftieth birthday, Josie Cruz Natori, an internationally renowned lingerie manufacturer, brought together an eighty-five-piece orchestra at Carnegie Hall in New York City, sat down at the concert piano, and played before a crowd of almost 3,000 invited guests ("Josie," 1998: 33). And why not? By the age of nine, this child prodigy had been trained as a classical pianist in her native Philippines and was playing before large audiences. Josie even performed with the Manila Symphony Orchestra (Taylor, 1988). She was a bright, artistic student schooled by nuns in traditional Catholic formality, as were her five siblings. However, as a teenager, she began to bridle at her cultural constraints. "When I was thirteen," Josie recalled, "my parents saw me dancing with the neighbor's son, and I was grounded for two months" ("Josie Natori," 1991: 74).

When she was seventeen, her mother took her on a world tour. From this broadening experience, Josie made the critical decision to attend the private, then all-female Manhattanville College in New York City. She majored in economics, graduated in 1968, and got her first job with Bache Securities for $6,500 a year. At age twenty-one, she was given the "ideal" assignment of going to the Philippines to open a branch of Bache there. After a few years, though, Josie wanted to return to the life she had come to enjoy in New York. She accepted a position with the Merrill Lynch investment firm. Within five years, she was a vice president making over $100,000 annually, often being referred to jokingly as "small but terrible." She elaborated, "I may look vulnerable, but I go straight in there and find my way through" ("Josie," 1998, 74). Josie had also met Ken Natori, another Wall Street executive, on a blind date arranged by friends. They fell in love, were married, and had a son, Kenneth, Jr.

Something was still missing from Josie Natori's life. She and her husband had planned to have a business of their own at some time. Both had entrepreneurship as part of their family background, but they were unclear as to which direction to take. They looked at franchises, car wash businesses, even a fertilizer company. But Natori wanted something to which she could personally relate, that would contribute to her homeland, and that would be unique enough to rise above the competition (Taylor, 1988). Then, the suggestions of two different people, in two different countries—one a friend in the Philippines, the other a buyer in New York—would give her the concepts that would become the focus of her future enterprise.

Her work focus changed unexpectedly in 1977 when that friend sent her a Filipino-embroidered blouse. Natori went on a "cold call" taking the blouse to the buyer at Bloomingdale's to consider the possibility of carrying this item. The buyer suggested that the garment be lengthened like nightshirts. From this simple comment, Natori then came up with the idea to make garments that could be worn both as lingerie and as outerwear—and that would help a woman feel her sensual self. "In the Philippines, we have always worn things at home that look like they could both go out and stay in—especially for entertaining. So that idea was natural for me" (Enkelis & Olsen, 1995: 13). But at first, this was a bit of a stretch for Natori considering her upbringing. "I'm a devout Catholic, and I believed that it was sinful to talk about sex, but as I ran out of synonyms, I finally had to let go," she explained ("Josie Natori," 1991: 74).

With $150,000 in personal savings and eventual support from her family, Natori initiated the Natori Company, hiring a freelance designer and working in the living room of the Manhattan apartment she shared with her husband and their one-year-old, Kenneth, Jr. Natori herself had no training in design, no manufacturing background, and clearly didn't understand the vagaries of the garment industry when she started. As she pointed out, "I was accustomed to Wall Street ethics—when they existed [but] I was unprepared for the rag trade. We got a twenty-five-hundred-dollar order from one major New York store, and after everything was made, they canceled it. On Wall Street, you cement a deal over the phone, but in fashion, you can sign in blood and it doesn't mean a thing" ("Josie Natori" 1991: 74). In spite of these difficulties, in just three years, the Natori Company was doing so well from national orders of companies like Saks, Neiman-Marcus, and Lord & Taylor that she built a factory in the Philippines to manufacture her lingerie line with the help of her father, who had a construction business there.

By 1985, Natori's husband joined the quickly expanding firm. This privately held company was reporting sales of $12 million, with this number doubling about every five years after that. By the late 1990s, Natori had added perfume, shoes, and jewelry to her line of offerings and was bringing her merchandise to television shopping audiences. Her philosophy about management's need to be open to change was clear: "If you stay put, you won't stay around. You have to keep innovating, keep generating fresh ideas" (Enkelis & Olsen, 1995: 15). Although Natori is glad she took business courses in college and has used that background in running her company, she noted that, "We've never done a formal business plan; we don't do formal market research. Everything was done just from a drive to actualize an idea. . . . I've always believed that if it's right, it will happen—everything is meant to be" (12).

In 1993, the Natoris sponsored an exhibition at the Metropolitan Museum of Art's Costume Institute on the historical influence lingerie has had on the ready-to-wear industry (Silver, 1994). Josie Natori's international entrepreneurial accomplishments have been recognized both in the United States and in the Philippines. She was appointed to the White House Commission for Small Business by President Bill Clinton, has won the highly valued Golden Shell award for excellent companies given by the Philippine government, and serves as chairperson of the Fashion and Design Council of the Philippines which she helped form. The Natori Company has also held charity fashion shows donating from just one, for example, over $150,000 to the Philippine-American Foundation, an organization with the goal of rural development. "I love my work," Natori stated. "I'm exhilarated by it, but it is not my calling in life. I am a Christian, a Catholic, and I have a goal to be able to give without limits—not just money—but what I can contribute to peoples' lives" (17).

SOURCES: Enkelis, L., & Olsen, K. (1995), *On Our Own Terms: Portraits of Women Business Leaders* (San Francisco, CA: Berrett-Koehler Publishers); "Josie Natori" (1998), *Crain's New York Business* [Online], March 30: 33 (available: Lexis-Nexis, accessed August 27, 1999); "Josie Natori: Queen of the Nightgown" (1991), *Cosmopolitan* [Online], December: 74 (available: Lexis-Nexis, accessed August 31, 1998); Silver, D. (1994), *Enterprising Women: Lessons from 100 of the Greatest Entrepreneurs of Our Day* (New York: AMACOM); Taylor, R. (1988), *Exceptional Entrepreneurial Women: Strategies for Success* (New York: Praeger).

ASSUNTA NG (1951–   )

"I don't get discouraged, and I don't take 'No' for an answer." (Assunta Ng, Publisher, the *Seattle Chinese Post* and the *Northwest Asian Weekly*)

Being born female in Canton, China, in 1951 limited a child's opportunities, and such cultural constraint was the early forecast for Assunta Ng. She and her family expected that she would marry and have children; there was no thought of college or a career. However, when Ng was sixteen, she took a standardized test given in Hong Kong. "The results initiated a new chapter in my life," she recalled (Monchik, 1998). Ng had scored in the top ten percent in all areas. Because of this, her teachers encouraged Ng and her parents, Hoi Sau Wong and Eric Woo, to consider her attending college in the United States. The parents faced a number of obstacles— permitting their daughter to go to college, thus leaving home and traveling to a foreign country, and financing such a decision. For Ng, the dilemma was finding a way to convince her parents to permit her to do so, considering the cultural norms of the time, and helping them find the monetary support.

Since Ng had heard that it was easy to get a job in the United States if a person were willing to work hard, she negotiated with her parents for them to give her enough money for one year, promising she would support herself after that. They agreed, and she left family, home, and country at age eighteen. Ng had decided to go to college in Portland, Oregon, but after one year, she moved to attend the University of Washington in Seattle where she studied journalism, education, and history and completed both her bachelor's and master's degrees. She became a public school teacher, married George Liu, and had two sons. Although teaching was fulfilling, Assunta Ng wanted to have a greater impact on society. "During Watergate [scandal during President Nixon's term of office], I remember long lines of people waiting to get the only Chinese paper which was published in San Francisco. This is what led me to think about starting my own paper in Seattle," she explained.

Ng tried to find information about other women who had started news-papers. Unsuccessful at that, she turned to learning about successful men in the field. Once she had formulated her ideas for an ethnic, community-based paper written in Chinese, she asked her husband for support. Al-though he was not initially in favor of her plan, he consented to her using family money to start the paper. Thus, in 1982, the *Seattle Chinese Post* hit the stands, followed by an English edition, the *Northwest Asian Weekly*. According to information provided on the company's Web site, Ng had established somewhat different strategic goals for these two weekly news-papers. "The Chinese edition is a primary news source with local, national, and Asian news for those who read Chinese. The English edition focuses on providing a voice and empowering the Asian American community" (*Northwest Asian Weekly*, 1998). As these publications were the first of their kind in the Seattle area, advertising in these papers enabled businesses to reach this specific market segment. Getting started was a struggle. For the first two years, the only money Ng took from the business was for operating expenses including staff salaries, none for herself. She poured whatever funds were left back into the business.

Between subscriptions and newsstand sales, the 1998 circulation was over 20,000 per week, resulting in annual revenues surpassing the half million dollar mark. Ng has employed twelve full-time staff, with part-timers hired as needed. Her policy has always been that when her employ-ees needed to bring their children to work, Ng was flexible enough to permit them to do so. Also, for some Asian professional immigrants who had only been able to find full-time jobs as manual laborers because of the language barrier, doing reporting, editorial, and features writing for the newspapers has provided them with an opportunity to use their intellectual skills.

Both papers have had economic impact on the community in other ways. The business stories or advertisements affect the bottom line of a local enterprise. "A review of a restaurant brings in new customers and new businesses have gained much needed attention after advertising in either the *Seattle Chinese Post* or the *Northwest Asian Weekly*," Ng pointed out. Three other services offered to businesses by her organization are transla-tions into Chinese, Japanese, Korean, and Vietnamese languages; typeset-ting in these languages; and compilation and publication of the *Seattle Chinese Yellow Pages*, which lists Asian organizations.

Consistently, Ng has been devoted to community service. In 1992 her newspapers' campaign raised more than $40,000 for a nursing home. Ng then initiated a "Women of Color and Power" group in 1993 that sponsors luncheons so that diverse women and men can build up their network and hear prominent guest speakers. As many as two hundred women have attended these events. Then, in 1994, Ng established the Northwest Asian Weekly Foundation, an organization that sponsors summer programs for Seattle youth to learn about Asian American history, role models, and resources. This is free to participants, who are also then eligible for $1,000 in college scholarship money.

Ng's philanthropic and business successes have garnered her much-deserved recognition. Not only is she listed in *Who's Who Among Asian Americans* and *The Complete Marquis Who's Who Biographies*, but she was honored by the newspaper *Eastsideweek* as the recipient of the Influential People under 40, 1991, award. In 1992 she received both the International Women's Forum Award and the Minority Business Advocate of the Year Award. To what has she attributed her success? "When something goes wrong, I don't get discouraged and I don't blame myself. When an earthquake and snow storm caused a building I owned to collapse, the damage cost over $100,000 to clean up. I didn't lose any sleep over it; I just dealt with it." And how does she assess her decision-making record? "Ninety percent of them are correct. I make very good decisions," she concluded.

SOURCES: Monchik, A. (1998), internal interview with Assunta Ng, February 2; *Northwest Asian Weekly* (1998), *http://www.nwlink.com/~scpnwan/biz.html* (accessed January 23, 1999).

ROSE O'NEILL (1874–1944)

"I had never imagined such an outcome of the venture. It was not in my rather vague temperament to 'look ahead' in a practical way. I think, in fact, I have never made a plan, but just blunder about doing or not doing what comes to hand with more or less enthusiasm." (Rose O'Neill, Creator of the Kewpie Doll and Founder of Rose O'Neill's Kewpie Shop)

According to feminist historical researcher Miriam Formanek-Brunell, Rose Cecil O'Neill "was an educated and informed, socially conscious, culturally critical, politically active New Woman who defied conventional expectations about gender roles in the life she lived and the work she created" (O'Neill, 1997: 1). But how could she have become such a nonconformist and a woman who earned at least a million dollars in the creative industry of caricatures and dolls when she was born female and poor in the nineteenth century? Credit must clearly be given to the unorthodox way in which she and her siblings were raised by their flamboyant Irish father, William Patrick Henry O'Neill, and their beautiful intellectual Dutch/German/English mother, Alice "Meemie" Aseneth Smith. Rose described her father as "a romantic with lucid intervals" (61) and her mother as a woman with a "kissing eye" who "couldn't see why being a parent should entitle one to treat children with lack of respect. . . . We thus enjoyed a childhood of 'high-thinking' fun and undamaged dignity" (30–31).

At first, O'Neill's father refused to allow her to attend a regular school as her mother would have wanted. She recalled him saying, "[Rose] shall have no studies except those conducive to the Arts . . . [because] she will have no occasion for an ordinary education" (O'Neill, 1997: 27). He emphasized, "My daughters will have their careers" (67). Rose was taught at home until she was eleven; then she spent a few years under the tutelage of Sacred Heart nuns, who taught her French, among other subjects, since most of them had come from France. Under their father's direction, most of the O'Neill children learned how to read and quote Shakespeare before they were nine years old. In addition, there were volumes of classics throughout the house, and their mother would regularly be reading one of them as she sat nursing a baby. Rose lovingly recalled that "Papa also placed tablets of drawing paper in handy spots, accompanied by beautifully sharpened pencils" (47) so that whenever the children got the urge to draw, they were free to do so. Their "models" were the pictures of works by da Vinci, Michelangelo, Raphael, and Greek sculptors they found in the books.

Though she had been born in Wilkes-Barre, Pennsylvania, most of O'Neill's childhood was spent on the road as the family kept relocating. Her father was not able to manage the finances of the businesses he would start and couldn't hold a regular job. "My playful father had always looked upon money as a projectile, as little boys do pebbles, and its destination the wind," she explained (O'Neill, 1997: 67). It was her mother, Meemie, who was the stable force in the family—taking jobs as a teacher even though she was bearing and raising seven children. Meemie became the classic pioneering woman, not by choice, but because she so loved the eccentric man she had married.

When her father was home, Rose loved playing theatrical roles with him in his frequent household renditions of the classics. She originally wanted to be an actress, but the family quickly recognized her gift as an artist. At fourteen, O'Neill entered her first art contest. It was held by the *Omaha World-Herald* newspaper, and she won a five-dollar gold piece, but not without having to prove that she could draw freehand so well. The judges were convinced that she must have traced the drawings, but they could find no similar originals. They then had her render several pictures as they watched. The editors were so impressed with her talent that she then became a freelancer for the paper.

At seventeen, she met and fell in love with the handsome, debonair Gary Latham, an aristocrat from Virginia. With the endorsement of Thomas Edison, Latham and his father were working on the first moving picture, a movie about bullfights. O'Neill and Latham married in 1896. Though they shared a very passionate love, the marriage lasted only five years, because her husband would collect the money she earned before she could, and spend it. O'Neill wanted to support her family, who continued to be impoverished, though now in the Ozark Mountains of Missouri at the place they named Bonniebrook.

During this first marriage, O'Neill had been illustrating for the magazine *Puck*. Here she had met writer Harry Leon Wilson, who had fallen in love with her. When he learned of her divorce, he began courting her, and she married him in 1902 on the rebound from Latham. He turned out to be a controlling, moody man who once said to O'Neill, "It's easy for me to be kind to a dog or a child, but there is something about a woman that makes me hard" (O'Neill, 1997: 79). By 1907 they were divorced, and O'Neill went to be with her family at Bonniebrook, the place that became her lifelong refuge. Here she wrote her first novel, *The Lady in the White Veil*, which came out in 1909. The publisher, *Harper's*, gave O'Neill a thousand-dollar advance. With this money, she and her sister, Callista, moved to New York City and began a phenomenal rise to fame and fortune.

O'Neill was well known as an illustrator by 1909, when Edward Bok of the *Ladies Home Journal* asked if she would draw a cupid for the magazine. Recollecting some pen-and-ink drawings she had made in 1898, O'Neill came up with an androgynous "Kewpie—a benevolent elf who did good deeds in a funny way. I invented the name for little Cupid, spelling it with a K because it seemed funnier" (O'Neill, 1997: 94–95). These illustrations and accompanying poems or stories appeared in many publications such as *Women's Home Companion* and *Good Housekeeping* magazines as well. Then letters started pouring in from children asking O'Neill if she would create a Kewpie they could hold. In response, she created first kaolin and feldspar dolls, then later, ones made of porcelain or celluloid and woodpulp. Rose and Callista, who became her business manager, opened a store on Madison Avenue in New York, Rose O'Neill's Kewpie Shop. Her dolls were made and also distributed internationally by the George Borgfeldt Company. O'Neill described the reaction to her newest creations: "Within twenty-four hours after the first Kewpies were shown in New York the telephones were vibrating with inquiries and orders from shops and department stores. . . . In the summer of 1913 thousands [were needed] . . . it was a problem to make deliveries. . . . Factory after factory had to be put into action . . . in France and Belgium" (109) in addition to the original plants in Germany. She remained active in her many ventures until her mother's death in 1937. Then O'Neill retired to Bonniebrook, where she began to write her memoirs.

In a letter to author Rowena Ruggles, O'Neill's nephew, Paul O'Neill, spoke of his aunt's many accomplishments: "She was a very productive artist, making some fifty-five hundred drawings, besides sculpturing the Kewpies and other statuary, writing literally hundreds of poems, novels, and making innumerable paintings in oils and water colors. . . . She made a fortune from the dolls, one company alone paying her $485,000 in royalties" (Ruggles, 1964:30). O'Neill died in 1944. She had made the decision not to have children, perhaps because she remembered the pain of having held in her arms for many hours the dead body of her beloved little two-year-old brother, Edward, and later mourning the loss of another brother she cherished, Jamie. Though childless by choice, she earned her fortune by making children and adults from around the world happy through the cavorting of her "little people," the Kewpies.

SOURCES: O'Neill, R. (1997), *The Story of Rose O'Neill: An Autobiography*, Miriam Formanek-Brunell, ed. (Columbia: University of Missouri Press); Ruggles, R. (1964), *The One Rose: The Mother of the Immortal Kewpie: A Biography of Rose O'Neill and the Story of Her Work* (Oakland, CA: Rowena Godding Ruggles).

KAY OWEN (1944–   )

"With my children grown and gone and my marriage ended, I realized that I had a blank canvas. I could create just about anything in my life at that point with that level of freedom." (Kay Owen, Founder of Nostalgia, Lifestyles Retail Stores)

Kay Smith recalled how her parents were warm and supportive to their two children. "They were both very loving and neat, clean, organized hard workers. My mother was the kind of mom who greeted you at the door after school with the chocolate eclairs. And she had a gift, an artistic eye, for decorating even though we didn't have a lot of money so our home was beautiful as well as very immaculate" (Rodriguez, 1998). From the values of her two parents, young Kay developed a sound work ethic as well as an appreciation for beautiful surroundings—standards she later incorporated into her own businesses.

During the 1950s when Kay was in high school, "guidance counselors didn't encourage girls to go to college." However, as her parents insisted that she had to have skills to support herself, she took a one-year accelerated program at the Albany Business College, not too far from their hometown of Gloversville, New York. Here she met and started to date another student, Ron Owen. Then Kay was offered a job in Washington, DC, and she accepted. However, the separation was not acceptable to her young suitor, and he gave her an ultimatum: "If you love me, I want you to come home and get married." She accepted, they got married, and moved to Saratoga, New York. Nine months later, they had their first child, Ron, Jr., followed a year later by daughter, Heidi.

In the twenty-three years of her marriage, Kay Owen was working hard at being a good wife and mother. Though she held full- or part-time jobs while her children were growing, she managed also to be a founding member of the Saratoga County Animal Welfare League, teach elementary religious education classes in the Sunday School program of the Methodist Church, and sing in the choir. Owen was also active with the Cub Scouts of America and the Parent Teachers' Association. Ultimately, the couple drifted apart, and they mutually decided to separate and divorce followed.

Owen was working for the Empire State College, getting good job performance reviews and receiving promotions. However, she grew more and more restless in the bureaucracy of state government. Owen was forty-five when she finally recognized that what she needed was "autonomy, work with meaning, consistent challenge, fulfillment, learning and growing" (Rodriguez, 1998). "I did not know what I was going to do then, but all I needed to know was what I did *not* want to do. My philosophy is that, if it doesn't work out, you just move along." She took a leave of absence from her job and opened a candy shop in Saratoga, New York, called Indulgence. Her daughter, Heidi, joined her in this venture. After about a year, she sold this business for a small profit to a competitor.

Owen then went to work for a couple of different retail shops. It was through these experiences that she learned that she loved retail but was reminded that she didn't like working for someone else. "I want to do things my own way, and I need a beautiful environment whether it's my office, my store, or my home, or I can't function well." Then an unusual occurrence took place. Owen received a book in the mail by Paul Hawken titled *Growing a Business*, written for entrepreneurs. She didn't order it and, to this day, doesn't know how it came to her. Coincidentally, two shops in Saratoga were both going out of business. Owen saw this as a niche opportunity and opened a store that offered handcrafted, high-quality, unique items. "I had no one to consult with, no one to talk to. I just made the best decisions I could. I rented a storefront, got on the bus to New York City to attend a trade show. I had no clue about what I was doing," she laughed.

In 1991 with her personal savings of $10,000 and a small loan from her mother, Owen opened Nostalgia, a gift shop with decorative accessories for the home. This was her opportunity to create the beautiful environment she craved. Owen decorated the shop in a feminine and romantic style with flowers, white linens, soft music. "Ambiance and presentation are everything. It looks beautiful, it smells good, it sounds pretty, and we try to keep it as clean and organized as possible." As sales grew, Owen added a women's clothing line. She turned the profits back into the business once she had met her own minimal needs. Her store quickly outgrew the physical space of one location so Owen opened a second store in 1994, called it Lifestyles, and invited her daughter to manage the establishment; her daughter accepted and moved back to the area. Lifestyles was later recognized by *Metroland Magazine* as the "Best Elegant Clothing Women's Store in the Capital District"—an important distinction because of the competition in women's apparel stores in this large geographic area. When the children's clothing line became popular, another store was opened in 1996, called the Bunny Patch. This shop was eventually sold so that Owen could concentrate on her core businesses. In April 1998 she opened another Lifestyles store, this time in Manchester, Vermont. She explained, "When self-employed, if you want to grow financially as a retailer, you either get a larger store or multiple locations. We have chosen multiple locations."

Today, the financial indicators for Owen's enterprise continue to be good. Nostalgia has been growing at a ten percent annual rate, and Lifestyles at twenty-two percent. She is looking at several additional locations for expansion. Her suggestion to others is "Do what you love, and the money will follow. How can this not help? How fortunate it is for any of us to do work that we love, and I've always loved decorating. It took me a long time to acknowledge that I'm gifted visually, but now I understand it because I've learned that you can teach people how to do a display, but you can only teach so much. You can tell when people are gifted. It's a passion; hours can go by and you're deeply absorbed, and you'd rather be doing nothing else."

SOURCES: Rodriguez, M. (1998), interview with Kay Owen on February 20, in Saratoga, New York; Smithgall, K. (1996), "Entrepreneurial Spirit: Kay Owen," *Glens Falls Business Journal*, July: 3.

SUSAN LA FLESCHE PICOTTE (1865–1915)

"As for myself, I shall willingly and gladly co-operate with the Indian Department in any thing that is for the welfare of the tribe. But I shall

fight good and hard against . . . anything that is to the tribe's detriment, even if I have to fight alone, for . . . I owe my people a responsibility." (Dr. Susan La Flesche Picotte, First Female Native American Medical Doctor)

Dr. Susan La Flesche Picotte lived only fifty years, dying from what was originally believed to be an infection in her facial bones but was later diagnosed as cancer. Yet, in those five decades, what she achieved was phenomenal. She became the first Native American woman to receive a medical degree, advocated for sound health-care practices on her reservation in Nebraska, and established a hospital in the town of Walthill, always ministering to any person in need regardless of race or color.

Susan La Flesche was the youngest of five children born into the family of Omaha Chief, Joseph La Flesche, whose father was a French trader and mother a Native American Indian of the Nebraska tribe. He was known as "Iron Eye" and militant in his fight to eradicate alcoholism from among his people. As he also believed that his children, including his daughters, needed to be educated, Susan was able to go to school on the reservation. Clearly talented, she went to study for three years at the Elizabeth Institute for Young Ladies in New Jersey, two years at the Hampton Normal and Agricultural Institute in Virginia, and was later accepted by the Women's Medical College in Philadelphia, Pennsylvania, where she received her medical degree. This type of cross-country travel and extensive education was atypical of what most young people in the country would have experienced, but for it to have been made available to a female born in 1865 to a tribe in Nebraska was truly unique.

When she was just a little girl, Susan heard the story of her brother, Louis, who died at the age of twelve, before she was born. She remembered her sister, Suzette, saying many times, "He should never have died" (Brown, 1995: 13). Susan also was affected by seeing her beloved father on his wooden leg, having lost the limb from an infection. These two family-related medical incidents had to have had an impact on this observant and impressionable girl, but she would not know until a number of years later the actual direction of this influence. Because she was so bright, Susan received grants to attend school, aided by the efforts of Alice Fletcher, a historical researcher studying the Omaha nation, its language, and its customs, who took a personal interest in this prodigy. While at the Hampton Institute, a school originally established for children of color, Susan discovered that she loved studying about and drawing the human body, trying to learn how it functioned. When she graduated as class salutatorian, General Cutchem, the superintendent at Hampton, presented Susan with the gold medal for having earned the highest score on the senior examinations. He said to her before the audience present: "This is for the excellence with which you have laid a foundation . . . you will become a part of the foundation work of your people. It is a great thing to be one of the first women of your race to lay this foundation. . . . I charge you to regard it as your duty to live for your people. To devote yourself to them" (Green, 1969: 128).

La Flesche took this message to heart. Following her success at the Hampton Institute, she went to the Women's Medical College and did extremely well there, because she loved what she was doing. "I've found my niche in the world now. It won't bring me fame, but it will bring me satisfaction," she told her sister (Brown, 1995: 125). While progressing with her medical classes, Susan managed to save enough money to send home for her father to buy a new wooden leg. She also had her sister send her descriptions of illnesses on the reservation, and she would practice diagnosing long distance; then her sister would report back on whether or not Susan's assessment matched the local doctor's.

Susan La Flesche received her medical degree in 1889 and was valedictorian of her class. She then got an internship at Woman's Hospital in Philadelphia. Following this assignment, she returned to her reservation, first given the task of medical doctor for the school and then, at her insistence, for the whole tribe. The Indian Bureau was willing to give her more responsibility but no more pay, saying they didn't have the funds. Dr. La Flesche accepted anyway because the need of her people was so great. She spent half a day at the school and the other half making house calls riding her faithful horse, Pie. " 'I'm not accomplishing miracles,' she told her sister Rosalie, 'but I am beginning to see some of the results of better hygiene and health habits. And we're losing fewer babies and [having] fewer cases of infection' " (Brown, 1995: 166).

Originally, Dr. La Flesche had made the decision not to marry and dedicated her life to the well-being of the tribe. For years, she worked extremely hard and under adverse conditions. "She was nurse, teacher, interpreter, social worker and general advisor as well as doctor. . . . Many times she faced the blizzards when she was overtired and she constantly drove herself [for] long, long hours as she hunted out the widely scattered families. . . . She talked of resigning but the Agent wouldn't listen—he needed her too badly" (Brown, 1995: 144). Dr. La Flesche's health began to deteriorate, and a pain developed in her ears, becoming ever more severe until she eventually went deaf.

Quite suddenly, in 1894, she resigned her position as physician and, at the age of twenty-nine, married Henry Picotte, a man she had gotten to know who like herself was part Indian, part French. She moved with him to Bancroft, a town still on the Omaha Reservation. They had two sons, Caryl and Pierre. All during this time, Dr. La Flesche Picotte continued her medical practice and was available day or night [putting] "a lighted lantern where it shone on the doorstep to guide anxious messengers in the dark" (Green, 1969: 147). Her husband, who had been ill for two years, died after only eleven years of marriage. She was also taking care of her invalid mother at the time, and her own physical pain was spreading from her ears down her neck. Susan was forty, widowed, and had two small boys to raise. She moved her family to Walthill and, somehow, kept practicing medicine. Dr. Picotte "made regular examination of the children in the Walthill school at no charge to the school district . . . [she also] was a charter member of the Medical Association of Thurston County and a member of the Nebraska State Medical Society" (158). She had always wanted to have a hospital that the Indians trusted enough to use and began to lobby for this goal. With the financial assistance of the Presbyterian Church and the Society of Friends as well as a land gift, the Walthill hospital was opened in 1913. Dr. Picotte only had a short time to enjoy the new medical facilities before becoming a patient there herself. The pain in the upper part of her body was now consistently intense. Her colleagues operated on her in early 1915, but it was useless because the cancer was already too invasive. She returned home to spend what time she had left with her sons and her sister Marguerite, dying in September 1916. As her family name, La Flesche, the arrow, signifies, Dr. Susan La Flesche Picotte never lost sight of her target—better health and health-care practices. She remained true to her people and her patients and hit her mark in the establishment of her practice and of the hospital that was named in her honor after her death, the Dr. Susan Picotte Memorial Hospital.

SOURCES: Bailey, B. (1994), *The Remarkable Lives of 100 Women Healers and Scientists* (Holbrook, MA: Bob Adams, Inc.); Brown, M. (1995), *Homeward the Arrow's Flight: The Story of Susan La Flesche* (Grand Island, NE: Field Mouse Productions); Green, N. (1969), *Iron Eye's Family: The Children of Joseph La Flesche* (Lincoln, NE: Johnson Publishing Company).

ELIZA PINCKNEY (1722–1793)

"I have planted a figg orchard, with design to dry them, and export them. I have rekond my expense and the prophets to arise from these figgs, but was I to tell you how great an Estate I am to make this way, and how 'tis to be laid out, you may think me far gone in romance. . . . I love the vegitable world extreamly [sic]." (Eliza Pinckney, Agriculturalist)

Elizabeth Lucas, nicknamed "Eliza," was the eldest of two daughters born to Colonel and Mrs. George Lucas. Her father was a British Army officer

stationed in Antigua, the West Indies, who encouraged his daughter's education by sending her to an English boarding school where she read Virgil,
studied French and music, but most important, fell in love with botany. In
1737, the family moved to South Carolina to become plantation owners,
but shortly after, Colonel Lucas had to return to the islands because of the
war with Spain. Because Eliza's mother was too ill to shoulder the burden
of taking care of her children and the plantation, all was left to this young
girl. Finding herself at age seventeen in charge of her father's plantation,
Eliza began to envision new possibilities that she might achieve.

Eliza used letters to keep her father informed: "I wrote my father a very
long letter on his plantation affairs . . . on the pains I have taken to bring
Indigo, Ginger, Cotton, Lucern, and Cassada to perfection" (Dexter, 1924:
120). It was her research and resulting success with indigo—the plant from
which a very marketable blue dye could be produced—that was the most
important factor leading to Eliza's fame. In order for the colonies to import
what they needed from Europe, the colonists had to produce something
exchangeable in return. Prior to her work, rice was the "cash crop" for the
state of South Carolina. It was far easier to raise than indigo. Among the
problems with trying to perfect this dye plant was getting seeds from the
West Indies. By 1745 Pinckney was able to harvest the indigo seeds herself
and gave them freely to any of her neighbors who wanted to raise this
crop. At the time, a bushel of indigo seed was worth ten pounds, so such
generosity was laudable.

The significance of Eliza Lucas' agricultural research accomplishment
and contributions need to be understood not only in the framework of her
being an eighteenth-century female who was very young, but also in light
of the complex process that was involved in the growing and harvesting of
indigo:

The leaves had to be cut at exactly the right time and then soaked in vats until they
had fermented just long enough to get the proper color. The liquid was then drawn
off into a second vat and beaten until it began to thicken, then led into a third vat
and allowed to settle. The clear water was drawn off and the sediment formed into
lumps or cakes, which, after being carefully dried in the shade, were finally ready
for market. . . . Eliza succeeded in bringing the plant to perfection. (Spruill, 1972:
309–310)

While her process was a great achievement, Eliza had suffered a cruel
blow from someone she thought trustworthy. There was a deliberate attempt to sabotage her efforts by the plantation's overseer, Nicholas Cromwell, whom her father had hired from the island of Montserrat. It's believed
Cromwell didn't want the colonies competing against his native land with
this plant. The English, on the other hand, were thrilled to no longer have
to negotiate for indigo from the French colonies. They offered the South
Carolina indigo growers a bonus to encourage its production, and indigo

quickly became this state's chief crop. In just two years of Pinckney's initial success, the South Carolina annual export of indigo increased from 5,000 pounds to 130,000.

In the midst of all of these endeavors, Eliza married Charles Pinckney, a lawyer and widower who was much older than she; they had five children in four years. He became the state's Chief Justice but died after only eight years of marriage. Eliza Pinckney had continued to manage her father's plantations and now, in addition, she was the owner of her husband's estate, which included "land and negroes in various parts of the colony" (Dexter, 1924: 123). Pinckney now had the complications of large-scale land management. These included the "uncertainties of colonial affairs, ignorant and dishonest overseers, and an unprecedented drought" (Spruill, 1972: 311). These didn't discourage her from continuing to experiment with hemp, flax, and the cultivation of silk.

Eliza Lucas Pinckney died of cancer at seventy-one years of age. Because of the heroism of her sons and son-in-law during the Revolutionary War and because of her contributions to the economy of the nation, President George Washington chose to be a pallbearer at her funeral.

SOURCES: Dexter, E. A. (1924), *Colonial Women of Affairs: A Study of Women in Business and the Professions in America Before 1776* (Boston, MA: Houghton Mifflin Company); Spruill, J. C. (1972), *Women's Life & Work in the Southern Colonies* (New York: W. W. Norton & Company).

LYDIA PINKHAM (1819–1873)

"Only a woman can understand a woman's ills." (Lydia Pinkham, Founder, the Lydia E. Pinkham Medicine Company)

This slogan rang true to the women of Lydia Estes Pinkham's time. In this era, which some historians have labeled the "Age of the Womb," male doctors referred to women as "mutilated men" and even went so far as to suggest that God created the uterus and then built a woman around it. When a woman had difficulty with her menstrual flow, the treatment could be bloodletting or applying leeches on the cervix or in the vagina (Stage, 1979). It's quite easy to understand why women were uncomfortable going to a male doctor, much less talking about female problems with one. According to biographer Sarah Stage:

False modesty not only kept women from doctors; it encouraged physicians to sacrifice sound medical practice to the dictates of Victorian prudishness. An illustration in a nineteenth-century gynecological text shows a doctor examining a fully-dressed female patient by kneeling in front of her and, with his eyes averted, reaching under her skirts. Accepted standards of medical modesty permitted doctors to touch female genitalia, but not to expose them to view—a procedure which helps explain numerous cases of misdiagnosis. Even after the introduction of the speculum in the 1850's, many doctors refused to employ the instrument because they feared it would sexually arouse their patients. (Stage, 1979: 78)

Lydia Estes was one of twelve children born of Rebecca and William Estes, an Italian farming couple in Lynn, Massachusetts. Her father, originally a shoemaker, had invested in real estate and become wealthy. The children were raised in the Quaker religion, and, by the time Lydia was a teenager, she and her family became Quaker radicals who stood for the abolition of slavery. At age sixteen, Lydia was a student of the Lynn Academy and an active member of the school's Female Anti-Slavery Society. After graduation, she was a teacher until 1843, when she met and married widower Isaac Pinkham, who had a five-year-old daughter. Within the next half dozen years, Lydia gave birth to four children. She lost her second son, Daniel, to cholera infantum. Like most mothers, Lydia had a host of home remedies for cures, but the death of one of her babies focused her attention even more dramatically on homeopathic treatment. Pinkham, expanding her knowledge of herbs and other substances, developed what was to be her world-famous medicine as a home remedy. She freely shared this potion with her neighbors.

The triggering event for marketing her remedy, which became known as Lydia Pinkham's Vegetable Compound, was the nationwide financial collapse in 1873. The panic and depression that followed had consequences for the Pinkhams that included the failure of the speculative investments of her husband, Isaac, who really never recovered from this blow, and following this, the forced closure of the grocery store owned by her son Dan. The family was close to destitution and strategizing for ways to bring in income. It was Dan who suggested that she try to sell her "medicine." Pinkham, because of their hard times, had to start accepting money for her potion.

Pinkham's botanical recipe consisted of unicorn root, life root, black cohosh, pleurisy root, and fenugreek seed. These herbs were softened by soaking and percolated in cloth bags; the liquid was filtered and then preserved in a nineteen-percent-alcohol mixture. Using alcohol as a preservative was not an unusual practice. Some other patent medicines even contained morphine, opium, mercury, or arsenic. Though the Pinkhams were temperance advocates, it was permissible in their minds to use alcohol for medicinal purposes.

In 1876 the Lydia Pinkham Medicine Company was set up formally in the name of her son William, because he was the only one in the family without debt; the Pinkhams didn't want past creditors coming after whatever profits the company might make. Dan had another genius of a marketing idea in 1879. He suggested that his mother had the perfect woman's face to grace the products they were selling since she was in good health, was a stately woman (tall for her time—five foot ten), and had a motherly look about her. The results of this marketing scheme could not have been predicted. "About six months after the ad began to run, the family refused an offer of $100,000 for the business and the new trademark" (Stage, 1979: 41). Lydia Pinkham's face became the most recognized of her century. Her picture was even used by newspaper editors for other famous women, including Queen Victoria.

In her widely distributed pamphlets, Pinkham was also breaking the silence surrounding women's ailments. She wrote frankly about all stages of women's health cycles—from childhood through menopause; she stressed the importance of cleanliness, exercise, and fresh air. Her customers were also encouraged to write to her and ask any questions they might have. Pinkham had a female staff in her Department of Advice to respond to the many letters she received. Among her products was an herbal douche, the Sanative Wash, that was promoted as a hygienic practice; however, women actually were douching in an attempt to prevent pregnancy. Since the sale of contraceptives was a violation of the Comstock laws, Pinkham found a way to circumvent them. "Ads for the Sanative Wash referred the reader to a footnote which recommended Ruth Paxton's 'Improved Fountain Syringe' available by mail for $1.50. The Paxton company existed on paper only. Sales of the fountain syringe brought in a revenue averaging $1700 annually to the Pinkham company" (Stage, 1979: 127).

Then one tragedy after another hit the family. In 1880, Dan Pinkham died of tuberculosis; he was not yet thirty-three years of age; less than two months later, Will, only twenty-eight, died of consumption. These losses were too much for Lydia Pinkham. She suffered a stroke in December of 1882 and died five months later. She was sixty-four.

Lydia Pinkham was fifty-seven when her venture started. In the short span of seven years, she initiated a business, brought it to national and international fame with the help of her sons, had annual sales of 200,000 bottles of her Vegetable Compound, was a household name and face, lost two of her sons, and then succumbed herself. Nonetheless, her business lived on; by 1925 sales had climbed to $3 million. The Great Depression, the ridicule of herbal approaches to health, and a marketing scandal— along with disagreements within her surviving family—took their toll on Lydia Pinkham's Medicine Company; it was eventually sold to the pharmaceutical group Cooper Laboratories. A century later, with today's renewed interest in herbal approaches to maintaining good health and holistic medical practices once again in vogue, Pinkham's products and methods do not seem as odd as her maligners portrayed them.

SOURCES: Sobel, R., & Sicilia, D. B. (1986), *The Entrepreneurs: An American Adventure* (Boston, MA: Houghton Mifflin Company); Stage, S. (1979), *Female Complaints: Lydia Pinkham and the Business of Women's Medicine* (New York: W. W. Norton & Company).

MARY ELLEN PLEASANT (1814–1904)

"I hold the key to every closet in town with a skeleton in it." (Mary Ellen Pleasant, Founder and Owner of several boarding houses in San Francisco, with other enterprises)

The life of Mary Ellen Williams Pleasant was filled with intrigue, real or fabricated, that included involvement with the Underground Railroad helping slaves escape, running houses of prostitution, selling illegitimate babies, and even the suggestion that she may have murdered her business partner when she was in her eighties. Yet Pleasant, a mulatto female born into slavery herself, was able to survive and prosper for almost ninety years because of her business acumen. According to author Quintard Taylor, "Pleasant's success flowed from three attributes . . . the ability to advise and . . . the courage to challenge the most powerful members of San Francisco's economic elite . . . a devoted following of young marriageable white women [and] 'insider information' from her contacts with the city's most successful white males" (Taylor, 1997: 117). But the question remains: How could a female slave born in 1814 on a plantation in Georgia end up on the other side of the continent and become, perhaps, the first female African American millionaire?

Clearly Pleasant's personal attributes were impressive. She was intellectually gifted. She had a natural sales ability and a willingness to take significant risks. Moreover, she was strikingly attractive and even able to pass for white when she chose to do so. How she parlayed these characteristics is what led to her ultimate successes.

A turning point for this slave child came when she was in her early teens. By chance, a wealthy man, Americus Price, happened to be riding past the plantation, had occasion to speak with her, and was so impressed with Mary Ellen's precociousness that he bought her for $650. Price's intentions were honorable. He believed that such a bright child should be educated regardless of race, and he sent her to a convent of the Ursaline religious order. There she learned how to read, do math, and speak French. Since educated blacks were not accepted in the South, Price then sent her to friends in Ohio so that Mary Ellen would not be in danger. However, when Price died shortly thereafter, Mary Ellen was sold into bondage and sent to New England. Here she worked in the shop of a Quaker woman, Mrs. Hussey, and learned how to sell to customers. "I was a girl full of smartness . . . people used to come in to hear what I had to say . . . few people ever got by that shop without buying something from me," Pleasant reminisced (Taylor, 1997: 118). She worked off this obligation in five years, earning her freedom, and then went to Boston to find work.

After a year of employment in a tailor's shop, Mary Ellen met and then married James Smith, a wealthy tobacco plantation owner from West Virginia who was a widower and an active abolitionist. It is not clear whether Smith knew that his bride was black (Williams, 1978). He died in 1844, leaving Mary Ellen with a sizable inheritance that she continued to use in their work for the Underground Railroad. By the end of the 1840s, she had married John Plaissance, the black overseer of the Smith plantation; moved to New Orleans where she became both a culinary and ceremonial student of voodoo queen Marie Laveau; and then headed to the West Coast because of the more extensive opportunities for people of color. Mary Ellen decided to go to California by ship; it was on this journey that she met Scottish banker Thomas Bell, with whom she would ultimately have a financially successful lifelong relationship.

Soon after she arrived in San Francisco in 1852, Mary Ellen changed her last name to Pleasant and started working for the wealthy. For a black female, the only employment available was serving, cleaning, or cooking for white employers. "Gender and racial restrictions in San Francisco allowed no place for a black woman other than as a domestic servant. Pleasant simply could not have worked in any other capacity" (Taylor, 1997: 126). In the largely male-dominated, increasingly wealthy social scene of mid-nineteenth century California, Pleasant auctioned off her services to the highest bidder and started earning $500 a month—more than even some miners were making. Within a relatively short period of time, this shrewd businesswoman was investing her inherited and earned money in real estate, starting or purchasing various enterprises such as a restaurant, a laundry, and a livery stable. She also set up other African Americans in business. In addition, Pleasant used much of her money to support the abolitionist movement of the West, as she had already done for a decade in the East. "Oral history collections of other black San Franciscans place Pleasant at the center of virtually every abolitionist and civil rights campaign in the Bay Area between 1852 and 1868" (132).

By the end of the 1870s, Mary Ellen, referred to by some as "Mammy Pleasant," had started three laundries and three boarding houses. One of these became her first "house of assignation," what some might refer to as a high-class house of prostitution. This facility, run by Eleanor Weile, had such famous clientele as the governor of the state, Newton Booth. Pleasant also supported the Lying-in Hospital and Home for Foundlings managed by midwife Laura Wilson. This was the vehicle for the birthing and then placement into wealthy families of the hundreds of children being born out of wedlock; at this historical point in time, it was not illegal to sell babies. In exchange, the mothers would give four months of "service" at one of Pleasant's "houses" (Holdredge, 1954: 259). Mammy Pleasant also owned property and mining stock with an estimated value of $300,000. She had a Victorian mansion built at a construction cost of $100,000 and furnished it for approximately $200,000.

Mammy Pleasant was privy to competitor financial information through the network of ex-slaves she had helped bring to California and Nevada where they worked in the homes of the very wealthy white businessmen and politicians, listened carefully, and then reported back to Pleasant. She maintained this control over naive blacks because she had cultivated the image in this closed community that she was a "voodoo queen" who could do them harm if they weren't loyal to her. In the more wordly black population, she was feared and/or respected because of her extensive power base in the white community. Because of her shrewd insider trading arrangements with Thomas Bell, co-founder and vice president of the Bank of California, the state's largest bank, she became a very wealthy woman.

Conflicting reports of her accumulated wealth ranged from hundreds of thousands of dollars to fifteen million, but it is impossible to get an accurate picture because, like many people of color, she "intermingled" her assets "with white friends and employers to protect it from racially inspired creditor harassment" (Taylor, 1997: 132; see also Holdredge, 1953). As she aged, though, many tried to legally rob Pleasant of her businesses, properties, and money, forcing her to fight legal battles for the last twenty years of her life. She died at the age of ninety.

Mary Ellen Pleasant had risked her life, her financial resources, and her personal freedom to free slaves, sometimes disguised as a man or a white woman. She supported the elderly, widowed, and orphans; financed the first African American newspaper in the West, *Mirror of the Times*. She helped build black churches and a school for black children; she fought streetcar discrimination. Pleasant enabled many black people to find work or start businesses, many white girls and women to literally survive—some more affluently than others; she initiated a number of enterprises, and she enabled many men to become very rich—this is the legacy of Mammy Pleasant.

SOURCES: Holdredge, H. (1953), *Mammy Pleasant* (New York: G. P. Putnam's Sons); Holdredge, H. (1954), *Mammy Pleasant's Partner* (New York: G. P. Putnam's Sons); Holdredge, H., (1970), *Mammy Pleasant's Cookbook* (San Francisco, CA: 101 Productions); Hudson, M. L. (1996), "When 'Mammy' Becomes a Millionaire: Mary Ellen Pleasant, an African-American Entrepreneur," Master's thesis, Indiana University; Taylor, Q. (1997), "Mary Ellen Pleasant: Entrepreneur and Civil Rights Activist in the Far West," in Riley, G. & Etulaine, R., eds., *By Grit and Grace: Eleven Women Who Shaped the West* (Golden, CO: Fulchrum Publishers); Williams, B. (1978), *Legendary Women of the West* (New York: David McKay Company).

FAITH POPCORN (1943–   )

"A channeler once told me that I had been a scout, a trailblazer, in a former life. I'm certainly trying to be one now . . . it's no longer enough just to dream about how we want to live." (Faith Popcorn, Founder and Chair, BrainReserve, Inc.)

Like some of her predictions about the future, Faith Plotkin Popcorn appears to be a contradiction in terms. Her work is focused outward, on consumerism, yet she prefers spending her weekends in a small, almost minimalist environment; she may be sporting chrome yellow or fuschia spikes of color in her hair one day or choose all-white hair the next while transacting business with traditional corporate executives. These ostensible incongruities don't faze Popcorn in the least; she's a master marketer who brings in $75,000 to $1.5 million per project for predicting trends for many Fortune 500 companies, and she receives from $30,000 to $45,000 for public speaking engagements.

Even her name is a marketing device. Faith was born in Manhattan into the Plotkin family; her parents were lawyers, and she had one sister, Mechele. The girls were raised primarily by their paternal grandparents, which, at least in Faith's case, was an advantage since it was the experience of working in her grandfather's haberdashery that taught her to keep a focus on the consumer. From her grandmother who also worked in the city, she learned "street smarts": "Nobody scared my grandmother. . . . She was the cowgirl of the East Side. 'Walk tall, look people in the eye, and nobody will ever hurt you,' " Popcorn recalled. "That's what she told me, and it held true" (Treen, 1991: 109). After she graduated from New York University with a degree in English, Faith took a job with Grey Advertising. Her first boss nicknamed her "Popcorn" as a tease on her last name. When Faith decided that this name fit her more appropriately, she legally adopted it as her own in 1969. "It's a name created to cause attention," she says, "and it does" (109).

Because of what she observed in the ad-agency business, Popcorn "became convinced there was a niche for a service that would provide an honest resource that comes only from the consumer, reporting directly how the consumer responds to different ideas" (Taylor, 1988: 28). The result was that, in 1974, with the limited savings she had, Popcorn founded the marketing consulting firm BrainReserve, with Stuart Pittman; she bought him out seven years later. The real breakthrough for her business came in the early 1980s, when she predicted the trend of what she labeled "cocooning"—the concept that consumers, because they feel that their outside world is unwelcoming and harsh, will retreat into their homes or into a homelike environment. She eventually explained this and other trends in her book *The Popcorn Report: Faith Popcorn on the Future of Your Company, Your World, Your Life*, issued by Doubleday in 1991; within seven years this book had been published in sixteen countries. The 1997 book she co-authored with Lys Marigold, *Clicking: 17 Trends That Drive Your Business and Your Life*, became available in seven languages.

Popcorn has been labeled Trend Guru, the Queen of Futuristic Consumerism, and the Nostradamus of Marketing because of the accuracy of her trend predictions. "In the Popcorn world, a trend is not a passing fad, but a long-lived force that is shaping the future inexorably and must not be ignored," writer Connie Koenenn explained (Koenenn, 1998: E3). Precise predictions have enabled Popcorn's firm to acquire an impressive list of clients. Among them are Campbell's Soup, Target, Pillsbury, BMW, Eastman Kodak, RJR/Nabisco, AT&T, American Express, IBM, and Philip Morris. She has done this with a staff of 28 and a computer bank of some 5,000 people (her TalentBank) in a wide range of occupations: housewives, lawyer, editors, scientists, environmental analysts, other futurists, doctors, entrepreneurs. "Experts from each discipline can glimpse maybe one or two parts of the puzzle of what's coming. But if you bring those experts together, the pieces fit together," Popcorn noted (Gustke, 1997: 47). In addition, over 3,000 consumer interviews are conducted each year, with the data collected and analyzed in the company's Trendbank.

The three primary "divisions" at BrainReserve have been marketing consulting primarily to Fortune 500 firms, managing the multiple lines of Popcorn Products such as books and tapes, and coordinating her speaking engagements. "We only take approximately four assignments at a time because I get very involved in each one. They usually have to do with refocusing our clients on future needs of consumers, or repositioning existing brands to better fit what consumers really are going to be needing, wanting, demanding," Popcorn noted (Guzman, 1998: 1).

Examples of the trends she predicts for the twenty-first century are:

The home will be the learning centre, the emotional centre, the food centre and the economic centre of your world. . . . Web purchases by the year 2010 will equal $300 billion a year . . . in every home there will be a virtual reality room. . . . You could even have a virtual date to see if you like the same movies. This will be the singles bar of the year 2000. . . . Time will be the new currency. We'll spend it, save it, invest it and trade it, the way we did with money in the 1980s and '90s. People want to simplify their lives, save time, reduce stress. For employee bonuses, people will prefer time over money. They want to spend time with their families; they want sleep. (Moore, 1999: 46)

Popcorn has made her business the center of her life and attributes her success to such dedication. "My life is my work. Fortunately all my best friends [including her sister] work with me" (Treen, 1991: 109).

SOURCES: Gustke, C. (1997), "Previewing the 21st Century," *Industry Week* [On-line], May 5: 47 (available: Lexis-Nexis Library: Academic Universe—Document, accessed, January 30, 1999); Guzman, E. (1998), "The Ultimate Trend-Spotter," Microsoft Investor, *http://www.investor.msn.com/Prospect/articles/inter/622.asp* (accessed August 31, 1998); Koenenn, C. (1998), "Trend Guru Has Her Eye on 'Atmosfear,' " *St. Louis Post-Dispatch* [Online], March 18: E3 (available: UMI—ProQuest Direct, accessed August 31, 1998); Moore, M. (1999), "Future Shock Need a Spouse? A New Suit? Just Click onto Your Microwave, Says Trend-Spotter Faith Popcorn," *Toronto Sun* [Online], January 17: 47 (accessed January 30, 1999); Popcorn, F. (1991), *The Popcorn Report: Faith Popcorn on the Future of Your Company, Your World, Your Life* (New York: Doubleday); Popcorn, F., & Marigold, L. (1997), *Clicking: 17 Trends That Drive Your Business and Your Life* (New York: HarperBusiness); Taylor, R. (1988), *Exceptional Entrepreneurial Women: Strategies for Success* (New York: Praeger); Treen, J. (1991), "Search for Tomorrow; As a Professional Trend Setter for America's Biggest Firms, Faith Popcorn Has Seen the Future—and It Sure Works for Her," *People Magazine* [Online], December 2: 109 (available: Lexis-Nexis Library: Academic Universe—Document, accessed, January 30, 1999).

SYDNEY REYNOLDS (1940–   )

"I have a personal philosophy which comes from my life experiences. I've labeled it the 'R-rule': Rejection, Rejection, Rejection—to be followed up with Regrouping, Regrouping, Regrouping. You learn from one rejection after another. They're blessings in disguise . . . crisis IS an opportunity." (Sydney Reynolds, Founder and CEO, Sydney Reynolds Associates)

Sydney Reynolds Associates (SRA) was incorporated in 1970 with the specific goal of recruiting women for professional positions in companies. At the time, it was the only female-owned retainer executive recruiting firm in the United States. By the 1980s, Reynolds specialized in the identification of middle- and senior-level executives for a select group of clients in such industries as oil, chemical, pharmaceutical, aerospace, electronics, communications, information systems, transportation, and power generation. Clients have also included government agencies. "It took me three years to sell my first contract," recalled Reynolds. "Every obstacle was there. I was a woman in a field dominated by men. It was rather naïve of me to get into their field . . . where men were twice my age and had far more experience."

Reynolds' early professional experience had been with the Young Presidents' Organization (YPO), a group of men under forty who were CEOs of their own companies. Her specific position there was to develop programs designed to advance their knowledge on running their businesses. "This is when the entrepreneurial spirit awakened in me," Reynolds recalled. "One of the presidents suggested that I become an executive recruiter. However, when I tried to find such a position, the firms only wanted me to be a secretary." Refusing to accept such a constraint, Reynolds aggressively searched for all possibilities, as she would recommend to a client, and landed her first job in the field of recruitment—placing male lawyers. Recognizing the ongoing need for corporate America to recruit women, she wrote a business plan with helping to satisfy this objective as a goal. As this was during the early days of the women's movement, there was heightened awareness of the small numbers of women in corporate America. Even though Reynolds conceived of the idea and wrote the plan, they hired someone else to carry it out. "In hindsight, their decision was correct, but at the time, it was devastating!" explained Reynolds.

Reynolds "regrouped" and decided to start her own company. She immediately encountered an obstacle because, in the field she was proposing, a company head would need bonding. Reynolds was refused bonding because she was under thirty and didn't have any credentials. "Remember, it was the late 1960s and very much a man's world," she pointed out. "Then I found out that I didn't need a bond if I were placing people in jobs paying more than $12,000 a year. Since I wanted to focus on women, this limited the playing field considering what women were being paid at that time."

With an original investment of $1,000, Sydney Reynolds started her executive recruitment firm "for women only." After three unsuccessful years, she analyzed her business plan and realized she was approaching recruitment in a kind of reverse order—trying to "sell" a woman to a company without knowing exactly what positions were available and what requirements the company needed. This led to a new strategic direction for Reynolds. "What I would do is conduct a search using guidelines provided by the client company, and then, since I knew how to find the women, make the referral. Now I had a product to match my expertise."

By 1974 Reynolds was also placing minority males, ending any candidate restrictions based on sex. "Finding individuals interested in pursuing other opportunities isn't difficult when you understand that the typical salary increase when you change jobs is 25 to 30 percent . . . not the 3 to 6 percent companies are giving out. The challenge is identifying the *unique* person who will give the company what they are looking for and more . . . that's how you get repeat business." More than two-thirds of SRA's business comes from clients with whom they have already worked. "Our policy is to guarantee that each assignment accepted will be brought to a successful close," Reynolds added. "What that means is that we work on an assignment until the client company has successfully hired a person for the position."

Reynolds' company serves clients in the private and public sectors as well as not-for-profit philanthropic organizations. She has successfully placed executives both nationally and internationally with organizations such as Mobil Oil, McDonnell Douglas, the *New York Times*, Citibank, *Newsweek*, and Smith Kline. Reynolds was also one of the founders of Women Business Owners of New York. She has served as chair of the New York Chamber of Commerce Women's Council and is a member of the board of directors for Graham Windham, a $30 million child-care agency for abandoned children. "The key to success," Reynolds concluded, "is having a passion for what you're doing. It's unconnected to the money. No matter what I do, it is driven by passion and the satisfaction that comes with knowing I am making a difference. My energy and motivation are fed by this."

SOURCES: Feinberg, M. (1985), "Searcher Cracks 'Bastion of Males,' " *New York Post*, May 13; Oppedisano, J. (1997), interview of Sydney Reynolds in Castleton, New York, on September 22; Reynolds, S. (1975), "Women on the Line: What Happens When Women Supervise Men—and Women," *MBA Magazine*, February; Reynolds, S., & Sape, G. (1982), "Equal Opportunity Employment in a Nonregulatory Environment," *IAPW Journal* (Winter): 1–5; Travis, G. (1979) "Head Hunters," *USAir Magazine*, October: 28–32.

PLEASANT ROWLAND (1941–)

"We could make some mistakes today and probably survive it. What is the scary thing about being an entrepreneur is that, in those early

years, you have no idea which piece could put you under so there's this hypervigilance that makes an entrepreneur very difficult to work for . . . that is the exhaustion and the stress of building an idea from nothing." (Pleasant Rowland, Founder, Pleasant Company)

Pleasant Thiele Rowland graduated from Wells College in Aurora, New York in 1962 with a bachelor of arts degree and then taught for six years at the elementary school level, where she found herself designing innovative ways to reach the children under her care and supervision. After deciding she wanted a change of scenery, she moved to San Francisco, California, and fortunately was able to get a job as a reporter for KGO-TV. "While working on a story about a new bilingual education program, Rowland met a publisher who became interested in the work she had done as a teacher and asked her to develop some reading textbooks for his company" (Silver, 1994: 265). She agreed, and by 1971 her work was so respected that it earned her the position of vice president of the Boston Educational Research Company. Then, in 1976, she met Jerry Frautschi, owner of Web-crafters, Inc., and decided to have one of her books printed by his firm. As he tells it: "We met in late May, fell in love over four days, and by November we were married. . . . We knew it was right" (Kassulke, 1998: 1A). They settled down in Madison, Wisconsin, and Rowland became step-mother to Frautschi's three sons.

Rowland now became even more committed to children's education, which led her, by 1981, to put out a publication she called *Children's Magazine Guide*. Then two triggering events narrowed Rowland's commitment to children's education, focusing it exclusively on girls aged seven to twelve. First, she and her husband traveled to Colonial Williamsburg, Virginia. She greatly enjoyed learning more about what took place historically at these sites, which started her thinking about making history relevant to today's youngsters. Then, in 1984, she went to buy Christmas presents for her nieces that they would treasure from their "Aunt Pleasant." Agitated by the homeliness of the Cabbage Patch dolls and the sexuality of Barbie dolls, she decided to create a whole new line of dolls.

Rowland started a toy business, the Pleasant Company, in 1986 with $1 million from personal savings, bank loans, and a private investor. Her Middleton, Wisconsin–based business had just twenty-four employees at first, but its mission was clear. "Our whole essence is holding off that onslaught of mass culture trying to sexualize little girls too early" (Kagan, 1993: D1), Rowland emphasized. She contracted with the Gotz family, doll manufacturers in Germany, for her first order of 1,000 dolls and had the clothes made in China, because that's where she could get small orders manufactured. Sales started to soar, yet Rowland thought of this quite simply: "I'm in the little girl business. And anything that can make this fragile time of a girl's childhood . . . better, is something we have a responsibility to do" (*Forbes*, 1998).

With her new business taking off so quickly, Rowland sold the *Children's Magazine Guide* to R. R. Bowker to concentrate on her new venture. Working in her own way, she broke all the rules taught in business schools. Rowland did not copy the doll-manufacturing leaders like Mattel. Trusting her own instincts, she decided to use the "softer voice" rather than the hard sell. She initiated her own mail-order catalogue with a circulation of 500,000 because she couldn't afford television or other mass-marketing devices. She didn't establish arbitrary financial goals. Instead, she "starved" the target audience—that is, staggered new productions to keep demand ahead of supply. The results were phenomenal. By 1993 sales were $74 million; in 1994, $108 million; in 1995, $152 million; in 1997, $287 million; and by 1998, $300 million. Rowland explained that, "at Pleasant Company we come from a point of sincerity, of wanting to change lives, not from a point of wanting to sell a whole lot of product. . . . The market came to us because it's starving for what we offer—quality, values, excellence. It's not that hard. What we did is not that complex" (*Forbes*, 1998).

In less than a dozen years from the initiation of Rowland's business, the Pleasant Company had sold over 4 million dolls, 45 million books, and initiated a magazine, *American Girl*, which garnered a circulation of over 700,000 the first year of publication. In a rare interview, granted to a public broadcasting station, WGBH, she explained the growth. "This [business] is about making a difference. We didn't happen overnight. This is an eleven year journey of being recognized as an industry leader or pioneer. There have always been dolls out there for girls . . . we are not the first . . . we are unique for one thing. We have targeted little girls as intelligent important people, and we have talked to them that way. . . . That's what matters; that's why we are successful" (*Forbes*, 1998).

In 1998, Rowland sold her business to the Mattel toy company for $700 million, remaining as vice-chair and member of the board. This sale made her one of the richest people in the United States. Rowland is considered by many to be a marketing genius. For whatever of this is true, she credits her indirect exposure to this field by her father, Edward Thiele, now deceased, a past president of Leo Burnett, one of the largest advertising agencies in Chicago. She recalled that as a little girl she would excitedly watch and listen to her father talk about projects and clients at home. "We saw the Jolly Green Giant and the Marlboro Man around the dining room table. . . . I learned from my father that the great ideas are executed in the fine details" (Kagan, 1993: D1). Her latest project is in her hometown of Chicago. The American Girl Place opened in 1998 on Chicago's "Magnificent Mile," just two blocks from the hospital where Rowland was born. It offers more than 35,000 square feet of shopping space filled with items to thrill little girls—from a girl's clothing line to the dolls, of course. This tourist destination boasts as many as "8,000 visitors on peak days" (Chicago, 1999).

Since 1992, Rowland has been very generous in her philanthropy, as has her husband. She has helped raise more than $4 million for children's charities (*Forbes*, 1998) and gave half a million to help fund the Monona Terrace fountain at the Madison Civic Center. In 1999, Pleasant Rowland gave $5 million to the Chicago Botanic Garden in Glencoe, Illinois, saying, "My hope is that this gift will provide visitors with a place of tranquility" (Sadovi, 1999: 21).

For those who contemplate starting a business, Pleasant Rowland has these words of encouragement. "Go do what you believe you're going to do. Come from a place of heart. Come from a place of mission. There will be people out there who will love this and admire it, if *you* love it and admire it" (*Forbes*, 1998).

SOURCES: "Chicago: The American Girl Line Has Local Roots" (1999), *Copley News Service* [Online], April 15 (available: Lexis-Nexis, accessed July 27, 1999); *Forbes Great Minds in Business* (1998) [Videorecording], WGBH, Executive Producers, Tim Smith & Steve Atlas; Kagan, S. (1993), "Rejecting Barbie, Doll Maker Gains, *New York Times* [Online], September 1: D1 (available: Lexis-Nexis, accessed July 27, 1999); Kassulke, N. (1998), "What Does He Want? Jerry Frautschi's Big Arts Gift Is about Family Roots, His Dream of a Rejuvenated State Street, and the Role of the Private versus Taxpayer Money in Our City," *New York Times* [Online], October 18: 1A (available: Lexis-Nexis, accessed July 27, 1999); Sadovi, C. (1999), "A $5 Million Dollar Gift of Green; Donation Is Botanic Garden's Largest," *Chicago Sun-Times* [Online], January 6: 21 (available: Lexis-Nexis, accessed July 27, 1999); Silver, D. (1994), *Enterprising Women: Lessons from 100 of the Greatest Entrepreneurs of Our Day* (New York: AMACOM).

MARGARET RUDKIN (1897–1967)

"I believe that success is often the result of an accidental circumstance and an opportunity to take advantage of it." (Margaret Rudkin, Founder, Pepperidge Farm)

One of the earliest and fondest memories for Margaret Fogarty, a small, redheaded Irish girl born in New York City, was the sight and smell of food cooking in the large brick kitchen of her grandmother's house. She lived there with her parents, Joseph and Margaret, and her five siblings. "My grandmother used to corn her own beef . . . [this along with her] cabbage and plain boiled potatoes made a divine dish—the melting corned beef, simmered for hours with spices and herbs, and the potatoes cooked soft . . . until the 'taters opened up and smiled at you" (Rudkin, 1963: 5). Her grandmother was the one who instilled in Margaret that fresh food was better than any artificial ingredient for a meal, a credo Margaret followed and that eventually led her to achieve far more success than this Irish immigrant family could ever have imagined.

While cooking became Margaret's hobby, in school she took business courses in finance and mathematics, graduating from high school as the valedictorian of her class. Her first job was for a local bank, and then she went to work for the brokerage firm of McClure, Jones, & Co. in New York City, where she met one of the partners, Henry Rudkin, a polo-playing Irishman, who was twelve years older than she. They fell in love, were married in 1923, and had three sons. As Henry Rudkin did very well in the stock market, they moved to an expansive, 125-acre piece of land in Connecticut, which they named Pepperidge Farm after the lovely trees they now owned. Then the Great Depression hit the country, and Henry had a serious polo accident by which he was disabled for six months. They sold their twelve horses and four of their five cars and let the servants go. Now, when Margaret had to think of new ways to make money, her first thoughts focused on what she could raise on the farm. If she didn't know enough about the particular fruit, vegetable, or animal, Rudkin would write to the Department of Agriculture for information and instruction pamphlets. Recalling a later experience, she wrote, "During the war we made our own butter. As usual I knew nothing about the subject, so again I wrote to Uncle Sam for a free booklet and found it very easy to follow instructions" (Rudkin, 1963: 66).

Then, because her youngest son, Mark, had asthma, Rudkin became very interested in the relationship between this condition and food additives. She recalled, "In 1937 the most amazing period of my life started purely by chance. I had become intensely interested in the study of proper nutrition, particularly for young children. Searching for medical advice about treating a special allergic condition, I was told by an allergy specialist that a basic diet of natural foods was most important" (Rudkin, 1963: 199). This quest for her son's relief triggered Rudkin's experimenting with making bread from fresh, stoneground whole wheat. "I had never made a loaf of bread in my life, but I got out all the cookbooks I owned, read all the directions, and started." Then she described the results: "That first loaf should have been sent to the Smithsonian Institution as a sample of bread from the Stone Age, for it was hard as a rock and about one inch high" (199). However, in her typical competitive style, Rudkin kept at it until the results were praised by her family. Then she told her son's doctor what she had baked, but he didn't believe she could make an edible loaf of bread from the ingredients she described. To convince him, she brought in a loaf for him to try. He thought it was so good that he began to supply the bread to his other patients. This was the beginning of the fast rise to fame of the Pepperidge Farm bread, even though it was a more expensive loaf than others on the market because Rudkin used only fresh ingredients, as she had learned from her grandmother.

At first, Rudkin didn't think of herself as having started a business, and money was very tight. She wrote, "I didn't spend a dollar if I could avoid it, and just used odds and ends I had in the house. I had a small gas stove in which we could make eight loaves at a time, an old table, a few mixing bowls, the old baby scale brought down from the attic to weigh the dough" (Rudkin, 1963: 210). Rudkin approached a local grocer and asked him to taste her bread—with her homemade butter, of course. He took all the loaves she had with her, and by the time she got back home, he had already called for more since every loaf had been sold. She then approached the manager of Charles and Company in New York with the same technique; the taste test won another customer. But she had the problem of how to deliver the bread order from Connecticut to New York by early morning; however, as her husband was now recovered and back to work in the city, he became her first deliverer of the baked goods. Before long, Rudkin needed to hire a delivery service because the demand was so high. Within just two months of having sold her first loaf of bread, so many loaves of bread were demanded that Rudkin needed to move into the larger buildings on the farm and hire more bakers. She demanded high-quality product and service from her employees and, in return, gave them better than average compensation packages. Three years later, she borrowed $15,000 and moved the business to expanded space in Norwalk, Connecticut, where the 50,000 loaves needed to meet demand could be baked and distributed. "There was no planning, no theory," Rudkin explained, "just: What is necessary to do next? Well, let's do it and see what happens. It was fun" (204).

Though she had planned more expansion in the early 1940s, this was halted because of World War II, as was the production of certain of their products. "Serious shortages plagued Pepperidge Farm during the war years, as essential ingredients such as honey, butter, sugar and flour were dramatically rationed. Products whose quality Mrs. Rudkin could not ensure were discontinued [as she had learned from her grandmother] until only the highest quality ingredients could once again be found" (Pepperidge Farm, 1999). By 1949, a new plant was opened in Pennsylvania, producing almost 80,000 loaves of bread a week. Four years later, another bakery was opened in Illinois, and the Pepperidge Farm company was now turning out over a million loaves a week. Rudkin herself was appearing in television commercials for her Pepperidge Farm baked goods.

By the early 1960s, annual sales were over $30 million, and Pepperidge Farm was acquired by the Campbell Soup Company. Rudkin served on the board of directors until her death in 1967. Thirty years later, the Pepperidge Farm division had eight plants in the United States and sales exceeding half a billion dollars.

SOURCES: Rudkin, M. (1963), *The Margaret Rudkin Pepperidge Farm Cookbook* (New York: Grosset & Dunlap); Pepperidge Farm: From Country Kitchen to Multi-Million Dollar Company (1999), *http://www.careermag.com/employers/pepperidge farm/index.html* (accessed July 13, 1999).

DEBRA ST. CLAIR (1953–   )

"What I can do is take a seed idea and carry it through to gestation and full manifestation. I take an original intuition and turn it into a reality." (Debra St. Clair, Founder, EcoNatural Systems)

Debra St. Clair's father was the first to recognize that his daughter didn't fit into any ordinary molds. He would tell her that she "better learn how to make [her] own business because she was so stubborn that she probably wouldn't be able to work for anyone else" (Kellogg, 1999). Only seventeen when she graduated from high school in Bloomington, Indiana, St. Clair went to college right away, attending Indiana University. She left after a year because she found herself restless with the standard college subjects. What really interested her were the possibilities for healing that lay hidden in plants and herbs, an interest passed on to her by her mother. This led St. Clair to study with the Dominion Herbal College in British Columbia and the School of Natural Healing in Utah while also taking courses in anatomy and physiology. With her interest in natural healing now having become a passion, St. Clair went to work with Dr. Edmond Bordeaux Szekeley, the author of over fifty books on natural medicine. He became her mentor, guiding her in the study of biogenic living and the development of a life-generating lifestyle.

In 1976, after her father died and left her an inheritance, St. Clair decided to use the money to start a business, the Sun Spirit Trading Company, selling herbal potpourris. However, Debra St. Clair wouldn't start just one enterprise. Over the course of the next twenty years, she would initiate three more ventures.

The products and gifts offered by Sun Spirit Trading Company quickly became desired merchandise in stores like Nordstrom, Nieman-Marcus, Lord & Taylor, and Saks Fifth Avenue in New York City. In less than a year, St. Clair took her line national and rapidly learned how to price, market, finance, and distribute her company's offerings. Six years later, she sold the company and became a research assistant for Dr. Bernard Jensen to acquire more knowledge of nutrition and experience in the field she loved. St. Clair also took courses in massage therapy and graphic design, receiving certificates in both fields.

By 1983, Debra St. Clair was lecturing nationwide in her chosen field and teaching classes on herbal medicine. She moved to Boulder, Colorado, the following year, where she still resides, and formed the company Mother Tinctures, with her own line of herbal extracts. Within five years, she was offering more than 150 different plant extracts used for nutritional support, for fighting disease, or for homeopathic medicinal remedies. Then *Self-Care Magazine* asked her to develop a first aid kit they could offer to their readers, which led to her to redesign her packaging and rename her company Nature's Apothecary. She also developed an instructional video, *Herbal Preparations and Natural Therapies: Creating and Using a Home Herbal Medicine Chest* so that she could cut down on her travel, since she had gotten married and had two small children.

Within a few years, however, St. Clair was confronting major changes in her life. She was now divorced and a single parent, running a company with over two hundred products. It seemed like good luck when she was approached by investors interested in becoming a part of her venture. But, unfortunately, the deal went sour. "I had issues with my stockholders—I didn't like the way they were utilizing the company. . . . [They bought me out and] I have had nothing to do with that company since 1991." St. Clair bitterly noted that she lost more than $6 million from this learning experience, but there was no way that she would stay down for long.

By the end of 1993, St. Clair's current company, EcoNatural Solutions, was up and running. She developed a product called Athletic Recovery Oil, testing it on a knee injury she herself had sustained. The results were noticeably positive, saving her from having to undergo the $12,000 surgical procedure the doctors were recommending. "Within four months, my knee was healed and I had full range of motion," she pointed out. St. Clair had also become concerned about the use of animal products in what she was personally using; when she found out that her favorite breath mint, Altoids, had a nonorganic ingredient, she decided to create her own line of all-natural, organic breath mints. Even before she was able to mass-market her new product, more than $60,000 of the mints were sold, and that sales number reached a quarter of a million dollars by the end of 1994. As of 1999, EcoSolutions had launched twenty-two products with forecasts of gross annual sales rising to almost two million dollars.

This time around in her entrepreneurial ventures, St. Clair wanted her business to be socially responsible. While lecturing in Canada, she had met Dr. Jose Cabannilla, a medical doctor from the Peruvian Amazon. After finding out that they shared a common interest in preserving the medical traditions of the indigenous peoples of Peru, they formed the Ethno-Medicine Preservation Project. This organization has purchased more than 1,600 acres of rainforest for the now 6,000-acre Isula Biological Preserve and Research Station in that country. St. Clair is particularly proud that the "harvesting, preservation, and preparation methods as well as thera-peutic application of their herbal remedies" have been recorded on film. Recently she completed a documentary on this subject called *Where Elders Meet*. For St. Clair, "success is not letting obstacles and hardships keep you from living your dreams."

SOURCE: Kellogg, A. (1999), telephone interview of Debra St. Clair on April 8, with additional notes from St. Clair on April 20.

HELEN SCHULTZ (1898–1974)

"The railroads and interurban companies are determined to 'get' me if they can. . . . Well, I'm not going to be gotten unless I have to be. And if they put me out of business here, well, I'll just simply take my little buses some place else and start a few new lines." (Helen Schultz, Founder, Red Ball Transportation Company)

Bus transportation came into existence around 1910, when Helen Schultz was just entering her teen years. She was born into an Iowan farm family, the eldest daughter of Joseph and Mary Schultz. They probably were not surprised when their determined daughter left the farm right after high school to attend a Duluth, Minnesota, business college. Like many young women of her day, Helen became a stenographer, but she broke the mold by going to work in various parts of the country instead of staying close to home. These experiences made her quite an independent woman, holding positions in California with the Santa Fe Railroad company and the Cunard Steamship Lines in San Francisco and, in Minnesota, with the Duluth, South Shore and Atlantic Railroad Company. With strong experience in the transportation industry, she decided to start her own business in this field. Helen Schultz let nothing stop her, even though she was only twenty-four years old, had no savings to invest, and was female.

But Schultz wisely let none of these facts deter her. She approached a man she felt would help her, asking Emmett Butler, her former boss from Minnesota, to invest in her dream. Schultz needed $500 for her first bus, money for a few months' salaries, advertising, rent, and a location. She obviously had made quite an impression on Butler because he chose not only to make start-up funds available to Schultz but later to provide expansion monies. Thus, in April 1922, the first intercity bus line in the state of Iowa was initiated and owned by a woman. Schultz called her business the Red Ball Transportation Company, the name of a six-hundred-mile route between St. Paul, Minnesota, and St. Louis, Missouri. This title represented her long-term goal of providing bus transportation along that route.

The obstacles to running a transportation business at this time and in this area of the country became quickly evident to this young entrepreneur. Schultz's first bus, like similar vehicles of the day, broke down regularly, ending up with flat tires and getting stuck in either mud or snow because so few roads were paved. She fought discouragement when, after just such an incident, her brother, Magnus, whom she had hired as a driver, quit after he was stranded for two weeks because his bus ran into "mud up to the axles" (Walsh, 1994: 334). Yet, these were minor problems compared to the tactics used against her by her bus and railroad competitors, as well as government officials. For example, emotions became so intense with the Speedway Motor Coach Company, a Chicago firm, that "several altercations between the bus drivers of the two companies and occasional overnight jail visits . . . became 'like a nightmare' to Schultz." However, as always determined and strong willed, she pointed out that "my jaw was set and my drivers were loyal" (336). Her battles with railroaders and legislators followed the same pattern. Schultz and her drivers faced arrest, fines, and/or jail on other occasions as well. On Independence Day 1924, she wrote out " 'thirty-two $100 checks to free my drivers each time they were jailed' for their attempts to take excursionists to and from Clear Lake" (340).

These cantankerous issues were not related to Schultz's gender; they occurred as well with other bus company owners who were male. However, the newspapers enjoyed pointing out her diminutive size, as this description from *Opportunity for 1924* pointed out: "a wisp of a girl [she was twenty-six at the time], she has accomplished more in three years than most men do in an entire lifetime . . . [she had] six powerful railroads fighting her as their keenest competitor in the state of Iowa. But . . . she knew how to fight—and won. . . . [It's] the hardest part of her work, but she loves it" (Walsh, 1994: 332). Within just a few years, the Red Ball Transportation Company had become the leading bus company in Iowa with more than "eleven 24-seater coaches, some of which were up-to-date models costing eleven thousand dollars each" (342).

By 1925 Schultz had also gotten married to Donald Brewer and was starting a family. Her sister, Margaret, became the household manager and later even took care of Schultz's two children, Donald and Mary, so that

Helen could continue to run the business. Schultz developed a hard, tough reputation—like the men in her industry—in terms of her rough treatment of employees, the language she used, her need for control, and her ability to tackle heavy tasks. For example, Schultz could repair and change tires and, on one occasion, "recruited a gang of eighteen men and personally superintended the clearing of the snow on three highways" (Walsh, 1994: 346) rather than wait for officials to do it. However, by 1930, the Great Depression, which for farmers such as those in Iowa had started during the 1920s, forced Schultz to reevaluate her dream. Over sixty percent of the bus carriers were operating at a loss by 1927. "Financial problems surfaced following the high wheelage taxes on buses, failures among rural banks and . . . competition of major [regional bus] companies" (Walsh, 1996: 44). Together, these brought Schultz to the realization that it was time to get out of the business. She sold her company to Edgar Zelle, owner of the Jefferson Highway Transportation Company, for $200,000. Although she retired from this industry, Schultz stayed in business, first investing in an automobile service station, then a Firestone tire company. Later, she and her family returned to the family farm. Helen Schultz, mass transportation pioneer, died at the age of seventy-six.

SOURCES: Walsh, M. (1994) "Iowa's Bus Queen: Helen M. Schultz and the Red Ball Transportation Company," *Annals of Iowa* (Fall), the State Historical Society of Iowa; Walsh, M. (1996), "Not Rosie the Riveter: Women's Diverse Roles in the Making of the American Long-Distance Bus Industry," *Journal of Transport History* 17, no. 1 (March); *Women in Transportation: Changing America's History* (1998) (Washington, DC: U.S. Department of Transportation, March).

LUCY SCRIBNER (1853–1931)

"I felt an even greater responsibility than ever before to give my best; my financial resources, my strength, my mind and heart. In this effort, I have had wonderful blessings." (Lucy Scribner, Founder, Skidmore College)

For many people, the kind of multiple tragedies that haunted the early years of Lucy Skidmore Scribner's life might have turned them into bitter, selfish individuals. She was the only child of wealthy coal merchant, Joseph Russell and Lucy Hawley Skidmore. Her mother died shortly after Lucy was born. Her father then married Anne Holmes Krebs, and life seemed to stabilize for Lucy, a shy, modest, and friendly young woman, as she went to school and traveled in the typical fashion of privileged young Victorian ladies. When she met John Blair Scribner, the eldest son of the publishing tycoon, they fell in love and were married shortly afterward in 1875. But tragedy lay ahead. In less than three years, she lost her two babies, and her beloved husband died suddenly of pneumonia at only twenty-six years of age.

For a while, Lucy tried to distract herself with travels and quiet pursuits, but when her father died in 1882, her own health began to deteriorate. She traveled around Europe for a while, and then, at the invitation of concerned friends, in 1900 she visited Saratoga Springs, New York, to see if the world-renowned mineral springs located there would help her regain health. She found much more. Because the environment was airy, bright, and welcoming to this weary woman she spent more time there than she had originally planned, finally deciding to set up permanent residence on North Broadway. Lucy Scribner also noticed that the young women of the area didn't have many opportunities to learn skills that would enable them to become self-supporting, she decided to do something about this.

In 1903 Scribner initiated the Young Women's Industrial Club (YWIC) in Saratoga. The early courses offered included cooking, dressmaking, typing, stenography, music, French, and German, and some of them were taught by local women. Eventually, the study of teaching was added because of the expressed interest and needs in this field. Other unique characteristics about the school were that it was integrated and did not have a religion restriction. These policies were clearly stated for all to read in Appendix A of the school's constitution: "This club shall be nonsectarian and open to girls and young women of good character, Protestant or Catholic, white, negro, or Indian" (*Classes*, 1910). The administration also didn't restrict admission based on marital status, an unusual position at this time in the history of women's education. The primary goal of the club was to develop a graduate who was self-sufficient, hard-working, diligent, socially conscientious, and thus employable.

Yet Scribner's bad luck still plagued her. During the early period of starting her educational establishment, she suffered from a series of illnesses that included an eye disease and a painful back stiffened because of illness. Then, in 1906, she was stricken with typhoid, from which she was sick for ten months. But she remained dedicated to her work for the school. She risked not only her health but her personal wealth as well, often curtailing her own personal expenses to give more and more to the college, paying off deficits when the college didn't break even.

By 1911 the Club had become the Skidmore School of Arts, with both full-time and part-time female and male students being accepted into the programs. The school was doing very well, and although she was the driving force behind its initiation, Scribner did not want it named after her because she felt that the entire endeavor had been the work of many. She was pleased, however, when the board of trustees named the educational organization after her father. The school's articulated goal was for each student who graduated to be "free from ignorance or prejudice [and] having the power to judge for herself and her fellow beings kindly and fairly and to be able to do good to herself and the world" (Hoffman, 1975: 36). A year later the school became a single-sex institution and remained so for sixty years. In 1922 Skidmore became a four-year, degree-granting college. The first eleven women graduated not with bachelor of arts degrees but with bachelor of science degrees, because they were taught "technical" subjects. At the time of Lucy Scribner's death in 1931, the college had more than six hundred students (Traeger, 1994).

The legacy of Lucy Skidmore Scribner is the initiation of a renowned liberal arts college whose faculty educate over 2,000 students a year and whose 24,000 alums are located all over the world. The daughter of Skidmore College's first president, Maud Keyes Decker, recalled the spirit of Lucy Scribner when she wrote in her father's biography, "Mrs. Scribner was one of the pioneers in this country in establishing clubs and extension courses for girls and women employed by business and industry. . . . I found her quiet, poised, experienced, and possessed of that warmth of enthusiasm for her work which is always contagious and, coupled with it, a fine sensitiveness, an awareness of the other person" (Decker, 1937: 104–105). Certainly Scribner's commitment to quality education confirms this observation.

SOURCES: *Classes of the Young Women's Industrial Club, 1910–11* (1910), Archives of Skidmore College; Decker, M. (1937), *Charles Henry Keyes: A Biography* (Minneapolis, MN: University Printing Company); Hoffman, A. (1975), "History of an Idea: Skidmore College 1903–1925," Ph.D. diss., Columbia University; Traeger, J. (1994), *The Women's Chronology: A Year-by-Year Record, from Prehistory to the Present* (New York: Henry Holt and Company).

MARY SEYMOUR (1846–1893)

"It is the desire of the directors to found a publishing house in which, not only the management, but the printing and every possible detail of the work may be in the hands of women." (Mary Seymour, Founder and Publisher, the *Business Women's Journal* and the *American Women's Journal*)

Mary F. Seymour was already the owner of a stenographic business, the Union Stenographic Company, located on Broadway and Park Row in New York City, when she published her first edition of the *Business Women's Journal* in January 1889. An excerpt from the *Albany Argus* quoted in the first edition of her paper described Seymour as "an indefatigable and successful business woman . . . [who] employs a large staff of experts. The work done by her is largely on law documents, and she is as well posted on law forms as a lawyer. She is a notary public and the first woman commissioner of deeds appointed for New Jersey" (*Business Women's Journal*, 1889: 32). According to an advertisement run in her newspaper, she employed twenty regular employees and up to fifty temporary typists as demand warranted. In addition, she was president of the Union Stenographic and Typewriting Association, which was located at the same address and through which students were trained in the requisite skills to provide transcriptions for lawyers and architects.

The masthead of Seymour's bimonthly newspaper read: "A Magazine devoted to the interests of all Women, especially those engaged in active pursuits." In the prospectus that began the first edition, Seymour eloquently declared her vision for the paper, its market, and its strategy:

For ten years we have tried to demonstrate that there is no sex in good work. Now we hope to broaden our influence and show that success is possible not in one sphere alone, but in all. Enough examples of prosperous women can be gathered in every business and profession to prove that success is the birthright of all who take the path which nature points out, and follow it fearlessly, persistently, and in a womanly way . . . in each new field of labor she must struggle hard to win. She who first reaches the stake will take the prize, and we wish to cheer her on in the unequal race, to tear away all the obstacles that custom has placed in her path, and to be among the first to place the laurel wreath on her brow. By recording the deeds of the brave we hope to inspire the feeble. (Seymour, 1889: 2)

The content of the *Business Women's Journal* included stories of now historically significant women such as reformer Frances Willard and American Red Cross founder Clara Barton. In addition, there were articles encouraging women to enter what at the time were considered nontraditional fields, like architecture and medicine. For those women choosing to follow more socially acceptable paths, there was information on how to be an efficient, effective, and professional clerical worker. Other examples of topics covered were women who fought in the Revolutionary War, women from California to Bologna, women in the offices of civil engineers, hospital nursing in England, how poor girls may learn a profession, and practical hints to students of stenography. In addition, short stories authored by women and articles about clothing of the times were featured. Seymour articulated the objectives for the newspaper: "[to] advocate the adoption of some avocation by every woman whose time is not occupied in household duties . . . to help all those who are seeking employment to select the most fitting . . . to stimulate those already employed to do their work in the best possible manner . . . to suggest new fields of labor . . . [to champion] the poor working girl and all women who suffer from unjust laws or customs . . . [to] look at the woman's side of every question" (Seymour, 1889: 2–3).

The paper was published only until 1892 because Seymour had health problems; she died the following year at the age of forty-seven, and the *Business Women's Journal* ceased to exist. But its pages contain a wealth of valuable information about women's lives and contributions during this historic period that were fortunately preserved by Seymour through her initiative and the comprehensive content of her publication.

SOURCE: Seymour, M. (1889), *Business Women's Journal* 1, no. 1: 1–32.

REBECCA SHAHMOON SHANOK
(1943–   )

> *"Everything worthwhile that I've done took far more investment than I ever could have imagined. But why would you want to live a life if you didn't have deep investments and commitments? I never thought 'I wish I didn't get into something.' I've always just said, 'I'm lucky to have this responsibility because it's so interesting, so worthwhile.'"*
> (Rebecca Shahmoon Shanok, M.S.W., Ph.D., Psychotherapist Founding Director, Institute for Clinical Studies of Infants, Toddlers, and Parents)

Rebecca Shahmoon was the second of four daughters born to Solomon and Hannah Shahmoon, Jewish immigrants from Baghdad who had not come to the United States by choice. When he was just eighteen, Mr. Shahmoon had left Baghdad for East Asia and eventually became a very successful importer/exporter of opium [legal then] and raw silk in Shanghai. He returned in 1938 when he was in his mid-forties to marry Hannah, nineteen at the time. They moved to Paris and welcomed their first child, Rachel, but then had to leave France because of the escalation of World War II. Jews were in great jeopardy, and the Shamoons just barely made the "last train out." They ended up on dangerous high seas trying to seek refuge in America. Luckily, when they arrived at Ellis Island in New York, they were able to get word to relatives who facilitated their processing and permission to stay. Rebecca acknowledged, "I got strengths from both my parents. My

father made grand plans; my mother was hard working and extremely creative. Both of my parents were generous and intelligent. From them I also
learned to appreciate all kinds of people and to be frugal. They were risk-
takers, and I like doing 'new' things" (Oppedisano, 1997). Yet, the isolation she experienced would stay with Rebecca. "I always felt like I was on
the outside . . . being an 'immigrant' was always there."

The Shamans moved to New Rochelle, New York. There they protected
their family in a large home behind iron gates, but this only heightened the
sense of difference their daughters felt. By sixteen, Rebecca experienced
serious emotional problems, and, following a reply letter from Ann Lan-
ders, began psychotherapy. Her parents, while not formally educated, accepted the idea that their daughters would get a college education, as long
as it was within five hundred miles of home and at an all-female college.
Rebecca took a compass, put it on a map, and drew a circle of that radius.
"The farthest was Elmira College and that's where I went." However, during her freshman year, Rebecca had a "mini-nervous breakdown" and went
into psychoanalysis. She summarized having gotten this timely help as
"lucky . . . I was very lucky." Her later professional choices were shaped
by these early struggles.

At this time, since Rebecca had been interested in theater in high school,
she set her sights on a career in acting. At eighteen, she moved into a New
York City apartment with two friends, took acting classes at the Herbert
Bergoff Theater, enrolled in the Martha Graham School of Contemporary
Dance, and took courses at the New School and at Columbia and New
York universities. "Theater contributed to my becoming effective with others," she later realized. "You have to put yourself in another's shoes when
you're acting, just like when you're a therapist." However, since she was
only in her late teens, there was still an undercurrent of insecurity in Shahmoon. "I never thought of myself as smart because I'd manage to succeed
in the courses I liked, but fail all those I didn't find interesting."

Her life shifted when she got a job as an assistant teacher in a nursery
school. She loved it and over time, "got interested in the kids I couldn't
help." While working, she pursued her college education in earnest so she
could go to graduate school and become a child psychotherapist. At twenty-
one, she married Charles Shanok, a long-time friend she thought of as her
"secure base." By 1968, Shahmoon Shanok had a bachelor's degree in early
childhood education, and, two years later, a master's in social work. She
then quickly became senior social worker with the Jewish Board and Family
Children's Services (JBFCS). Her first son, Noah, was born in 1974. She
began private practice the next year, almost by accident. In 1975, a colleague asked if she would consider taking on a private patient—the girl-
friend of one of his clients; she accepted and gradually found she had a
steady stream of referred private patients.

Shortly thereafter, Shahmoon Shanok had her second child, a daughter,

Arielle, and decided to extend her professional boundaries once again by going for her doctoral degree in clinical psychology at Columbia University. For her dissertation, she focused on how women grow and change when they became mothers. She expanded upon Erikson's work on lifelong maturation. "What I observed, researched, and wrote about were that physiological changes slow down starting in our early twenties so that the nature of adulthood differs greatly from the burgeoning developmental unfolding of childhood and adolescence. In adulthood, there is a deepening, shifting, and modifying of identities and of relationship capacities in response to internal and external events. Parenting is one among many of these 'marker processes or marker principles' as I called them. Having a child, being responsible for another life, affects you on all levels."

While Shahmoon Shanok was working on her degree and maintaining a part-time work schedule at the Madeline Borg Community Services and Child Development Center of JBFCS, she was also trying unsuccessfully to find a progressive Jewish school for her children. Then she learned that a man named Peter Geffen also had the same goal. They joined forces, and in 1981 the doors of the Abraham Joshua Heschel School opened, with Shahmoon Shanok as the founding president, a position she held until 1991. Twenty-eight children were in those first classes, but the numbers quickly grew to over four hundred. She is still on the board of trustees, and they are now planning a high school, again with social responsibility and critical thinking at the core of their educational philosophy.

Through her work as a board member of Zero to Three: The National Center for Infants, Toddlers, and Families, Shahmoon Shanok also was gaining a national reputation as an expert regarding children with developmental delays—those with what she terms "constitutional challenges." An expert in peer play psychotherapy and in interweaving mental health approaches in schools, she strongly espoused that children needed to be approached with respect, beginning where they are and cultivating their initiative and their strengths. Shahmoon Shanok become a frequent speaker at conferences and symposia. At one of these events, she was approached by a writer from *Parents'* magazine, who asked her to submit a sample column. She did one on "Sharing Family Stories" and became a contributing editor to the magazine for several years.

In 1993, Dr. Shahmoon Shanok received an intriguing and challenging letter from Chicago-based philanthropist Irving Brooks Harris, who had initiated the Erikson Institute and the "Ounce of Prevention Fund" in Chicago. He was interested in improving the training of professionals working with infants and young children. In his small survey of leaders, he asked: "What would you do with your training program if you were to get $50,000 a year guaranteed for five years? $100,000? $200,000? What else does this bring to mind?" Although she knew it was just a survey, Shahmoon Shanok responded passionately about what she felt could be done.

When he called to thank her, she believed that was all that was going to happen. To her great surprise, he decided to award her a five-year grant of $1 million a few months later. With this money Shahmoon Shanok strengthened the Early Childhood Group Therapy Training and Service Program and became the Founding Director of the Institute for Clinical Studies of Infants, Toddlers, and Parents. She describes Harris as "an American hero, the only person I've ever referred to this way. He is single-handedly changing the face of training and services to benefit our nation's youngest children."

With her children grown and her marriage ended, Dr. Shahmoon Shanok has since brought aboard an associate for her private practice and plans to write a book on her peer play psychotherapy as a strength-centered model to support children's wholesome development, reach out to their parents and teachers, and improve schools. "We need to spot the children *before* they begin to fail," she emphasizes." Though her plate is full, she concluded, "I'm a bit of a missionary at heart. Preschools and schools in general can become a safety net, catching kids, cherishing their strengths, partnering their vulnerabilities, and cultivating their initiative. My goal is to spread the know-how we've gained." Shahmoon Shanok's programs have recently received a substantial grant from Head Start/New York to do just that on a research and demonstration basis in three of their agencies.

SOURCE: Oppedisano, J. (1997), interview with Rebecca Shahmoon Shanok, M.S.W., Ph.D., on February 28, in Saratoga, New York, with additional notes July–August 1999.

MURIEL SIEBERT (1930–   )

> *"I happen to think women are our country's secret weapon. If we did not have the educated women in the work force, we all would be second class citizens. And without them, we could not compete on a global basis."* (Muriel Siebert, Founder, Muriel Siebert and Company, Inc.)

To understand the personal drive behind the successes of Muriel "Mickie" Siebert, the "First Woman of Finance," it is necessary to look back at her early family life. Siebert was born in Cleveland, Ohio, the youngest of two daughters. She recalled, "My mother had a God-given voice, and she was offered a place on the stage, but nice Jewish girls didn't go on the stage in those days, so I grew up with a woman who was frustrated her entire life.

I certainly wasn't going to play that role. I vowed I would do whatever I wanted to do" (Kempton, 1993: 41). While Siebert was attending Case Western Reserve University, her father was "dying of cancer and it was a long, hard death. Three years with nurses around the clock and he died broke," she remembered painfully (MacLean, 1997: 203). Siebert dropped out of college to support her mother and her older sister, who had psychological problems and was eventually institutionalized. Since there were limited opportunities for women in Cleveland, Siebert went to New York City in 1954 with only $500 in her pocket. She was hired as a research analyst for the financial firm of Bache and Company, starting at $65 a week.

When Siebert received her first commission stock order from the administrators of the Madison Fund, who wanted to show their appreciation for having made money on a report she wrote, her career took a dramatic turn. Siebert related that she was "slugging it out with the boys . . . [and fighting] like a son-of-a-bitch" (Kempton, 1993: 40); that's what it took. She built up an impressive commission business, then became a partner at Stearns and Company, followed by a partnership with Finkle and Company. She was successful because she had a keen ability to analyze data. "When I look at a page of financial data, the numbers speak to me. I know a balance sheet; I can understand cash flow and depreciation. It's always been this way for me" (Siebert, 1997).

It didn't take long, however, for Siebert to become frustrated with working harder than her male counterparts, bringing in more business but still making less, no matter what she did. She turned to a colleague she trusted for advice, Gerald Tsai, founder of the Manhattan Fund. He told her that she "would have to buy a seat [on the New York Stock Exchange (NYSE)] . . . that was the triggering point for me. . . . He didn't help me, but I was able to buy the seat" (Siebert, 1996). No rules had prevented a woman from becoming a member, yet the historical practice had been to discourage such an action. Thus, in 1967, Muriel Siebert became the first woman to hold a seat on the NYSE; it cost her $400,000.

Muriel Siebert and Company, Inc., was set up in offices on Third Avenue in New York and structured as a sub-chapter S company. In 1975 Siebert's firm became a retail discount brokerage company. Two years later, then New York State governor Hugh Carey asked her to serve as the state's banking commissioner; she accepted, but to do so she had to place her firm in a blind trust. When she returned in 1982 after five years in public service, Siebert found her business in disarray. "Three of her employees had walked out with tapes of her customer lists, and she had to rebuild her company in every department" (Siebert, 1998: 3).

Not only did Siebert rebuild her company but, by 1996, it had reached a market value of $160 million, employed 120 people, and had over 80,000 accounts. As Siebert would explain it, "That is what I do for a living. I do a lot of pro bono for my soul" (MacLean, 1997: 200). She has set up three foundations: the Muriel Siebert Foundation, the Los Angeles Women's Entrepreneurial Fund, and the Siebert Entrepreneurial Philanthropic Plan. To date, contributions of over $4 million have been donated to various organizations through Siebert's generosity; however, her goal is for this level to reach $5 to $10 million annually. "My mother raised us to believe that with success comes obligation," she explained (Kempton, 1993: 41).

In 1996 Siebert made a significant strategic move with her firm; she took the company public by a merger with a furniture company that was liquidating—in essence, a "shell" company. The renamed Siebert Financial Corporation now was traded on the NASDAQ stock exchange. One of the reasons for this merger was that Siebert wanted to expand her business through acquisitions. "To do so she need[ed] a currency to pay for those deals. Sellers of rival brokerage firms or asset management companies are more likely to accept publicly traded stock that share in a private company than to accept a cash deal that could create a tax obligation" (Wyatt, 1996: 6). By 1998 the market value of Siebert's firm was $191.67 million; she was still the president and chief executive officer and owned approximately ninety-six percent of the company's stock.

Muriel Siebert has received numerous prestigious recognitions, including ten honorary doctorates, as well as being inducted into the Ohio Women's Hall of Fame and the International Women's Hall of Fame. She has also served as the director of the New York State Business Council and sits on a number of boards of trustees. In answer to the inevitable question about retirement, Muriel Siebert declared: "I had an uncle who worked until he was 95. . . . I'll keep going until I get bored. . . . I take pride in what I do and as long as I'm enjoying myself, I'll work" (MacLean, 1997: 208).

SOURCES: Herera, S. (1997), *Women of the Street: Making It on Wall Street— The World's Toughest Business* (New York: John Wiley and Sons); Kahn, L. (1963), *Women and Wall Street* (New York: MacFadden Books); Kempton, B. (1993), "What Does Success Really Mean? A Conversation with Muriel Siebert," *Executive Female* (January/February): 38–41; MacLean, B. (1997), *I Can't Do What? Voices of Pathfinding Women* (Venture, CA: Pathfinder Publishing); Siebert, M. (1998), *http://www.msiebert.com/html*; Siebert, M. (1997), speech, Governor George Pataki's Economic Summit for Women, May 19, Albany, New York; Siebert, M. (1996), Conversation with Jeannette Oppedisano, December 13, in New York; Taylor, R. (1988), *Exceptional Entrepreneurial Women: Strategies for Success* (New York: Praeger); Wyatt, E. (1996), "Wall St.'s Top Woman Slips in the Back Door," *New York Times*, February 11: 5–7.

GLORIA STEINEM (1934–   )

"You empower yourself by freeing yourself from the external authority that depends on undermining your self-authority in order to function . . . you start to question history. . . . You realize that you really didn't learn it all." (Gloria Steinem, Co-founder of *Ms.* magazine)

In a 1996 interview with reporter Don George, Gloria Steinem identified the three important factors that shaped her lifecourse: leaving Toledo, which made possible different educational experiences than would otherwise have been available to her; travel, particularly her two years in India; and "the belated time at which feminism began to dawn on me . . . around 1969" (George, 1996: 2). Steinem's childhood and teen years were full of disorder and trauma. Her mother, Ruth, had a series of nervous breakdowns and became progressively more mentally ill; her father was a traveling salesman who barely eked out a living. Though she had a much older sister, this sibling lived in Washington, DC; Steinem became nursemaid to her mother. To her father, she was more a friend than a child. She loved him: "Against all he had been taught a man's life should be, against all convention for raising children and especially little girls, he loved and honored me as a unique person. And let me know that he and I—and men and women—are not opposites at all" (Heilbrun, 1995: 21–22).

Her father left the family when he could no longer tolerate his wife's degenerating mental condition; at that point, Steinem's life became one of raw survival. According to a childhood neighbor, Lillian Barnes Borton, quoted in the *Toledo Blade* newspaper, Gloria Steinem lived in a house that "was in a bad state of disrepair and very definitely overrun with rats. The rats would even get up on our beds at night, they were in our kitchen range and sink cabinet. . . . I remember when Gloria was bitten by the rats. Mrs. Steinem was so terribly upset that she cried" (Heilbrun, 1995: 25).

In 1951, when Gloria was seventeen, Suzanne, her older sister, strongly suggested to their father that he give Gloria a break from the responsibilities of caring for her mother. He made a commitment to do so for a year so that Steinem could go back with her sister to Washington, DC, to finish high school. This opportunity put Steinem's life on a very different and exciting path. She finished high school and was accepted at Smith College. When she graduated from college, she spent two years in India and wrote *The Thousand Indias* for the Indian Tourist Bureau. After this experience, she returned the states and worked as a journalist for a number of magazines.

During the latter part of the 1960s, Steinem was working for *New York* magazine when she was sent to cover a hearing on whether or not New York State laws on abortion should be liberalized. "I was hearing women stand up and tell the truth about this [abortion] experience and realizing that it was something that one in three, or one in four American women had needed even then. It made me understand why I had gone through life identifying with the wrong groups, because I was a wrong group too" (Heilbrun, 1995: 3).

Culturally, Steinem realized that a burgeoning women's social movement—what many called the feminist perspective—was under way. Yet, there was no vehicle for documentation and distribution of this "new" realization of women's experiences. Steinem determined that a magazine could be a powerful vehicle for social change, yet she didn't want to be the one to start such a venture; she was, after all, a journalist. However, the background she had gained as one of the initiators of *New York* magazine, coupled with her soul sister Pat Carbine's expertise garnered from being executive editor and editor-in-chief of *Look* and *McCall's* magazines respectively, was the kind of professional experience needed for such an effort to be successful. Another forward-focused woman, Katherine Graham, publisher of the *Washington Post*, put up $20,000 as seed money to start such a magazine.

A sample issue, appropriately titled *Ms.*, first came out in December 1971 as a supplement to *New York* magazine. The response received was a clear demonstration of the potential for a significant readership. The first full issue of 250,000 copies, which came out in the spring of 1972, sold out within eight days. By 1979 the magazine was part of the Ms. Foundation for Education and Communication and, as such, was a nonprofit entity. For most of the time that *Ms.* was published, Steinem had been pouring money into the magazine from the income she received as a public speaker and author. In 1986 she responded to a *People* magazine story that alleged her income to be six figures: "It's more rewarding to watch money change the world than to watch it accumulate. That's why most of my royalty and speaking income is given to the Women's Movement, why my editing at *Ms.* is unsalaried" (Heilbrun, 1995: 365).

In 1987, the magazine was sold to an Australian-based company, John Fairfax, Ltd.; subsequent owners have included Lang Communications in 1989 and, in 1996, MacDonald Communications Corporation. The magazine's circulation has ranged from a high of 700,000 to a low of 200,000—a point at which MacDonald shut the magazine down. However, a contract condition with Steinem stated that she would be given the right of first refusal if the magazine were ever to be sold. In December 1998, she, along with the editor-in-chief of *Ms.*, Marcia Ann Gillespie, joined with

Liberty Media, a group of women investors who gave her the money to keep *Ms.* alive. Steinem recalled, "All those years of begging. *Ms.* never had enough money, ever. We were underfunded to begin with, and we couldn't get advertisers because we wouldn't cater to them. . . . Now there were networks of women with money. They were so amazing. I had never imagined I would come across so many people who cared and were willing to invest" (McNamara, 1999: D4). Coinciding with Steinem's sixty-fifth birthday in March 1999, the relaunching of *Ms.* magazine occurred.

Steinem continues to work for the full economic empowerment of women. "Consciousness, the first stage of big time consciousness change, has been completed and we've made important incursions into all kinds of areas where women were not present before. But we are just beginning institutional change because, for instance, we haven't changed the work pattern. We haven't changed who cares for children" (George, 1996: 8). Thus, she continues to throw out challenges for still needed change in society to bring women into equal status with men.

SOURCES: George, D. (1996), "Gloria Steinem—on the Web," *http://www.ms. foundation.org/* (accessed July 22, 1997): 1–15; Heilbrun, C. (1995), *The Education of a Woman: The Life of Gloria Steinem* (New York: Dial Press); McNamara, M. (1999) "*Ms.* Magazine's Future Tied to Gloria Steinem: Redesigned Publication Due This Month," *Times Union*, Life and Leisure, March 12: D4; Thom, M. (1997), *Inside Ms.: 25 Years of the Magazine and the Feminist Movement* (New York: Henry Holt and Company); Zeff, L. (1995), *Gloria Steinem: Ms. America* [Videorecording], A&E Home Video.

ELLEN STEWART (1920–   )

"Pick up your head, baby. You aren't gonna see anything staring at your feet." (Ellen Stewart, Founder, La Mama E.T.C.—Experimental Theater Club)

Ellen Stewart came to New York City in 1950 to be a fashion designer, but she found herself on a labyrinthian path that led her to a surprising deed—creating a world-renowned experimental theater that has survived for almost forty years. Stewart had left Chicago and been in the Big Apple for only a few days when she saw a beautiful church. A devout Catholic, she decided to go in, light a candle, and pray that she would find a job soon since she had little money left. When she came out, Stewart saw Saks

Fifth Avenue, went across the street, and asked if they had any openings. They hired her as a porter, one of the few jobs available to blacks in the 1950s (Anderson, 1997).

In short order, Stewart was recognized for her creative designs. She had befriended an elderly fabric dealer in the garment district, Abraham "Papa" Diamond. "He recognized her raw talent and supplied her with material and encouragement as she honed her design skills. He also exhorted her to always have a 'pushcart'—a dream to propel her creativity and action—and to use it to help others" (Sharp, 1997). She would wear her creations to work. When a customer noticed the quality and brought it to the attention of her employer, Stewart was offered the opportunity to advance from her menial job to work in the lingerie department, where she could finish garments. She soon became a fashion designer at Saks and ultimately ran the sportswear department. But racism came at her from both sides of the color line. When Stewart was no longer required to wear the smocks other black employees had to wear, they asked her to intervene for them. She did so but was unsuccessful. She remembered their response. "They ran the elevators, and when I went to get on, they'd close the door in my face. If I went into the cafeteria, they'd all get up and leave. They really punished me. I was boycotted for the whole eight years I was there" (Anderson, 1997: 31). The U.S. white workers gave her a hard time too because they didn't want to work with a black woman. The one group of people who accepted her were the World War II refugees from Europe. They even nicknamed her "Mama," the label that she carries still today. Even when Saks tried to recognize Stewart formally for the notable accomplishment of being the "only American to have two gowns at the coronation of Queen Elizabeth II" (Sharp, 1997), racism reared its ugly head once again. Saks planned a lunch in her honor in 1953, but the restaurant refused to seat her (Harris, 1992).

By 1960, Stewart needed a new direction and suddenly got overwhelmed with the idea of opening a basement coffeehouse on the Lower East Side of Manhattan. "I just do what I'm told to do. I listen to the ideas that come to me and go willingly where I sense I'm to go," she explained. "I don't wonder how it's going to turn out" (Anderson, 1997: 31). She gave the cafe her nickname, La Mama. As she and her friends were fixing up the cafe for opening night, one of them suggested that she also use the space for a theater. That idea really caught her attention as she remembered what happened to her foster brother. A playwright, he had become so dejected by his experience with Broadway producers that he had even stopped writing (Sharp, 1997). In less than a year, Stewart initiated the La Mama—Experimental Theater Club to give those like her foster brother a chance to succeed. Remembering Papa Diamond, she put a pushcart wheel over the doorway.

The timing and the venue were right for the New York City of the 1960s, and the theater quickly became a producer/artist haven, though not a profitable venture. Stewart moonlighted as a designer for the next thirteen years to support her productions. She had a clear vision: "I started encouraging people to try to find ways to communicate through means that went beyond language so that if, say, some Chinese people were sitting in the audience, they would feel inside rather than outside of what was happening on the stage. That's our goal" (Anderson, 1997: 29). By 1965, her troupe was traveling to Europe to present their theater productions.

But political differences, both locally and abroad, created personal and professional risks for Stewart from the beginning. When she started out with La Mama in 1961, Mayor Edward Koch "saw to it that I went to jail for doing entertainment without a license" (Anderson, 1997: 31). In 1965, the French authorities took away her passport and charged her with pornography for Jean-Claude van Itallie's production of *America Hurrah* (Texier, 1990: 2). Stewart was also censored by the State Department for her troupes' travel to Poland and Romania. And, in the late 1960s and early 1970s, "blacks didn't want to be with me at La Mama unless I'd be all black. I refused. The Black Panthers even had me on a hit list. Without my knowing about it, McNeil Lowry at the Ford Foundation put a tail on me for protection" (Anderson, 1997: 31).

The Ford Foundation had started helping Stewart in 1967. The first grant of $35,000 enabled Stewart to purchase the building at 74-A East Fourth Street, an old sausage factory, and convert it into two ninety-nine-seat theaters. A second grant of $165,000 in 1968 permitted Stewart to buy a seven-story building in which she provided La Mama artists with free rehearsal space. The Ford Foundation also supported the travel of international artists, like Romanian director, Andrei Serban, to come to La Mama. Stewart's productions have appeared in countries worldwide, including Italy, Turkey, Macedonia, Croatia, and Austria; international troupes have come to La Mama from Bulgaria, Montenegro, Serbia, and other countries.

Many famous writers, directors, producers, and actors have had their start with Ellen Stewart. Among them are Harvey Fierstein, Harold Pinter, Billy Crystal, Danny DeVito, Robert De Niro, and Bette Midler. Composer/author Elizabeth Swados wrote of Stewart's passionate dedication to global exchange and of her doing what she feels is right for each individual artist. "She prescribes countries for the doldrums and makes sure an artist can get to the desert or ancient chapel she thinks will help him or her grow. She matches composers, actors, and dancers with director, designers and choreographers from halfway across the globe. Nothing stops Ellen when she senses a fitting combination" (Swados, 1986: 1).

In 1985, Ellen Stewart received the MacArthur "genius" award, with a grant of $300,000. With the money, she purchased a house in Spoleto, Italy, where she set up an artists' colony. Swados pointed out that Stewart's style of "theater [has] taught audiences to open up. She endured insults and poverty. Her gift of possibility is what resonates and persists" (Swados, 1986: 1). The arts community recognized Stewart's lifelong commitment by inducting her into the Theater Hall of Fame in 1993.

Ellen Stewart's personal philosophy is a unifying force for all. "I believe that we are one big world and that all of us are connected. It's as if there were some kind of genetic residue in each of us that binds us all together. If we could find a way to communicate through that part of our common geneticism, so to speak, there'd be an almost umbilical understanding among people. To find a way to do that—to strike a chord inside you that makes you respond to me, is what should be happening" (Anderson, 1997: 30).

SOURCES: Anderson, G. (1997), "Visiting La Mama's Founder: An Interview with Ellen Stewart," *America*, February 8: 28–32; Harris, W. (1992), "Phoenix or Ashes for La Mama," *New York Times* [Online], September 6: 2 (available: Lexis-Nexis, accessed July 28, 1999); Sharp, S. (1997), *Women Who Dare* (Washington, DC: Library of Congress Publishing Office); Swados, E. (1986), "Stretching Boundaries: The Merlin of La Mama," *New York Times* [Online], October 26: 1 (available: Lexis-Nexis, accessed July 28, 1999); Texier, C. (1990), "At La Mama, the Avant-Garde Buttons Up," *New York Times* [Online], October 28: 5 (available: Lexis-Nexis, accessed July 28, 1999).

MARTHA STEWART (1941–   )

"I felt the need to integrate my efforts under one roof so that we can be the most effective and information-centered company in media. We needed to be free in order to follow our dreams into new areas of endeavor." (Martha Stewart, Founder, Martha Stewart Living Omnimedia, Inc.)

Martha Kostyra Stewart has climbed to the top of the mountain, both literally and figuratively. She began her meteoric rise to fame in the late 1970s with a small catering business in Westport, Connecticut. In the span of just twenty years, Stewart's "information server" corporate conglomerate, Martha Stewart Living Omnimedia, Inc., "includes two magazines, a television show, 27 books, a Web page, radio spots and newspaper columns. In 1998, retail sales of her merchandise topped $1.1 billion—96 per cent more than a year ago" (*Martha's Millions*, 1999: 42). Stewart's second climb was to the top of Mount Kilimanjaro, the highest peak in Africa, with four other women. One of them, Sharon Patrick, quickly became her best friend and strategic advisor. As a result, Stewart hired her to be "president, a member of my Board, and our chief operating officer—and her English bulldog, Norman, often accompanies her to the office" (Stewart, 1998: 14).

Martha was the second oldest of six children born to Edward and Martha Ruszkowski Kostyra. Her father taught physical education in the New Jersey public school system; her mother, who was also a schoolteacher, gave up her profession to be at home full time. Entrepreneurship was demonstrated by her paternal grandfather, Franz (Frank) Kostyra, who, while serving Poland, his native land, in military service, "learned everything from baking to running a mess hall . . . he knew the meat and potatoes of food preparation and restaurant management" (Oppenheimer, 1997: 12). He immigrated to the United States, and when he settled in Jersey City, New Jersey, he opened a butcher shop, Kostyra's Meats, paid for in cash from the money he had frugally saved. He also had a second venture later, a tavern. Frank Kostyra was a tough taskmaster with his children. Martha's brother Eric explained, "Grandfather would hold a lit cigarette under Dad's elbow to force him to keep his arm up when he was practicing the violin" (13). Not surprisingly, Martha's father learned to be stern with his family, too.

According to Frank Kostyra, Martha's younger brother, "Dad was physical with us. . . . He had a fiery temper, and when we misbehaved or got out of line, we got the stick or the belt. Martha resented Dad. She *hated* him in many respects. I know she never forgave him for kicking her in the back one time on the front sidewalk for some incident. She said, 'I'll *never* forgive him' " (Oppenheimer, 1997: 25). Childhood friends were also afraid to spend much time at the Kostyra house, according to Gail Hallam Charmichael, because their father was "a tyrant" (29). Martha found comfort and security in school. As she was bright, capable, competitive, artistic, and high achieving, she quickly attracted the positive attention of teachers. Her favorite teacher, Irene Weyer, recalled, "She was a child of superior intelligence. She would make such lovely pictures. Her English, her grammar, her whole makeup showed that this child loved to learn and was creative. I'll never forget the way she carried herself, the way she spoke" (36).

These academic capabilities and personal qualities enabled Martha to gain entrance into Barnard College in New York City, where she majored in art history. To support herself, Martha both modeled and worked as a full-time maid and cook for two widowed sisters. Since she was a perfectionist and a compulsive cleaner, Martha more than met their standards. Though she didn't have a lot of time for a social life, her college friend Diane Stewart convinced both her brother, Andy, a Yale law school student, and Martha to go out on a blind date. They quickly became a couple, marrying in 1961. Martha left college to become the breadwinner while her husband completed his last year in law school. Then he continued at Columbia University, earning a master of laws degree in January 1964. Martha completed her Barnard degree program six months later. The following year, their daughter, Alexis "Lexi" Gilbert, was born.

In 1968, Martha took the stockbroker's exam and was registered with the New York Stock Exchange, at the age of twenty-seven. She went to work for Monness, Wilimas, and Sidel, starting at $100 a week plus commissions but quickly ran that number up to a six-figure salary. With both of the couple having good jobs, the Stewarts decided to move out of New York City in 1972 to a lovely "farmlette" with an 1805 Federal period house in Westport, Connecticut—a location where there was no state tax at the time. The economic troubles of the mid-1970s caused some negative interactions for Martha at work; disillusioned, she resigned in 1973. At thirty-two, she was suddenly being shaken by circumstances out of her control; some suggest she had a nervous breakdown.

By the mid-1970s, though, Martha Stewart was in the catering business, first with Ann Brody, then with Norma Collier. Stewart and Collier called their service the Uncatered Affair. "Their selling point was that the client's guests would never know the meal had been made by someone else. . . . Another marketing strategy was that they would use only natural ingredients in their concoctions. Business soon boomed" (Oppenheimer, 1997: 155). But a year later, the partnership ended abruptly, and Martha was on to her next venture, the Market Basket, a small gourmet shop. By 1978, her kitchen was gracing the cover of *Country Living* magazine, and Martha was predicting that she would have her own magazine one day.

She has been on a nonstop treadmill of achievement ever since, under the umbrella of a company bearing her name, Martha Stewart Living Omnimedia, Inc. In the summer of 1999, she took her company public in an effort to bring in $150 million from the stock sale to support the company's strategic direction. Explaining some of her future plans to the readers of her own magazine, *Martha Stewart Living*, she pointed out, "The world of online services is of great interest to us at the company, and in the near future, you will be offered television programming six days a week that is 'interactive' with your computer" (Stewart, 1997: 12). Communication with her clients, customers, and fans is a critical component for the Stewart enterprise. In just one month, over one thousand letters and two thousand e-mail messages were sent to them (12). Stewart has also initiated a new line of products with Kmart—lawn and gardening furniture; a new line of fabrics to be carried at Calico Corners and Jo-Ann Fabrics and Crafts, with eighteen patterns and an expectation that over 350 fabrics will be offered by 2002; and she has become a venture capitalist, joining other investors in funding the Internet-based business, ibeauty.com. As she pointed out in her high school yearbook: "I do what I please, and I do it with ease" (Oppenheimer, 1997: 60).

SOURCES: "Martha's Millions" (1999), *Maclean's* [Online], August 9: 42 (available: Lexis-Nexis, accessed August 24, 1999); Oppeneimer, J. (1997), *Martha Stewart—Just Desserts: The Unauthorized Biography* (New York: William Morrow and Company); Stewart, M. (1997), "A Letter from Martha," *Martha Stewart Living*, March/April: 12; Stewart, M. (1998), "A Letter from Martha," *Martha Stewart Living*, May: 14.

EMMA STINSON (1868–1940)
KATHERINE STINSON (1891–1977)
MARJORIE STINSON (1896–1975)

"The men thought I was a regular old maid about it. . . . But I wanted to see the conditions [of the plane she was going to fly]. It's all right if your automobile goes wrong while you are driving it. You can get out in the road and tinker with it. But if your airplane breaks down, you can't sit on a convenient cloud and tinker with that!" (Katherine Stinson, Co-founder of the Stinson Aviation Company)

They were savvy enough to design, build, rent, and sell airplanes. They could even train the pilots who were going off to use planes in warfare for the first time during World War I. But they weren't good enough to serve in the military themselves because they were women—specifically, the Stinson women. Their aviation saga started when young Katherine wanted to make money to go to Europe to study music so that she could become a teacher in that field. Women of the early 1900s weren't able to command high salaries; however, Katherine learned that stunt pilots could earn as much as $1,000 a day, a small fortune in comparison to what a clerk or secretary might make, and so she set her sights on the field of aviation. From the time she was a small child, Katherine had learned from her mother, Emma, that all things were possible. "My mother never warned me not to do this or that for fear of being hurt. Of course, I got hurt, but I was never afraid" (Rogers et al., 1983: 12).

Though a young woman of the early twentieth century, Katherine was moving to the beat of a different drummer. In 1910, she was driving one of the first automobiles. Once again, it was her mother who gave her permission to learn how. Her father was more protective, especially when Katherine suggested that she wanted to become a pilot. Recalling how the planes were constructed in their infancy, how dangerous they were, and what the social mores for young women were at that time, it isn't difficult to understand her father's trepidation. "My father didn't approve in the *least*. He was like the hen with an unmanageable duckling in its brood. But I finally gained the consent . . . and I set out to be an aviator" (Rogers et al., 1983: 11).

But even getting someone to teach her was a daunting task. Katherine was a mere five feet tall and weighed about one hundred pounds, hardly the kind of physical stature presumed to be necessary to maneuver those early open-air biplanes. "Max Lillie thought it was too much for most men to handle—but it would be impossible for this curly-haired girl!" (Rogers et al., 1983: 13). Nonetheless, Katherine convinced Lillie, the famous aviator from Chicago, to take her up in the air, and, with less than four hours of actual flight time, she was able to master the complexities of the machine and had learned enough to fly alone. In 1912 Katherine Stinson became the fourth woman in America to earn a pilot's license—the first being Harriet Quimby, in 1911. In short order, Katherine was a stunt pilot and was nicknamed "The Flying Schoolgirl" because she looked so young.

In 1913, Katherine and her mother, Emma Stinson, decided to start their own aviation business in Hot Springs, Arkansas, where they were living; thus the Stinson Aviation Company was formed. However, soon after, Katherine's mentor, Max Lillie, who had moved to San Antonio, Texas, because the weather permitted year-round flying, convinced the Stinsons to follow suit. They moved themselves and their business to Texas, originally leasing city land at Fort Sam Houston to begin the Stinson School of Flying. They later moved to "a 750 acre former municipal sewer farm as the site. . . . The aviation family quickly turned the farm into a thriving aviation operation" (Purificato, 1997: 14).

Katherine also taught her three siblings how to fly. Her sister Marjorie earned her pilot's license at age eighteen and soon became known as "The Flying Schoolmarm" because she was running the Stinson pilot training school. During this time, Katherine was also setting records and amazing audiences. By 1917 she had "flown longer and covered more miles than any aviator in the world, man or woman . . . her place in the history of aviation was assured" (Rogers et al., 1983: 20). Among her firsts were: first pilot to skywrite at night, first woman to fly mail in the United States, first woman to perform the loop-to-loop, and first woman pilot to fly in the Orient. In the United States she was now referred to as "The Daring Bird-Girl," and Charles Lindbergh "declared her to be the world's greatest woman flier" (Danini, 1997: 3). In Japan, they called her "The Air Queen"; in one demonstration alone, almost 25,000 Japanese came out to watch her daring feats, and fan clubs started up all over that country. In China, she made more than thirty exhibition flights.

By this time, World War I was raging in Europe. Katherine wanted to fly for the United States but was rejected. She began to do volunteer work for the Red Cross, dropping fundraising leaflets and collecting pledges as she flew various public relations trips. By the time she completed her fundraising tour of the summer of 1917, she was able to present to the secretary of the treasury over $2 million in pledges. Now she tried to become a reconnaissance pilot for the U.S. war effort but was rejected once again. In her typical determined way, Katherine headed to Europe and became an ambulance driver. Back home, Marjorie was training Canadian and American pilots for war duty; it's estimated that she trained more than eighty such pilots. While in Europe, Katherine contracted what would eventually be identified as tuberculosis, and although she was eventually cured, she never flew again. In 1929, the renamed Stinson Aircraft Company was merged with the Lycoming Motor Company. In a reminiscent moment, Katherine recalled, "In the early days, it was fun to fly. You could soar over the rooftops and trees or drop down to meet a train and wave at the engineer. . . . The whole sky belonged to you. Now they have so many regulations, and the sky is crowded. All is gone" (Danini, 1997: 3). The sisters never had children. Katherine Stinson did marry attorney and judge Miguel Otero, Jr., settling in Santa Fe, New Mexico, where she went on to study architecture, becoming an award-winning designer of homes. Marjorie never married; she went to work as an aeronautical drafter for the U.S. War Department, remaining there for fifteen years. Then she became a researcher of aviation history. Both sisters lived long lives—Marjorie until she was seventy-nine and Katherine, eighty-six.

SOURCES: Danini, C. (1997), "World Flight—Amelia Earhart to Linda Finch 1937–1997," *San Antonio Express-News*, March 9 (available: Lexis-Nexis Academic Universe, accessed February 21, 1999); Purificato, R. (1997), "A Legacy of Flight: After 81 Years, Stinson Field Remains as the Second Oldest Continually Operating Municipal Airport," *Leading Edge* [Online], *http://www.afmc.wpafb.af. mil/public/HQ-AFMC/PA/leading edge/feb97/age14.htm*, February (accessed March 19, 1999); Rogers, M., Smith, S., & Scott, J. (1983), *We Can Fly: Stories of Katherine Stinson and Other Gutsy Texas Women* (Austin, TX: Texas Foundation for Women's Resources); "Stinson S. Junior: From the Golden Age of Aviation" (1999), Arkansas Air Museum [Online], *http://www/users.nwark.com/arkairmuseum/ stinsonj.html* (accessed March 20, 1999); *Women in Transportation: Changing America's History* (1998) (Washington, DC: U.S. Department of Transportation, March).

HARRIET STRONG (1844–1926)

"My attitude was that of a humble searcher after truth. This attitude of humbleness in a woman is sometimes an advantage. When she goes forth in a rural community to make inquiries from her neighbors, she will find that they often tell her the truth about what she wants to know. Whereas the man new at ranching will nearly always assume that he knows it all, by intuition, no doubt." (Harriet Strong, Rancher, Inventor, "Walnut Queen of Southern California")

One of six children, Harriet Russell was born in Buffalo, New York, and lived there until her family moved to California when she was ten. She spent most of the rest of her life out west. From the time she was small, though, "Hattie" suffered much pain from what was then considered a female malady called "hysteria." In spite of this illness, she was able to complete two years of education at a female seminary while she was a teenager. Then, in 1863, when she was nineteen, she met a successful mining engineer named Charles Lyman Strong. Much older than she, he appeared to everyone to be a stable person who could provide well, and with her family's blessings, they were married. She was to learn later that he had a history of mental illness that soon caused his work with the Gould and Curry Mine Company to deteriorate, forcing him to leave his job. Charles then brought his family to the San Gabriel Valley of southern California not far from Los Angeles in the hopes that living on this 320-acre farm might bring him peace. In an unusual decision for a Victorian male, he put this real estate in Harriet's name. He also continued to be active in mining when his health permitted him to do so.

Though the Strongs were married for twenty years and had four daughters, whom Charles affectionately referred to as "little chicks," he was unable to have a loving relationship with his wife. She painfully recalled, "You have told me too many times you have no love to give me" (Albertine, 1994: 172). They both suffered with serious illnesses and bouts of depression, sometimes going for treatments to the same health spas when they could afford to do so. Her difficult marriage caused Harriet Strong to resent her lot in life as a wife, for she later wrote, "I do assert that marriage as a rule is the grave of every high thought & noble motive in life" (173). Since she couldn't do so publicly, Harriet rebelled against her fate in her own, then quiet way. As one example, when her husband ridiculed her for being too weak to raise a window, Strong responded by inventing and patenting a pole with an end hook to raise and lower windows as well as a screw fastener to keep windows open. Fresh air was important to her spirit.

Some of Charles Strong's health problems may have been the consequence of his work. In the mining industry, mercury poisoning was a common resulting illness. He once wrote to his wife, "Yesterday I handled considerable quick silver and it had such an effect upon my nerves that I hardly slept any all night, and this morning I feel twitchy from the crown of my head to the soles of my feet" (Albertine, 1994: 172). His mental instability coupled with a rumor he heard in 1883 about his new mining investment having been "salted"—that is, ore placed strategically to appear to be part of a rich lode—pushed Charles Strong to his emotional limit. He put his affairs in order and then shot himself to death.

Harriet had been east for a "cure." Now, at age thirty-nine, she found herself widowed with four daughters to raise and in a legal battle to retain the rights to property that was in her own name. However, her husband's death turned out to be a liberating event for Harriet Strong. Once she was in control of her destiny, her illnesses disappeared. This second half of her life was clearly established in a forward entrepreneurial push for economic independence for herself, her daughters, and women in general.

After eight years of estate litigation, Harriet Strong finally won the case. Now that her farm, Ranchito del Fuerte, was legally her domain, Strong began experimenting with raising various crops, including native fruits, pampas grass, and walnuts—new to California and thought to be impossible to grow. This was not an easy task for any farmer. Researcher Susan Albertine explained the dilemma: "Los Angeles rests in a natural drainage basin surrounded by mountains. As the city began its rapid expansion, with the boom of the 1880s water management became its most serious problem. Every three to four years much of the basin might be under water; in the dry periods, crops could not be grown without irrigation" (Albertine, 1994: 161). Since Strong was already an inventor, she combined her intuitive strength with more self-education by studying irrigation and flood-control methods and systems. Strong's ideas for flood-control dams and reservoirs were patented in 1887. She became politically active in the struggle to get approval for irrigation projects. In fact, it was Strong who originally proposed that the Colorado River be dammed so that California could get the water it needed for irrigation. In 1894, she received another patent, this one for the processes she developed to trap debris and store water. Her methods were responsible for making development in the Los Angeles basin possible, according to Albertine. The consequence of her irrigation approaches was that Strong and other farmers became very successful, especially in growing the "impossible" crop—walnuts. By 1912 the California Walnut Growers Association was formed with over one thousand members.

Strong was also a skilled, intuitive marketer. In order to increase demand for the pampas grass she was growing, she traveled east, making several stops. In Philadelphia she decorated a department store with the tall, filmy, grass plumes. The customers were so impressed that the owner ordered 134,000 plumes at a dollar a piece. In New York she convinced the Republican Party to use her plumes as their national emblem by presenting them in the red, white, and blue colors. Then, she approached the Democratic Party using a neutral plume in a different design and got another contract. Money was pouring in. Wherever she went, her marketing approach worked, and she was dubbed "The Pampas Lady" (Rasmussen, 1999). Strong was now a nationally renowned businesswoman and became the first female member of the Los Angeles Chamber of Commerce.

Harriet Strong also established several other organizations during her lifetime. One was the National Business League with its journal, the *Business Folio*. The goal of this group was for women to learn the theory and practice of business. Strong was an oil baron, too, establishing and serving as president of the Clarendon Heights, Inc., Oil Land and Petroleum Company when she successfully prospected for and found oil in the surrounding hills (Albertine, 1994: 175). Though not quantifiable, it is said that she made a fortune in her enterprises and that, although she worked with men and women, she did not want the next generation of women in her family to marry, instead creating for them at her "Ranchito del Fuerte—the little ranch of the Strong—a matriarchal home, a 'golden' haven for her family" (173).

From age forty to her death at age eighty-two from a traffic accident, she was an active feminist. In a position paper she presented at the National Suffrage Congress, Strong "argued that women could apply domestic skills to their work in the marketplace; they were excellent, experienced managers and, she maintained, naturally more honest than men" (Albertine, 1994: 175). She later declared, "It isn't any more masculine for women to vote than for men to cook dinner, and it would be all right for either to do both" (Rasmussen, 1999: B3).

Historical researcher Albertine suggests that the invisibility of Harriet Strong in recorded history might have come about because she was so successful at so many endeavors—"rancher, horticulturist, inventor and engineer, irrigation expert, financier, philanthropist, suffragist, and fiercely matriarchal head of a household" (Albertine, 1994: 180). It does not explain her absence in the entrepreneurship literature, though, for few could deny that she would be a truly incredible entrepreneurial force for any time.

SOURCES: Albertine, A. (1994), "Self Found in the Breaking: The Life Writings of Harriet Strong," *Biography* no. 17, 2: 161–185; Rasmussen, C. (1999), "L.A. Then and Now: 'Walnut Queen' Broke Lots of New Ground," *Los Angeles Times* [Online], February 28: B3 (available: Nexis-Nexis, accessed July 30, 1999).

LUCILLE TREGANOWAN (1930–   )

*"Years ago, a divorced woman with children was persona non grata
here. . . . Some neighbors didn't want their children to play with mine
because they were from a broken home. That's how bad it was."* (Lucille Treganowan, Founder of Transmissions by Lucille)

Lucille Treganowan was born and raised in Iola, Kansas, a town of about
7,000. She went away to college, attending the University of Arizona, but left
school to get married and followed her husband back to his hometown of
Pittsburgh, Pennsylvania. But in 1960, after ten years of marriage, they were
divorced. She was "too proud to return to Kansas . . . so she stayed in Pittsburgh even though it was a tough place for a single mother" (Lawson, 1996:
1). Treganowan had to figure out how to raise and support three children,
who were "then ages 6, 3, and 18 months, by herself. Her job search got her
nowhere until she drove her battered 1946 Plymouth into Scuro's Auto Repair shop . . . and overheard the owner say he had just fired a mechanic
whose wife was the bookkeeper" ("Mechanical Woman," 1996: 143). Treganowan knew that she could handle the clerical work, remarking as she recalled this moment, "I was in the right place at the right time."

Because customers kept asking her questions about the car repairs that
were being done and she didn't want to look "stupid," Treganowan began
reading automotive repair books. Though at first, she just wanted to learn
enough to "fake it," she soon discovered that she had an affinity for re-
pairing transmissions and genuinely enjoyed this work. Treganowan described the moment she came to this reality: "A little light came on and
said 'so that's how a car works.' I became fascinated and started to learn
for real" (Busk, 1997: 27). She became a mechanic in 1962, with "the boys
in the shop" saying things to her like, "Go back to the office. What do you
know?" ("Mechanical Woman," 1996: 143). A couple of years later, she
became their shop manager and then became a partner in the business. But
in 1973 a dispute erupted among the partners; this became the catalyst that
led to the opening of her own business. Her angry partner warned her that
she was "going to look like Josephine the Plumber [and be] laughed off
the streets" (Thomas, 1994: A1).

With a second mortgage and a small business loan, Treganowan was
able to open her first "Transmissions by Lucille" in an abandoned gas sta-

tion. She was the first woman in western Pennsylvania to get a small business loan. As her business grew and was profitable, she opened a second location. But after fourteen years, the responsibilities began to take a toll. "By 1987 I felt burned out. I hated getting up in the morning. To revitalize myself, I tried taking two courses at Chatham College. It was a tremendous experience so I decided to go back to school full time. . . . It got me back on track. . . . I had always had a hard time delegating, and through my courses, I developed better management skills." She graduated magna cum laude in 1991. As Treganowan approached the year 2000, she had two shops, employed nearly thirty people who serviced approximately seven hundred cars a month, and her businesses were bringing in estimated sales of $1.25 million.

Nearly seventy but in fine health, Treganowan starts each day with a half-hour walk before going in to her office, which is above the garage in what used to be her living room. She recalled that "instead of having a normal life, my kids grew up in the garage" (Lawson, 1996: C1). Her son Kip now works for the business; her other son, Todd, and daughter, Tana, chose different paths. Treganowan has five grandchildren, of whom she is very proud, but she confesses, "I get supersensitive [when the media] play up the grandma bit. ["Greasemonkey Grandma" and "Grandma Good-wrench" are two such examples.] They would never do this to a man" (Reeder, 1996: C01). For hobbies, Treganowan grows flowers and makes decorations from car parts. In fact, the shop parking lots are lined with transmissions turned into flowerpots with impatiens and petunias. She also creates clocks from pistons and tie racks from engine valves.

Treganowan's many accomplishments include publication of her book, with Gina Catanzarite, called *Lucille's Car Care: Everything You Need to Know from Under the Hood by America's Most Trusted Mechanic*; a host spot on the weekly HGTV cable television show, *Lucille's Car Clinic*; and acting as spokesperson for Jiffy Lube. Among Treganowan's assignments for this company was a trip to North Dakota in 1997 to help residents with their flood-damaged vehicles. "I think I'm successful because it's part psychological. . . . Cars and repairs are extremely expensive and a woman is comforting and soothing to talk to—almost like when a child skins a knee," she concluded (Busk, 1997: 27). Treganowan credits her father, who owned a plumbing and heating business, with helping her envision possibilities. "He treated me just like my two brothers . . . I was taught to believe that I could do anything. It never occurred to me that I shouldn't be in the transmission business because I'm a woman. That's how I was raised" (Lawson, 1996: C1).

SOURCES: Busk, C. (1997), "Lucille Knows What's Up under the Hood; Grandmother with a Wrench," *Chicago Sun-Times* [Online], February 4: 27 (available: Lexis-Nexis, accessed June 5, 1999); Lawson, C. (1996), "Under the Hood with

Lucille Treganowan: Life's Miraculous Transmissions," *New York Times* [Online], June 6: C1 (available: Lexis-Nexis, accessed June 5, 1999); "Mechanical Woman," *People Weekly* (1996) [Online], October 14: 143 (available: Proquest, accessed June 5, 1999); Reeder, S. (1996), "Ms. FIXIT," *Indianapolis Star* [Online], October 23: C01 (available: Lexis-Nexis, accessed June 5, 1999); Thomas, P. (1994), "Lucille Used to Cook Beef on Car Engines; Now She's a TV Star—In Brave New World of Cable, Ms. Treganowan Dispenses Tips on Automobile Care," *Wall Street Journal* [Online], December 30: A1 (available: Proquest, accessed June 5, 1999).

LILLIAN VERNON (1927–   )

"If a pregnant 21-year-old immigrant can start a company from scratch and turn it into a dynamic $238 million corporation, you can too." (Lillian Vernon, CEO, Lillian Vernon Corporation)

On March 18, 1927, Lilly Menasche was born in Leipzig, Germany, the second child of an aristocratic Jewish family. Before she was ten, Hitler's reign of terror had begun, and her whole world would become one of fear and flight. To escape the Nazis, her father, Herman, a businessman, took the family to the Netherlands. Before long, he knew that they would not be safe there either, and he managed, fortunately, to get them all to the United States. Even though no one in the family could speak English yet, Mr. Menasche attempted to continue the type of manufacturing business he had had in Europe—producing lingerie. This wasn't successful enough to support the family, but not one to give up, he turned to manufacturing leather goods.

In the meantime, Lilly and her brother, Sigfried (Fred), were trying to understand this foreign culture and learn how to fit in. "I was lonely," Vernon recalled. "Now as a businesswoman, I understand that there are advantages to being an outsider peering in. Outsiders see with a special clarity" (Vernon, 1996: 16). It was Fred who helped to alleviate this sense of isolation, and she adored him. These two young people were raised in a strict German Jewish household where it was expected that the son would go into business and the daughter would get married and have children. World War II changed this parental goal. While Fred was in college, he was drafted into the army. After the Normandy invasion, the Menasche family learned that Fred had been killed in action; Lilly, now the only child, ended up leaving college to go to work for her father. One of her tasks was to salvage zippers from old clothing; it was a very difficult time for the country and for this family.

It was at the dinner table that Lilly learned about the reality of day-to-day business. "Dinner was filled with nonstop talk of shipments, orders, invoices: the details of business. I sat, listened, and absorbed. Every meal was like a class" (Vernon, 1996: 26). However, while these lessons were going on, another contradictory message was being given to this young woman by her mother. "She often made me unhappy with criticism that undermined my self-confidence and left me feeling inadequate. She frequently criticized my appearance, comparing my looks unfavorably to her own. I grew to feel that whatever went wrong was somehow my fault" (27). These powerful messages—discipline, financial stringency, business monitoring, bottom-line responsibility, and the need for absolute control—later became inherent characteristics of the Vernon management style.

In 1949, Lilly met and married Sam Hochberg, a man nine years her senior. Two years later Lilly Hochberg became pregnant with their first child. "I knew we would need more income. But a working wife was an embarrassing commentary on her husband's earning power. It was a dilemma: I had to earn money, but I couldn't leave the house to do it. Restless and anxious, I spent a lot of time flipping through magazines. It was the ads that intrigued me. Which items would I buy if I had the money?" (Vernon, 1996: 41). Concentrating on that question, she came up with the two innovative ideas that would create her unique niche in the market: starting a mail-order business from her kitchen table and offering personalized/initialized items. Both her husband and her mother rejected the idea, but her father continued his support as always and became her manufacturer. With seed money of $2,000, Lilly began her business. She placed a $495 ad in *Seventeen* magazine, a vehicle targeted to teen women, for two items: an initialized handbag for $2.99 and a matching initialized belt for $1.99. The results were phenomenal. Within the year she had received orders for over 6,000 items with sales totaling approximately $32,000. "Before long, I was zipping through one hundred pieces of mail an hour . . . I typed address labels, banging at the old typewriter keys with two fingers. [Then] I took the train into New York and worked in my father's factory, embossing every item with the appropriate gold initials. Then I packed each order and hauled it to the post office" (49). The year was 1951.

In the short span of just twelve months, Vernon gave birth to a business and a baby boy. The company, Vernon Specialties, was named after the place where the family lived, Mount Vernon, New York. Her first son was named after her beloved brother, Fred. In later years, Lilly also took the company name as her own, thus becoming Lillian Vernon. By 1956 sales had risen to almost $200,000, and she opened her first manufacturing plant in Providence, Rhode Island. During this time, Vernon also gave birth to her second child, David. Product sales to date had generated a mailing list of over 125,000 names, the "building blocks" of such a business. Again Vernon followed her "golden gut." Against the advice of others, she started a mail-order catalogue. Between 1960 and 1990 sales rose from $500,000 to $238 million, and the mailing list grew to over 17 million names. In this same period, Vernon divorced Sam Hochberg, giving him the manufacturing end of the business while she retained the mail-order division; she married and divorced Robert Katz; and she confronted a critical threat to the business caused by its exponential sales growth:

Sudden increases in orders require considerable cash and capacity, and it takes time for revenues to catch up. In 1983, I had to expand our facilities and add to the payroll, but everything cost money . . . our obsolete computer system failed to keep up with an 80 percent increase in business. Fulfillment was dangerously slow . . . I found myself in a hole. Some $20 million worth of inventory was sitting in a warehouse . . . I couldn't pay my bills . . . I needed millions to stay afloat. I wasn't used to debt, but I was determined not to declare bankruptcy. I got a $13 million loan which I repaid months before the due date. . . . We also installed a customized computer system. Sales reached $100 million in 1986. (Vernon, 1996: 52)

Having made the difficult decisions necessary to get the business back on track, she also took the company public in 1986. Hers was the first woman-owned business to be offered on the American Stock Exchange. Within ten years it was listed as the nation's seventh largest gift cataloguer by *Catalogue Age Magazine* (Pressler, 1996).

The slogan for such accomplishment could be "women making women" since the profile of the average Vernon customer has been over ninety percent female, with "the average age [being] 44, and the average household income . . . more than $53,000—33 percent above the national average" (Burney, 1996: 8). With more than 10,000 competitors in the mail order business (Belton, 1996), Vernon has been strategically aggressive by entering other distribution channels. In 1985 she opened the first retail outlet store. By 1995 Vernon's corporation distributed 179 million catalogues to 18 million people that resulted in 49 million orders. This same year her products became available over the Internet, and by 1998, sales through the Web site passed the million-dollar mark. In addition, Vernon entered both the America Online and QVC home shopping networks; total sales for 1998 reached the $258 million mark. According to the Market Guide Report for this same year, the Lillian Vernon Corporation employed 1,500 and had a market value of $141.58 million (Lillian Vernon, 1999).

But the story of Lilly Menasche, aka Lillian Vernon, has other important elements. The company and its founder have a long and significant philanthropic record, with over 500 charities as recipients. Vernon has been active on over twenty boards, including New York's Lincoln Center, the Virginia Opera, and New York University's College of Arts and Science. She has received numerous honors, including the NAACP Medal of Honor;

being inducted into the Direct Marketing Association Hall of Fame, the Connecticut Women's Hall of Fame, and the National Women's Hall of Fame; being named by the National Foundation for Women Business Owners as one of the fifty leading Women Entrepreneurs of the World; and having a number of honorary degrees bestowed upon her as well from, for example, Baruch College, Old Dominion University, Mercy College, and the College of New Rochelle.

However, all has not been sublime. "Looking back at my life . . . it was too hard," she admitted (Cruice, 1998: 10). Yet, one of the difficult dimensions is said to be Vernon's inability to relinquish her leadership and control; this has had serious consequences on her family relationships and on the corporate dilemma of succession planning. Her son Fred became estranged from his mother and left the company when she wouldn't relinquish control, while son David has remained with the firm, making it clear that he does not want to lead it. He described the company as "a family business with no family" (Burney, 1996: 8). Lillian Vernon has scoffed at the concept of stepping down as CEO. "I feel retirement is ridiculous. In Europe when someone owns a business, they *never* retire. . . . Staying in business, I stay involved. It gives my life continuity and a purpose" (Daddona, 1998: 21).

SOURCES: Aig, M. (1992), "Her Catalogue Has the Right Stuff; Shopping: With Her Thousands of Useful Products, Lillian Vernon Has Helped Revolutionize the Mail-Order Business," *Los Angeles Times*, October 13: D6; Belton, B. (1996), "Catalog Queen Has More up Her Sleeve," *USA Today*, November 29: 7B; Burney, T. (1996), "The Matriarch of Mail Order," *St. Petersburg Times*, December 23: 8; Cruice, V. (1998), "Starting Simply, the Story of a Business," *New York Times*, May 24: 10; Daddona, D. (1998), "Celebrating Women: New Awards at the Connecticut Women's Hall of Fame," *Woman Magazine*, August: 20–21; Lillian Vernon Corporation, Market Guide. (1999), *http://www.marketguide.com/mgi/snap/5401A.html* (accessed January 12, 1999); Lillian Vernon Online (1996) *http://www.lillianvernon.com* (accessed January 17, 1999); Pressler, M. (1996), "The Lillian Vernon Way; Catalogue Firm Sticks to Tradition, Stays Strong in Tough Times," *Washington Post*, November 24: D01; Vernon, L. (1996), *An Eye for Winners: How I Built One of America's Greatest Direct-Mail Businesses* (New York: Harper Business); Vernon, L. (1996), "An Eye for Winners," *Success Magazine*, November 9, 45–52.

LAURA VOGTLE (1969–)

"As is the case always, we ended up doing a LOT of late nights!"
(Laura Vogtle, Co-founder, Laura Kathryn, Inc.)

Laura Keith was a college student at the University of Alabama in Tusca-
loosa when she incorporated her first business. Combining her interest in
fashion and her artistic talent, she started making jewelry, barrettes, belts,
and other accessories. These items quickly caught attention and were in such
high demand that she had to hire classmates and get her family involved to
keep up with the sales. Then, just after she earned her bachelor's degree, she
met a Birmingham attorney, Jesse Vogtle, Jr. They fell in love and were married, but her new marital status didn't end her entrepreneurial dreams.

Laura Keith Vogtle had been born in Monroe, Alabama, one of Kathryn
and Dan Keith's three children. When Laura was five years old, the family
moved to Birmingham where her father, a doctor, established his medical
practice. Her brother, Stephen, followed in their father's footsteps, and the
daughters, Laura and Meredith, became entrepreneurs in a different way.
Meredith chose the path of artist, designer, and painter, while Laura,
shortly after marriage, decided to open her second enterprise, a fashion
boutique, with her mom. However, even though it was now near the end
of the twentieth century and the women would be running this boutique,
when Laura went to the bank for a loan, they refused to give it to her
unless her father signed for it. "The person at the bank, and others too,
thought I was crazy to try to open my own business," she explained (Elliot,
1998). Finally, with both the loan and some personal savings, the doors to
Laura Kathryn, Inc., were opened in Birmingham, with mom managing the
financial end and daughter, the merchandise.

The mother-daughter team soon learned that the fashion boutique business is highly competitive, demanding diligence and hard work. As Vogtle
pointed out, "My staff and I try to keep a fresh, new look in the store at all
times so that there is a rapid merchandise turnover rate. We keep the display
window as fashionably appealing and alluring as possible. I bring in different
brands that I believe will be attractive to our customers, but as soon as I do,
they appear in the stores of our competitors." The first few years that the
store was in operation were lean ones, but by 1998 the boutique had a steady
stream of customers, fluctuating by season, and profits were rising. Her sister
Meredith's work is regularly displayed in the store, too.

During the early years of the Laura Kathryn boutique, Vogtle became
the mother of three children, a responsibility she took most seriously. "One
of the advantages of having your own business is flexibility. I enjoy being
able to care for my children and work at the boutique," enthusiastically
adding, "I absolutely love what I'm doing!"

In addition to being both a business owner and a parent of small children, Laura Vogtle is an active community volunteer. She participates in
the Birmingham Ballet Guild, sometimes helping with the advertisements
of performances and other events; and she is a member of the Junior
Women's Committee, a group of one hundred women who donate their
time and other resources to charities in the area. Though she admits that

the path she has chosen is very hard work, Vogtle suggests to other women that there is a satisfaction in making customers happy that makes her efforts worthwhile. "There is contentment in being 'at rest' with what you're doing," she concluded.

SOURCE: Elliott, C. (1998), interview of Laura Vogtle in Birmingham, Alabama, on February 18.

DIANE von FURSTENBERG (1946–   )

"What I'm trying to do with the rebirth of my business is a renaissance. I'm reinventing myself and my lifestyle. The seeds are planted. . . . It's time for the harvest." (Diane von Furstenberg, Founder, Diane von Furstenberg Studio)

Diane Halfin was born into a well-to-do Belgian family, but because her mother, Lilly, had spent fourteen months in a German concentration camp, she was raised very strictly, not even allowed to wear makeup or date. Lilly did, however, emphasize independence in her daughter so that, by the time Diane was eleven, she had declared: "I will always get what I want" (Francke et al., 1976: 55). Her parents sent her to finishing schools, and she later attended the University of Geneva, where she met Prince Egon von Furstenberg of the Fiat family. They married in 1969 because she was pregnant with his child, but his family was furious. "Everyone was saying Egon was young, attractive, beautiful, good name, rich. How could he be marrying this Jewish girl who's absolutely nothing. I was really hurt," recalled von Furstenberg (57). To ease the pain, Diane went to work for an Italian textile manufacturer. This apprenticeship with Angelo Ferretti taught her about fabric printing. When the young couple moved to New York, she brought several dresses she herself had designed using the silk jersey Ferretti fabric (Taylor, 1988).

Diane von Furstenberg, now officially a "princess," started making the rounds to market her dress designs. She had two breaks. The first was with *Vogue*'s editor-in-chief, Diana Vreeland, who ran one of the designs in this internationally read magazine. As the demand for von Furstenberg's dresses started to increase, she tried to get a manufacturer to accept her line as a division; the efforts failed. Then John Pomerantz from the Leslie Fay company suggested she start her own business; he also introduced her to an investor, Richard Conrad. This help, coupled with $30,000 of seed money, a gift from her father, launched her dress manufacturing business.

However, Diane von Furstenberg was still a relatively new immigrant. "I was learning about the country, how stores work. I am a very motivated person when I start something . . . and here I was, this woman entrepreneur, so young" (Bosco, 1988: 25). But she was driven to do whatever it took and even to push herself to questionable limits: "Because she had no office and no staff, she spent hours in the freezing cold Customs' warehouse at Kennedy Airport breaking down the orders from Italy to reship to her clients. In 1971, von Furstenberg even coerced her obstetrician into delivering her daughter ten days early by Caersarean section in order to be ready for the warehouse chores a week later" (Francke et al., 1976: 57).

Within a year, the business was grossing over a million dollars in sales. By 1975 300,000 of her wrap dresses, which became the design hit of the season, were sold. From von Furstenberg's perspective, "I wanted something sexy, but comfortable. I just didn't realize every woman in America was looking for the same thing. It seemed to me a sociological thing. It had to do with the changes women were going through at the time as much as anything else" (Finkelstein, 1998). An example of this design is on display in the Smithsonian Institute in Washington, DC.

Within ten years, her business was grossing over $250 million. In the 1980s, the Diane von Furstenberg (DVF) name was selling over a billion dollars worth of licensed products; the market was saturated with DVF! The meteoric rise that von Furstenberg was experiencing took its toll. "Sometimes I wake up in the night in terror of all I carry on my shoulders," she confided to a reporter (Francke et al., 1976: 53). She also realized that she had lost quality control—a value she prized highly—so she ended some of the licensing agreements, explaining, "There was no coherence to anything being done by the licensees. . . . It's important to me that there be coherence between who I am, my lifestyle and my merchandise" (Gordon, 1992: 8).

In 1984, Diane von Furstenberg sold off her businesses and went to live in Paris, where she initiated a publishing company called *Salvy*. She returned to the states in 1992 when she signed an agreement to market her clothing line on the QVC home shopping television network. "I was a has-been and now I'm a pioneer again. I'm getting a second chance—this time I am going to be smarter," she declared (Finkelstein, 1998). Once again, her wrap dress was launched along with other lines; the result was unprecedented and stunning. In the short span of a two-hour broadcast, $1.2 million of her Silk Assets line was sold.

When she was asked what kind of advice she might offer, von Furstenberg responded: "Listen to [your] instincts. At the same time, let people help you; listen to what they have to say and consider it. . . . So many people try to sway you and discourage you. Don't let it happen; if you have a gut feeling about something, go with it . . . recognize that there are going to be failures.

There are good moments and there are bad. You have to eat humble pie sometimes, but you have to be a survivor" (Finkelstein, 1998).

SOURCES: Bosco, A. (1988), "Diane von Furstenberg of New Milford," *Litchfield County Times*, January 29: 17, 25; Finkelstein, A. (1998), "Talking Dresses with Diane von Furstenberg," *http://www.insidefashion.com/feat_diane.html* (accessed August 6, 1998); Francke, L., Whitman, L., & Gilbert, S. (1976), "Princess of Fashion," *Newsweek*, March 22: 52–58; Gordon, M. (1992), "Von Furstenberg in Deal with QVC," *Women's Wear Daily*, November 2: 8; Schneider, K., & McNeil, E. (1997), "Wrap Artist; Riding the Retro Rage, Diane von Furstenberg Relaunches the Dress That Made Her Famous," *People Magazine* [Online], August 25 Update: 150 (available: Lexis-Nexis); Taylor, R. (1988), *Exceptional Entrepreneurial Women: Strategies for Success* (New York: Praeger).

MAGGIE WALKER (1867–1934)

> *"Time and conditions change so rapidly that unless we keep on the alert, ever working, watching, improving and learning, we will be left behind in the race of progress. Eternal vigilance is the price of success."*
> (Maggie Walker, First Female President of a chartered bank in the United States; Founder of the St. Luke's Penny Savings Bank and the *St. Luke Herald* Newspaper)

Maggie Lena Draper was the illegitimate child of a former slave Elizabeth Draper, and a white Northern abolitionist writer, Eccles Cuthbert. She was born on the Richmond, Virginia, plantation owned by abolitionist and Civil War spy Elizabeth Van Lew and raised in an environment that encouraged her to become educated and develop into a self-confident young woman. Because Van Lew also permitted freed blacks living with her to have businesses on the side, Maggie's mother had a laundry business that she continued even after she married William Mitchell, Van Lew's butler, and had their son, Johnnie. The Mitchells subsequently moved to town because William could earn more money there as a waiter. But one night, her stepfather didn't come home from work, and the family was plunged into tragedy when he was found robbed and murdered a few days later. To survive, Maggie's mother had to increase her workload of laundry and ironing. It became Maggie's job to take care of her little brother and to deliver the laundered items to customers, while still managing to stay in school. As she described herself: "I was not born with a silver spoon in [my] mouth, but instead, with a clothes basket almost upon my head" (Maggie L. Walker, 1999).

At sixteen, Maggie Lena Draper Mitchell demonstrated her determination to fight for equality by organizing the first recorded school strike over segregation. For graduation, the blacks in the class of 1883 at the Armstrong Normal School decided that they would no longer tolerate having their ceremony in a church while the white students got to have theirs in the theater. With Maggie leading them, they argued that their parents were taxpayers, too, and got results. From then on, all students received their diplomas in the school auditorium. For the three years following graduation, Maggie taught at the Lancaster School. During this time, she helped initiate the Women's Union, an insurance company for black women. This was a notable achievement for those days, when few such services were available to people of color in America.

In 1886, Maggie married Armstead Walker, Jr. Her husband was a Richmond building contractor who worked with his father. They had three sons—Russell Eccles Thomas, Armstead Mitchell, who died at seven months of age, and Melvin Dewitt. For twenty-five years, life for the Walkers was quite comfortable. Maggie continued her community activities working for her church and for the Grand United Order of St. Luke (I.O. of St. Luke). This was a service organization started in 1867 in Baltimore, Maryland, by Mary Prout, an ex-slave who originally wanted to help black women care for their sick and arrange for appropriate burials; men were later admitted. Since Walker had taken some business courses and was innately intelligent, she rose through this organization, holding various offices. Then, in 1899, the Right Worthy Grand Secretary-Treasurer of the organization, its highest position, resigned. His stated his reasons: "The order was at its lowest ebb . . . there was no money in the treasury . . . the order was not spreading as it should . . . [and] there was a lack of cooperation" (Daniel, 1931: 34). While the organization numbered over 3,000 members in 57 chapters, the treasury showed a balance of only $34.65, with unpaid bills of $500. Walker was offered the position, and she accepted the challenge for an annual salary of $100. She then went to work reviving the organization, deciding first to increase the visibility of the organization through its own newspaper.

Walker explained to the membership: "What we need is an organ, a newspaper to herald and proclaim the work of the Order. No business, no enterprise, which has to deal with the public, can be pushed successfully without a newspaper. . . . We have the men, we have the women, we have the brains. Let us form a partnership of heads and brains, and actually do something" (Maggie L. Walker, 1999). Thus, the *St. Luke Herald* was founded in 1902. Next, though she had no experience or training in finance or financial institutions, Walker taught herself about the banking industry and quickly followed the newspaper publication with the 1903 chartering of a bank after another of her rousing oratories: "We need a savings bank, chartered, officered, and run by the men and women of this Order. Let us put our moneys together; let us use our moneys; let us put our money out at usury among ourselves and reap the benefit ourselves" (Maggie L. Walker, 1999). Over the years, the St. Luke Penny Savings Bank was restructured several times, but it still exists today as the Consolidated Bank and Trust Company, the oldest bank continuously run and owned by blacks in the United States.

Walker believed that pennies became nickels, which became dollars, which could then create a good life for the people of her community. She had already initiated a Juvenile Division to encourage young children to save. Next she worked on home ownership by bank employees. "When any one of our girls is advanced to making as much as fifty dollars a month . . . we begin to persuade her to buy a home. As soon as she saves enough for the first payment, the bank will help her out" (Daniel, 1931: 37). In 1904 Walker began a department store, the Saint Luke Emporium, which lasted only seven years because of a backlash from the Retail Dealers Association. As the emporium threatened white retailers, their association notified wholesale merchants as far away as New York City that they would lose business from all white retailers if merchandise was supplied to the black-owned and-operated store (Brown, 1990: 188).

The second decade of the new century were dramatic years for Walker. She had an accident falling from the front steps of her home. Her knees were severely injured, resulting in constant pain. In 1915 came an unbelievable calamity when her son, "Russell, mistook his father for a prowler on the porch and shot him. . . . [A long trial ensued, during which time her mother died.] Russell was acquitted of the murder charge but never quite recovered from the ordeal. He died in 1923, leaving his wife and child to live with Maggie" (Duckworth, 1993: 571). Suffering intense psychological pain and progressively more physical debilitation from her worsening knee condition, Walker found herself by 1928 confined to a wheelchair. In spite of these conditions, she remained active in the I.O. of St. Luke. She also saw the bank absorb all of the other black banks of Richmond, Virginia, with assets having grown from the original $30 to millions. At one point, the bank even rescued the Richmond public schools with a $100,000 loan—the only bank that could afford to do so. Walker served as chair of the board of the bank almost until her death in 1934. The governor of Virginia, E. Lee Trinkle, said of her life and contributions: "If the State of Virginia had done no more, in fifty years, with the funds spent on the education of Negroes than educate Mrs. Walker, the State would have been amply repaid for its outlay and efforts" (Ovington, 1927: 134).

SOURCES: Brown, E. (1990), "Womanist Consciousness: Maggie Lena Walker and the Independent Order of Saint Luke," in Malson, M., Mudimbe-Boyi, E., O'Barr,

J., & Wyer, M., eds., *Black Women in America: Social Science Perspectives* (Chicago, IL: University of Chicago Press); Daniel, S. (1931), *Women Builders* (Washington, DC: Associated Publishers); Duckworth, M. (1993), "Maggie L. Walker," in Smith, J., ed., *Epic Lives: One Hundred Black Women Who Made a Difference* (Detroit, MI: Visible Ink Press); Maggie L. Walker National Historic Site (1999) *http://www.nps.gov/malw/* (accessed July 4, 1999); Ovington, M. (1927), *Portraits in Color* (New York: Viking Press).

SARAH WALKER (1867–1919)

"It is not for me [her mansion, the Villa Lewara]; it is for my people so that they can see what can be accomplished no matter what their background is." (Sarah Walker, Founder, Madame C. J. Walker Manufacturing Company)

Her parents were newly freed slaves when Sarah Breedlove was born on the Burney cotton plantation near Delta, Louisiana. She was orphaned at six and went to live with her sister in Mississippi; had little formal education; married Moses McWilliams at fourteen, allegedly to escape the cruelty of her brother-in-law; and was widowed six years later with a daughter, A'Lelia, to support. To survive, she moved to St. Louis, Missouri, and worked as a servant, cooking and cleaning. From all of this adversity came the first American woman to be a self-made millionaire, according to the *Guinness Book of Records*. Remarkably, she was a black woman who achieved this while blacks and whites were segregated, blacks were being lynched, and women did not have the right to vote! What was the triggering event that caused this thirty-eight-year-old black washerwoman to become an inventor and businesswoman?

It may have been the bad luck of beginning to lose her hair. To try to discover something to stop this, Sarah Breedlove McWilliams found someone who could analyze the contents of the current hair products on the market for black women. Then she began to experiment with them in her kitchen. Years later, she told of praying to God and then, through a dream, envisioning how to develop the hair-growth treatment that would begin her amazing voyage.

In 1906 Sarah and A'Lelia moved from St. Louis to Denver, Colorado, where she met and married Charles J. Walker, a newspaperman. He is credited with teaching her how to use mail order and advertising. She developed a three-pronged approach that worked: a door-to-door sales force (the first of its kind) of black female agents, a mail-order campaign, and promotions in black churches. Madame Walker had found an unfulfilled void—a "market niche" in today's business terms—black women who couldn't comb their unruly "nappy" hair yet wanted to find a way to be beautiful. She not only created her "Wonderful Hair Grower" but also developed the process of washing the hair, oiling it, and then pressing it with the steel "hot comb" she had invented; prior to this, some black women would try to "press" their hair with a flat iron. In time Walker built her line up to twenty-three products, which included a pomade for men, had up to 3,000 mostly female employees, and had reported annual gross earnings as high as $276,000 (1917)—at a time when there were no taxes (Latham, 1993; Nelson, 1987).

Madame Walker set strict standards for her employees. First, they were never to refer to the process as hair "straightening"; they were to follow the exact hygiene standards she established long before any were required by law; and the sales agents were to wear a "uniform" of white blouses and long black skirts. These "uniforms" served several purposes: they enabled those living in the areas being served to quickly identify Walker agents, they helped these salespersons become role models for other women and girls, they were marketing devices, and they helped the generally poor female employee, who did not have to be concerned about what to wear to work.

Walker products were also used internationally. The most famous personage identified with these hair softeners was Josephine Baker, the American black nightclub performer who was so admired and celebrated in France. (It was not unusual for black entertainers to leave the states to live and perform in Europe since they were treated far better in foreign lands than in their birthplace.) To handle the rapidly increasing business, Walker established an additional office in Pittsburgh under the management of her daughter and, in 1910, set up headquarters for the expanding company in Indianapolis. In addition to employment, Walker provided education for her "beauty culturists" at the Walker College of Hair Culture. Through her various enterprises, Madame Walker enabled hundreds of black women to also become entrepreneurs and educators.

Philanthropy was an inherent characteristic of Walker as well. Among the organizations to which she gave were Mary McLeod Bethune's Daytona Literary and Industrial School for Training Negro Girls, the National Association of Colored Women, the National Conference on Lynching, the National Association for the Advancement of Colored People (NAACP), and the Palmer Memorial Institute. She wanted to plant the concept of charitable work in her workers as well. "Beginning in 1913 Walker organized her agents into 'Walker Clubs,' and gave cash prizes to the clubs that did the largest amount of community philanthropic work" ("Madame C. J. Walker," 1997).

Madame C. J. Walker's commitment to both philanthropy and women's independence did not end with her death, which was hastened by hypertension, her unceasing hard work for her company, and her untiring dedication to helping others. Walker set aside two-thirds of the company stock under trusteeship to assure that certain charities would continue to be supported, targeted an additional $100,000 for selected charities, and articulated that the company was to always be headed by a woman. Because of legal issues regarding the conditions of her will, the final disposition didn't occur until 1926. Walker's wishes were generally followed until 1985, when the company was bought by an Indianapolis businessman.

SOURCES: Bundles, A. (1992), *Madam C. J. Walker* (New York: Chelsea House); Latham, C. (1993), Madam C. J. Walker (1867–1919) Collection (1910–1980): Historical Sketch, Indiana Historical Society—Manuscripts and Archives, *http:// www2.ihs1830.org/ihs1830/walker1.htm* (accessed July 14, 1998); "Madame C. J. Walker (Sarah Breedlove McWilliams Walker): Inventor, Businesswoman" (1997), Mitchell C. Brown, LSU Libraries, Louisiana State University, Baton Rouge, *http:// www.lib.lsu.edu/lib/chem/display/sources.html* (accessed July 14, 1997); *Two Dollars and a Dream* (1987) [Videorecording], J. Nelson (Producer & Director), New York, Filmmakers Library.

MARILYN WEINSHEL (1947–   )

"Success is being happy with what you do; it is a style of life. So what if you lose? You just try again." (Marilyn Weinshel, Founder and President, Holdings Fine Accessories, Inc.)

As the women's movement was in its early stages, Marilyn Grand Weinshel found herself with a master's degree in counseling, two children, and an unfulfilling job as a women's group counselor in Marblehead, Massachusetts. She decided to try work in sales, and, although she liked the actual selling to customers, Marilyn still felt restless. What changed her work life around was something almost inconsequential—a request from her mother for a knitting bag that would hold all her knitting needles. Marilyn had a friend make the bag. The idea to go into this kind of business, however, was an article in *New York Magazine* about the best knitting shops in New York City. With the help of her friend, she made seven more bags, took them to one of the shops mentioned in the article, and sold six bags. With this success, the business, later named Holdings Fine Accessories, Inc., was born in 1980. "My mother [Hilda Grand Koweek] gave me $500 to start.

Since I was still married, I had the security of knowing I was not the primary breadwinner; my efforts were for second income" (Oppedisano, 1999). By 1989 this was not the case; the Weinshels were divorced.

Weinshel purchased her early fabrics from a company called Fabrications. When she showed her bags to the managers there, they began purchasing them for their chain of stores. Since Weinshel was not a skilled sewer, she hired local home sewers to produce the quantity required for these growing sales and then had to add factory stitchers as well. However, this dependence on a single large client soon taught her a major lesson. Fabrications went out of business, and she had to develop a new client base. Weinshel turned to trade shows, where she could demonstrate her bags and make sales. It was at one of these shows that she met sales representatives who not only wanted to market her product but suggested she enter the gift industry. To do so, Weinshel would have to expand her line.

The product line expansion that Weinshel decided upon consisted of tote bags, garment bags, shoe totes, handbags, and a line of what she labeled "valuables" cases. Again it was a fortuitous meeting that led her to another major business decision. As she was picking up her products from the factory, she met a man in the golf industry who used the same manufacturer. When he saw her products, he suggested that she go into the women's golf industry. In doing so, Weinshel became the first to make unique golf bags for this segment of the industry, thus carving her own market niche. "Most of the golf professionals to whom I sell are men who want to make their female customers happy but don't know how. I make sense of my products to these men because I know my business well so they take me seriously," she explained (Santer, 1998).

The business side has operated out of Weinshel's home basement since its initiation even though it has grown into a million-dollar plus enterprise over the twenty years it has existed. As with many entrepreneurs, she has remained a "hands-on" manager, one who designs all her fabrics, makes sales, supervises, answers phones, lifts heavy boxes of product, packs, and ships. Weinshel employs two full-time office staff supplemented by one part-timer, two local female sewers, a local graphic designer who creates the original designs, and a number of sales representatives who market her line in addition to other related product lines. She utilizes two local factories—one that produces items that are too complicated and time consuming for the home sewers and the other for the manufacture of the leather goods. Holdings Fine Accessories contains seven tapestry collections with all of these fabrics woven in Italy. In addition to tapestry and leather, fabrics used in her other collections are glazed cotton chintz, sailcloth, and a microfiber.

The Holdings Fine Accessories merchandise is sold at golf and specialty stores as well as at trade shows. At the 1998 trade show in Las Vegas, for example, Weinshel received one order for $50,000. "My counseling career gave me the critical skill of learning how to establish relationships with people by listening to others' needs. I'm a very good listener" (Oppedisano, 1999). Her accounts include the U.S. Open, the National Basketball Association (NBA), Universal Studios, and the Walt Disney Company. In connection with the U.S. Open, Weinshel produces a special fabric for the club hosting the annual event. The Disney contract came about after one of Weinshel's representatives showed the Holdings line to a company representative. The Disney person simply wanted to have a Mickey Mouse pin added to an already existing floral tote bag, but this didn't seem marketable or classy enough to Weinshel so she asked, "If I designed a product with Mickey and Minnie Mouse woven into the fabric, would you look at it?" Not only did Disney look at it, but she now has a license to sell Disney products in the open market and sells her Disney accessory line at three golf stores in Disney World and in other Team Mickey stores in Florida. She also produces one line of products in a fabric that is solely for the Disney parks and cannot be purchased elsewhere.

Weinshel remains a made-in-the-USA manufacturer primarily because of a negative experience she had in the mid-1990s. She had some small leather wallets, checkbook covers, and the like manufactured overseas, but the quality was poor so that supplier was eliminated. Her competitive edge has always been high quality at competitive price points. Weinshel explained two recent strategies she has initiated: "We are establishing brand identity through such vehicles as the Ryder Cup and the PGA Championship events and have recently begun development of a Web site for the company so that Internet users can have easy access to our products" (Oppedisano, 1999). Overall, her experiences in business have been positive, and her sales have shown steady, consistent growth. Weinshel has not experienced financial problems because of her early decision not to take on anything for which she didn't have the resources. "I don't jump into anything unless I've thoroughly researched the idea and sought out input from my employees. I value their opinions," she noted (Santer, 1998).

As she approached the new millenium, Weinshel began to consider selling Holdings Fine Accessories because she felt that she lacked the business experience and formal training to position the company for expansion. "I believe I've taken it as far as I can so it's getting to a time when I should sell it to someone who can take advantage of its growth potential," she concluded.

SOURCES: Holdings Fine Accessories Inc. (1999), *http://www.holdingsgolf.com* (accessed July 14, 1999); Oppedisano, J. (1999), interview with Marilyn Weinshel, February 4; Santer, L. (1998), interview with Marilyn Weinshel, March 16.

DAWN WELLS (1945–   )

"Times have changed and my career has changed right along with them." (Dawn Wells, Founder, Wishing Wells Collections)

Dawn Wells would no doubt be a familiar face to many. She played the starring role of Mary Ann on the *Gilligan's Island* television show, which ran from 1964 to 1967 and is still in syndication. But acting is only one of the careers in which Wells has achieved. She rates her contributions as entrepreneur, community activist, and writer equally as important as television fame.

Wells was born in Reno, Nevada. "I came from good stock," she noted proudly, "ethics and morals, church and honor rolls" (Scott, 1996: 1). Typical of her generation, she "was raised on the all-American principles of the '50s—kindness [and] consideration" (Moss, 1995: 6B). When Wells was in high school, her grandmother came to live with the family after having a stroke. This two-year period had a profound influence on the impressionable young girl. She watched as her mother cared for her grandmother, with each of the women suffering through this debilitating life experience. What she found especially humiliating was the difficult experience that dressing becomes for those with disabilities. The young teen didn't know then that one day she would find a way to change this.

Wells left Nevada to attend Stephens College in Missouri—a small, private women's college—where she originally planned to study chemistry so that she could become a doctor. But a college counselor suggested she switch to theater, an idea that intrigued the receptive student. Wells went on to earn an associate degree from Stephens and a bachelor's degree in drama from the University of Washington. Then, in 1962, she won the Miss Nevada contest; this opened many doors in the entertainment field for her. The cautious Wells decided that she would give herself two years to make it in acting. "If I didn't make it, I would go back to college and my pre-med courses. I was lucky. I was the right age and had the right looks to be a perfect ingenue"—qualifications that landed her the starring role of Mary Ann on *Gilligan's Island*. "That was a time when life was sweet and things were nice," she recalled (Scott, 1996: 1).

Visibility as a female television celebrity has had its rewards and its hazards. "Strangers routinely act as if they know [me], but [I] accept it. 'Why would you not want to have that feeling from somebody?' she asks. 'It's love that they're coming at you with. Well, a little lust, too!' " But she added, "I've had some stalkers that you wouldn't even want to talk about. One man wrote me an 11 page letter about sex and sin in Hollywood, and every single word is in a different color pencil" (Seiler, 1997: 2D).

After her television series ended, Wells went on to perform in stage productions. It was here in all of the quick changes actors had to go through that she remembered her grandmother's problems with dressing. Wells got the idea to use Velcro fastening wardrobe techniques for a clothing line for the disabled. She asked members of the fashion design department at Stephens College to help her create the clothes. She wanted her line to include items for both men and women, clothing that was brightly colored, comfortable, and machine-washable, so that seniors and the disabled could maintain their dignity and independence. The ease of using such clothing would also relieve some of the difficulties that caregivers and home health aides experience in dressing those for whom they are responsible. She asked, "Why shouldn't the elderly . . . be treated as the young people they were 30 years ago? . . . It's an event for a woman when she can wear a new dress with a little style to it [and] men don't want to be seen in bathrobes and pajamas. Their self-esteem is very important" (Arkush, 1992: 20).

Wishing Wells Collections, as she called her enterprise, was begun in 1989 in Studio City, California. It was a "dream five years in the making. Initially it was difficult for Wells to find financial support. '[New York] garment district guys were curt until they found out what it was,' " she pointed out (Telingator, 1992: 7). Interest in the items offered by Wishing Wells Collections grew, and by 1999 the catalogue company also had established a Web site, had a contract for her clothing line for the J. C. Penney Company special needs catalogue, and had a contract with a nursing home chain. The importance of her efforts was once again reinforced in 1996, when Wells' own mother suffered a stroke at the age of eighty-four. "I'm all she's got and she's all I've got," Wells commented sadly (Gasior, 1996: 6B).

Wells has remained active in other professional work in addition to the design, manufacture, and promotion of the clothing collection. She has hosted the Dawn Wells' Reel Adventures, a woman's fishing show; appeared in the TV movie *A Higher Place in Heaven*; hosted an Australian TV show, the *Castaway Correspondent*, filmed in Los Angeles; managed the Dawn Wells Film Actor's Boot Camp in Idaho; and written *Mary Ann's Gilligan's Island Cookbook*, with proceeds from sales going to such charitable endeavors as the Missy Braden Scholarship Fund and the Stephens College Dawn Wells Scholarship fund.

Community involvement is critically important to Wells. "Our lives come back to us in many ways. . . . I want to put something back into this world," she explained (Berdan, 1996: 1). Her service commitments have included co-producing and co-hosting the Children's Miracle Network Telethon; serving on the advisory board of the University of Missouri Children's Hospital; serving on the boards of one of her alma maters, Stephens College, and Artsgenesis—an organization whose aim is to put professional artists together with students and teachers; and fundraising for Daybreak—a Dayton, Ohio, shelter for homeless and runaway youth. As a hobby, she likes to paint.

In reflection, Wells suggested, "If I had to do it all over again, I'd probably have become a pediatric surgeon because they make such a difference in the lives of people in so many walks of life" (Scott, 1996: 1). Certainly the health and well-being of people has been a lifelong focus for this celebrity. In fact, one of the most profound experiences for Dawn Wells came from her volunteer work for the Children's Miracle Network. There she met seventeen-year-old Missy Braden from Poplar, Missouri, who had cystic fibrosis and needed a heart and lung transplant. Missy stayed in California with Wells for the two weeks before receiving the transplant. However, her body rejected the organs and she died, but not before promising Wells to be her guardian angel. "She's on my shoulder all the time now," Wells said. "When I'm having a bad day, she's there to make it better" (Forgrieve, 1996: 1).

SOURCES: Arkush, M. (1992), "Star's Role as Designer," *Los Angeles Times* [Online], September 25: 20 (available: Lexis-Nexis, accessed June 7, 1999); Berdan, K. (1996) " 'Mary Ann' Is Still Sewing and Cooking: Just Sit Right Back for a Tale about Dawn Wells, Who Played Mary Ann on 'Gilligan's Island'," *Des Moines Register* [Online], February 12: 1 (available: Lexis-Nexis, accessed June 2, 1997); Forgrieve, J. (1996), " 'Mary Ann' Leaves Coconut Pies for Career as Volunteer," *Tampa Tribune* [Online], July 4: 1 (available: Lexis-Nexis, accessed June 2, 1997); Gasior, A. (1996), "Dawn Wells; Once-Carefree Castaway Copes with Real-Life Crisis," *Dayton Daily News* [Online], January 29: 6B (available: Lexis-Nexis, accessed June 2, 1997); Moss, M. (1995), "More Than 'Mary Ann'; Dawn Wells Visits Dayton to Promote Her Book and the Welfare of Local Kids," *Dayton Daily News* [Online], February 13: 6B (available: Lexis-Nexis, accessed June 2, 1997); Scott, V. (1996), "Hollywood," *United Press International* [Online], October 31: 1 (available Lexis-Nexis, accessed June 7, 1999); Seiler, A. (1997), "All Ashore after 'Gilligan's Island' Dawn Wells Finds Mary Ann Role Still Follows Her," *USA Today* [Online], November 5: (available: Proquest, accessed June 2, 1997); Telingator, S. (1992), "Caring Couture: Dawn Wells Designs with Special Clients in Mind," *Chicago Tribune* [Online], July 12: 7 (available: Lexis-Nexis, accessed June 5, 1999).

JUDY WICKS (1947–   )

"When I get up in the morning and open my closet door, I see a sign that says, 'Good Morning, Beautiful Business.' It is a reminder of just

how beautiful economic exchange can be when we put forth our best effort and creative thought and energy into providing the best possible product or service for our customer. That we do, in fact, use our business relationships as a way to express our love for people. That's what makes it a thing of beauty." (Judy Wicks, Founder and President of White Dog Enterprises, Inc.)

Doing good while "breaking bread" is what makes Judy Wicks, the founder of the White Dog Cafe, a world-renowned eatery in Philadelphia, Pennsylvania, such a unique personality in the international restaurant arena. From the purchase and use of organic foods to the visiting and support of her "international sister restaurants," this flower child of the 1960s dishes out social awareness and political activism while tempting palates. Her customers don't mind; they keep coming back for more, as evidenced by her annual sales of approximately $4.5 million. "Bringing people together around food is a family tradition," recalled Wicks in her newest book, *White Dog Cafe Cookbook: Multicultural Recipes and Tales of Adventure from Philadelphia's Revolutionary Restaurant*. Crediting the big meals her grandmother, Grace Scott, cooked when she was running a guest house so that she could put her daughters through school and her own parents having monthly "Friday Night Hungry Club" gatherings, Wicks said that's how she learned the connective power of food.

Wicks grew up in Ingomar, Pennsylvania, and showed signs at a young age of an early entrepreneurial leaning. Before she was a teenager, she was selling her own products such as handpainted scenes on scraps of wood she got from a local construction site. She learned to be an independent thinker from her mother, an outdoorswoman and leader of the local Girl Scouts troop. It was around this same time that young Judy Wicks learned what it felt like to be excluded. "When I was ten I loved to play softball, but I wasn't allowed to join the team because it was for boys only . . . that experience taught me the destructive effects of discrimination. I learned the importance of finding a way to include everyone according to their own strengths and interests and how the whole group suffers when some are left out of the game" (Wicks, 1999).

After graduating from Lake Erie College, Wicks married her childhood sweetheart, Neil Schlosser, and in 1969 they joined VISTA, a volunteer program of giving service where needed in America. Their assignment was to live and work in an Eskimo village, another event that was to further define the tenor of Wicks' personal and professional philosophy. "The Eskimos have a communal economy; wealth accumulation is not a goal; they share everything equally," she explained. After returning from this work, Wicks and her husband used the $3,000 stipend they had received to initiate the Free People's Store (known later as the Urban Outfitters). They not only offered items such as dyed tee shirts and unique boxes but had a "ragman" bin "so everyone could leave with something."

An automobile accident led Wicks to her next destination. "At the time I needed to be on my own and not be Mrs. Anybody. I needed to find out what had become of the little girl named Judy Wicks." She and her husband were divorcing; she had become a single parent with two children and had been separated from her business. In this distressed state, she drove her car through a red light and crashed it. She needed a job right away to pay for the damages, and someone who was just passing by suggested that she could go to a nearby restaurant and work as a waitress. For the next thirteen years, Wicks worked at La Terrasse, eventually becoming the business manager. Wicks had also believed the owner when he said that they were partners, but he never formalized this relationship. Once the business had grown and was successful, he told her that she was fired because she was mixing her personal opinions in the business. "It was the best thing that ever happened to me," Wicks pointed out. "I went on to discover that expressing what I believe in through my work, expressing my values through my business would become the most important aspect of my career."

Wicks began to sell muffins and coffee from her house in 1983. As the business grew she added more American foods, cooked on the backyard barbecue, served her customers on her home furniture on the cramped first floor while the dishes were being washed nearby, and had them use the family bathroom when they needed such facilities. By 1985 Wicks had received a bank loan, expanded her operation to a connected rowhouse, put a kitchen in the basement, and added restrooms. Facility improvements continued over the next decade. Wicks has continued to live upstairs. It is her insistence on keeping the very homey, cozy atmosphere that has created a particular ambience and has contributed to the loyalty of White Dog Cafe customers.

However, it is not just food that keeps this business in the forefront of today's success stories. Judy Wicks manages a series of community action projects through her enterprises. "People come to the White Dog because they're hungry, but it's not simply hunger for food. It's a hunger for meaningful relationships, it's a hunger for sharing your values with others, it's a hunger for community, it's a hunger for being a part of something bigger than oneself," she passionately stated. This is exemplified by customer participation in Wick's programs such as the monthly Community Service Days, when they might work on local gardens or rehabilitate houses, or the Prison Garden Tour, where customers visit and eat dinner with prisoners who grow organic foods, herbs, and flowers. Another initiative is the Philadelphia Sister Restaurant Project, where Wicks arranges events that encourage customers to visit minority-owned restaurants in neighborhoods they might not go to otherwise. The list of events and opportunities for learning and activism are so extensive that Wicks puts out a triannual news-letter, free to all who request to be on the mailing list or to subscribe through her Web site, *www.whitedog.com.*

Wicks has a vision of how the world should be that she labeled her Table for Six Billion. She imagines people from all around the world sitting around one big table, joining hands, and sharing a feast prepared by all, "with enough for everyone . . . We might offer this grace":

Heavenly father, mother of our earth, universal spirit who dwells here in each of our hearts, forgive us for the harm we have done to our planet and the plants and animals who live here with us. Forgive us for the harm we have caused each other. Thank you for giving us the courage to put aside our fears of not having enough for ourselves so that we could make room for everyone of us around this table of great abundance and nourishment. Thank you for the creativity it has taken to find ways for each of us to participate in the making of this great feast so that we can each join in the satisfaction of our work well done. Bless this food that we now eat with the greatest joy knowing that you are present in the pleasure of every bite and in the love we see all around us in each and every smiling face. Amen. (Wicks, 1999).

This picture captures the mission that Judy Wicks established for her en-terprises: to serve fully—to serve customers, each other, community, and nature.

SOURCES: Wicks, J. (1999), "The Lifegiving Workplace," speech given May 14, at the Eastern Academy of Management Conference in Philadelphia, Pennsylvania; Wicks, J., & Von Klause, K. (1998), *White Dog Cafe Cookbook: Multicultural Recipes and Tales of Adventure from Philadelphia's Revolutionary Restaurant* (Philadelphia, PA: Running Press).

EMMA WILLARD (1787–1870)

> *"The education of women should always be relative to the men; to please us, to be useful to us, to educate us when young and to take care of us when grown up, to console us, to render our lives easy and agreeable; these are the duties of women at all times."* (Emma Willard, Founder, Troy Female Seminary, now the Emma Willard School)

Emma Hart Willard was a teacher by the time she was sixteen, the principal of a girl's academy at twenty; and, at the age of twenty-seven, she started her first school, the Middlebury Female Seminary, in her Vermont home.

The year was 1814. "When I began my boarding school in Middlebury, my leading motive was to relieve my husband from financial difficulties. I had also the further motive of keeping a better school than those about me; but it was not until a year or two after that, I formed the design of effecting an important change in education by the introduction of a grade of schools for women higher than any heretofore known" (*Harper's Bazaar*, 1893: 20).

Willard was the one of the youngest of sixteen children, born into an unusually encouraging family for a female of her time. Her parents, Lydia and Samuel Hart, placed a high emphasis on education regardless of gender. In a time when most girls weren't even lucky enough to have the opportunity to get an education, she was able to learn subjects not normally included in the few schools girls of her day could attend. Willard's father encouraged her to go to the exclusive Berlin Academy for girls, and within a few years, because of her natural abilities and gift for learning, she became one of the teachers there. At the age of twenty-two, Emma Hart married Dr. John Willard, a widower who was twenty-eight years older than she. Like her father, Dr. Willard enjoyed and encouraged his wife's intellectual pursuits. They had one child of their own in addition to those from his first marriage, but these responsibilities did not hinder Emma's quest for knowledge. In fact, when she read what her stepson was being taught at Middlebury College, she was struck by the vast differences in education for women and men. This motivated her to expand the breadth of her own self-instruction by reading his textbooks in such subjects as geometry and philosophy. When she opened her schools, she incorporated these subjects as well as science, history, and astronomy into the curriculum. In fact, she was the "pioneer in the teaching of science, mathematics, and social studies to girls, antedating Mary Lyons' Mount Holyoke Seminary by 16 years and the first public high schools for girls (in Boston and New York City) by 5" (McHenry, 1980: 446).

This is not to say that Willard didn't subscribe to the more traditional elements of a girl's education like homemaking, hygiene, and dance. She even discouraged her students from taking part in political discussions because she felt that politics was the domain of men. However, she was nontraditional in most other ways; she "even dared to introduce into the course of study the indelicate subject of physiology. [At the insistence of parents] the modesty of their daughters had been preserved by the pasting of heavy paper over the pages in their textbooks which depicted any part of the body" (Wilson, 1970: 102).

At the invitation of then governor DeWitt Clinton, Willard moved to New York State and started her second female seminary in Watervliet in 1816. Her husband accompanied her and was supportive of her advocacy to educate girls and women. Five years later, with $4,000 of financial support from the Troy Town Council, Willard began the Troy Female Seminary, considered to be one of the most influential of America's schools, with a class of ninety students at the annual tuition rate of $200, which included room and board. For some students who were worthy of admission but couldn't afford this fee, Willard herself provided scholarships. She also encouraged entrepreneurship, too, since graduates of such schools often went on to establish seminaries of their own.

Willard was also a widely read author in her field. Her publications included *History of the United States or Republic of America* (1828), *The Fulfillment of a Promise* (1831), *Universal History for Schools* (1849), and *Morals for the Young* (1857). But Willard was most widely known for *An Address to the Public, Particularly to the Members of the Legislature of New York, Proposing a Plan for Improving Female Education* (1819). In addition, she traveled extensively to spread the word of the viability of girls' and women's educational ability and society's responsibility to see that it was developed.

To assess Willard's entrepreneurial impact, we might begin by looking at the economic reality of providing education to the thousands of students who have graduated from her school in Troy, New York, renamed the Emma Willard School. However, a complete evaluation is not possible when we consider the reality of how many people, particularly girls and women, she had to have benefited by her advocacy and tenacity in the pursuit of accessible quality educational opportunities; these benefits to society are incalculable and, indeed, international in scope.

SOURCES: Dunlap, D. M., & Schmuck, P. A., eds. (1995), *Women Leading in Education* (Albany: State University of New York Press); "Emma Hart Willard's Legendary Life" (1998), *http://www.emma.troy.ny.us/wlcm/article.htm* (accessed February 13, 1999); Goodsell, W. (1970), *Pioneers of Women's Education in the United States: Emma Willard, Catherine Beecher, Mary Lyon* (New York: AMS Press); Lutz, A. (1929), *Emma Willard: Daughter of Democracy* (Boston, MA: Houghton Mifflin Company); McHenry, R., ed. (1980), *Famous American Women: A Biographical Dictionary from Colonial Times to the Present* (Springfield, MA: G. & C. Merriam Company); Wilson, D. C. (1970), *Lone Woman: The Story of Elizabeth Blackwell, The First Woman Doctor* (Boston, MA: Little, Brown & Company).

TERRIE WILLIAMS (1954–   )

"Don't give up five minutes before your miracle. It takes prayer, perseverance, and staying in the race. There are no excuses for not being

able to do what you want to do." (Terrie Williams, Founder, Terrie Williams Agency)

Terrie Williams was one of two daughters born to Marie and Charles Williams of Mount Vernon, New York. Her mother, though the daughter of a sharecropper, found a way to complete high school and then earn both an undergraduate and a graduate degree. Williams honors her mother, saying that she "is one of the strongest and most inspiring women I know" (Williams, 1994: 21). But there was another woman who had such an impact on Williams' life that she dedicated her book, *The Personal Touch*, to her; that was her grandmother, "Lady D," who was abandoned by her husband and had to raise her nine children alone. Williams poignantly wrote to her grandmother in the dedication, "I miss you."

Entrepreneurship was a familiar trait in the Williams household. When her father lost his job because the trucking company he worked for had closed, he opened his own with a partner. He had learned responsibility at an early age when his own abandoned mother needed him to quit school to help her support five children. Terrie's parents also taught their daughters the importance of helping others. She recalled that "for several years my family went to the St. Agatha Home—a refuge for disadvantaged and orphaned children . . . and, we'd bring a little girl home . . . with us on [the] weekends. . . . Her joy made me realize that I want to—as much as possible—find a way to make a difference in people's lives" (Williams, 1994: 24). This need to help others was the underlying reason Williams later chose the educational path in college that she did.

As education was important to both of Williams' parents, they saw to it that their daughters went to "good" schools. Interestingly, for two little black Christian girls, these turned out to be Jewish institutions, starting with the nursery school sponsored by the Young Men and Young Women's Hebrew Association to Brandeis University in Waltham, Massachusetts, where Williams earned her bachelor's degree cum laude in social work. She followed this by attending Columbia University in New York City, receiving a master's degree in the same field. Her first job was with New York Hospital. She worked there two years, and in that time she became convinced that "Human beings want and need to work with people who treat them well," she said. "After food, air and water, people are starved to be recognized" ("Celeb," 1997: 82).

While Williams recognized that her experience in the hospital was invaluable in gaining understanding of the human condition, she also realized that this was not the professional life that was right for her. By chance, she read in an ad in the *Amsterdam News*, a black newspaper, that the local YWCA was offering a course in public relations. As she was able to fit it into her work schedule, she signed up and thus began her education in an entirely different field from her undergraduate and graduate studies.

While taking the course and still working at the hospital, Williams recognized that she needed some media experience; she volunteered at WWRL, a local radio station. Here she met Bob Law, who "showed me all kinds of ropes and facilitated introductions to many people" (Williams, 1994: 12), which enabled her to take a new job as program administrator for the Black Filmmaker Foundation. In time, this opportunity and the subsequent contacts Williams made led to her next positions—executive director of the Black-Owned Communications Alliance (BOCA) and director of the World Institute of Black Communications. "Then I got the PR job of my life at Essence Communications, Inc." The people with whom she worked there and what she learned under their guidance gave her the courage to go out on her own in less than five years.

In 1988 Williams started her public relations business out of her home, having "no agency experience whatsoever. . . . None," she emphasized, adding, "And I didn't have any money" (Williams, 1994: 2). However, what she had was a "formula for success that combines a distinctive work ethic—involving attention to detail, drive, determination, honesty, and integrity—with a way of life that revolves around . . . my philosophy [that] we are on this planet to support one another as human beings, first, last, and always" (2–3). Two of her initial major clients were internationally acclaimed comedian and film star Eddie Murphy and the jazz great Miles Davis. Coincidentally she had met Davis when she was working at the hospital. She had learned that Miles Davis was a patient on another floor. She swallowed her fear, walked into his room, and introduced herself, which began a valuable friendship that lasted until his death. To get Eddie Murphy she had to be savvy and impressive. Williams first strategically met his aides and producers. "I sent them notes, letters, articles of interest— whatever it took to further establish and cement the relationship," she explained (16). She hadn't even opened her firm yet, but by the time Murphy received her material, he knew about her, knew those whom he trusted felt the same way about her, and he said to her on the telephone, "I got your package and I would love you to represent me"—words she will remember till the day she dies (18).

Fortuitously, another New York city public relations practitioner wanted to find someone to share space in his Manhattan office because he was going to be spending much more time in Washington, DC. Williams jumped at the chance; now she had an office. She used her personal savings to purchase the few items she needed and for her initial capital expenditures, which she kept to a minimum. Her friend Joe Cooney, former publicity coordinator at Essence, joined her in this new venture. After a decade as a highly visible public relations expert, Williams' client list is now even more impressive and includes performers such as Janet Jackson and Sinbad; politicians David Dinkins and Sharon Pratt Kelly; NBA sports stars; and even astronaut Mae Jemison. Williams has learned to be direct and brutally honest with her clients when the situation warrants. "Dealing with celebrities egos is challenging. If you do not level with them, you are doing them a disservice. You must point out the clients' metaphorical nakedness," which she labeled the "Emperor's new clothes phenomenon" ("Celeb," 1997: 82). This has the potential of causing client walkouts. For example, she "has quit [Eddie] Murphy and he has fired her, but they have stuck it out. For her 40th birthday, Murphy sent 'an incredible basket with a bottle of Geritol and epsom salts' Williams added, 'It really made me laugh' " (Harper, 1994: D16).

Williams' workdays are long and fast-paced, starting at six in the morning and often going late into the night at the necessary social gatherings. She also speaks regularly at functions that encourage minorities and women to go after their dreams. Her rapid climb to a highly respected pinnacle in her field was highlighted in 1992 when she received the prestigious New York Woman in Communications Matrix Award, the first African American woman to be so honored in twenty-five years. When asked by writer Martha Southgate about the three most important things Williams had learned in her years in business, she responded, "First, that every problem always works itself out some way. Second, that it's important to schedule some time for yourself. . . . Third, and most important: What goes around comes around. That keeps me treating people as I'd like to be treated. Amazing things happen when you're nice to people others overlook" (Southgate, 1994: 52).

SOURCES: "Celeb PR Is All Business, Say Pros, Who Scoff at Starry Image" (1997), O'Dwyers PR Services Report, January (available: Lexis-Nexis, accessed August 2, 1999); Godfrey, J. (1995), *No More Frogs to Kiss: 99 Ways to Give Economic Power to Girls* (New York: Harper Business); Harper, P. (1994), "How Use of 'Personal Touch' Has Built a Minority Public Relations Firm," *Los Angeles Times* [Online], October 2: D16 (available: Lexis-Nexis, accessed August 2, 1999); Southgate, M. (1994), "Becoming Your Own Boss," *Essence*, October: 54 (available: Lexis-Nexis, accessed August 2, 1999); Williams, T., "Forge on to the Next Millennium" (1997), Governor Pataki's Economic Summit for Women, talk presented on May 20, in Albany, New York; Williams, T. (1994), *The Personal Touch* (New York: Warner Books).

OPRAH WINFREY (1954–)

"If you are struggling and it doesn't seem to be coming together, you can't look outside yourself for why it isn't working. You just have to

stop right where you are and look right inside yourself." (Oprah Winfrey, Founder, Harpo Productions, Inc.)

The story of Oprah Gail Winfrey—one of the acclaimed media stars of the
late twentieth century—is legend. She was born on January 29, 1954, to
an unmarried, young, and poor black woman, Vernita Lee. Her biological
father might have been a twenty-year-old black soldier named Vernon Winfrey, who came briefly into Vernita's life. After Oprah's birth, her mother
went to Milwaukee, Wisconsin, because of the promise of more work opportunities for blacks. She had to leave her baby girl with her mother,
Hattie Mae, on her pig farm in Kosciusko, Mississippi. Oprah's grandmother saw to it that the little girl was able to read, write, and do arithmetic by the time she was three years old. As Winfrey later recalled,
"Somehow, with no education, my grandmother instilled in me a belief
that I could aspire to do great things in my life" (Mair, 1996: 8). But it
was also in this household that the little child got her first whippings. Biographer George Mair wrote: "Hattie Mae would send Oprah into the
piney woods where they lived to find and bring back a switch. It had to
be a sturdy, lithe switch or she would be sent back again" (9).

Oprah was so bright that she began to do public readings. In school,
teachers enjoyed having her in the class, but her peers made fun of her
because, while they wanted to fool around, she wanted to learn. For pleasure, the lonely little girl rode pigs bareback and escaped into the world of
books. When she was six years old, her mother came back into her life,
taking the child from the safety and surety of the Mississippi farm to the
crowded inner city of Milwaukee where she lived for almost ten years.
When she was nine, though, her mother sent her to live in Nashville, Tennessee, with Vernon Winfrey, who had a barber shop, and his wife, Zelma.
Though his biological paternity might have been questionable, Vernon willingly assumed fatherly duties for the child he fully accepted as his daughter.
Finally, Oprah had a real home. Since the Winfreys stressed reading and
vocabulary, Oprah's natural abilities in these areas began to shine. She soon
won $500 for a speech she gave to a church group at the age of seven. But
this idyllic arrangement was abruptly ended after just a year when her
mother brought her back to her cramped city dwelling.

Within two years, Oprah was living a young girl's nightmare. She was
raped, and then became the object of inappropriate sexual attention from
many men and boys. Oprah was also threatened by peers at Lincoln School
because she was so smart. "On several occasions, classmates cornered her
and threatened to beat her up. She talked her way out of the confrontations,
but it left her fearful of the next time, when maybe she might not get away"
(Mair, 1996: 15). The teenager became so openly rebellious that, by the
time she was fourteen, her mother sent her back to live with the Winfreys.

What they soon learned was that she was pregnant by an uncle. The male child died soon after birth; the painful memory remains.

Oprah Gail Winfrey did a complete turnaround under the loving and watchful eyes of Vernon and Zelma Winfrey. By now, her father had a small grocery story attached to his barbershop, and the teenager had to work in the store after school. Then she heard about a March of Dimes walkathon and volunteered. Who could have guessed that this simple act of charity would put her on the path that would lead to worldwide celebrity? The drive made money by getting businesses to pay for the miles volunteers walked, and Oprah chose WVOL, a radio station. When disc jockey John Heidelberg heard her voice, he recommended that the station manager meet the teenager. Oprah was hired immediately and started earning $100 a week. Heidelberg also began to teach her about the broadcasting business. Graduating from East Nashville High School, she went to Tennessee State University, studying there for a year. Then, in 1973, at the age of nineteen, Oprah Winfrey was offered an on-air television job with Channel 5, WTVF-TV, for $15,000 a year as the first female and the first black newscaster in Nashville (Mair, 1996: 36).

In just a few years, Winfrey's next opportunity came from Baltimore's WJZ-TV, where she stayed for seven years. Then Chicago beckoned. She answered and remains centered there today. Her first opportunity was as host of the program *A.M. Chicago*. Oprah related, "Everybody, with the exception of my best friend [Gayle King Bumpas], told me it wouldn't work. They said I was black, female, and overweight. They said Chicago was a racist city and the talk-show formula was on its way out" (Mair, 1996: 73). Winfrey signed a four-year contract for $200,000 a year with WLS-TV. How wrong they were. It is estimated that she soon will be worth a billion dollars.

In addition to television, Oprah Winfrey wanted to be an actor. Years earlier she had read *The Color Purple*. She's fond of saying that when preparation and opportunity meet, "luck" happens (Mair, 1996: 51). One such lucky moment came when she was approached by Quincy Jones to play the role of Sofia in a film version of the book. She also felt that this was, in a sense, preordained, since the name of Sofia's husband was Harpo, which is Oprah spelled backward. The movie was released in 1986, the same year she started her own company, which she named Harpo Entertainment.

Winfrey is the first black woman to own a television and movie production company. The two famous women who proceeded her in this type of business were Mary Pickford and Lucille Ball (Goodman, 1991). The Harpo Entertainment Group now includes Harpo Productions, Harpo Films, and Harpo Video—the primary property is the creative work of the CEO and chairperson, Oprah Winfrey. Though started with just five employees, by 1994 Harpo had more than 130 employees and was grossing over $100 million. The preceding year, *Forbes* magazine had declared Oprah Winfrey to be the richest entertainer in the United States and, thus, the world. By 1999, she was reaching over 33 million viewers a day in the United States and being watched in over 130 countries.

But the Oprah Winfrey story is not just about public acclaim and financial success. While she was filming a movie, she met a twelve-year-old boy from the inner-city projects she has labeled the "war zone." Her personal interest included even checking that he was doing his homework and doing it well. From this relationship, Winfrey decided to establish Families for a Better Life (FABL), a two-year program that gives 100 families $60,000 each to help them to improve their skills, get jobs, and move out of the projects. She simply said, "Being able to save families for a better life feels like one of the things I was meant to do. . . . That's how I'm supposed to be using myself" (Gerosa, 1994: 280). In 1997 Oprah also started the Angel Network. In this effort, she asked her fans and viewers to save pennies and dimes that would be collected in sites around the country to provide college scholarships for deserving students. Her educational philanthropy has also extended to Tennessee State University, where she established ten annual scholarships in her father's name valued at $250,000, and she gave a $1 million gift to Morehouse College in Georgia.

In 1998, Winfrey joined with other female television executives to structure Oxygen Channel, a station "to superserve women who are the most underserved audience in cable television," according to partner Geraldine Laybourne. For her part, Winfrey agreed that any shows that her company owns, once they are no longer under other contracts and the rights have reverted back to her, will be available to the Oxygen Channel. She will also produce new programming as well. This same group has become a major supporter of the renewed *Ms.* magazine.

Winfrey has attributed her successful life to a few simple rules: "Don't try to please others and don't let others control you. Count on yourself and surround yourself with good people. Have harmony in life, dispose of betrayers, be nice, and don't ever give up. And from the richest black woman in the world: Don't do anything for the money" (Mair, 1996: 149–150).

SOURCES: Carter, B. (1998), "Three Female TV Executives Plan to Create Cable Channel for Women," *New York Times* [Online], November 24: C1 (available: Lexis-Nexis, accessed August 26, 1999); Gerasa, M. (1994), "What Makes Oprah Run?" *Ladies' Home Journal*, November: 200+; Godman, F. (1991), "The Companies They Keep: Madonna and Oprah Winfrey," *Working Woman* 16, no. 12: 52+; Mair, G. (1996), *Oprah Winfrey: The Real Story* (Secaucus, NJ: Citadel Stars); *The Oprah Winfrey Show* (1999), *http://www.oprah.com*.

SELECTED BIBLIOGRAPHY

Aldrich, H. (1989). "Networking Among Women Entrepreneurs." In O. Hagan, C. Rivchum, & D. Sexton, eds., *Women-owned Businesses*. New York: Praeger.

Anzilotti, C. (1994). "In the Affairs of the World: Women and Plantation Ownership in the Eighteenth Century, South Carolina Lowcountry." Ph.D. diss., University of California.

Ashby, R., & Ohrn, D. G. (1995). *Herstory: Women Who Changed the World*. New York: Viking.

Baron, A., ed. (1991). *Work Engendered: Toward a New History of American Labor*. Ithaca, NY: Cornell University Press.

Bonner, T. N. (1992). *To the Ends of the Earth: Women's Search for Education in Medicine*. Cambridge, MA: Harvard University Press.

Bowen, C. C., & Hisrich, R. D. (1986). "The Female Entrepreneur: A Career Development Perspective." *Academy of Management Review* 11(2): 393–407.

Branch, M., & Rice, D. (1984). *Miss Maggie: A Biography of Maggie Lena Walker*. Richmond, VA: Marlborough House Publishing.

Brewer, A. (1992). *Richard Cantillon: Pioneer of Economic Theory*. London: Routledge.

Brush, C., & Chaganti, R. (1996). "Cooperative Strategies in Non-high-tech Ventures: An Exploratory Study." *Entrepreneurship Theory and Practice* 21(2) (Winter): 37–55.

Burr, S., & Strickland, M. (1992). "Creating a Positive Business Climate for Women: An Approach to Small Business Development." *Economic Development Review* [Online] (Winter): 63. Available: Proquest. Accessed August 31, 1999.

Capowski, G. (1992). "Be Your Own Boss? Millions of Women Get Down to Business." *Management Review* [Online] (March): 24. Available: Proquest. Accessed August 31, 1999.

Casteneda, A. I. (1992). "Women of Color and the Rewriting of Western History: The Discourse, Politics, and Decolonization of History." *Pacific Historical Review* 61: 501–533.

Chaganti, R. (1986). "Management in Women-Owned Enterprises." *Journal of Small Business Management* (October): 18–29.

Collins, N., Gilbert, S., & Nycam, S. (1988). *Women Leading: Making Tough Choices on the Fast Track*. Lexington, MA: Stephen Greene Press.

Cooper, A. (1998). *"A Woman's Place Is in the Kitchen": The Evolution of Women Chefs*. New York: Van Nostrand Reinhold.

Daniel, S. I. (1931). *Women Builders*. Washington, DC: Associated Publishers.

Davisson, R. A. (1993). "Invisible Owners of Painted Ladies and Other Houses: Women Property Owners in Nevada City, California." Master's thesis, University of California.

DeCarlo, J., & Lyons, P. R. (1979). "A Comparison of Selected Personality Characteristics of Minority and Non-minority Female Entrepreneurs." *Journal of Small Business Management* (December): 22–29.

Dexter, E. A. (1924). *Colonial Women of Affairs: A Study of Women in Business and the Professions in America Before 1776*. Boston, MA: Houghton Mifflin Company.

Dhillon, P. K. (1993). *Women Entrepreneurs: Problems and Prospects*. New Delhi: Blaze Publishers & Distributors.

DiBacco, T. (1987). *Made in the U.S.A.: The History of American Business*. New York: Harper & Row.

Drucker, P. (1985). *Innovation and Entrepreneurship*. New York: Harper & Row.

Duncan, B. (1991). "A Profile of Female Home-Based Sewing Entrepreneurs Who Participated in the Mississippi Cooperative Extension Service Sewing as a Business Program." Ph.D. diss., Mississippi State University.

Dunlap, D. M., & Schmuck, P. A., eds. (1995). *Women Leading in Education*. Albany, NY: State University of New York Press.

Ferguson, M. (1995). *Women in Religion*. Englewood Cliffs, NJ: Prentice-Hall.

Fucini, J. J., & Fucini, S. (1985). *Entrepreneurs: The Men and Women behind Famous Brand Names and How They Made It*. Boston, MA: G. K. Hall & Co.

Godfrey, J. (1992). *Our Wildest Dreams: Women Entrepreneurs Making Money, Having Fun, Doing Good*. New York: HarperBusiness.

Goodsell, W. (1970). *Pioneers of Women's Education in the United States: Emma Willard, Catherine Beecher, Mary Lyon*. New York: AMS Press.

Green, P. (1997). "A Resource-based Approach to Ethnic Business Sponsorship." *Journal of Small Business Management* 35(4) (October): 58–72.

Grover, M. (1998). "Starting a Company Is Like Going to War." *Forbes* [Online] (November 2): 184–193. Available: Proquest. Accessed February 13, 1999.

Harry, L. (1994). *Stressors, Beliefs, and Coping Behaviors of Black Women Entrepreneurs*. New York: Garland Publishing.

Herera, S. (1997). *Women of the Street: Making It on Wall Street—The World's Toughest Business*. New York: John Wiley and Sons.

Hisrich, R. D., & Brush, C. G. (1980). "The Woman Entrepreneur: Management Skills and Business Problems." *Journal of Small Business Management* 22 (January): 30–37.

———. (1986). *The Women Entrepreneurs: Starting, Financing, and Managing a Successful Enterprise*. Washington, DC: Heath & Co.

Hisrich, R. D., & O'Brien, M. (1981). "The Women Entrepreneurs from a Business and Sociological Perspective." Frontiers of Entrepreneurship Research. Proceedings of the 1981 Conference on Entrepreneurship, pp. 21–39. Wellesley, MA: Babson College; Englewood Cliffs, NJ: Prentice-Hall.

Kurato, D. F., & Hodgetts, R. M. (1995). *Entrepreneurship: A Contemporary Approach*. Fort Worth, TX: Dryden Press.

MacLean, B. (1997). *I Can't Do What? Voices of Pathfinding Women*. Ventura, CA: Pathfinding Publishing.

Maman, M., & Tate, T. (1996). *Women in Agriculture: A Guide to Research*. New York: Garland Publishing.

McClain, J. (1995). "Women-Owned Firms Grow." *Times Union*, April 12: C16.

McHenry, R., ed. (1980). *Famous American Women: A Biographical Dictionary from Colonial Times to the Present*. Springfield, MA: G. & C. Merriam Company.

Moore, D., & Buttner, E. (1997). *Women Entrepreneurs: Moving Beyond the Glass Ceiling*. Thousand Oaks, CA: Sage Publications.

National Women's History Project. (1991). *Las Mujeres: Mexican American/Chicana Women: Photographs and Biographies of Seventeen Women from the Spanish Colonial Period to the Present*. Windsor, CA: National Women's History Project.

———. (1985). *Women as Members of Groups*. Windsor, CA: National Women's History Project.

Nelton, S. (1998). "Women's Firms Thrive." *Nation's Business* [Online], August: 38–40. Available: Proquest. Accessed August 31, 1999.

Nichols, N. A., Ed. (1994). *Reach for the Top: Women and the Changing Facts of Work Life*. Boston, MA: Harvard Business School Publishing Corporation.

Niethammer, C. (1977). *Daughters of the Earth: The Lives and Legends of American Indian Women*. New York: Macmillan.

Purcell, C. W., Jr., ed. (1990). *Technology in America: A History of Individuals and Ideas*. Cambridge, MA: MIT Press.

Rebolledo, T. D., ed. (1992). *Nuestras Mujeres: Hispanas of New Mexico, Their Images and Their Lives, 1582–1992*. Albuquerque, NM: El Norte Publications.

Rolka, G. M. (1994). *100 Women Who Shaped World History*. San Francisco, CA: Bluewood Books.

Sicherman, B., & Green, C., eds. (1980). *Notable American Women: The Modern Period*. Cambridge, MA: Radcliffe College.

Signorielli, N., ed. (1996). *Women in Communication: A Biographical Sourcebook*. Westport, CT: Greenwood Press.

Silver, A. D. (1994). *Enterprising Women: Lessons from 100 of the Greatest Entrepreneurs of Our Day*. New York: AMACOM.

Smith, J. C. (1993). *Epic Lives: One Hundred Black Women Who Made a Difference*. Detroit, MI: Visible Ink Press.

Tierney, H., ed. (1991). *Women's Studies Encyclopedia, Volume III: History, Philosophy, and Religion*. Westport, CT: Greenwood Press.

Trager, J. (1994). *The Women's Chronology: A Year-by-Year Record, from Prehistory to the Present*. New York: Henry Holt and Company.

Wagner-Martin, W. (1994). *Telling Women's Lives: The New Biography*. New Brunswick, NJ: Rutgers University Press.

INDEX

Page numbers in bold indicate main entries.

About the Author

JEANNETTE M. OPPEDISANO is Director of Camp Start-up at Skidmore College, an entrepreneurship program for teen women and founder and president of the Whispering Wynds, a life strategy management consulting practice.

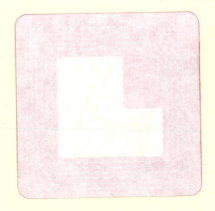

c2000   8-15-01   1/06